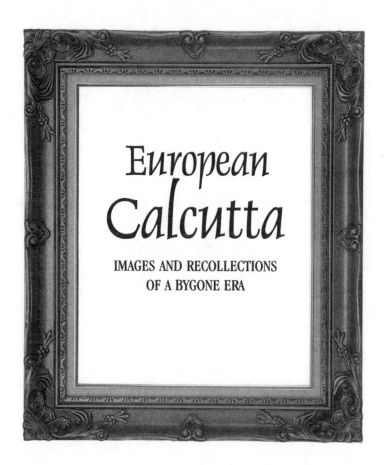

European Calcutta

IMAGES AND RECOLLECTIONS
OF A BYGONE ERA

European Calcutta

IMAGES AND RECOLLECTIONS
OF A BYGONE ERA

Dr Dhrubajyoti Banerjea

UBSPD®

UBS PUBLISHERS' DISTRIBUTORS PVT. LTD.

New Delhi • Bangalore • Kolkata • Chennai • Patna • Bhopal
Ernakulam • Mumbai • Lucknow • Pune • Hyderabad
Ahmedabad • Nagpur • Coimbatore • Bhubaneshwar • Guwahati

UBS Publishers' Distributors Pvt. Ltd.

5 Ansari Road, Daryaganj, **New Delhi**-110 002
Phones: 011-23273601-4, 23266646-47, 23274846, 23282281, 23273552
Fax: 011-23276593, 23274261 • E-mail: ubspd@ubspd.com

9, Ashok Nagar, Near Pratibha Press, Gautam Buddha Marg, Latouche Road,
Lucknow-226 018 • Phones: 0522-4025124, 4025134, 4025144, 6531753
Fax: 0522-4025144 • E-mail: ubspdlko@lko.ubspd.com

Z-18, M.P. Nagar, Zone-I, **Bhopal**-462 011
Phones: 0755-4203183, 4203193, 2555228 • Fax: 0755-2555285
E-mail: ubspdbhp@bhp.ubspd.com

1st Floor, Shop No. 133-134, Aust Laxmi, Apparel Park, Outside Dariyapur Gate,
Ahmedabad-380 016 • Phones: 079-29092241, 29092248, 29092258
E-mail: ubspdahm@ahm.ubspd.com

2nd Floor, Shree Renuka Plaza, Tilak Road, Mahal, **Nagpur**-440 002

2nd Floor, Apeejay Chambers, 5 Wallace Street, Fort, **Mumbai**-400 001
Phones: 022-66376922-23, 66102067, 66102069
Fax: 022-66376921 • E-mail: ubspdmum@mum.ubspd.com

680 Budhwar Peth, 2nd floor, Near Appa Balwant Chowk, **Pune**-411 002
Phone: 020-24461653 • Fax: 020-24433976 • E-mail: ubspdpune@pun.ubspd.com

Crescent No. 148, 1st Floor, Mysore Road, **Bangalore**-560 026
Phones: 080-26756377, 26756362 • Fax: 080-26756462
E-mail: ubspd@bngm.ubspd.com

60 Nelson Manickam Road, Aminjikarai, **Chennai**-600 029
Phones: 044-23746222, 23746351-52 • Fax: 044-23746287
E-mail: ubspdche@che.ubspd.com

2nd & 3rd Floor, Sri Guru Towers, No.1-7 Sathy Road, Cross III, Gandhipuram,
Coimbatore-641 012 • Phones: 0422-2499916-17
Fax: 0422-2499914 • E-mail: ubspdcbe@cbe.ubspd.com

No. 40/8199A, 1st Floor, Public Library Building, Convent Road, **Ernakulam**-682 035
Phones: 0484-2353901, 2373901, 2363905, 4064706 • Fax: 0484-2365511
E-mail: ubspdekm@ekm.ubspd.com

3rd & 4th Floors, Alekhya Jagadish Chambers, H.No.4-1-1058, Boggulkunta, Tilak Road,
Hyderabad-500 001 • Phones: 040-24754473-74 • Telefax: 040-24754472
E-mail: ubspdhyd@hyd.ubspd.com

1st Floor, Plot No. 145, Cuttack Road, **Bhubaneshwar**-751 006
Phones: 0674-2314446-47 • Fax: 0674-2314448
E-mail: ubspdbbh@bbh.ubspd.com

8/1-B Chowringhee Lane, **Kolkata**-700 016
Phones: 033-22529473, 22521821, 22522910 • Fax: 033-22523027
E-mail: ubspdcal@cal.ubspd.com

1st Floor, House No. 4, Kanaklata Path, Lachit Nagar, Bharalupar, **Guwahati**-781 007
Phones: 0361-2461982-84 • E-mail: ubspdguw@guw.ubspd.com

Ground Floor, Annapurna Complex, Naya Tola, **Patna**-800 004
Phones: 0612-2672856, 2673973, 2686170 • Fax: 0612-2686169
E-mail: ubspdpat@pat.ubspd.com

Visit us at www.ubspd.com & www.gobookshopping.com

© Dr Dhrubajyoti Banerjea

First Published	2005	Second Reprint	2008
First Reprint	2006	Third Reprint	2011

ISBN   978-81-7476-506-2

Dr Dhrubajyoti Banerjea asserts the moral right to be identified as the author of this work.

Editorial Consultant: Barnali Roy

Cover Design: Dushyant Parasher

Printed at: International Print-o-Pac Limited,

To
My Daughter Jyotishmita
and all those who love
the city

Foreword

Calcutta, distinct from Kolkata, which is as the city is now called, is a British creation. The political classes may not like this but it is a fact that one cannot ignore. Rudyard Kipling's famous quip about Charnohk's mid-day halt becoming a city only reflected what was an evident fact. From three small hamlets grew a city through the initiative of British traders and rulers and some Indian collaborators of the British who, for reasons of self-interest, chose to stay near the centre of power, and built their own mansions and institutions, and thus contributed to the making of the city. The city of Calcutta has very little history prior to the coming of the East India Company and Job Charnohk's somewhat accidental arrival in the village of Sutanuti.

This book thankfully does not seek to deny the British heritage of Calcutta. On the contrary, it celebrates that aspect through some rare photogrpahs and detailed annotations about some of the more important areas of what was the 'White Town'. Even today, despite the enormous—and most of it horrible—changes that have taken place in the city's landscape, the most beautiful and the best laid-out part of Calcutta is that the British had made for themselves and their institutions. Tree-lined avenues, spacious bungalows, grand mansions and office buildings in imitation of those in London were the features of the White Town. Not so long ago, even in the fifties, those features were all there. I remember as a child how much I enjoyed a drive down Chowringhee staring at the buildings on one side and the green of the Maidan on the other—a gleaming white balustrade, which ran the length of the road, separated the road and the green. Alipore seemed a world apart with its magnificent houses with lawns and gardens. Looking back, I realize that Calcutta was a very gracious and charming place to live in. This book captures some of that ambience through photographs and text.

A proper history of Calcutta is yet to be written. It is a history that cries out for narration and analysis. When that history comes to be written, this book will be an indispensable source. It will be indispensable for two reasons; one, for the detailed annotation it provides for the buildings and the areas it studies. Some of the material is new in the sense that it was scattered in many books and articles. The author has brought these together in one place. The other is the graphic aspect. The history of European Calcutta is represented here through pictures, and some of these are rare. Dr Banerjea has displayed a collector's passion. It is obvious that his love affair with Calcutta is a long and ongoing one.

The preservation of the heritage of Calcutta has suddenly acquired a new urgency. Mindless government construction and marauding realtors are obliterating the city's heritage. It is nobody's argument that the city's landscape should remain unchanged ever and nigh. But changes should keep in mind history and aesthetics. A beautiful colonial bungalow should not be pulled down and replaced by a concrete monstrosity. There are other more appealing ways to use that space. Moreover, there are some buildings which should never be broken down because they are part of the city's history. There is a need for greater awareness in this regard. This book helps to build that awareness. Moreover, when the task of preservation and maintenance moves from files to implementation, this book will provide a rich documentation of what the city was like in the past.

Rudrangshu Mukherjee
The Editor, Editorial Pages
The Telegraph

Preface

I was born in North Calcutta, spent my early years in Central Calcutta and most of my life thereafter in South Calcutta. The city has been the only constant in an otherwise chaotic world.

I have vivid memories of the Second World War, the Bengal Famine, the Great Calcutta Killing and the Partition of India, which changed forever my beloved city.

I have always loved Calcutta. But the idea of penning its history had never crossed my mind. It is probably thanks to two experiences in my life that this book exists. The first was Darjeeling. I was posted there in 1975 at the Victoria Hospital. Following the tradition of senior government officers, I joined the Darjeeling Gymkhana Club as a Special Member. Its prime attraction was its vast, well-stocked library: a marvellous collection of books on Calcutta, Lord Curzon, C.E. Buckland, Busteed, H.E.A. Cotton and lots more. The more I read, the closer I came to the City of Joy. Returning to Calcutta, I started my own collection: books, photographs, post cards, maps—anything with the remotest Calcutta connection!

The other experience, which is still going strong, was the Calcutta Club. I became a member in 1987, again mainly for its splendid library. Bound volumes of *Bengal: Past and Present*, the magazine of the Calcutta Historical Society...those shelves were a goldmine. I started collecting anecdotes and all kinds of detailed information about the city. The obsession drove me to roam about the European part of Calcutta, ready to pounce on the tiniest bit of history. I will never forget my first entry into Clive Row—digging out the past of the city's commercial hub. The old churches—St. John's, the Armenian Church, the synagogues—what a fascinating world I discovered there!

And then one day it just seemed to be a very natural thing to do to put all those discoveries down on paper. So here it is, my tribute to Calcutta's 'White Town', the world in which the Europeans lived, its past and its present.

I am not a historian. I am a lover who just has to give something back to the city he loves. I've enjoyed every minute that went into this book and all the surprises it had up its sleeves.

I just hope it proves to be of help to historians everywhere. But most of all I hope it touches the common chord of pride and wonder in the hearts of my fellows lovers of Calcutta.

Dhrubajyoti Banerjea

Acknowledgements

Thanks are due to Mr. Shameek Bandyopadhyay for going through the manuscript and editing it in his own inimical style.

Mr. Debajyoti Dutta for getting the edited manuscript in to the computer and the final compact discs.

Dr. C.R. Panda, the Curator of the Victoria Memorial Hall for his kind suggestions.

Dr. Ranjit Sen and Calcutta Historical Society for permission to use some of the photographs published in several numbers of *Bengal Past and Present*.

Mr. Rathin Mitra for permission to use some of his sketches. Bengal Club, Secretary Gautam Guha and Librarian S. Chakraborty for using their library for primary research.

Mr. N.R. Bose for the recent photographs and arrangements for reproducing older photographs.

Mr. B.M. Varma, Senior Steward of Royal Calcutta Turf Club for information.

Sister Bernardette and Loreto House for the sketch and general information.

Calcutta Club for permission to reproduce various William Wood lithographs and Daniell prints in their possession. Calcutta Club librarains Mrs. Runa Banerjee and Mrs. Lily Chatterjee and library assistant Md. Nissar for constant help.

Calcutta Cricket & Football Club and Mr. Prodipto Banjerjea for the photograph of the Clubhouse.

ITC for their photographs.

Thanks are due to the following for their help with information: Late Dr. Partha Banerji, Late Mr. Dilip Roychowdhury, Late Mr. Chandrasekhar Rudra, Mr. Arun Bhattacharyya, I.A.S., Dr. Subir Chatterjee, Mr. P.B. Sinha, Mr. Sidney Kitson, Mr. Madhav Goenka, Rajmata Gayatri Devi of Jaipur, Mr. Meena, PRO of South Eastern Railways, Mr. Sam Luddy, Mr. Pradip Dasguta, Mr. T.C. Chowdhury, Mrs. Subhadra Roychowdhury, Mr. Pradip Lall, Mr. Amaresh Gooptu, Mr. Amiya Gooptu, Mr. Sunil Gangopadhyay, Shatrujit Banerjee and many others.

My daughter Jyotismita for helping with her perfect word and my wife Aruna for bearing with the monotonous sound of typing till late at night.

Finally Smt. Barnali Roy for acting as a Literary Agent, finding a publisher and the final cut.

List of Illustrations

Figure 1:   Charnock's Mausoleum at St. John's Church, Photo courtesy Calcutta Historical Society

Figure 2.   Charnock and his Daughter Catherine White's Headstone Photo N.R. Bose

Figure 3:   Dalhousie Square and St. Andrew's Church

Figure 4:   Wellesly Place, Statue of Marquis of Wellesley and Writer's Building, Photo courtesy Calcutta Historical Society

Plate 1:   George Lambert (attributed), Old Fort William from the land side with St. Anne's Church in front. 1730

Plate 2:   Plan of old Fort William by Lt. William Wells in 1753.

Figure 5:   Replica of Holwell's Monument, Old Customs House in background

Figure 6:   The General Post Office and the Royal Insurance Building on the left

Plate 3:   A pre-postage stamp era letter to London bearing Calcutta G.P.O. Ship Letter Postmark in red dated 9 August 1843

Figure 7:   Calcutta Collectorate Today, Photo Mr. N.R. Bose

Figure 8:   Old Custom House

Figure 9:   The Small Causes Court

Plate 10:   The Metcalfe Hall, Photo courtesy Calcutta Historical Society

Figure 11:   The Central Telegraph Office

Figure 12:   Government Place East

Figure 13:   Peliti's Restaurant, Government Place East. Photo Bourne & Shepherd

Figure 14:   The Great Eastern Hotel

Figure 15:   Government Place East and Horse-drawn Tramcars, Photo Bourne & Shepherd

Figure 16:   The Currency Building. Photo Bourne & Shepherd

Plate 4:   Thomas Daniell, views of Calcutta north side of the Tank Square, Writer's Building and the Old Court House 1786

Figure 17:   The Writer's Building across Dalhousie Square before renovation

Figure 18:   The Writer's Building after renovation.

Figure 19:   Sir Charles D'Oyly's View of Clive Street, 1835

Figure 20:   The Same Area after 50 Years. Photo Johnston & Hoffmann

Figure 21:   Clive Street 1910

Figure 22:   The Chartered Bank

Figure 23:   The old building of the Bengal Chamber of Commerce, Photo courtesy Calcutta Historical Society

Figure 24:   The Armenian Church of St. Nazareth, Photo courtesy Calcutta Historical Society

Figure 25:   The Epitaph of Rezabebe on the oldest Christian grave in Calcutta, Photo courtesy Calcutta Historical Society

Figure 26:   The Shield of David Synagogue. Photo courtesy Mr. Samuel Luddy

Figure 27:   John Palmer's House in Lal Bazar at the site of the present Police Headquarters, Photo Bourne & Shepherd

Figure 28:   The newly erected Imperial Secretariat Building seen from the Government Place North

Figure 29:   The Treasury Building at the southern end of the Imperial Secretariat

Figure 30:   The Bank of Bengal, Strand Road

Figure 31:   The Burmese Pagoda, Eden Gardens

Figure 32:   The Bandstand, Eden Gardens

Figure 33:   The Bengal Council House 1931, Photo courtesy Calcutta Historical Society

Figure 34:   The Buckingham House, Photo courtesy Calcutta Historical Society

Figure 35:   The High Court, CalcuttaFigure 36: The Town Hall

Figure 36:   The Town Hall

Figure 37:   The Government House, North Front

Figure 38:   The Government House, Throne Room

Figure 39:   The Government House, Ball Room

Figure 40:   Thacker Spink & Co. Photo Bourne & Shepherd

Figure 41:   Curzon Garden and the Imperial Military Office

Plate 5:   Thomas Daniell, Views of Calcutta, Houses on the Chowringhee Road, 1787

Plate 6:   The same scene a few years later. The small pond has now been extended and beautification done by a Benares banker.

Figure 42:   Bristol Hotel, Chowringhee, Photo Johnston & Hoffmann

Figure 43:   The Metropolitan Building, originally built by the Whiteaway and Laidlaws Departmental Stores. Sketch Rathin Mitra

Figure 44:   Grand Hotel, Chowringhee

Figure 45:   New Market

Figure 46:   Christmas Morning in the New Market

Figure 47:   Sudder Street

Figure 48:   Speke's House, Sketch courtesy Rathin Mitra

Figure 49:   The Old United Service Club Building, Photo courtesy Johnston & Hoffmann

Figure 50:   The United Service Club

Figure 51:   William Wood, the junction of Chowringhee and Park Street and the Asiatic Society Building in 1830

Figure 52:   The Tomb of Hindoo Stuart in South Park Street Cemetery, Photo courtesy Calcutta Historical Society

Figure 53:   St. Xavier's College, Park Street, a picture postcard with a postage stamp postmarked on the first day of issue 12.4.1985

Figure 54:   Loreto House, the old building dating back to Eliza Impey, in 1842 Sketch courtesy Loreto House

Figure 55:   Sir. A.A. Apcar's House in Russell Street, now the Royal Calcutta Turf Club, Photo courtesy RCTC

Plate 7:   The New Spanking ITC Centre, Courtesy ITC Ltd.

Figure 57:   William Wood, Chowringhee Road, south of the junction with Park Street The house on the left was owned by Babu Kaliprasanna Singha, 1830.

Figure 58:   The Bengal Club (old building on the Chowrighee)

Figure 59:   The Virginia House, Photo courtesy ITC

Figure 60:   The Army & Navy Stores, Chowringhee

Figure 61:   Willam Wood—The Chowringhee Road and the Theatre 1830

Figure 62:   La Martiniere School

Figure 63:   Calcutta Club, Sketch courtesy Rathin Mitra

Figure 64:   The Presidency General Hospital

Figure 65:   Victorial Memorial Hall

Figure 66:   The Grandstand, Race Course

Figure 67:   St. Paul's Cathedral with the Old Steeple

Figure 68:   The Equestrian State of General Outram in the Maidan and the Ochterloney Monument

Figure 69:   Chowringhee Gate Fort William

Figure 70:   Plassey Gate Fort William

Figure 71:   Dalhousie Barrack Fort William

Figure 72:   Bengal Nagpore Railways Head Office at Garden Reach, Photo courtesy South Eastern Railway

Figure 73:   A View of the Zoological Gardens

Figure 74:   Belvedere House, Alipore

Figure 75:   Woodlands, The Maharaja of Cooch Behar's Palace in Alipore "during my father's time", writes Rajmata Gayatri Devi of Jaipur. Photo Courtesy the Rajmata

Figure 76:   Hastings House, Alipore

Figure 77:   Thackeray House, Alipore, Photo couresty Mr. Arun Bhattacharya I.A.S.

Figure 77A: The Club House, Calcutta Cricket & Football Club, Ballygunge, Photo courtesy C.C.F & C.

Figure 78:   A view of Barrackpore Government House. Photo courtesy Calcutta Historical Society

Figure 79:   The Strand Calcutta

Figure 80:   The Old Pontoon Howrah Bridge

Contents

Foreword   *vii*

Preface   *ix*

Acknowledgements   *xi*

List of Illustrations   *xiii*

1. Calcutta: The Beginning   1

2. Europeans at Calcutta and Job Charnock   7

3. Lal Dighi, The Great Tank, Tank Square:
   Dalhousie Square to Binoy Badal Dinesh Bagh   12

4. The Old Fort and the Black Hole   17

5. The Changing Face of the Old Fort Area   24

6. Villages to Metropolis: Calcutta 1757–1800   30

7. Around Lal Dighi   38

8. Esplanade Row and its Environs   109

9. The Government House, Calcutta   149

10. Esplanade East to Park Street   160

11. From Burying Ground Road to Park Street   190

12. Chowringhee Road from Park Street to Lower Circular Road   223

13. Lower Circular Road   245

14. The Vast Expanse of the Maidan   264

15. The Fort William of Today   282

16. Here and There   292

Epilogue   343

Index   345

Chapter One

Calcutta: The Beginning

There is no conclusive evidence as to how old Calcutta is. Investigations by geologists and scientists in other disciplines over the years have pointed to the possibility of Calcutta and lower Bengal having been hill stations. An oyster bed discovered at the very heart of the modern city in its turn pointed to yet another possibility. A committee of scientists, who conducted a series of bore hole operations in the vicinity of Calcutta between December 1835 and 1840, reached significant conclusions recorded by Henry F. Blanford:

There appears every reason for believing that the beds traversed, from top to bottom of the bore-hole, had been deposited either by fresh water or in the neighbourhood of an estuary. At a depth of thirty feet below the surface, or about ten feet below mean tide level, and again at three hundred and eighty-two feet, beds of peat with wood were found, and in both cases there can be but little doubt that the deposits proved the existence of ancient land surfaces... .

A peaty layer had been noticed at Canning Town on the Mutlah, thirty-five miles to the south-east, and at Khulna in Jessore, eighty miles east by north, always at such a depth below the present surface as to be some feet beneath the present mean tide level. In many of the cases noticed roots of the Sundri were found in that peaty stratum. This tree grows a little above ordinary high-water mark in ground liable to flooding; so that in every instance of the roots occurring below the mean tide level there is conclusive evidence of depression. This evidence is confirmed by the occurrence of pebbles; for it is extremely improbable that coarse gravel should have been deposited in water eighty fathoms deep, and large fragments could not have been brought to their present position unless the streams, which now traverse the country, had a greater fall formerly, or unless, which is perhaps more probable, rocky hills existed which have now been partly removed by denudation and covered up by alluvial deposits. The coarse gravel and sand, which form so considerable a proportion of the bed traversed, can scarcely be deltaic accumulations; and it is therefore probable that when they were formed the present site of Calcutta was near the margin of the alluvial plain.[1]

A.K. Ray, a noted historian of Calcutta, writes:

It will thus appear that the description of lower Bengal (including Calcutta and its neighbourhood) in Barahamihira's *Brihatsamhita* as *samatata* or tidal swamp, and the inference that it was gradually raised by alluvial deposits into a habitable kingdom about the seventh century after Christ are in perfect accord with the trend of modern physical researches, while there is nothing in the social history of Bengal, which commences with King Adisur, between the seventh and the ninth century after Christ, that appears to militate against the inference.

1. That in remote antiquity, gneissic hills stood out from the sea where Calcutta now is.
2. That at a later date—probably during the tertiary period—these hills were depressed and a tidal swamp extended up to the foot of the Rajmahal hills.
3. That the Lower Gangetic plains below the Rajmahal hills began to be elevated by fluvial deposits about four or five thousand years ago.
4. That the extension of the delta was from north and west to the south and east.
5. That, near Calcutta, an elevation of the area has alternatively been followed by a subsidence.
6. That in historical times the extreme south-eastern portion, including the districts of Khulna, Jessore, the Sunderbans and Calcutta, was not fully formed in the seventh century of the Christian era, when East Bengal was sufficiently inhabited to form the nucleus of a kingdom.[2]

The legend of ancient Calcutta has been well narrated by Mr. C.R. Wilson:

Like other cities Calcutta has its legend. Long, long ago, in the age of truth, Daksha, one of the Hindu Patriarchs, made a sacrifice to obtain a son, but he omitted to invite the God Siva to come to it. Now Sati, the daughter of Daksha, was married to Siva, and she was indignant that so great an insult should have been offered to her divine husband, and deeply grieved that such a slight should have been passed upon him through her kindred. In vain did she expostulate with her father. 'Why,' she asked, 'is my husband not invited? Why are no offerings to be made to him?' 'Thy husband,' was the reply, 'wears a necklace of skulls; how can he be invited to a sacrifice?' Then in grief and indignation, and shrieking out, 'This father of mine is a villain; what profit have I in this carcase sprung from him?' she put an end to her life; and Siva, 'drunk with loss,' transfixed her dead body on the point of his trident and rushed hither and thither through the realms of Nature. The whole world was threatened with destruction; but Vishnu, the preserver, came to the rescue. He flung his disk at the body of Sati and broke it into pieces which fell scattered over the earth. Every place where any part of her body fell, became a sanctuary, a sacred spot full of the divine spirit of Sati. The names of these places are preserved in the garlands of sanctuaries. Some of them are well-known places of pilgrimage, others are obscure and forgotten; but today the most celebrated of them all is Calcutta, or rather, Kalighat, the spot which received the toes of the right foot of Sati, that is, of Kali.[3]

Recently, during an excavation in the Bethune College compound in Calcutta, while digging for the foundation of a new college auditorium, some ancient earthenware pots, figurines and other artefacts were found. Further digging led to some brick structures. It has been conjectured that these may belong to the Gupta era. In 1783, about two hundred Gupta era gold coins were found, and an excavation in the Blind School compound in Behala resulted in the discovery of the upper part of a Gupta era figure of Lord Vishnu, at a depth of eight feet. While digging for tanks in the Chowringhee area upright stumps of Sundri trees (found mainly in the Sunderbans) were found at a depth of 4 to 5 feet.

A biography of Guru Nanak states that he came to these parts in 1503, while on a tour of India to preach and spread his religion. The place where he lived and preached was near the crossing of Chitpore Road and Harrison Road. The site was later bought by Guru Tegh Bahadur in 1666, where he built the Bada Sikh Sangat Gurdwara.[4] The *Ain-i-Akbari*, written between 1585 to 1596 by Abul Fazal, mentions Calcutta under Satgaon. Around 1575 Monohar Ghosh, a *gomasta* or land collector of Raja Todarmal during the reign of Emperor Akbar, settled at Sutanuti, soon after Bengal became a part of the Mughal Empire. His descendants lived in North Calcutta and one of them, Sri Hari Ghosh, is commemorated in a street named after him.

Gradually three villages grew up on the eastern bank of the river Hooghly—Kalikata, Sutanuti and Gobindapore—with a population of two to three hundred inhabitants. Nearby was the old temple of Kalighat. In 1560 a Portuguese merchant, Van den Broucke, drew a map of Bengal, locating Calcutta on the eastern bank of the river. *Chandimangal*, a ballad in praise of the goddess Chandi, written by Mukundaram towards the end of the sixteenth century, mentions Kalikata, Salkia, Chitpore and Kalighat. He also mentions Betor, later known as Bantra. Betor was a major port at that time. *Manasamangal*, written by Bipradas Piplai, mentions Kalikata and Kalighat as sites that come in the course of the voyage of his hero, Chand Saudagar. In 1687, Krishna Das in his book, *Narada Puran*, introduces himself at the end as living in the Bow Bazar area of Calcutta and belonging to the Subarna Banik Sampraday. When the Portuguese first came to Bengal in 1530, the two great centres of commerce were the ports of Chittagong in the east, which they called *Porto Grande*, or Great Haven, and Satgaon (*Saptagram*) in the west, named *Porto Piqueno* by them. Business thrived in these regions, and many European merchant princes came to these waters for trading. When the river near Satgaon was silted up and the traders moved to greener pastures, mostly to the river port of Hooghly, the Porto Piqueno was reduced to a desolate village of a few thatched huts (the present-day Adi Saptagram).

But four families of Basaks and one of Setts chose to utilize the facilities of the upcoming port of Betor on the western bank of the river Hooghly, and came to settle in the village of Gobindapore. They cleared the jungle by the river and built dwelling houses and a temple of their family deity, Gobindajee. An offshoot of the Setts moved away from Gobindapore to found a new village further north across the creek, by the side of the river, naming the site Kalikata. They had their houses at or near the site of the present day General Post Office. The East India Company bought their property when the Old Fort William was being built. The Setts and not Job Charnock should be regarded as the founding father of the city.

In a short time, they opened a trading centre in North Calcutta for the sale of cotton bales and cloth. This came to be known as Sutanuti or Cotton Bale Market.[5]

In the seventeenth century, the port of Betor too disappeared from history and the Calcutta area rose in importance. The English East India Company had their headquarters at Hooghly, with isolated factories in Dacca, Balasore, Cossim Bazar and Patna. The French were settled in Chander Nagar, the Dutch at Chinsurah and the Danes at Serampore. In 1686 Job Charnock became the Chief Agent of the British at Hooghly, but after a skirmish with the Mughal Fouzdar, he was compelled to sail down river and halt at Sutanuti. But as the Fouzdar's army came pursuing, the English fled to Hijli, the low deadly swamp near the mouth of the river. In three months, half of Charnock's troops were dead. An overture was made to the Fouzdar Nawab Shaista Khan and the English were back to Sutanuti.

In 1688, the Court of Directors of the Company sent a squadron of ships under the command of Captain Heath, who reached Sutanuti in September. He compelled Charnock to close down operations in Bengal, and took him to Fort St. George in Madras. But fifteen months later, the new Nawab, Ibrahim Khan, allowed the English East India Company to come back to Bengal.

So, finally, Job Charnock landed at Sutanuti, for the third time, on 24 August, 1690, and there began the saga of a great metropolis.

CALCUTTA IN 1690

One can reconstruct a view of the three villages and the surrounding areas at the time when Charnock landed at Sutanuti. Besides the three, there was a fourth village, Chitpore, from which a long road went up to Kalighat in the south. On the way, in the middle of the jungle, there was a Shiva temple probably erected by a hermit named Chowranghi, on the site now occupied by the Asiatic Society at 1 Park Street.[6] The river then was closer to the Strand Road and the part adjacent to it, on the east, still lay in the riverbed. The Setts and Basaks had their dwellings on the side of the river, west of Lal Dighi. But their weaving looms and paddy fields were a part of the present day Maidan. A creek originating from the river ran along the area immediately north of Government House along the present Creek Row and ended at the Salt Lakes. The creek was navigable and large boats used to ply through the creek. The early settlers used a bridge to cross the creek to reach their looms. In a cyclonic storm in 1737, many boats were destroyed on the creek, and a large sea-going vessel was hurled from the river, sailing over part of the town to its destruction in the creek. Accordingly, a part of the creek was called Dinga Bhanga. Later the creek was filled up, but the names Creek Row and Creek Lane bear testimony to its earlier existence.

It was probably Lalmohan Sett, son of Mukunda Ram Sett, one of the early settlers, who dug the Great Tank or Lal Dighi. Lalmohan also established a market east of Lal Dighi, which was called Lal Bazar.[7]

West of Lal Dighi, a descendant of the Zamindar Lakhsmi Kanta Majumdar (Sabarna Roychowdhury) built a *cutchery* (land-rent collection office). Later, Job Charnock rented this *cutchery* to establish the Company's office, which functioned up to 1706.

The climate of Calcutta at the time did not suit the Europeans. According to Charnock's contemporary, Alexander Hamilton, 'he (Charnock) could not have chosen a more unhealthful place on all the river; for three miles to the north-eastwards is a salt-water lake that overflows in September-October, and then prodigious number of fish resort thither, but in November and December when the floods are dissipated, those fishes are left to dry, and with their putrefaction affect the air with thick stinking vapours, which the north-east winds bring with them to Fort William, that they cause a yearly mortality. One year I was there, and there were reckoned in August about 1200 English, some military, some servants of the Company, some private merchants residing in the town and some seamen belonging to the shipping lying at the town, and before the beginning of January there were four hundred and sixty burials registered in the clerk's book of mortality.'[8]

The figures of 1200 English at this time has been disputed by English historians, according to whom the number could not be more than 51.

Charnock's selection of the site of the future headquarters of the East India Company in Bengal bears testimony to his long experience in Bengal. Unlike all the other European trading centres on the Hooghly, it was situated on the east bank of the river and therefore well defended on one side in case of an attack by the Nawab's army. On the east it was defended by the Salt Lake swamps and on the south by a deep impenetrable jungle. Being farthest downstream from the Mughal seat of power also ensured lesser interference. And the command of the river gave them the opportunity to keep an eye on the activities of other European competitors.

References

1. Blanford & Mendicot. *Manual of the Geology of India*, Part I, pp. 397-400.

2. Ray, A. K. *Census of India*, 1901, vol. VII.

3. Wilson C. R. *The Early Annals of the English in Bengal*, vol. I, pp. 128-29.

4. Deb, Raja Benoy Krishna Bahadur. *Kalikatar Itihas* (Bengali), edited by Subal Chandra Mitra, Calcutta 1982, p. 11.

5. Roy, Samaren. *Calcutta: Society and Challenge, 1690-1990*, Calcutta 1991, p. 8.

6. Cotton, H.E.A. *Calcutta Old and New*, Revised Edition, Calcutta 1980, pp. 2.

7. Sur, Atul. *Kalkata* (Bengali), Calcutta 1981, p. 15.

8. Losty, J.P. *Calcutta, City of Palaces*, London 1990, p. 15.

Chapter Two

Europeans at Calcutta and Job Charnock

About the year 1530, twenty years after Albuquerque's conquest of Goa, the Portuguese sailors began to open up trade in Bengal. The river to Calcutta was easily navigable and the Portuguese sailors would not anyway venture further up the river. Their usual anchoring places were Garden Reach and Betor on the opposite bank of the river Hooghly. Every year when the ships arrived from Goa, innumerable thatched houses were erected, markets were opened and all sorts of provisions and stores brought to the waterside. An immense number of galliasses lay at anchor in the deep water waiting, while the small budgerows made their way up the river past Baranagore, Dakshineswar and Agarpara to Satgaon, and returned filled with silk and muslin, lac, sugar and rice. During these months the banks on both sides of the river were alive with people and a brisk trade was carried on. But no sooner had the last boat come back from Satgaon, and its cargo safely shipped aboard the galliasses, than they set fire to the temporary and improvised houses of bamboo and straw, and the place vanished almost as suddenly as Aladin's palace when carried off by the genie. Away sailed the Portuguese back to Goa, leaving no traces of their coming except the burnt straw and ruined huts. And yet a careful observer might have noticed more important consequences, for in those dying embers the nucleus of the future city of Calcutta was already taking shape.[1]

The Dutch had a stint in the area, but left it for Chinsurah up the river for their trading centre and factory. The Armenians came to Calcutta before the English and set up a flourishing business. The oldest Christian grave discovered in the city in 1895 is the grave of Rezabebe dating back to 1630, still standing in the Armenian Church graveyard.

The English came to Bengal in 1651, when Bridgeman and Stephens were sent in charge of a party to establish a factory at Hooghly and purchase saltpetre. When the Mughal *Fauzdar* of Hooghly attacked the English factory, Job Charnock came to settle at Sutanuti, 24 miles downstream. Later they moved their trading centre to Hijli, but skirmishes continued. After a treaty, the English returned to Sutanuti. But some time later they left the place to set up a permanent trading centre at Chittagong.

Many European sailors died either in the villages or in the ships passing through the river. For their burial a site near the river in Calcutta was used and the site assumed the name of The Old Burial Ground. This remained the European burial ground until 1767 and twenty years later the graves were dug up and the site was used for building the St. John's Church.

JOB CHARNOCK

Job Charnock was born in Lancashire, England. He came to India in 1655/56. He was posted at the Patna factory from 1658 to 1680 and was chief of the Cossim Bazar factory from 1681 to 1685.

He was the only servant of the Company who was above criticism in service and monetary matters. There is the story of his rescue of a beautiful young Indian lady from performing *sati* (i.e. ascending the funeral pyre of her dead husband to die with him), and marrying her. Sources put this happening either in Patna or in Bengal. But there is no proof of their marriage, or records of baptism of any of his children. The grave of Mrs. Charnock, who pre-deceased him, was never found. But they lived together for nineteen years. Alexander Hamilton, writing on this episode of Charnock's life, says,

> Instead of converting her to Christianity, she made him a proselyte to paganism, and the only part of Christianity remarkable in him, was burying her decently, and he built a tomb over her, where all his life after her death, he kept the anniversary day of her death by sacrificing a cock on her tomb, after the pagan manner; and this was and is the common report, and I have been credibly informed.[2]

The ritual of sacrificing a cock on his wife's tomb, if true, seems to be related to the cult of the Panch Pir or Five Saints in Bihar, a ritual observed there by low-class Muslims as well as by Hindus, that may have been picked up by Charnock when he was the Chief of Patna in Bihar.

On 24 August 1690, when he landed in Sutanuti again, Charnock found the old living quarters in an uninhabitable state. To find shelter from the pounding rain Charnock and his men had to go back to the ship. Eventually some thatched houses were built at Sutanuti for them. They settled there and trading thrived. Accounts of the location and species of the tree under which Charnock would sit, smoke his *hookah*, and conduct official business differ considerably. According to some, it was a *peepul* tree at the place later called *Baithak*-khana. According to others, it was a tamarind tree near the old burial ground. One only wonders why Charnock would venture so far nearly to the end of the city to indulge in his *hookah*![3]

Job Charnock died in Calcutta on 10 January 1693 and was interred in the Old Burial Ground, which later became part of St. John's Church. Charnock's eldest daughter Mary married Charles Eyre, who was Chief Agent of the East India Company in Calcutta from 1694 to 1699, and probably erected the mausoleum between 1695 and 1698. Mary died in Calcutta on 19 February 1696 or 97. She was interred beside her father and they share the same tombstone. Charnock's two other daughters Elizabeth and Katharine also died in Calcutta and were interred in the St. John's Churchyard, probably in the family mausoleum.

Figure 1: Charnock's Mausoleum at St. John's Church
Photo courtesy Calcutta Historical Society

Figure 2. Charnock and his Daughter Catherine White's Headstone
Photo N.R. Bose

But there is no mention of Charnock's wife in contemporary records. No attempts were made to preserve his residence, which was auctioned off for Rs. 575.

The Charnock mausoleum is a massive edifice, octagonal in form, with a double dome and an urn at the top. This is probably the oldest piece of masonry in Calcutta. At each face there is a low and narrow archway. It is likely that it contained, when first erected, two table monuments, side by side, whose covering slabs of shining black stone now fill up the western arches of the chamber. The slab, which bears Charnock's name, also has the name of his daughter Mary. It is commonly believed that Charles Eyre erected the mausoleum after his wife's death, but possibly that is not true, as the inscription of Charnock's name on the slab seems older, cut around 1695.[4] The inscriptions for Mary were added later, in the vacant portion of the same stone, after her death. There are four black stone slabs now, within the mausoluem. The two in the centre are in memory of Charnock and his daughters, Mary Eyre and Katharine White; the latter's husband Jonathan White's stone lies among those which encircle the mausoleum, outside. Flanking them, on the right, is a slab in memory of Mrs. Maria Eyles, and on the left, is a tablet which recalls the name of Surgeon William Hamilton. The inscriptions on Charnock's tomb are in Latin, the English translation of which runs thus:

> May the Lord remember the dead, Job Charnock, an English Gentleman, and lately, in this most worthy kingdom of Bengal, Agent of the English, has deposited the remains of his mortality beneath this marble, that they may rest in the hope of the blessed resurrection unto the coming of Christ, the Judge; who, after he wandered abroad on soil not of his own, returned to the home of his eternity on the 10th January 1692 (93).[5]

The tombstones of Surgeon Hamilton, Maria Eyles and others were transferred to the Charnock mausoleum when the old European Burial Ground was dug up to lay the foundations of St. John's Church.

In 1892, two hundred years after Charnock's death, the Public Works Department, engaged in a thorough repair of the mausoluem, dug up Charnock's grave, up to a depth of six feet, one does not know why. Was it to ascertain whether his wife was also in the same grave, or to unearth hidden treasures, or may be a hidden vault? No explanation is recorded for this intriguing act of digging. But the Reverend H.B. Hyde, then Chaplain of St. John's Church, informed a meeting of the Asiatic Society in 1893, that no other coffin or vault was discovered. Digging up to a depth of six feet, a part of the bones of a left forearm was found, in the same position that a left hand is kept, in a coffin, across the breast. After this discovery further digging was stopped and the grave was filled in.

P. Thankappan Nair has some interesting information: Charnock's tombstone was probably brought from Pallavaram, near Madras. All the old tombstones in St. John's Churchyard were of the same type. Thomas H. Holland, a noted geologist, examined these stones, and found that they were of a stone hitherto unknown to geologists. Holland named it 'Charnockite'.[6]

References

1. Wilson, C.R. *The Early Annals of the English in Bengal*, Part 1, p. 134.
2. Losty, J.P. *Calcutta, City of Palaces*, London 1990, p. 16.
3. *Bengal Past & Present*, 1914, vol. VIII, Part 2, p. 168.
4. Cotton, H.E.A. *Calcutta Old & New*, p. 433.
5. Nair, P. Thankappan. *Calcutta in the Seventeenth Century*, Calcutta 1986, p. 440.
6. Ibid. p. 442.

Chapter Three

Lal Dighi, The Great Tank, Tank Square:
Dalhousie Square to Binoy Badal Dinesh Bagh

Lal Dighi was the nucleus of the transformation of three sleepy villages to a great metropolis. Around this tank the English East India Company established their factory, fort and business houses and under the Crown, the Capital of India and the city of Calcutta.

According to Bengali historians, this tank was dug by a wealthy Bengali merchant, Lal Mohan Sett, east of his residence by the river. The Setts used to hold the Holi Festival, or Doljatra as it is known in Bengal, with great pomp and splendour. Two platforms would be erected in the Lal Dighi, one in the north for the deity of Sri Radha, and one in the south for Gobindajee. A temporary market, called Radha Bazar, would come up every year for *abir* or powdered colours. Some historians have suggested that as the tank waters used to turn red with the red Holi colours, the tank assumed the name Lal Dighi.[1]

Figure 3: Dalhousie Square and St. Andrew's Church

There are other explanations however for the name. Kathleen Blechynden suggests that the name probably came from the reflections of the red wall of the Old Fort William on the tank waters (the fort was later built west of the tank).[2] There is a view that attributes the name to the reflection of the red walls of the Old Mission Church. Lord Curzon refuted the 'reflection theory,' on the ground that the name Lal Dighi or Lal Bagh is quite common in Bengal.[3]

The Dutch Admiral Stavorinus, who visited the settlement in 1770, writes: 'It was dug by the orders of the Government, to provide the inhabitants of Calcutta with drinking water, which is very sweet and pleasant. The number of springs which it contains, keeps the water at the same level.'[4]

The tank covered 25 acres of ground at that time. In 1709, the Company carried out restoration and extension of the tank. Old records show that the monthly upkeep of the tank was only ten rupees; rupees twenty-four went for planting orange trees and rupees twenty for cleaning the tank and repairing the walls.[5] In May 1755, Mr. Holwell requested the Board of Directors of the Company that he might have permission to repair and enclose the tank and prohibit the washing of people and horses therein.

The Lal Dighi and its surroundings are vividly portrayed in the paintings of European artists who visited Calcutta during the later part of the eighteenth century.

The Maidan then was a tiger-infested jungle, but the walks by the Lal Dighi were safe for evening promenades, moonlight picnics or just a brief romance.

During the reign of Warren Hastings the tank was cleansed and completely embanked. The water was always esteemed the sweetest in Calcutta and, until the introduction of the municipal water supply, remained the chief source of drinking water for the European community.[6]

Figure 4: Wellesly Place, Statue of Marquis of Wellesley and Writer's Building
Photo courtesy Calcutta Historical Society

Theodore Forresti and John Oliffres drew a plan of Calcutta in 1742 in pen and ink and wash. Among other features of the area it shows Lal Dighi now called the Great Tank stretching from the Old Fort in the west to the Rope Walk in the east. On the eastern side of the tank stood the rope factory of the East India Company; the road next to it called Rope Walk (later Mission Row). Building on the eastern side of the tank up to the Rope Walk was prohibited, but from 1779 to 1784 Antonio Angelo Tremamondo ran a riding school in the area. In 1780 a new road was built, running from the Old Court House in the north along the eastern side of the tank, ending at the Esplanade.

A coloured etching by Thomas Daniell painted in 1786 shows the eastern side of the Tank Square, the old Mission Church and some contemporary houses, and the eastern gate of the tank from which stairs run down to the water. On the southern side can be seen three company soldiers loitering in the park, in the part of the park then used as a training ground for the militia.

Other works by Thomas Daniell, from 1786, offer views of the Tank Square looking north, including part of the Old Fort, the Holwell Monument, Writers' Building and a part of the Old Court House; the eastern side of the Old Fort, Clive Street, the Theatre and the Holwell monument. A coloured etching painted by William Bailey in 1794 shows the Tank Square and the rapidly changing skyline of the area.

The coloured aquatint by James Baillie Fraser in 1819 shows the marked changes in the eastern side of the tank. In place of the Old Court House we see a new church, St. Andrew's Kirk (Scottish Church); on the eastern boundary of the Tank Square we see a new aqueduct running throughout for supply of water to the natives. (In 1820, the Company installed a steam engine at Chand Paul Ghat to supply water to different parts of the city through similar aqueducts.) In another aquatint by the same artist in 1819, we see part of the tank and the western side of the park where people are seen relaxing with the changing skyline on the western side. A fine picture by Frederick Fiebig in 1845 gives a remarkable view of the Old Court House Street from the portals of St. Andrew's Kirk. On the right one can see the ornamental railings of the Tank Square, with lamp posts adorning the corners. On the street pedestrians vie with an assorted collection of carriages, bullock-carts and palanquins.

On the southern side of Tank Square, a marble portico was erected in 1824, with a statue, by Chantrey, of the Marquess of Hastings, facing the entrance to Wellesley Place. Sir Charles D'Oyly's painting of 1835 makes the statue the centre of the picture, but a part of the Writers' Building is also visible. The Portico and the statue were later incorporated into the Dalhousie Institute, which was built in 1865. Probably at this juncture the name of the Tank Square was changed to Dalhousie Square, after Dalhousie who was Governor General just before the mutiny.

The Dalhousie Institute contained a large hall 90 feet by 48 feet with walls lined with marble, a semi-circular roof, richly decorated. It also had a library, a reading room and a billiard room. It was erected as a monumental edifice, to contain, within its walls, statues and busts of great men. The Dalhousie Testimonial Fund, the Havelock, Neill and Nicholson Fund and the Venables Fund supplemented by public subscription to the extent of   Rs. 30,000 were 'appropriated' for its erection. The foundation was laid on 4 March 1865, with full Masonic honours, in the presence of Sir Cecil Beadon, the Lt. Governor of Bengal, and a large assemblage. Mr. John Remfry, founding Secretary of the Institute, took great pains to establish and run the institution. Unfortunately, after Independence, this beautiful edifice was demolished and the present day Telephone Bhavan was erected on the site. The croquet and tennis courts of the Calcutta Trades Club next to the Dalhousie Institute also disappeared on the boundary of the Telephone Bhavan.

Attempts have been made to beautify the Dalhousie Square at different times. In 1868, a fountain was erected on a pedestal at the south-west corner of the Square. When Lord Curzon became the Viceroy of India in 1899, he took great pains to identify the historic landmarks of Calcutta and beautify them. He spelt out his improvements of the Dalhousie Square:

Regarding Dalhousie Square—the Tank Square and Park of old Calcutta—as a spot of historical sanctity as well as natural charm, I laid out the ground afresh, squared the famous Lal Dighi or Red Tank, surrounded it with a pillared balustrade and a beautiful garden, swept away the unsightly sheds and public conveniences, and converted it into an open-air resort for the public and Valhalla for the Bengal Government.[7]

The Square was again cleansed and some beautification done, when Sir Andrew Fraser was the Lt. Governor of Bengal in the early twentieth century. There were some statues and memorials in the Square; an obelisk was erected on the north-east corner in memory of Mr. Colesworthy Grant, founder of C.S.P.C.A, (Calcutta Society for Prevention of Cruelty to Animals), and the writer of *Annals of Rural Bengal*. There were statues of Sir Ashley Eden, Lt. Governor of Bengal (1877-82), Sir John Woodburn and the Maharaja of Darbhanga at the south-west corner. Over the years, the square has been encroached upon many times, first, with the laying of tram tracks inside, during the British regime. After Independence, the Telephone Bhavan came up on the site of Dalhousie Institute, along with the eyesore of tinsheds, for the parking of government vehicles opposite Writers' Buildings, and the minibus terminus on the north-west corner.

From Lal Dighi to the Great Tank, to Tank Square and to Dalhousie Square, the name changed after Independence to Binoy-Badal-Dinesh Bagh, to commemorate the historic adventure of three young Bengali revolutionaries. On 8 December 1930, three young members of the Bengal Volunteers, Binoy Basu (1908-30), Badal (Sudhir) Gupta (1912-30) and Dinesh Gupta (1911-31) made a daring entrance into the Writers' Buildings, Headquarters of the Bengal Government, and shot dead Mr. Simpson, the Inspector General of Prisons. Binoy and Badal committed suicide in the Writers' Buildings, but Dinesh, who shot himself, survived and was hospitalized. He was hanged in Calcutta on 7 July 1931.[8]

Though attempts have been made from time to time to fill up the tank for various reasons, good sense has prevailed, and the Lal Dighi is still there.

References

1. Sur, Atul. *Kolkata* (Bengali), Calcutta 1981, p. 29.
2. Blechynden, Kathleen. *Calcutta past and present,* Calcutta 1905, New Edition 1978, p. 18.
3. Curzon, The Marquis of Keddlestone. *British Government in India,* London 1925, vol. i, p. 3.
4. Cotton, H.E.A. *Calcutta Old and New,* Calcutta p. 268.
5. Blechynden, Kathleen. op. cit. p. 18.
6. Cotton H.E.A. op. cit. p. 269.
7. Curzon. op. cit. p. 91.
8. *Muktir Sangrame Bharat* (Bengali), Compilation, Calcutta 1986, p. 131.

Chapter Four

The Old Fort and the Black Hole

S
ir John Goldsborough, the Company's Chief Governor of all the Settlements, came to Sutanuti in 1693 after Charnock's death. Credit must be given to Goldsborough for shifting the nucleus of the settlement from Sutanuti to Calcutta. For the lines drawn by him became the walls of the factory compound. In 1668 permission was obtained from Azim Us Shan, grandson of Aurangzeb, and then the Mughal *Subahdar* in Bengal (in consideration of a gift of Rs. 16,000) to purchase the right of renting the three villages, Sutanuti, Kalikata and Gobindapore, from the existing landlords, the Majumdars (Sabarna Roy Chowdhurys). The latter were given a sum of Rs. 1300. The Company thought that they had obtained the *zamindari* rights of the villages and they could collect rent from the inhabitants, and the annual payment to the *Subahdar* was just under Rs. 1200.[1] Ralph Sheldon, a member of the Council, was appointed in 1700 to be in charge of collecting the revenues of Calcutta, while acting as a magistrate, with a police force under him, for the native population. Thus he became the first Collector and Magistrate in British India. The English were always concerned with fortifying their interests in Bengal. When Raja Sobha Singh rebelled against the Nawab, the latter permitted the English, the French and the Dutch to take steps to defend their interests. In the mean time the English bought the properties of the Setts north and west of Lal Dighi to extend their factory and offices. The Setts went over to a place north of Burra Bazar and settled there on the bank of the river. They later built a bathing *ghat*, made of stone, giving the area its present name, Pathuriaghata.

The building of the fort began in 1699; in 1700 a walled enclosure and a bastion was completed. It was named Fort William after the reigning English King William III. The actual site of the fort is the plot now occupied by the General Post Office, Calcutta Collectorate, The Reserve Bank Building and the East Indian Railways premises on the east. To the north of the fort lay the Fairlie Place and on the south the present day Koilaghat Street where they had their warehouses. On the west flowed the river Hooghly, which was much nearer than it is now. The eastern ramparts looked on the Lal Dighi. The fort was an irregular tetragon in shape. Its north side was 340 feet long, the south side 485, its east and

Plate 1. George Lambert (attributed), Old Fort William from the land side with St. Anne's Church in front. 1730

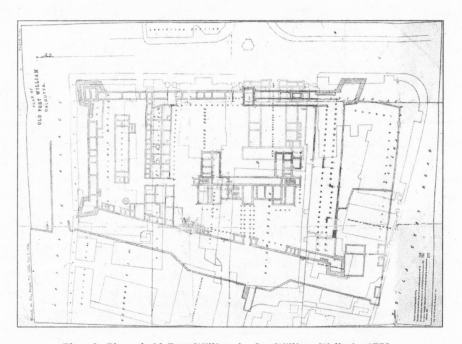

Plate 2. Plan of old Fort William by Lt. William Wells in 1753.

west sides each 710 feet. At the four corners were small, square bastions, each mounting ten guns, with the projecting main east gate carrying five guns. Curtain walls about four feet thick and eighteen feet high connected the bastions. The wall to the riverside was of solid masonry, with embrasures for heavy guns, and the space between this river wall and the west curtain was closed at each end by small cross walls with palisaded gates. Within, the fort was cut into two unequal sections by a block of buildings running east and west, damp and unhealthy, and known as the Long Row, in which were housed the Company's young officers. The smaller northern section contained the magazine and armoury, the dispensary and various shops and stores. It had a small river gate, near which stood the flagstaff. The south section had two gates, one leading to the river, the steps, and the landing stage; the other opening on the present day Koilaghat Street. The south section was used for storing the Company's goods, import and export warehouses and for the carpenters' yard.

In the middle of the south section was the Governor's House that Alexander Hamilton, a contemporary, found the best and the most regular piece of architecture that was ever seen in the East. This building formed three sides of a rectangle, the best and principal face being 245 feet long. At the centre of the western face was the great gate, from which a colonnade ran down to the water gate and the landing stage. The large hall and the main rooms of the factory lay on the first floor, which was approached by a grand staircase to the left of the great gate. The south-east wing contained the apartments of the Governor. A raised cloister ran round the three corners of the court enclosed within the building.

On either side of the east gate of the fort and looking on to Lal Dighi there extended a double row of arches parallel to the east curtain wall. The first row of the line of arches to the left had a range of rooms built against the wall, the second row forming a verandah or piazza, west of the rooms. Each of these arches measured 8 feet 9 inches. The first four between the gate and the south-east bastion were used as the court guard and were left open to the piazza in front. The next nine arches formed intercommunicating rooms, employed as soldiers' barracks. They were separated from the piazza by a small parapet built between the arches. The fourteenth and fifteenth arches adjoined the stairs leading to the bastion and were completely walled in. This was the military prison that would later become notorious as The Black Hole.[2]

The first known pictorial view of the fort was painted about 1730 by George Lambert, from the perspective of the west bank of the river; another oil on canvas, painted in 1730 and attributed to George Lambert, depicts the eastern face of the fort with St. Anne's Church in the foreground. It also shows the eastern face of the magnificent Governor's House inside the fort. An Anonymous View of Calcutta in 1756, which was published in Robert Orme's *History*, vol. II in 1778 in London, shows a panoramic view of the city from the river showing the fort, the Company's office (old) and some buildings that came up on the river front. In 1753, William Wells drew a plan of Fort William and part of Calcutta in pen and ink and water colour.

The fort was not constructed according to any of the established norms, Indian or European, followed in the architecture of forts or fortifications. Hence it proved to be vulnerable in the face of the first assault by a superior force. Initially, the garrison had about 100 soldiers, but when it fell, it had a larger number.

Once Siraj-ud-Daulah became the Nawab of Bengal, he became apprehensive of the increasing fortification of the English in Calcutta. In no uncertain terms, he warned them that they were in Bengal as traders, and that they were misusing the power given to them for collecting the rent of the three villages, and that this was causing loss of revenue to the Nawab; and thirdly, that the English were sheltering fugitives from the Nawab's territory. In 1756, Siraj-ud-Daulah marched from Murshidabad to teach the English a lesson. In June the Cossim Bazar factory was captured and the Nawab began marching towards Calcutta. According to contemporary records, he had with him an army of 50,000 to 60,000 men, 250 cannons and 500 elephants. On 16 June, the actual attack began with the Nawab's army destroying all the Indian houses east and south of the fort. On 18 June the attacking army moved close to the eastern and northern batteries. A great struggle ensued, but the English gradually retreated to the fort. There was utter confusion inside the fort and a lamentable lack of leadership was evident. It was decided that the European ladies and children would be sent by ship to safety, but on 19 June the Governor Roger Drake and the military commander, Captain-Commandant Minchin, embarked on a ship and left for a safer haven leaving the others to their fate. John Zephania Holwell, the Third in Council, became the leader of the defenders. But after some vigorous defence they surrendered on 20 June. The Nawab entered the fort and held a *durbar*. The Nawab announced that no harm would come to the survivors. What happened actually on that fateful night of 20 June 1756 in the fort, will never be fully known, the facts lost in a great historical controversy. According to John Zephania Holwell, the Nawab, annoyed over the small amount of money found in the fort coffers, ordered 146 survivors to be confined in the military prison, a room about 18 feet x 14 feet. During the night 123 of them persished due to suffocation and lack of water. Next morning only 23 survivors were set free and the dead bodies were flung into the ditch. Thus the myth of the 'Black Hole' Tragedy was born. The British historians have ever since harped on the depravity of Nawab Siraj-ud-Daulah and the character of the Indians in general. Doubts have been raised about several claims made by colonial historians. Were there 146 survivors really left in the fort? Probably not. Could 146 persons be physically accommodated in such a small room? Probably not. None of the Council meetings of the Company mentioned anything about the tragedy nor adopted any resolution to condole the death of so many of their servants. The two most important Muslim historians of the period, Nawab Golam Hosain Khan, the author of the *Syer-ul-Mutakkherin* completed in 1783 (he was no friend of Siraj-ud-Daulah), and Golam Hosain

Salim of Maldah, the author of *Riaz-us-Salatien*, completed in 1787-88, did not make any reference to the Black Hole Tragedy. None of the Indian inhabitants of Calcutta knew about the tragedy, though in India news of a calamity travels fast by word of mouth. The accounts of the survivors, Holwell, William Tooke and Capt. Mills, contradict each other. One survivor stated that Capt. Mills was not present at the fort at all, having chosen the safer haven of Falta along with others. But the myth became a part of history, finding place in every colonial history book.

In 1916, Mr. J.H. Little wrote an article in *Bengal Past and Present*, the journal of the Calcutta Historical Society (established 1907), vol. XI, Part 1, Serial No. 21, describing the story of the 'Black Hole' as a 'Gigantic Hoax'. Controversy broke out again. A special meeting of the Calcutta Historical Society was held on 24 March 1916 at 9 p.m. in the hall of the Asiatic Society of Bengal to discuss the Black Hole Question. The Venerable Archdeacon Walter K. Firminger presided. Mr. J.H. Little, who had reopened the controversy in the pages of *Bengal Past and Present*, spoke first, pointing to the discrepancies in the different statements of Holwell and others, and defending his position with well-established facts. Professor E.F. Oaten, speaking next, challenged Mr. Little. The Hon'ble Mr. E.J. Monahan, speaking next, spoke in the same vein as Professor Oaten, but in a moderate manner.

But the last speaker Mr. Akshaya Kumar Maitraya supported Mr. Little's argument, concluding in his long speech:

> True it is that this gigantic hoax of Holwell is recorded in every textbook as an actual event of History, and we have to teach it, and generations after generations have to continue to learn it by heart. But it is also true, as Lord Acton told us, that "the historians of former ages, unapproachable for us in knowledge and in talent, cannot be our limit. We have the power to be more rigidly impersonal, disinterested and just than they; and to learn from undisguised and genuine records to look with remorse upon the past, and to the future with assured hope of better things; bearing this in mind that if we lower our standard in History, we cannot uphold it in Church and State.

Mr. Little replied in brief. The debate was over near midnight.[3]

Coming back to John Zephania Holwell and his Black Hole story, Holwell erected, at his own cost, an obelisk at the north-western corner of Lal Dighi, or Tank Square, in 1760. It was supposed to mark the site of the ditch where the corpses of the inmates of the prison were flung on 21 June 1756. The obelisk had a memorial tablet in which only 48 names were inscribed, and had a very vivid pictorial representation, as it appears in Upjohn's map of 1793 and in two of the paintings of Thomas Daniell, and in Fraser's *Views of Calcutta*, published in 1824. The memorial in the last named picture is about 50 feet high, without any railings, and people are seen resting against it and the barber plying his trade at the base. The East India Company never took the pains to maintain it. Falling into disrepair it became an ugly sight, till it was pulled down in 1821 under the orders of the Governor General, the Marquess of Hastings. When Lord Curzon came to Calcutta as Viceroy, he entrusted Dr. C.R. Wilson of the Indian Education Department to demarcate the sites of the old fort, the Black Hole and the Holwell obelisk. Dr. Wilson did a fine job. He discovered the site of the Black Hole, which is between the northern end of the G.P.O and the southern end of the Calcutta Collectorate just beyond the pavement. Lord Curzon had the site covered in black marble, enclosed with a railing and an inscription on the wall.

Under Curzon's order, a white marble replica of the original brick and plaster Holwell obelisk was erected on the same spot. This new obelisk was a personal gift from the Viceroy, and was unveiled by him on 19 December 1902. The obelisk was finally removed in 1940, when Netaji Subhas Chandra Bose led a movement for its removal.

ST. ANNE'S CHURCH

The first Anglican church was situated on the eastern side of the curtain wall of the old fort at the site of the present day Rotunda of the Writers' Buildings. The church was built by public subscription and a subsidy from the East India Company. The church was named

Figure 5: Replica of Holwell's Monument, Old Customs House in background

St. Anne's after the reigning queen of England. It was consecrated on 9 May 1709 by Bishop Anderson.[4]

Captain Alexander Hamilton notes that the 'steeple was very lofty, the Governor on every Sunday walked in solemn procession, attended by all the civil servants and all the military on duty.'[5]

An anonymous painting attributed to George Lambert shows the church in the foreground with the east side of the Fort William behind and the northern fringe of the Tank Square on the left. The church was situated within its compound. The nave of the church was about 20 feet wide by 80 feet long, with a slightly convex roof, terminating in an apse with five windows of full height. On each side were aisles, five bays with pitched roofs, separated from the nave by pillars. The handsome and very tall steeple, apparently of wood sheathed in metal, was built to house the bell which was acquired in 1712, and this was finished in 1716. In 1724 the steeple was severely damaged by lightning, but was repaired. It was finally thrown down by the great cyclone of 1737. Around this time the Europeans had begun to live round the Tank Square with the Fort and the church in the vicinity. St. Anne's Church was completely destroyed during the siege of the Fort William by Nawab Siraj-ud-Daulah in 1756 and never rebuilt.

References

1. Losty, J.P. *Calcutta, City of Palaces*, London 1990, p. 17.
2. Cotton, H.E.A. *Calcutta Old and New*, Revised Edition, Calcutta 1980, pp. 352–354.
3. 'The Black Hole Debate,' *Bengal Past and Present*, vol. XII, part. 1, no. 23, January-March 1916, reprinted in *Bengal Past and Present*, vol. CVI. parts i and II, Nos 202–203, 1987, pp. 71–112.
4. C.R. Wilson. *Early Annals of British India*, p. 215.
5. Cotton. op. cit. p. 381.

Chapter Five

The Changing Face of the Old Fort Area

Siraj-ud-Daulah left Calcutta, naming it Alinagar, under the charge of Raja Manik Chand as the Military Governor. But when the news of the debacle reached Fort St. George in Madras, an army under the command of Colonel Robert Clive was sent to Bengal. Robert Clive recaptured Calcutta on 2 January 1757. They found the fort indefensible, and the buildings inside badly damaged. St. Anne's Church, the Company's House and most of the big houses around the Tank Square were destroyed. After a few skirmishes a temporary peace was agreed with the Nawab. Within a few months, on 23 June 1757, Clive defeated the depleted army of Nawab Siraj-ud-Daulah (aided by the treachery of his most trusted commander Mir Jaffar), at the Battle of Plassey, and Siraj was murdered soon after. In Clive's presence, Mir Jaffar was installed at the Masnad in Murshidabad on 29 June. The new Nawab had to pay the English a huge amount of money; over 70 lac of rupees was delivered to Clive and his committee in Murshidabad and despatched to Calcutta in 700 chests in 100 boats. As most of the European Calcutta and the great Indian Bazar (Burra Bazar) had been destroyed by the Nawab's army a huge amount of compensation money arrived from the new Nawab, Rs. 100 lac for the Company, 50 for the European community, 20 for the Hindu inhabitants and 7 for the Armenians. New buildings began to appear, with Calcutta filling up fast. Although some plans were drawn up to build a new fort in the middle of the English Town, these were shelved, considering the siege of the previous year and the debacle. Captain Brohier, the Chief Engineer, chose instead Gobindapore, the southernmost of the three villages, for the new fort's site. Old inhabitants of Gobindapore were compensated with land in Sutanuti. Brohier laid out the lines of the new fort in August 1757 and work began in October. The jungle eastwards was cleared to form an Esplanade which continued northwards to a new road (now Esplanade Row) marking the southern border of the town; moving east the clearance met with the road to Kalighat and towards south to a new road in continuation of the Marhatta Ditch. The whole area was cleared to form a great expanse of lush green with absolute prohibition of building thereon. Thus was born the Maidan.[1] Coming back to the Old Fort William, part of the fort was repaired to house the Company's army, as the new fort was not yet ready. Some surviving buildings within the fort were used as the Customs House, while the remaining part of the old Factory House, i.e. the northern wing with its verandah in front of it, was used as the Customs Master's House. One of the buildings just behind the River Gate of the fort was given a new gabled roof, and this served the Protestant community as a church for 20 years before St. John's was built. In a painting by Thomas Daniell in 1786, the dilapidated south-eastern bastion of the old fort can be seen, along with the Holwell obelisk.

Another coloured etching by Thomas Daniell from 1786 shows the old Fort Ghat and a view of the western portion of the Old Fort. Next to the Old Fort Ghat was the Customs House Wharf depicted on a coloured lithograph by Sir Charles D'Oyly in 1835.

Now it was time to pull down the old fort to make way for new buildings to house the power centre of Imperial India. It was left to a whole line of early technocrats and historians to rediscover for posterity a near-exact demarcation of the Old Fort. Roskell Bayne of the East Indian Railway, while putting the foundations of a new office building (at the Fairlie Place Corner), was the first to expose the greater part of the northern end of the Old Fort in 1883; deducing the remainder from the measurements and drawings given in published works, he could recreate the southern part of the building, and believed he had discovered the actual site of the Black Hole. A white marble slab was fixed in 1884 on the interior of a great masonry gateway leading into the G.P.O. (for the latter had by then been erected on the greater part of the old Customs House site). Meanwhile in 1891, Mr. C.R. Wilson, profiting by the discovery in the British Museum of Lt. Wells' map of Calcutta of 1753, which gives an exact plan of the Old Fort, had started a fresh series of explorations for which the final removal of the old Customs House provided an opening. Beginning with the exposure of the foundations of the Eastern Gate, he proceded to reconstruct the Eastern Curtain from the Gate to the south-east bastion. He was thus able to find the exact site of the Black Hole, a few feet away from that marked by Mr. Bayne. Accusations have been made against the East Indian Railway and Mr. Bayne that he had made no attempts to preserve the part of the Old Fort he discovered. In 1895-96, when the old house which was used to store the post office records was pulled down to make room for a new building, Wilson was able to test the accuracy of his plan and trace out clearly the lines of the south-west bastion of the Old Fort. This time none of the walls was cut away, and excavations showed in clear unbroken continuity the line of the curtain, the slope of the bastion, the roof of the staircase with the river walls and gun platforms.

On 28 February, a special meeting was convened at the Yard of the G.P.O. at Lord Curzon's initiative to consider the whole question of demarcating the area of the Old Fort William. Curzon personally pinpointed the site of the fort.[2] Thanks to Lord Curzon's interest we are left with a clear picture of the site of the Old Fort as it was in the old days and how the site looks today with its new buildings.

Lord Curzon soon enough had both the outer and inner lines of the curtain and bastions of the Old Fort, wherever they had not been built over, traced on the ground by brass lines cut into the stone of the pavement (some of them are on the main steps of the G.P.O.); and white marble tablets were inserted into the walls of the adjacent buildings with inscriptions indicating the parts of the Old Fort that originally stood there.

First, a marble tablet with the following inscription was placed on the wall of the G.P.O. outside the new iron gateway:

Behind the gateway
Immediately adjoining this spot
Is the site of the Black Hole prison
In Old Fort William.

This stone tablet has now been removed to the Philatelic Museum.

A little to the south, the big steps of the G.P.O., overlooking Dalhousie Square, are practically identical for a portion of their length with the outer wall of the south-east bastion. Here accordingly are brass lines let into the steps, the space between them being the exact thickness of the ancient wall. A tablet on the adjoining wall explains:

The brass lines
In the adjacent steps and pavement
Mark the position and extent
of part of the South-east bastion
Of Old Fort William,
The extreme South-east point being
95 feet
From this wall.

Entering through the new iron gateway there was a kitchen chamber, with a tablet on the outside wall:

The two lines of twelve arches
To the west of this tablet
Are all that remains above ground
Of Old Fort William and
Originally formed a portion of the arcade
Within the South curtain.
The Black Hole prison was a small room
Formed by bricking up two arches

Of a similar but smaller arcade
Within the East curtain
South of the East gate.

Close to this another tablet explains the neighbouring brass lines:

The brass lines on the stone
On the adjacent ground
Mark the Position and extent
Of the South curtain
Of Old Fort William.

At the corner of the red brick building of the Calcutta Collectorate next to the G.P.O. the tablet reads:

Sixteen feet behind this wall
Was the entrance of the East Gate
Of Old Fort William through which
The bodies of those who perished
In the Black Hole were brought and
Thrown into the ditch
On the 21st June 1756.

The site of the next tablet has changed, the Customs House where the tablet was inserted having given way to the Reserve Bank of India Building. The inscription read:

To the west of this tablet
Extended the range of buildings
Called the "Long Row"
Which contained the lodgings
Of the Company's Writers
And divided the Old Fort
Into two sections.

Further north we come to the East Indian Railways Office (now Eastern Railway), which was once the north-east corner of the Old Fort. A brass line in the stone pavement and tablet commemorates the fact:

> The brass lines in the stone
> On the adjacent ground
> Mark
> The position and extent
> Of part of
> The North-East bastion
> Of Old Fort William.

Entering Fairlie Place moving west, the wall on the left hand is identical with the line of the north side of the Old Fort, till we come to a tablet, which records the position of the north-west bastion:

> The brass lines
> In the stone on the adjacent ground
> Mark the position and size and part of
> The North-West bastion
> Of Old Fort William.

A little further on, we enter a gate on the left and reach the quadrangle inside the East Indian Railways Office. On the right hand wall there is a tablet:

> The brass lines
> In the stone of the adjacent ground
> Mark the position and extent of the
> Northern portion of the West curtain
> Of Old Fort William.
> This tablet marks the position of the
> North River Gate through which Siraj-ud-Daulah entered the Fort
> On the evening of the 20th June 1756.
> Behind this tablet to the South of the
> Gate stood the great flag-staff
> Of the Fort.

The remaining tablets are more difficult to access. If we were able to draw the line of the West curtain of the Old Fort southwards, we should come to a place where the buildings of the Long Row originally joined the Curtain walls. Immediately beyond this was the wharf, from which the river has now retreated far to the west.

Somewhere on the western boundary of the Reserve Bank of India building are two tablets:

1. The brass lines in the stone
    On the adjacent ground
    Mark the position and extent
    Of the continuation of the West curtain
    Of Old Fort William
    Near where it was met by the Long Row.

2. The brass lines
    In the stone of the adjacent ground
    Mark the position and extent
    Of a portion of the North wall
    Of the Factory, the principal building
    In the centre of Old Fort William.[3]

Curzon had a Map of Part of Calcutta marking the site of the Old Fort and the buildings that existed in his time. On the corner of Koilaghat Street stands the G.P.O.; next to it is the Calcutta Collectorate, behind which were the Opium Godowns. Next to the Collectorate we come to the Customs House with the new Import Godowns at its back. The Customs House has given way to the Reserve Bank of India building after Independence.

At the corner of Fairlie Place now stands the East Indian Railways Office which continues along the whole of the southern side of the street. As noted earlier, the river Hooghly used to flow much nearer than now; a part of the present Eastern Railway Office, including the Booking Office and adjacent buildings, and the Strand Road were once in the riverbed. In the Map we see the buildings on the west of the actual Fort in the west, with the East Indian Railways Booking Office, Goods Warehouse, etc. proceeding southwards along Strand Road till we find on our left the Post and Shipping Office and the Port Commissioners' Office at the corner with Koilaghat Street. Entering Koilaghat Street, we continue eastwards, passing the Port Commissioners' Office, to come to the southern end of the Old Fort. On our left we find an imposing building, the Office of the Comptroller General of Post Offices, and further on the Office of the Director General of Post Offices. Lastly we come to the General Post Office at the corner, thus ending a tour of the Fort William that was.

References

1. Losty, J.P. *Calcutta, City of Palaces,* pp. 35–36.
2. Wilson, C.R. 'A Short History of the Old Fort William, in Bengal,' Part III, published in *Bengal Past and Present,* vol. II, part 1, Jan-July 1908, p. 15.
3. Curzon, The Marquess of Keddlestone. *British Government in India,* vol. I, pp. 154–57.

Chapter Six

Villages to Metropolis: Calcutta 1757–1800

After the battle of Plassey Calcutta grew very rapidly. A large number of European traders settled here to make a quick fortune. Even the Company's servants, from the Governor to the chaplain, would engage themselves to something or the other. Many of them made millions and returned to England. But the English back home were soon tired of hearing the stories told by these neo-rich about their dining with a *raja* or strolling through Calcutta in their favourite palanqins. They came to be derisively called *nabobs*. The Europeans adopted much of Mughal culture: they would enjoy a *hookah* in the evening, relaxing in a Mughal robe, watching dancing-girls perform a native song. Many of them either kept or married native girls, as European women were still too few in Calcutta. But things gradually changed: when the news of the rich unmarried *nabobs* in India and their great wealth reached the shores of England, lots of unmarried ladies sailed for India to find a rich husband. They were known as the *Fishing Fleet*. Most of them found a husband, but some returned dejected and were called *Returned Empties*. There are some excellent descriptions of life in Calcutta during this period. Mrs. Kindersley's *Letters from the East Indies* published in 1777 describes life in Calcutta in 1768. Elizabeth Fay's *Original Letters from India* was published in 1817, but her memories of Calcutta centred on the town in 1780. The epistolary anonymous novel *Hartly House Calcutta... A Novel of the Days of Warren Hastings* was published in 1789 and describes Calcutta before Hastings' departure in 1785. Mrs. Kindersley writes:

Calcutta does not appear much worth describing; for although it is large, with a great many good houses in it, and has the advantage of standing upon the banks of a river, it is as awkward a place as can be conceived; and so irregular that it looks as if all the houses had been thrown up in the air, and felled down again by accident as they now stand; people keep constantly building; and everyone who can procure a piece of ground to build a house upon, consults his own taste and convenience, without any regard to beauty or regularity of the town: besides, the appearance of the best houses is spoiled by the little straw huts, and such sort of encumbrances, which are built by the servants for themselves to sleep in; so that all the English part of the town, which is the largest, is a confusion of very superb and very shabby houses, dead walls, straw huts, warehouses and I-know-not-what.[1]

The first horse-drawn carriage arrived from England in 1740, solely for the use of the Governor and members of the Council. Others had to stick to their palanquins mainly, till a large number of carriages arrived from England. For the experience of riding a coach in Calcutta, one could refer to Mrs. Christina Pringle, wife of John Alexander Pringle of the Bengal Civil Service. She arrived in Calcutta in 1829 and died in this city on 12 November 1830. She is buried in the South Park Street Cemetery. In a letter to her parents in England on 2 December 1829, she writes, 'It is very troublesome driving in Calcutta, for the black coachmen have no rules about keeping the right hand in passing, but drive on quite reckless of everything.'[2]

The town was filling up, with every rich household maintaining 25 to 30 servants, who would either build a shanty next to their master's house or live in the native town.

The Marhatta Ditch, which was dug in 1742, in a semi-circular shape, about seven miles in length, as a protection from the attacking Marhatta hordes, was not completed. The half-dug ditch came to be considered the outer boundary of the town. There were many Europeans in the city who would boast that they had never been to the other side of the ditch. But quite a few did cross the ditch: Warren Hastings had his house in Alipore, others in Kidderpore and Garden Reach and some even to the north in Barrackpore, Dum Dum, etc. The ditch was filled up in 1799 and in its place the Lower and Upper Circular roads were built. The Governor General's bodyguards had their camp at the Ballygunge Maidan.

The weather, particularly during the rainy season, was a killer to the Europeans. The Fever Hospital near the Old Burial Ground had an unsavoury reputation: 'Where many go to undergo the penance of physick but few come out to give account of its operation.'[3] Probably one-third of the European community in Calcutta died of malaria, enteric diseases or cholera during or immediately after the monsoon. Those who survived the rains used to have a gala celebration of their survival on 15 November every year.

The East India Company was trying to consolidate its position and keep the trade flourishing and looked for a stronger administration. The Supreme Court (the Old Court House) and other smaller courts, a police system, and postal services came into being. The 1690s were however soon forgotten. There would be no more mudhouses with thatched roofs—a great number of large mansions and palaces had begun to appear. In 1774 Warren Hastings proposed boundaries of Calcutta for policing purposes; in 1794, the Governor General Lord Cornwallis fixed the boundaries of Calcutta with the Marhatta Ditch to the north, the Circular Road (constructed along the eastern portion of the Ditch) to the east, the river Hooghly to the west, and the Lower Circular Road to Kidderpore Bridge and

Tolly's Nullah to the river, including the new Fort and Coolie Bazar (now Hastings) to the south.

East of the vast expanse of the Maidan, the Chowringhee area attracted many Europeans, who built large garden houses around the area. Lal Dighi and its immediate surroundings were left for the Government and business houses; the residential area moved south to the Esplanade Row. For the Governor there was a new palace, The Buckingham House on Esplanade next to the Council House. Both of these buildings were demolished in the closing years of the century to make way for the new Governor General Lord Wellesley's 'dream house', now the Raj Bhavan, completed in 1803. A Public Lottery Committee, set up for buildings and new roads, soon came up with St. John's Church and the Town Hall. Several new roads were built. There was a building boom and everywhere in town one could see brick kilns, and the new highways all blocked by bricks and house-building materials.

For entertainment, a playhouse was built near Lal Bazar, and later, one north of Lal Dighi. Taverns flourished in various parts of the White Town. The more notable ones were the Harmonic in Lal Bazar, and London near Lal Dighi. The first organized horse-racing took place in Akra near Calcutta on 16 January 1769 and continued until 1809, after which it shifted to the present course in the Maidan. Catastrophe struck Calcutta and Bengal in 1770 when plague and famine took a toll of one-third of the total population of 15 million. In Bengali this is described as *Chhiattarer Manvantar*.

The Court of Directors of the East India Company appointed Warren Hastings as the President of their Bengal Council on 13 April 1772. In October 1774 he became Governor General of Bengal and continued in office till 1785. In 1774 the Mayor's Court in Calcutta was elevated to a Supreme Court by a charter. Sir Elija Impey arrived in the same year as the first Chief Justice. Hastings and Impey soon came to be involved in the controversial death sentence passed on Maharaja Nandakumar, a Brahman, who by his ability and efficiency had risen to be an important official in the court of Nawab Mir Jafar of Murshidabad. Though the British historians of the time have upheld the justice of the order, Indians in general, and some notable English peers too, have expressed their reservations.

In a colourful career, Nandakumar, on the Nawab's recommendation, had been appointed to a high post by Lord Clive. The Emperor Shah Alam had bestowed upon him the title of Maharaja. He was quite influential in Calcutta among the Indians and English alike. He was an upright man who would not tolerate any nonsense. On 11 March 1775, Mr. Philip Francis laid before the Board a formal letter addressed to the Governor General and Council by Nandakumar. In this document Hastings was personally charged with accepting bribes from Munni Begum, widow of the Late Nawab, Mir Jaffar, and Mohd. Reza Khan and others. Two days later Nandakumar, in another letter, offered to appear before the board and give his evidence, both oral and documentary. The majority were in favour of accepting the offer, when Hastings declared the Council dissolved and left the room. The charge was that Hastings had amassed four million rupees in two and a half years by all manner of underhand means. Hastings did not wait; he engaged two persons, Kamaluddin and Mohan Prasad, to file a case against Maharaja Nandakumar for forgery.

Nandakumar was arrrested on 6 May and put in a common jail. There are differences of opinion about the location of this jail—it was either the jail in Lal Bazar or the one in Free School Street. Mr. H.E.A. Cotton is convinced that he was put in the common jail, at the site now occupied by the Victoria Memorial.

The trial started on 8 June 1775 at the Supreme Court. The judges were the Chief Justice Sir Elija Impey, Hyde, Chambers and Le Maistre. Chambers was of the opinion that the rules prevalent in England were not applicable in India, but the others did not agree with him. The intentions of the court were quite evident from the beginning; though a high caste Brahman, Nandakumar's application for a special separate jail was outright rejected by Impey. Nandakumar began a fast unto death.

Impey sent a physician to examine him. When the physician considered his condition to be grave, the court allowed the erection of a special tent in the jail for his accommodation. The jury consisted of ten Englishmen and two Eurasians. The three witnesses for Nandakumar were not believed, finally the jury gave their verdict: 'Guilty'; punishment: death by hanging. William Hickey, Attorney of the Supreme Court, is said to have recorded in his *Memoirs* that some of the jurors had confided in him that they did not find him guilty.[4] The vindictiveness of the new masters is evident in the judgement that recommended prosecution of Nandakumar's witnesses for false evidence. Calcutta was stunned. Many Brahmans left Calcutta to settle in Bally, Uttarpara, and other small towns.[5] All attempts to save his life went in vain. He was hanged on 5 August 1775 at a special scaffold erected at Coolie Bazar (Near Fort William), now Hastings, near the bridge.

The Sheriff of Calcutta, Alexander Macrabie, who accompanied Nandakumar from the jail to the gallows, has left a detailed account of his meeting with the Maharaja on the night before and the morning of the execution. The Maharaja was dignified and ascended the gallows with unusual calm.[6] A large gathering attended the execution and a universal shout was heard, and many of them took a bath in the Ganges. There was a great hue and cry both in India and in England. Hickey's *Bengal Gazette* of October 1781 quotes from an English paper:

> The human and intelligent reader will not fail to recollect that, in Bengal in 1757, the East India Company's servants, with Col. Clive at their head, were guilty of a most infamous forgery in counterfeiting the signature of Admiral Watson to a treaty by which they defrauded Omichund, a Gentoo merchant, of £ 250,000 promised him. Clive had even the malignity in person to inform Omi Chund of the deception by which he had

cheated him. The Colonel's words overpowered him like a blast of sulphur, and he fell fainting on one of his attendants.

We first committed a successful forgery on a native of Bengal, and gloried in it, though it occasioned his death. Soon after we sent out English judges to establish English laws in that country, and with a justice peculiar to wise and innocent men, a retrospective of past crimes is taken, and a native of the country, who knew nothing of English laws, is hanged for a crime which we had triumphed in committing. Clive was made a peer in England, though he committed in Bengal the same crime for which we hanged Nun Coomer.[7]

Immediately after this trial in Calcutta, addresses expressive of confidence and satisfaction were presented to the Chief Justice and the Supreme Court by various sections of the community, including Hindus. Dr. Busteed hastens to add that these addresses were got up with indecent haste: 'Mr. Impey the Chief Justice's son, with questionable discretion, has appended them to the defence of his father. One of them (presented to Chief Justice himself) is from the 'free merchants, free marines and other inhabitants.' It is nauseating in its bombast and its servility. At the head of the names of the eighty-four inflated persons who signed this imprudent panegyric stand those of Playdell, the Police Magistrate and Robinson the Foreman of the Jury. *Hickey's Gazette* of June 1781, while Elija Impey was still in Calcutta, refers to a play at the New Theatre, near the Court House that was in rehearsal: a tragedy called

TYRANNY IN FULL BLOOM, OR THE DEVIL TO PAY
WITH THE FARCE OF ALL IN THE WRONG.

Elija Impey (Sir F. Wronghead), the other judges, and Warren Hastings (Don Quixote charging at Windmills), are some of the characters. Nandakumar appears as a ghost in the drama. Busteed goes on to say that every schoolboy in England, if asked who Impey was, would reply glibly that he was the judge who once hanged a native in India to accommodate a Governor General. The Impeachment of Elija Impey at the British Parliament was held in 1782.

The questions arose again at the time of Warren Hastings' Impeachment. Burke and Mill were of the opinion that the Chief Justice had misused his office to put a man unjustly to death to serve a political purpose.

Hickey's Bengal Gazette or the *Calcutta General Advertiser*, the first newspaper in India, was published in English from Calcutta on 29 January 1780 by James Augustus Hickey. It was a weekly paper published on Saturdays. The paper went out of circulation when the editor Hickey was imprisoned for defamation.

Sir William Jones arrived in Calcutta in 1783, to take up the office as a Judge of the Supreme Court, but his knowledge of Asian studies had no equal. He founded the Asiatic Society of Bengal in 1784, with Warren Hastings as the chief patron.

Calcutta was growing, with large palatial buildings sprouting everywhere. Many old houses were pulled down in the Esplanade area in 1761, the records showing an amount of Rs. 5,727 given as compensation.[8]

Several European artists came to Bengal and other parts of India to make a fortune. We are indebted to them for paintings of different locations in Calcutta, documenting meticulously the slow evolution from the three small villages to the Second City of the British Empire. While Francois Balthazar Solvyns concentrated on the human types of the city and its neighbourhood, Major Antoine Polier, who became Chief Engineer of the Bengal Army in 1762, studied the changing cityscape more closely. His panoramic view of Calcutta extends almost from the northern limit of the still village-like Sutanuti to Fort William. The first topographic artist, William Hodges, arrived in 1780 and made a number of paintings, Warren Hastings acquired quite a few of them. On his return to London, he published *Select Views in India* in 1786, the first great book of aquatint prints of India. Another artist who visited India at this time was Ozias Humphry, who spent two years in India from 1785 to 1787 and recorded some of his impressions of Calcutta. But he is better remembered for his lawsuit against the Governor General, who had recommended him to the Oudh Court in Lucknow and other noblemen for painting their portraits. In the *Memoirs of William Hickey*, vol. III, 306, there is a reference to an action brought against the Governor General Sir John Macpherson, by Ozias Humphry, the artist, who endeavoured to make Sir John personally responsible for the payment of Humphry's fees for painting portraits of affluent Indians, who had commissioned him on Sir John's introduction and recommendations. The artist failed in his action, but Sir John did not press for payment of his own costs. Records of the case can be seen in the *Calcutta Gazette* of 12 March 1789. Another artist who could not make it was John Alefounder. In a letter to Ozias Humphry on 19 December 1786 Alefounder complained of his disappointment at the great expense which attended his journey and the uncertain profits, and which had left him melancholy mad. There was another painter who came to India and became more famous for the adventures of his wife than his paintings. Karl von Imhoff was a German baron, who had met and married Anna Maria Apollonia Chapuzet de St. Valentine, a descendant of a noble French family, in Nuremberg.

While travelling to India on the *Duke of Grafton*, they met Warren Hastings, who was going to Madras as a Member of the Council. During the long voyage a strong friendship sprang up between Baroness Imhoff and Warren Hastings. According to the story generally believed, an arrangement was made on arrival at Madras for the institution of divorce proceedings in the court. While Imhoff came to Calcutta, the Baroness stayed back in Madras as Hastings' guest. Imhoff was doing well in Calcutta as a painter, so his wife joined him in October 1771 and Hastings arrived at Calcutta in February 1772. Ultimately Imhoff was sent back to England in 1773 and the Baroness stayed back to marry Warren Hastings.

The foundations of Calcutta's topography, giving it for the first time the appearance of a large, expanding city, were laid in the set of 12 views of the city which were published in Calcutta between 1786 and 1788 by Thomas and William Daniell. Thomas Daniell and his nephew arrived in 1786, hoping to be able to produce aquatints in India itself, and immediately set to work on their twelve views of Calcutta. These were engraved and coloured with the help of Indian artists, and finished by 1788.

John Zoffany, one of the earliest Royal Academicians, was obliged to leave England, owing, it is said, to the ill feeling he had roused against himself through his injudicious indulgence in the habit of incorporating often in unflattering terms the faces of his friends and acquaintances into his paintings without the permission of the persons concerned. He arrived in India in 1781 and stayed in Calcutta till 1787. Here he painted 'The Last Supper' and presented it to the newly-built St. John's Church as an altar-piece. The painting caused a great sensation in Calcutta society, as the artist had not forgotten his old habit. Several Calcutta personalities can be identified in it.[10]

In the closing years of the century the widening gulf between Occidental splendour and Oriental squalor was quite evident. Native men and women came to Calcutta in boats only to be sold as slaves in the market. Sale advertisements would appear in the newspapers. Englishmen flocking to the city for making a quick million included senior Government personnel. The ubiquitous William Hickey, in his memoirs, writes about the death of   Mr. Thomas Davies (1792), the Advocate General, who stayed in Bengal another season to accumulate money, thereby sacrificing his life. Hickey says that his death 'brought to my recollection an epitaph I had formerly read upon the tombstone of a Dutch gentleman at Madras on the coast of Coromandel:

Mynheer Gludenstack is interred here
Who intended to have gone home next year.'[11]

Recently, Elton John's rendition of 'England's Rose' at Princess Diana's funeral service at the Westminster Abbey left the television-viewing world shedding copious tears, but Calcutta had its 'Rose' too.

Rose Aylmer is buried in the South Park Street Cemetery. The inscription on her grave reads:

To the Memory of the Honourable
Rose Whitworth Aylmer
Who Departed this Life March 2nd A.D. 1800
Aged 20 Years.

What was her fate? Long, Long before her hour
Death called her tender soul, by break of bliss.
From the first blossoms, to the buds of joy;
Those few our noxious fate unblasted leaves
In this inclement clime of human life.

Miss Aylmer came to Calcutta to visit her aunt, Lady Russell, wife of Sir Henry Russell, one of the Judges of the Supreme Court, and it was in their house in Chowringhee that she died.

Before Rose Aylmer left England for India, she had met the poet, Walter Savage Landor. On receiving the news of her death, he wrote:

Ah! What avails the Sceptred race?
Ah! What the form divine?
What every virtue, every grace?
Rose Aylmer, all were thine.
Rose Aylmer, whom these wakeful eyes
May weep but never see,
A night of memories and of sighs
I consecrate to thee.[12]

References

1. Mrs. Kindersley, quoted in Losty, *Calcutta City of Palaces*, p. 37.
2. *Bengal Past & Present*, vol. IV, July-December 1909, p. 468.
3. Mrs. Kindersley. op. cit. p. 20.
4. Sur, Atul. *Kolkata* (A complete history of Calcutta). Calcutta 1981, p. 81.
5. Cotton, H.E.A. *Calcutta Old & New*, p. 91.
6. Busteed H.E. *Echoes from Old Calcutta*, Calcutta 1882, pp. 63–67.
7. Ibid. p. 62.
8. *Bengal Past & Present*. vol. XLIII, 1932, p. 128.
9. Ibid. vol. XXXIV, 1927, p. 306.
10. Blechynden, Kathleen. *Calcutta, Past and Present*, Calcutta, New Edition 1978, pp. 119–20.
11. *Memoirs of Wiliam Hickey*, ed. A. Spencer, London 1913–25, Vol. IV, p. 22.
12. Blechynden, Kathleen. *Calcutta Past and Present*, pp. 140–41.

Chapter Seven

Around Lal Dighi

Today's Netaji Subhas Road contains three streets from the colonial period. From the corner of Hare Street up to Koila Ghat Street, there lay Dalhousie Square West; from G.P.O. to the Old Custom House it was Charnock Place; and from the Eastern Railways Office across Fairlie Place to the north it was Clive Street. From the corner of Hare Street, as we enter Dalhousie Square West, the first building (now 1, N.S. Road) in a dilapidated state, once numbered 29, housed Commercial Union Assurance Co. and Alliance Assurance Co. The next, Number 28, once occupied by the Mercantile Bank of India, now houses several companies with the ANZ Grindlays Bank on the ground floor. Number 3 Netaji Subhas Road is the Mcleod House, the Head Office of Mcleod & Co. Private Ltd. At the beginning of the twentieth century they had their premises in Dalhousie Square South at 31/1. They were one of the largest merchants and agents in Calcutta. Their interests

Figure 6: The General Post Office and the Royal Insurance Building on the left

Plate 3: A pre-postage stamp era letter to London bearing Calcutta G.P.O. Ship Letter Postmark in red dated 9 August 1843

were in tea, coal, rubber, steamer services, indigo, light railways, etc. At present their principal business is described as real estate, general merchants, investment in share and securities, loans and advances, etc. The next house on this stretch is the Royal Insurance Building, numbers 26 and 27. This large red brick building, erected towards the mid-nineteenth century, typifies the kind of building that made Calcutta a City of Palaces. The Royal Insurance Building stands even today under the same name and extends along Koila Ghat Street towards the west up to Bankshall Street. Across Koila Ghat Street we come to one of the finest buildings in Calcutta, the General Post Office.

This magnificent building stands on the site of the south-east bastion of the Old Fort William. Calcutta's first post office was situated in Old Post Office Street, functioning from 1774. The next post office was situated at the corner of Hastings Street and Church Lane. These were in the pre-stamp era, when postal dues were collected at the post office and a date stamp was affixed on the letter. The first postage stamp was issued in 1854, bearing the portrait of Queen Victoria. For the erection of the G.P.O., the remaining part of the bastion had to be removed, but removal was difficult as the old foundations and masonry were extremely hard, and could be removed only by blasting. The building was designed by the Government Architect Walter B. Granville, and completed in 1868. It overlooks Dalhousie Square in the east, Koila Ghat Street in the south. The ground floor covers 49,471 sq. feet and the first floor 29,713 sq. feet. The remainder is covered by outer offices. Its total cost came to Rs. 630,510. At the south-east corner is a lofty dome, on the outside a multi-dialled illuminated clock. The dome is supported by an octagonal base and 28 Corinthian pillars. From floor to spring of arch the space is 101 feet 9 inches wide. The tower itself is nearly 120 feet in height. The front towards Dalhousie Square has 11 pillars, and that facing Koila Ghat Street has 12, all Corinthian.

The east side is 160 feet exclusive of the tower, which has a diameter of 90 feet. The south side is 345 feet long and the west 200 feet. In the tower, under the lantern is a lofty circular hall containing the public letter boxes. The building has two storeys; the first floor once serving as the office of the Post Master General; the Presidency Post Master occupying the ground floor. At the back on the west, opening to a gate on Koila Ghat Street is the yard for mail vans. The offices of the Post Master General and Presidency Post Master have been shifted. On the southern side there is now the G.P.O. Philatelic Bureau, where stamp collectors can pick up newly issued stamps and first day covers. The marble tablets and the lines demarcating the lines of the old fort have already been dealt with in the chapter on the Old Fort.[1]

CALCUTTA COLLECTORATE

When the East India Company took over the three villages they appointed a Collector or *Zamindar*, as they were called in the Company's time. The first *Zamindar* Ralph Sheldon took charge in 1700, assisted by Govindaram Mitra, who was called a *Black Zamindar*.

Figure 7: Calcutta Collectorate Today
Photo Mr. N.R. Bose

Holwell, of the Black Hole fame, was, for some time, a *Zamindar* of Calcutta. The first collectorate was situated opposite Lal Bazar up to 1756. When the Company's administration gave way to imperial rule, the position of *Zamindar* was abolished. The collection of revenue became the responsibility of the Collector of Calcutta. In 1891, a part of the old Custom House was demolished to make way for the new Calcutta Collectorate. This was Number 3 Charnock Place, the G.P.O. being numbers 1 and 2. This three-storey building has beautiful cast-iron ornamentation and designs. The main gateway is very imposing. Recently, the West Bengal Government was seriously considering the demolition of the old building to build a skyscraper in its place to house its numerous offices. But good sense prevailed; the building still stands as a Heritage Building to be preserved for posterity. According to R.C. Sterndale, the Collector's *Cutchery* was located in Lal Bazar between the Old Play House and the Common Jail at the site of the later day Carlisle, Nephew & Co. In 1820 it was shifted to a house at the corner of Chowringhee and Park Street. About 1830 it was moved to the Old Mint premises in Church Lane, where it continued for fifty years before moving to Bankshall Street, in 1881.

OLD CUSTOM HOUSE

Old photographs show a double-storeyed building (Number 4 Charnock Place) built on a part of the site of the Old Fort. On 9 February 1819, the Governor General Lord Hastings

Figure 8: Old Custom House

laid the foundation stone of the building. In Independent India, the building was demolished to make way for the new imposing building of the Reserve Bank of India. A new Custom House in the mean time was built on Strand Road in 1942. The Income Tax Office functioned out of this building for a period in the early years of the twentieth century.

THE EAST INDIAN RAILWAY HEADQUARTERS
(NOW EASTERN RAILWAY)

Now we come to the site of the north-eastern bastion of the Old Fort William, at the corner of Clive Street (Netaji Subhas Road) and Fairlie Place. On the site stands the Headquarters of the East Indian Railways (now Eastern Railway), who started the first railway service in the eastern part of India. On 15 August 1854, the train steamed out of Howrah station towards Hooghly. The station was a temporary tin shed a little away from the muddy bank of the river. The carriages had to be made locally as those out from England as models were lost only a few weeks before the opening in a shipwreck at the Sandheads. But the official opening was scheduled for February 1855 with the extension of the line to Burdwan. Festivities were arranged at Burdwan for invited guests, but the Governor General, Lord Dalhousie, could not make the journey due to severe indisposition. He inaugurated the service however at Howrah station. The first headquarters was situated at 29 Theatre Road (Shakespeare Sarani), which was later taken over by the Calcutta Turf Club.[2] In 1905 the number of the building is shown as 40 Theatre Road, situated at the site of the present Air-Conditioned Market. In 1863, Mr. Roskell Bayne made the plans and designs for the new building, one of the finest in Calcutta with its ornate Italian design. In British days its address was 105 Clive Street. The huge building covers the whole length of the southern portion of Fairlie Place, from the corner of the main street up to the gate leading to the quadrangle which was a part of the old fort. The gate of the building occupies a site close to the North River gate of the old fort, through which Nawab Siraj-ud-Daulah had entered the fort on 20 June 1756. The two main pavillions at the north-east corner are impeccably Italian, with four ornamental panels depicting Architecture, Sculpture, Music and Business. The names of the main stations appear below the panels.[3] The part past the gate of the quadrangle up to the Strand Road is the Booking Office, built later, on land reclaimed from the river.

FAIRLIE PLACE

This street starts from the corner of the East Indian Railways office to meet Strand Road in the west. The whole southern part of the street is taken up by the Eastern Railway's offices. The street figures in Well's map of 1753, but without a name. The only house shown in this part was the mansion of Mr. Cruttenden, a Council member. It had a spacious garden.

Eduard Holden Cruttenden was second in Council at Fort William in 1753, but was dismissed from the Company's service two years later, becoming a free merchant. His house played a prominent part both in defence and attack in 1756. It was completely destroyed during the siege in 1756.[4] Fairlie Place owes its name to William Fairlie, a distinguished Calcutta merchant in the time of Lord Wellesley and a former Sheriff of Calcutta (1808). In the Calcutta Gazette of 25 April , 1799, he appears as a candidate for a contract for 'supplying and feeding elephants and camels for the service of the Army in the Bengal Presidency.' The full complement of elephants maintained appears to have been 200 and of camels 90 : while the charge for the keep and feed of a single animal is set down, for elephants at Rs. 30–40 per month, and for camels Rs. 11–13 per month. Fairlie's name occurs frequently as one of the 'Gentlemen of the Grand Jury.' On 5 December 1805, he had the privilege as foreman of presenting the address to Sir John Anstruther, the Chief Justice, in which permission was asked for the placing in the Town Hall of a portrait which now hangs in the High Court.[5]

William Fairlie married Miss Margaret Ogilvie at St. John's Church on 17 February 1798. They had extensive properties in Calcutta. On 13/14 October 1802, Fairlie and his wife sold to the Company for Rs. 60,000 their dwelling-house and ground (2 *bighas*, 1 *cottah*) near the Esplanade.[6] He appears to have been a senior partner of the firm of Fairlie and Gilmore and Co., and his name heads the list of the Commissioners of the Calcutta Exchange Lottery advertised in the *Gazette* in 1799. The Fairlies returned to England in 1812, selling off their Calcutta properties. The name of the firm Fairlie & Gilmore was then changed to Fergusson, Fairlie & Co. This firm was probably the forerunner of Macneil & Magor Ltd.

The northern side of Fairlie Place is occupied entirely by business premises. House number 1 on Fairlie Place, as one enters the street from Strand Road on the west, was originally a godown that in 1925-26 came to house Mackinnon Mackenzie, Williamson Magor, and later the Unit Trust of India. Next comes Fairlie House followed by number 3 containing several offices. Number 4, now the Kilburn and Company Building, once served as the head office of the Calcutta Electric Supply Corporation till it moved to Victoria House at the head of Chowringhee Street. Towards the close of the nineteenth century, houses numbers 5 and 5/1 were occupied by the Bengal Coal Company Limited and the Commercial Bank of India Limited. The original houses have disappeared. A new number 5 now houses the ANZ Grindlays Bank. The Bengal Coal Company, which had Prince Dwarkanath Tagore as one of its owners, was once a flourishing company issuing monthly dividends to its shareholders. In 1926 the Imperial Tobacco Company had its head office in the old number 5, where it had moved in from 14 Radha Bazar Lane.

STRAND ROAD UP TO
KOILAGHAT STREET

Strand Road, now one of the city's major thoroughfares, leading to the Howrah Bridge and the Howrah Station, was still in the riverbed when Job Charnock set foot in Sutanuti. The Port Commissioners' jetties and godowns line the street on the west. The Port railway system, meant to transport goods offloaded at the jetties, has now been converted to form part of the city's circular railway for public transportation. To the east of the road, till it meets Koilaghat Street, there are the Eastern Railways Booking Office, the new Custom House built in 1942 at number 15/2. Number 15/1, once serving as the Shipping and Port Offices, has since been demolished to make way for a new concrete structure housing the Collectorate of Central Excise. Number 15 is the office of the Port Commissioners.

CALCUTTA PORT COMMISSIONERS

Calcutta, with its rich hinterland drawing a continuous stream of foreign traders, was identified fairly early as the ideal location for a major port. The port of Calcutta is much older than the city. The Bengal Pilot Service was constituted by the East India Company in 1669. As the shipping channels in and out of Calcutta, this was an absolute necessity. The Company used to operate from the old Fort William and built *ghats* or wharfs to handle ocean-going ships. Later a dry dock was built near the Bankshall. The fort wharf was completed on 16 October 1710. Forty-one ships were engaged by the Company for trade with Bengal between 1709 and 1718. After the battle of Plassey the Port of Calcutta grew in importance.

The Government of India constituted a River Trust in 1863 to regulate the operation of the port. When the Commissioners for Making Improvements in the Port of Calcutta (Port Trust) were appointed on 17 October 1870 under the Calcutta Port Improvement Act of 1870 by Sir William Grey, Lt. Governor of Bengal, they inherited six screw-pile jetties and four sheds for the accommodation of the sea-going trade.[7]

Calcutta Port has had its zenith and is in decline now from increasing silting of the river Hooghly. Shipping of higher tonnage cannot come to the port any longer; a sister port complex at Haldia is doing well. At the corner of Strand Road and Koilaghat Street stands the Office of the Calcutta Port Trust extending east into the latter street. The building, more than 120 years old, is well maintained.

KOILAGHAT STREET

From Strand Road one enters Koilaghat Street, leading to Lal Dighi. The road has been renamed Babu Tarapada Mukherjee Sarani in 1982. The old name Koilaghat is probably a corrupted form of Killaghat (Fort Wharf). The origin of the name has also been ascribed to the large traffic of coal through this street in the earlier part of the nineteenth century. Upjohn, in his map of 1794, calls it Tankshall Street (probably from the original mint inside the Old Fort), but there is a view that the correct name should have been Tackshall, Dutch for Custom House, which then stood at the south-west corner of the Old Fort.

The southern wall of the Old Fort and the import and export warehouses were situated on this street. During the time of Warren Hastings, the Company's Council House was situated on this street next to the Export Ware House, probably near the Bankshall corner. Following a great controversy among Calcutta historians about the site of this Council House, the credit for finding the spot must go to Lord Curzon, who wrote: "The Locality of the dilapidated Council House was still an unsolved problem" when, just as these pages were going into print, there was unearthed an extract from the *India Gazette* or *Calcutta Public Adventurer* of 3 March 1781, to the following effect :

To be let or sold, The House known by the name of the Old Council House, next door to the old Export Ware House. For particulars Please to enquire of Mr. Edward Mulling at the Commercial Council House.

This short-lived Council House was famous for an incident that took place in this house on 9 June 1763, when one of the members of the Council, Stanlake Batson, lost his temper and struck Warren Hastings in the face. Batson was suspended, and Governor Vansittart and Hastings refused to sit with him even after he had apologized and been reinstated by the votes of the majority.

On 15 October 1764 the Council meeting resolved:

The present Council Room being from its situation greatly exposed to the heat of the weather, and from its vicinity to the Public Office very ill-calculated for conducting the business of the Board with that privacy which is often requisite, it is agreed to build a new Council Room at a convenient distance from offices, and that it shall be done under the inspection of Mr. Fortnum, the civil architect.

The old Council Room was shut in by houses on the south. There were no *punkhas* then, men had to endure heat in their white jackets with the slight degree of air the *chauries* gave.[8]

The entire southern side of Koilaghat Street up to the Bankshall Street corner is occupied by the gigantic red-brick mansion now occupied by the Railways. This used to be the Military Accounts Office when Calcutta was the capital of British India. On the northern side next to the Port Commissioners' Office there is a red-brick fortress which used to accommodate the office of the Comptroller General and Deputy Comptroller. Today it bears the sign of Postal Savings Bank. The upper storeys of the huge building look empty and abandoned with hanging doors and windows. Incidentally, these buildings mark the site of the north-western bastion of the Old Fort.

The next building before the G.P.O. is the Office of the Director General of Post Offices in India, now also the office of the Presidency Post Master and Director of Postal Services, with a newly opened Philatelic Museum containing many relics of the postal department on the ground floor. Standing before the G.P.O. Building we face the Lal Dighi. To the south of the street stands the red brick mansion of the Royal Insurance Co. From this point we turn west to come to a small road on our left, connecting Koilaghat Street and Hare Street—Bankshall Street.

BANKSHALL STREET

Bankshall Street derives its name from the Bankshall or Marine House, that stood at the site of the Small Causes Court. Originally this was known as the Company's House. Earlier still, it was the *cutchery* of the Sabarna Roychowdhurys, initially taken out on rent by the Company, and then bought. This house has been shown in William Well's plan and map of old Calcutta just south of the Old Fort, with the Governor's *Ghat*, Dock Head and the Dock, and the houses of Mr. Douglas, Mr. Amyatt close by, and that of Mr. Holwell a little further to the south. The Company's House used to be the Governor's residence outside the fort and had an extensive garden leading to the Lal Dighi. During the siege of 1756, the Company's soldiers made the first line of defence at Mr. Cruttenden's house on the north of the fort and at the Company's House, but they had to retreat from both into the fort. Under the attack of Siraj-ud-Daula's artillery both the houses were completely destroyed. After regaining Calcutta, the Company rebuilt the Company's House, but called it now the Marine House, with the Master Attendant's Office next to it.

There are several explanations for the name *Bankshall*. According to P. Thankappan Nair[9] the name is a corruption of the Sanskrit words *banik* and *shala*, a marine house where traders and buyers met to transact business. John Clark Marshman traced the name to a Portuguese word. The Dutch have been given credit for a similar word. Rev. James Long took a literal view and held it to mean 'Hall on the banks of the river' 'Banks Hall'. Some would trace it to the Bengali word for corner—*bank*—and the Sanskrit *shal*. As the road is quite short it has only a few houses on it. As we enter from the north we see on our left the eastern portion of the red brick building of the Chief Commercial Manager's Office of Eastern Railway (previously a part of the Military Accounts Offices), which is house no. 1. House no. 2 in the same compound used to be occupied by the Department of Commerce and Industry and the Government of India Patent Office. Now it is a part of the Railways offices. No. 3 houses the Small Causes Court. Opposite the Court on the eastern side of the street stands a very old dilapidated building, which used to be the Criterion Hotel towards the close of the nineteenth century; the building extends eastwards to Hare Street. No longer a residential hotel, it now has several shops and cheap eateries. Houses numbered 4 and 5 once housed North West Soap Co., Lipton Tea Godowns, Samuel Fitze Co. Ltd. Elgin Mills and Jambon Co. Ltd. Both the buildings were probably demolished to make way for the Shaw Wallace Building. The present owners of the property are descendants of Tipu Sultan.

David Thomas Shaw was already trading in Calcutta in 1868. Charles William Wallace joined him in London in 1881. Shaw's brother, R. Gordon Shaw, managed several tea gardens towards the close of the century. Shaw Wallace and Company commenced business in 1886 in piece goods, tea and silk; now it has interests in tea, oil, fertilisers, breweries, distilleries, cotton, metals, engineering, shipping, etc.[10] Before moving to Bankshall Street they had their office at 20 Strand Road. In 1836-37 several Government Offices including the General Post Office, The Board of Customs, Salt and Excise, the Superintendent of Stamps and the Master Attendants, were shifted to Bankshall Street.

SMALL CAUSES COURT

Old documents suggest that the court started functioning from a huge building near the Indian Museum in Sudder Street; about 1870 it shifted to a building in Mangoe Lane. In 1874 its new building in Bankshall Street was ready for occupation. The architect was Mr. W. H. White of the Government Public Works Department. The building has echoes of the contemporary French Palladean style, but has ionic columns. Later the court building was extended to the south, covering the site of the Marine Hosue, the Master Attendant's Office and the Ice House. The court building, an imposing edifice, has a historic setting, but most of the courtrooms are dingy, dark and gloomy.

Figure 9: The Small Causes Court

Mr. Montague Massey in his recollections gives a description of the Ice House, which had once stood on the site of the western edge of the court:

Before the introduction of artificial ice, Calcutta was entirely dependant for its supply on the importation of Wenham Lake ice in wooden sailing ships by the Tudor Ice Company from America. The Ice House was situated at the west end of the Small Causes Court, the entrance facing Church Lane and approached by a steep flight of stone-steps. There were no depots distributed about the town as there are now, and everyone had to send a coolie to the Ice House for his daily suply with a blanket in which it was always wrapped up.

.... . When the vessel's arrival was telegraphed from Saugor, great was the rejoicing of the inhabitants. The vessels used to be moored at the *ghaut* at the bottom of Hare Street, as there were no jetties in those days. The ice was landed in great blocks on the heads of coolies and slided down from the top of the steps to the vaults below.'

This was probably the beginning of Indo-American trade as the Dutt family of central Calcutta were the importers of the ice.

Massey goes on to record that the Small Causes Court was built on the site of the old General Post Office which moved from Lindsay Street to Bankshall Street in 1834-36, adjacent was the Postmaster's residence. Massey's description of the Post Office reads:

This is one of the very few buildings in Calcutta about which I have the least recollection, I suppose owing to it having been one of the first to be demolished. It was no longer in existence at the time of the great cyclone of 1864. As far as my memory serves me, it was a low-roofed, one storeyed building, having a decidedly godownish appearance, fenced in on the south side, which was the entrance, by a row of low, green-painted palings with an opening in the centre. It was however notwithstanding a place of great interest for the time being, more particularly to the boys like myself having recently landed in a strange country, for on the arrival of the mail steamer at Garden Reach, which occurred at about 3 o'clock in the afternoon, we used to go down after dinner to get our home letters, which in those days, I think, were more highly prized than they are now. I quite forget what occupied the site of the present post office building.

As we leave Bankshall Street and move south, we come to Hare Street, beginning at Strand Road and ending at the south-western corner of Lal Dighi. The street was previously known as Old Fort Ghat Street and is described in contemporary Directories as *Bankshall Ka Dukshin Rasta*. The street was a narrow lane from Lal Dighi leading to the river, which was closer then. The street came to an end with houses on the river bank. Hare Street is one of the Calcutta streets constructed by the Lottery Committee in the 1820s. It is believed to be named after the great philanthropist, David Hare. But it could have been named after John Hare, who was a Sheriff of Calcutta and a popular figure, before David Hare came to Calcutta. David Hare lived at the corner of Church Lane and the street named after him, at the site now occupied by Nicco House. His house had a large garden covering the area up to St. John's Churchyard. David Hare came to Calcutta in 1800 and set up business as watch-maker, but he soon came to realize that it was not his vocation in India. An advertisement appeared in the *Government Gazette* of 1 January 1820 (Supplement) for January 1820.

DAVID HARE
Watch Maker

Begs to inform his friends and the public in general that he has this day retired from business; and requests they will accept his most sincere thanks for the very liberal support with which they have favoured him for the last eighteen years.

He also takes this opportunity of respectfully and earnestly soliciting a continuance of their patronage to the successor, Mr. Gray, who came from England on purpose, and has been his assistant for five years; which has afforded D. H. such a knowledge of his character and abilities that he feels the greatest confidence in recommending him on their notice.

David Hare was an educationist in spirit. In May 1816, he was present at a meeting with his friends, Raja Ram Mohun Roy, Raja Baidyanath Mukherjee and others, with Justice Edward Hyde East of the Supreme Court for the foundation of Hindu College. The College came into being on 20 January 1817 at Gorachand Basak's house on 304, Chitpore Road, moving later to College Street via Bow Bazar. Hare is supposed to have donated the land for the building. In 1817 he founded the Calcutta School Book Society and was the main force behind it. Though he had donated the land and worked hard for the establishment of Hindu College (later Presidency College), he was not a member of the first Committee for the College, with Justice Sir Hyde East as Chairman. He was again the main force behind the establishment of Medical College, Bengal, on 1 June 1835. For some time he was Secretary of the College. The freedom of the press was yet another cause that he championed and upheld. He died of cholera on 1 June 1842, and the David Hare Training College in Ballygunge Circular Road perpetuates his memory. Recently, the Medical College authorities have very rightly renamed the Prince of Wales Hospital block within its campus after David Hare.

The northern side of Hare Street from the Bankshall Street corner is nearly entirely occupied by the Small Causes Court; this part, an addition made in 1882, demolishing the Company's House, the Master Attendant's Office and the Ice House. At the corner with

Strand Road stand two new buildings, viz. the buildings of the Shipping Corporation of India and the United Insurance Company at number 16, Hare Street.

METCALFE HALL

On the southern pavement of Hare Street at the corner it forms with Strand Road stands the imposing Metcalfe Hall, named after Acting Gvoernor General, Sir Charles Theophilus Metcalfe. Charles Metcalfe was born at Calcutta in 1785. His father was then a major in the Bengal Army. He was educated at Eton, and returned to India as a Writer in the Company's service in 1801. He succeeded to the family baronetcy in 1822 at the death of his elder brother. He was President of the newly found Bengal Club from 1827 to 1837. In 1827, he was member of the Supreme Council. In November 1833 he was appointed Governor of Agra, but was soon recalled to act as Provisional Governor General during the interval between the departure of Lord William Bentinck and the arrival of Lord Auckland (March 1835–March 1836).

Metcalfe is best remembered for the stand he took on the freedom of the Press which had been denied in a series of cases leading to the inprisonment of James Augustus Hickey, editor of the *Bengal Gazette*, and the deportation of the editor of *The Bengal Harkaru*, and finally the 1823 Press Ordinance for censorship of the Press.

Reverend William Adam was the first European employed by the British Government to enquire into, and report upon, the state of indigenous education in Bengal. Reverend Adam, in January 1827 started the *Calcutta Chronicle*. The success of the paper surpassed

Plate 10: The Metcalfe Hall
Photo courtesy Calcutta Historical Society

the most sanguine expectations; but reacting to some remarks on the question of the Calcutta Stamp Act, the Governor General Lord Combermere decided to suppress the paper. The Chief Secretary wrote to Rev. Adam on 31 May 1827, informing him that the comments have incurred the displeasure of the Government, hence his licence stands cancelled.[11]

One of Lord Metcalfe's notable acts as acting Governor General was to pass the Act XI of 1835, without reference to the Home Authorities. Press Censorship was abolished by this enactment. Though Metcalfe was hailed as the 'Liberator of the Indian Press', the East India Company headquarters in London took exception to his stand, and he was passed over by the Directors when the Governorship of Madras fell vacant in 1838. On the arrival of Lord Auckland, Metcalfe was appointed Lt. Governor of the north-western provinces, a post he resigned in 1838 in protest against being passed over for the Governorship of Madras, and retired from service. He died in England in 1846.

Lord Metcalfe enjoyed great popularity in India. He was universally recognized as an able administrator of unimpeachable integrity. He won the admiration of both Europeans and Indians, long before he 'liberated' the Press in India. On 18 February 1832, a meeting was convened in the Town Hall to honour Metcalfe. Mr. James Pattle proposed and Dr. John Grant seconded a motion that a subscription should be opened to erect a statue to Sir Charles Metcalfe, and present him with a service of plate. Mr. Longueville Clarke, a distinguished advocate, proposed and Dr. J.R. Martin seconded a proposal 'That by combining together the different public subscriptions which are now raising of offer testimonials to Sir Charles Metcalfe, it would enable the whole Indian community to express in a more distinguished manner their appreciation of the character to that eminent man.' The motion was unanimously carried out. Mr. Clarke went on to suggest the erection of a public building to be called the Metcalfe Hall, the ground floor to be devoted to the museum and committee rooms of the Agricultural and Horticultural Society, and the upper floor to the Calcutta Public Library, both these institutions having long been 'the peculiar object of the solicitude and bounty of Sir Charles Metcalfe'. This was also adopted and led to the appointment of a joint committee. Sir Edward Ryan was appointed President and Mr. Longueville Clarke, the Secretary.

A contibution of Rs. 10,000 from the Agricultural and Horticultural Society's fund opened the subscription list; individual members contributed another Rs. 3,000; the Public Library gave Rs. 6,000; and a sum of Rs. 70,000 was ultimately collected.[12]

The Government donated the site, which is also of historic importance. According to Pranatosh Ghatak, this had been the residence of Harinarayan Sett, a little after Job Charnock's days, before it was rented out to the Company's factors.[13]

The foundation stone for Metcalfe Hall was laid on 19 December 1840. The Governor General Lord Auckland, his sisters, the Misses Edens, all the Members of the Council and other distinguished invitees attended the ceremony. The work of construction was completed in 1844. It is a piece of Greece in Calcutta, as the architect, Mr. C.K. Robinson, chose the design from the portico of the Temple of Winds in Athens. A broad flight of steps lead to the portico or colonnade on the west on the riverfront, with a covered colonnade entrance in the east, with another similar flight of steps up to the entrance hall. The building stands on a solid ornamental basement, ten feet in height; with thirty columns thirty-six feet in height, rising from this basement and supporting the general structure of the building, giving it externally the appearance of a Greek temple of one lofty storey. The columns and colonnade nearly surround the whole building. It was intended to carry them entirely round, but the work had to be abandoned for lack of funds. Internally, there are two storeys and they were used for the purpose they were built for. The Public Library, using the upper floor, languished under lax management and inadequate support; the offices of the Agri-Horticultural Society failed to attract public interest; and the building itself fell into disrepair.

When Lord Curzon came to Calcutta in 1899 as Viceroy, he gave the Metcalfe Hall a new lease of life. After taking over, he visited all the Government Offices and Public Buildings in Calcutta. In his own words:

> One afternoon I paid this place a visit. I found that the lower storey was occupied by an institution known as the Agri-Horticultural Society, which had collected there a number of glass bottles and jars on shelves containing seeds and specimens, and some rusty implements and ploughs... . I dare say they were very useful in their own way and place. But it seemed to me that they were singularly out of place in the Metcalfe Hall; the financial condition of the Society was also dismal. Then I walked upstairs to the floor which belonged to the Calcutta Public Library, and I found the shelves in these rooms filled with books, the majority of which had parted company with their bindings; the rooms were occupied by a few readers of newspapers and light fiction, whose tenancy of the library was freely disputed by the pigeons who were flying about inside the room, and evidently treated it as their permanent habitation. Both of these experiences had a very disquieting effect upon me. Then about the same time, I visited the Home Department, and I found stacked there in a crowded and unsuitable building the large library of books belonging to the Government of India and known as the Imperial Library, practically accessible to none but officials, useless for purpose of study or reference, and unknown to the public at large.[14]

Lord Curzon thought that the capital of British India should have a library equal to the stature of the British Museum or the Bodlean at Oxford. Metcalfe Hall was his choice for the site of such a library. The Government of India bought the Metcalfe Hall from the two occupiers, and an Act was subsequently passed to validate the transfer. Metcalfe Hall was taken over, completely renovated and refurnished; a librarian was procured from England. The collection of books known as the Imperial Library was brought over and arranged in the new location. The Government of India created a staff and provided an annual sum for their payment, for the upkeep of the building and the purchase of new books. The Imperial Library in Metcalfe Hall was formally opened on 30 January 1903 by Lord Curzon. At the inauguration the library had nearly 100,000 books. But the fate of the Hall became uncertain when the Imperial Library shifted to the Foreign Department buildings in Esplanade East in 1924. The Metcalfe Hall was for some time the office of the Commissioner of Income Tax. After that the building has been used mainly as a godown or dumping ground, as the Asiatic Society of Bengal has been doing since 1998. The Metcalfe Hall is surrounded by a high ugly wall that hides from view the beauty of the lofty building. Recently, the Town Hall in Calcutta has been completely renovated for public use. I sincerely hope that the Metcalfe Hall is renovated and made useful, as part of our heritage.

In the old Calcutta Directories the Metcalfe Hall is shown as Number 1A, Hare Street. Early records assign the next building to Rallis India, bearing the address No. 1, Church Lane; this building has since been demolished to make way for a new office block. Here we cross Church Lane and come to the present building, Nicco House. This is where David Hare used to live, his gardens extending up to the walls of St. John's Church. The office building has two entrances, the one on Church Lane bearing the address 7, Church Lane, and the entrance on Hare Street, Number 2. The road numbers since have changed, so Metcalfe Hall has become Number 1 and the present Nicco House No 2. A later renumbering of the houses has marked Metcalfe Hall as No. 1, and the present Nicco House as No. 2. At the end of the nineteenth century the area was occupied by serveral offices, including those of Innes Watson & Co., 'Indian Field', W.S. Burke, W.C. Burke and G. Knowles & Co.

Mr. W.S. Burke seems to have been an active sportsman, associated with several sports bodies, including:

Bengal Cyclists' Association, 1, Hare Street
President: Mr. A.A. Apcar
Honorary Secretary: Mr. W.S. Burke
Bengal Presidency Amateur Athletics
Association, 1, Hare Street
President: A.A. Apcar
Secretary: W.S. Burke
Calcutta Clay Pigeon Club, 1, Hare Street
Secretary: W.S. Burke
Cyclists Touring Club, 1, Hare Street
Consul General for Bengal: W. S. Burke
Calcutta Rowing Club
Secretary: W.S. Burke

Between Nicco House and Garstin Place there are a few old buildings housing offices and shops. Once popularly known as *Garsting Sahib ka Barrack*, Garstin Place is a blind alley, leading from the southern side of Hare Street up to the northern boundary of St. John's Churchyard. It was a private passage, when it was taken over by the Calcutta Corporation, and named Garstin Place. The first hospital in Calcutta was situated in this passage. The present Government office at the corner of Hare Street was probably a part of the hospital compund. West of the hospital, extending up to the modern Hare Street was a large tank. The hospital was erected in 1707 to serve the Company's soldiers and sailors. The main building was 175 feet long and 60 feet wide; at first it was a single-storey building. In 1710 the hospital was walled round and barracks erected for the soldiers to live in. Curiously enough, the East India Company contributed only Rs. 2000 to build this hospital, the rest of the money was raised by public subscription. The hospital was surveyed and renovated in 1730, and in 1736 a couple of upper rooms were added as quarters for the resident doctors. The hospital seems to have been destroyed at the siege of 1756, though some sources claim that this hospital existed until 1763.

John Garstin, born in 1756, came to Calcutta in the East India Company's employ, and became Major General of Engineers and Surveyor of Bengal. He built the Town Hall of Calcutta, the Government House in Calcutta and the gigantic Granary at Bankipore, Patna. The Old Court House was demolished in 1792 under his supervision, and he used the materials and fittings for his Garstin Buildings. The houses were numbered 1, 2, 3, etc., Garstin Buildings. Number 1 was the headquarters and studio of the Indian Broadcasting Company, when it began radio transmission in Calcutta on 26 August 1927. After the Government took it over it came to be known as the All India Radio. After Independence it was named *Akash Vani*. The Akash Vani shifted to its own building at its present location at the Eden Gardens in 1962. At the end of the nineteenth century 1. Garstin Place was the address of Stewart Mackenzie and Company, and A.W. Figgis, the well-known tea brokers. The latter have shifted their offices now to the modern building at 16, Hare Street, which also houses Rallis India (previously Ralli Brothers, located at 1 and 2 Church Lane). The 1 Garstin Place building, rich with accociations, is in the process of being demolished.

Garstin Place had five buildings in all, numbers two to five holding residential flats and a few offices.

Coming back to Hare Street we come to 7, Hare Street, which for many years was the Calcutta office of the Reuters and Associated Press of India; now it houses the Press Trust of India and a commerical firm, Blue Star. Number 8 is also of historic importance for the beginning of Telephones in Calcutta.

On 12 March 1878, Father E. Lafont lectured on the telephone at St. Xavier's College. Calcuttans had to wait until 23 April of the same year for the watchmakers, Black & Murray, to arrange an exhibition. But the Viceroy Lord Lytton refused permission to intending telephone companies. His successor Lord Ripon was more progressive, and the Oriental Telephone Company Limited obtained its franchise in June 1880. The Central Exchange, in the magnetto system, was opened on 28 January 1882. The Calcutta exchange had three hundred lines, but only 79 subscribers; the lone Indian among the users was the philanthropist, Sagar Dutta.

In 1883 the concession was bought by the Bengal Telephone Company Ltd. for Rs. 7,60,000. In 1918, Bengal Telephone Company moved to the premises at 8, Hare Street, which still houses the commercial offices of the Calcutta Telephones. It was acquired by the Government of India on 1 April 1943.[15]

9 Hare Street used to be the office of the leading newspaper, *The Englishman*. Its predecessor *John Bull in the East* was founded by John Pascal Larkin in 1821 with other servants of the East India Company as a rival to *Calcutta Journal* established three years earlier by James Silk Buckingham as 'the organ of the merchants of the city.' After the deportation of Buckingham in 1823, the *Calcutta Journal* and the *John Bull* were placed under independent management. The celebrated Dr. James Bryce was in charge from 1825 to 1829. The paper prospered for a while, but it had become moribund when it was bought by Joachim Hayward Stocqueler in 1833. The rechristened first number of *The Englishman* appeared on 1 October 1833 and for many years it displayed on its first page the well-known lines from Milton's *Areopagitica*: 'This is true liberty when free-born men, having to advise the public, may speak out'—an allusion to Act XI of 1835 which granted freedom to the Indian Press. Stocqueler, a most remarkable man, took full advantage of the gift and collected a staff of brilliant contributors, mostly advocates of the Supreme Court, who were as outspoken as he was and became involved in many controversies and libel actions, even duels.

The history of the Bengal Club by H. R. Panckridge records one such case. *The Englishman* published a series of attacks upon certain measures taken by the Adjutant General Colonel Lumley. The tone of these attacks may be judged by the fact that Stocqueler, in reply to the accusation that they amounted to 'wanton defamation', could only answer, 'suppose they were—what is that to the purpose?' The position of a journalist, who conceives it his duty to criticize adversely the official actions of a fellow member of the Club must of necessity raise questions of ethics. To Colonel Lumley's friends Stocqueler's transgressions appeared heinous and, led by Mr. Longueville Clarke, they proposed expulsion of Stocqueler from the Club.

With an amazing disregard for the proprieties, both sides rushed into print, and for many months the Press was filled with comments on the schism that was bringing the Club near dissolution. Lord Metcalfe's tact finally saved the situation. Stocqueler was induced to resign his membership.

Now back to *the Englishman*. Charles Thackeray, uncle of the famous author William Makepiece Thackeray, was highly regarded as a leader writer in *the Englishman*. He was admitted as an advocate in the Supreme Court on 22 October 1827, but ultimately drifted to journalism. According to Stocqueler, his practice was to lock Thackeray into a room with pens, ink, paper and a full bottle of claret. The understanding was that he was not to expect release until he had finished both the leading article and the claret. The editor and the contributor had a difference of opinion, and Thackerary in 1836 joined the *Bengal Harkaru*, a much older newspaper, which began its career in 1780 as the *Indian Gazette* and *Calcutta Public Advertiser* and ended it as the *Indian Daily News* in 1924. Thackeray died in Calcutta in 1846. Stocqueler lost control of the paper in 1842. After that it passed through many hands including David Yule's. Under the ownership of John O'Brien Saunders (1852–1905) in 1878, *the Englishman* reached its apogee and was the most influential newspaper in India. When it celebrated its centenary on 21 July 1921, it had long occupied the premises at 9, Hare Street which overlooked St. John's Churchyard. Under Saunders the Hare Street office was the site for many symposia on literary and social subjects. In 1931, it ceased to be a daily paper and become a weekly magazine. But, when the new palatial offices of the *Statesman* in Chowringhee Square opened in 1933, it had passed under the control of the proprietors of that journal and migrated with them. *The Englishman* ceased publication on 26 March 1934.

9 Hare Street is now partly occupied by the Calcutta Telephones and by Blue Star. Before going to the next house, 10 Hare Street (in yesteryears and now 1, Council House Street), let us cover the buildings on the northern side of the street from the corner of Bankshall Street. The first building, 15 Hare Street, was the Criterion Hotel & Old Bombay Cheap Jack, the building continuing into Bankshall Street. Today there is no hotel, only cheap eateries and different kinds of shops.

The next two houses, numbers 14 to 12, were offices and residential flats. At the corner of Lal Dighi was No. 11, the famous restaurant of G.F. Kellner, the regular Railway caterers at one time. We have an account of 1920 by the Australian aviators, John McIntosh and Raymond Parer, who arrived at Calcutta on 14 March 1920 in their tiny aeroplane, landing at the Ellenborough Course in the Maidan. At Kellner's they were received in a cool atrium by a white-haired old Indian in the whitest of cotton suits and taken to the office. On their way they passed through shelves containing £ 20,000 worth Scotch whiskeys and delicious estables. Kellner is no more, but *biriyanis* are available on the pavement.

Now back to the other side of the street, we are at the convergence of Hare Street, Council House Street and Dalhousie Square (B.B.D. Bagh) South and West. There is no longer a 10, Hare Street. The red-brick government of India building is numbered 1, Council House Street, housing several Government of India offices. Previously, there was another building here, described as the Foreign Office, dismantled in the early part of the twentieth century.

Le us go back to the early years of the nineteenth century. William Doughty announced in the *Calcutta Gazette* in 1807 that he had taken that well-situated and most extensive house belonging to the Estate of General Martine, opposite to the College (College of Fort William), at the south-west corner of the Tank Square:

> Where he has spared no expense in fitting it up for the reception of families and gentlemen arriving from Europe and the upper stations, and also his long rooms for the accommodation of larger parties for which purpose proper assistants are engaged.

The house is to be conducted under the title of the Crown and Anchor Hotel and British Coffee House.

In a later advertisement it is announced that 'a Ball to celebrate the opening of the new House will be held on April 3, 1807'.[17]

The hotel probably did not last long, as the building was taken on rent for the College of Fort William, then situated just opposite to it at the site of the present-day Hong Kong Bank. The two buildings were connected by a gallery across the street.

We cross the Council House Street and come to Dalhousie Square South, now simply B.B.D. Bagh. The entire southern part of Lal Dighi was deliberately shorn off its beauty, the Dalhousie Institute was demolished to make way for the Telephone Headquarters. There were no plans to make its design compatible with the Raj era buildings it faces. On south the first building is the Hong Kong Bank, previously known as Hong Kong & Shanghai Banking Corporation, once the site of the office and godown of Bengal Nagpore Railways, and for many years before that the office of Messrs. Mackenzie Lyall & Co., prominent in the shipping business. The *Calcutta Gazette* of 12 March 1829 published a sensational news. The judges of the Supreme Court passed a sentence in the case of King vs. Pran Kissen Halder, who at one time was a man of great wealth, entertaining the Company's factors and other gentlemen at his house in Chinsurah. He was sentenced to be transported for seven years for forgery.

CALCUTTA EXCHANGE & COFFEE ROOM

A society of Gentlemen acquired the house 'lately occupied' by Mr. Raban situated at the corner of Tank Square opposite to Messrs. Ord and Knox's—the present site of the Hong Kong Bank—to set up on 19 June 1788 'a place of public resort for the purpose of meeting and transacting business.' The Calcutta Exchange & Coffee Room, as it was called, set down the following terms:

1. That the house will be open to the admission of all persons, whether European, native or others.
2. That two rooms will be apportioned, one for members and the other for non-members.
3. That separate apartments will be allotted to the subscribers for the transaction of business during the Change hours.
4. That Tuesdays, Wednesdays, Thursday and Fridays shall be the days for meetings.
5. That the doors be opened at ten in the morning, shut at twelve noon and the rooms cleaned by one p.m.
6. Subscription will be five *sicca* rupees per member per month.

But by 1799 the Calcutta Exchange was up for sale. For some time it served as a restaurant. Around the year 1800 the premises were rented by the Governor General Lord Wellesley and formed part of the Provost Chambers for the College of Fort William.

COLLEGE OF FORT WILLIAM

This unique college was founded by the Marquis of Wellesley, Governor General of India, in the year 1800. The objectives for setting up the college are to be found in the minutes of the Council Meeting held on 18 August 1800:

> European civil servants of the Company will have knowledge about India, its background, main languages for the dispensation of justice, administration of so vast a revenue system, the maintenance of civil order among millions of people of various languages and manners, usages and religions. The pleadings in the courts are conducted in the native languages, the law the Company judge administers is not the law of England but that law which the natives had been accustomed to under their former sovereigns, tempered and mitigated by the voluminous regulations of the Governor General in Council as well as by the general spirit of the British Constitution.
>
> As a consequence, qualifications of the highest order must be possessed by those upon whom these ampler duties devolve, if they are to acquit themselves honourably of the charge entrusted to them. The same is true for every department, be it judicature or revenue, political or financial or diplomatic. It is certainly desirable that all those stations should be filled by the civil servants of the Company and it is equally evident that the qualifications requisite are far outside the limits of a commercial education. The civilians can no longer be considered as the agents of a commercial concern.

By the regulations the Governor General was to be the Patron and Visitor of the College, and its Governors, the members of the Supreme Council and the judges of the Sudder Dwanny Adawlut (the High Court of Judicature) and of the Nizam Adawlut (the Central Criminal Court), The Advocate General and the Standing Counsel to the Honourable Company, its law officers, while its immediate government was to be vested in a Provost, Vice Provost and such other officers as the Patron and Visitor shall think proper to appoint with such salaries as he shall deem expedient.

The Provost was always to be a clergyman of the Church of England as established by the law, and his primary duties were to receive the junior civil servants on their arrival at Fort William, to superintendent and regulate their general morals and conduct, to assist them with his advice and admonition and to instruct and confirm them in the principles of the Christian religion according to the doctrines, disciplines and rites of the Church of England.

The first Provost was Reverend David Brown. One among the first batch of students was Charles Metcalfe, later the Acting Governor General. On 3 January 1799, a notification of the Public Department dated 21 December 1798 was issued, directing that 'From and after 1 January 1801, no servant will be deemed eligible for any of the offices hereinafter mentioned, unless he shall have passed an examination (the nature of which will be hereafter determined), in the laws & regulations and in the languages, a knowledge of which is hereby declared to be an indispensable qualification.'

The languages considered requisite were Persian and Hindoostanee for the office of Judge or Registrar of any Court of Justice, and Bengali for the Collector of Revenue or of Customs or Commercial Resident or Salt Agent in the provinces of Bengal and Orissa. The actual opening of the College of Fort William took place on Monday, 24 November 1800, with lectures in the Arabic, Persian and Hindoostanee languages.

The curriculum for a three year course was quite substantial, with

1. Languages:
    Arabic   Marhatta
    Persian   Tamula (Tamil)
    Sanskrit   Canara
    Bengali
    Telenga
2. Mahomedan Law
3. Hindoo Law
4. Ethics, Civil Jurisprudence and the Law of Nations
5. English Law
6. The Regulations and Laws enacted by the Governor General in Council at Fort St. George (Madras) and Bombay respectively for the civil government in the British Territorries in India
7. Political Economy and particularly the commercial institutions and interests of the East India Company
8. Geography and Mathematics
9. Modern Languages of Europe
10. Greek, Latin and English Classics
11. General History (Ancient and Modern)
12. The History and Antiquities of Hindoostan and Deccan
13. Natural History
14. Botany, Chemistry and Astronomy

The first three years of service of all civil servants appointed in the establishment of the Presidency of Bengal, from the date of these orders were to be spent at the college and during that period and time, the prescribed studies in the college were to constitute their sole public duty. Similar privileges were extended to all of the junior military servants of the Company in India.

The Governor General had not initially asked the permission of the London Headquarters of the Company for the college. When it was first referred they withheld permission; even when they later gave their approval, they insisted on modifications of the original proposal.

It appears from the records that a sanction had already been accorded to the purchase of the Writers' Buildings for the college, provided they could be obtained on reasonable terms.

But the Governor General informed the Court of Directors that the Writers' Buildings could not be obtained on such terms, nor could they be converted to the final purposes of the college. The Governor General selected and bought a site for the college at Garden Reach. The college never moved there as the project was vetoed by the Court of Directors. The land was resold at a small loss.

A student of the college was involved in a court case. He was charged before Mr. Martyn, one of the Justices of Peace on 16 February 1802 with having assaulted one Jagonnaut Singh, a *vakeel* of the Court of the Sudder Dewany Adawlut. The fact was that a cat had been sitting in a shop near the deponent's house. The student, Mr. Chisholme, set his dog at the cat, the cat ran to the deponent's house, the said Mr. Chisholme followed the cat and attempted to go into the *zennanah*, the deponent begged him not to enter the *zennanah*. Thereupon Mr. Chisholme gave the deponent two violent blows with his fist upon the deponent's forehead and he also assaulted in a similar fashion a boy named Saum Singh. Mr. Chisholme admitted the assault. In the end it was resolved that this conduct will be reported to the Acting Visitor for proper action.

As the college became popular the building formerly occupied by the Crown and Anchor Hotel was also taken on rent and a walking gallery was erected to reach the building across Council House Street. In the 1820s the college moved to the Writers' Buildings and later to a building in Lyon's Range.

There were several changes in the statutes of the college in 1841, when the college of Fort William was placed under the control of the Government of Bengal. For the qualifying examinations, there was an oral examination on certain text books:

Persian	:	*Anwari Soheilee* and *Goolistan*
Hindi	:	*Prem Sagar*
Bengali	:	*Hitopadesh*

In its lifetime of a little over fifty years, the Fort William College played a significant role in giving a new direction to Bengali culture and literature. Like so many of those colonial institutions set up to support colonial administration, the Fort William College too went on to achieve far more than what it was intended to accomplish. The College brought together a band of dedicated British and Indian scholars who went into close collaboration to produce and publish a rich list of titles covering popular stories, chronicles and legends, as well as definitive editions of literary texts, in both Bengali and English.

Mrityunjoy Vidyalankar was the first Pundit on the college faculty. Iswarchandra Vidyasagar taught at the college between 1841 and 1846, and again in 1849. Under the leadership of William Carey, Sanskrit *pundits* and Persian and Arabic *munshis* joined hands to create a new Bengali prose capable of meeting the requirements of the new times and more accessible to the common people.[19]

This unique institution was dissolved by Lord Dalhousie on 24 January 1854, though it had ceased to function in 1852.

To come back to the house, we find the Calcutta Exchange revived in 1818. The upper storey had a lofty hall with marble pillars used for balls and gala parties before the Town Hall was built. The first Secretary of the Exchange was a Mr. Brodie, who in 1822, was succeeded by Mr. Murdoch Mackenzie. The latter, finding his duties becoming somewhat onerous, applied for permission to have an assistant, a position filled eventually by Mr. James Napier Lyall. Messrs. Mackenzie & Lyall were appointed in 1823 Joint Secretaries, while being at the same time allowed to trade upon their own account. Their business grew and in 1827 they took another partner and the name was styled Mackenzie, Lyall & Co. Auctions were periodically held at the premises by all who had goods to dispose of in this manner. The East India Company found an outlet for their opium and salt in these auctions.

Messrs. Mackenzie, Lyall & Co. did a flourishing business from the upper storey offices at the Exchange for a long time, before they moved their office to Lyon's Range in 1888. There were cases when the rivalry between the buyers at the auction sales, each trying to outbid the others, led to pandemonium and violence, and the police had to be called to restore peace. The Exchange was very popular at the time and used to publish *The Exchange Gazette* and *Daily Advertiser*.[20]

At one time the Calcutta Exchange had its eastern boundary in Vansittart Row, with the site of the old Mcleod & Co. (it used to be the Bishop's Palace in the days of Bishop Middleton, when St. John's was the Cathedral Church) as part of its premises.

Next we come to Vansittart Row, a little cul-de-sac, with an arched gateway formed by the Standard Insurance Building as its entrance. The Vansittart Row has been named both in Mark Wood's and Upjohn's maps. It is named after Henry Vansittart, who succeeded Holwell as Governor of Bengal in 1760, and served until 1764. Vansittart owned properties in the Row named after him and had a garden house at Middleton Row at the site of the present Loreto House. There are several offices in Vansittart Row. In 1841 and 1842 W. Rushton & Co. published from their office at Vansittart Row two successive issues of the *Bengal & Agra Guide*, the earliest known guidebook of Calcutta. The printers at their Ballantyne Press also published the *Planter's Journal* and specialized in pirated editions of popular novels. On 27 March 1837, the *Calcutta Courier* announced the publication by Mr. W. Rushton of a 'reprint' 'of the most amusing and witty production, *The Posthumous Papers of the Pickwick Club*,' with a frontispiece which was 'so good a copy of the original' that the *Courier* 'had some difficulty to believe that the original plate had not been obtained from England.' Pirated copies followed in 1838 of novels by Bulwer Lytton and Capt. Marryat and plays by Sheridan Knowles.

THE CENTRAL TELEGRAPH OFFICE

We leave the Standard Insurance building and come to the road leading to the Government House (Raj Bhavan today)—Red Cross Place (previously Wellesley Place). On our left is the Telephone Bhavan built on the site of the Dalhousie Institute, on the right we can see the majestic north entrance of the Government House. We cross Red Cross Place and come to the Central Telegraph Office, one of Calcutta's surviving notable Victorian buildings. Situated at the corner of Dalhousie Square South and Old Court House Street, the original design was made in 1868, the ground cleared in 1870 and building commenced in 1873. The style of architecture is admirably suited to the requirements of the climate. The building stands upon a plinth, 4 feet 6 inches high, and consists of a main block facing Lal Dighi, with a tower at the east, and three wings; the east wing facing Old Court House Street, the other two forming a centre; and the west wing on Red Cross Place. The total height of the building is 66 feet above plinth, and of the tower, which resembles an Italian Campanile, 120 feet. The central entrance of the main northern front is well-designed. The columns are well proportioned, the balconies and cornices bold and rich in decoration, and the general effect is exceedingly good. The tower is carried up as a part of the main buildings as far as the roof; strengthened, however, at its four corners, by buttresses, which are continued to the top. The Telegraph Office also houses the Dead Letter Office in the eastern wing.

Figure 11: The Central Telegraph Office

THE ROAD FROM THE OLD COURT HOUSE TO ESPLANADE

In 1781 a road was built leading from the Old Court House Street by the side of the eastern end of Lal Dighi, the newly constructed Fort William and across the Maidan to Surman's Bridge in Kidderpore. The road was built according to plans made by Colonel Henry Watson. The long road was later given three names, from the Lal Bazar corner to Currency Office was the Tank Square East renamed Dalhousie Square East and in 1969 to Binoy-Badal-Dinesh Bagh East. From Manton & Co (now demolished) to the north-eastern end of Government House was the Old Court House Street; and the last stage up to Esplanade was Government Place East. According to the Calcutta Corporation Street Directory of 1981 they have renamed BBD Bagh East, Old Court House Street and a part of Government Place East, Hemanta Basu Sarani.

Hemanta Basu, Chairman, All India Forward Bloc and a close lieutenant of Netaji Subhas Chandra Bose, was murdered by unknown assassins near his house in North Calcutta on 19 February 1971. The Calcutta Corporation sanctioned Rs. 30,000 on 20 March 1971 for the installation of a statue of Basu at the junction of B.B.D. Bagh East and Lal Bazar Street.

Strangely enough, none of the establishments on this stretch uses the name Hemanta Basu Sarani, not even the Tourism Department of the Government of West Bengal, whose address still is 3/2, B.B.D. Bagh East.

The Company put an embargo on any building activity on the eastern side of Lal Dighi, as evident from Thomas Daniell's *View of the Eastern side of Tank Square;* with no houses on the eastern side and the newly built Mission Church clearly visible.

This embargo was lifted in 1806, but it is on record that a riding school run by one Antonio Angelo Tremamondo had been based there from 1779 to 1784. There is an interesting history attached to the premises No. 4 on the eastern side of Lal Dighi (a very important address, which we shall visit shortly). By a deed dated 6 September 1780, the land described as 'One biggah and 16 cottahs of the Honourable Company's 'Camar' or untenanted land situated in *Dhee* Calcutta is the Anglicised versionof *dehee* meaning a cluster of villages was granted to Charles Weston, the benefactor of the poor of Calcutta and friend of Holwell in his old age, with a condition that 'no House, wall or other erection of any kind whatsoever shall be built upon the ground excepting a palisade, fence or railing.' And, 'on failing of this condition, the ground shall revert to the Company.' In 1795 Weston sold the land for Rs. 6,000, with the prohibition attached thereto; and in 1799 it passed to the Barrettos. It remained waste for another nine years. After the prohibitory period was over, a house was built upon it, which was sold in 1836 for Rs. 82,000. In 1882, the premises was bought by Sir Walter Desouza for Rs. 1,80,000; a few years later he sold it for Rs. 3,50,000.[21]

Another view of Old Court House Street looking south from Larkin's Lane was painted by Thomas Daniell in 1788. Hickey points out that the second house from the right belonged to John Prinsep. The larger house further south belonged to Mr. Grand, a factor of the

Company, who married a French girl of sixteen in Chandernagore. Mrs. Catherine Grand was a great beauty. On the night of 8 December 1778, Sir Philip Francis, Member of the Council, was 'surprised' in this house. Grand was away, dining with Richard Barwell. Francis climbed into the house by a bamboo ladder, assisted by three friends, including Sir George Shee and Sir John Shore, a future Governor-General. The friends kept watch outside, while Francis gained access to Mrs. Grand. In the meantime Grand's servants had discovered the ladder, and secured Francis when he attempted to leave the house. He was able, however, to summon his friends, who assisted him to escape, but who were in their turn secured by Grand's servants until their master returned home. Since Francis refused to meet Grand in a duel, Grand took him to court. The action was tried before Chief Justice Impey and Judges Hyde and Chambers, who found for the plaintiff, with Chambers dissenting, that though no actual guilt was proved, the damage done by Francis to Mrs. Grand's reputation should be liberally compensated. Impey delivered a fine of 50,000 sicca rupees. Grand returned his wife to her family in Chandernagore.

There is a dispute however about the place of occurrence. Grand's own narrative written some years later states that he 'was then living at a garden house, a short distance from town, with my recently acquired consort', and evidently close to Warren Hastings' house at Alipore. The notebooks of Mr. Justice Hyde record that for ten months after their marriage, the Grands lived in the house of Robert Sanderson, Barwell's father-in-law, and this was possibly Grand's garden house near town. Hyde's notes on this case also reveal that Barwell's dinner that night had been, not at his house in Kidderpore, but at the tavern of Francis Le Gallais in town. That the Grand house was in town is corroborated by William Hickey's account of the episode in his memoirs, where he details the stratagems to which he was reduced in order not to act for Grand, including having to leave town himself.

William Hickey himself made a water-colour sketch of Old Court House Street, depicting the houses standing in 1789, one of which, Hickey states, was the house 'Mr. Francis made his entree into, which cost him 50,000 Rs'. Mrs. Catherine Grand disappeared from the Indian scene and a few years later emerged in Paris as the wife of Prince Talleyrand.

The following poem appeared in Calcutta papers about Mrs. Grand:

Was it that half Danish air
Of your birthplace made you fair?
Surely some ambitious star
Watch'd that night at Tranquebar
And a more than human hope
Cast the childish horoscope
How you were reserved to reign
Queen of Ganges, Queen of Seine.
Does your spirit haunt the floor of that house in Alipore

Vis a vis to Francis set
In the spectral minuet
All Calcutta came to you—
Fit obeisance to do
What a story would you tell
Girlish ghost, Jades si belle.

Next was the house of Mr. Harding, one of the paymasters. Behind these two houses may be seen houses in Wheler Place behind Buckingham House. On the left the first house was that of Mr. Ellis, the Surgeon General, followed by a library and a school. The furthest buildings are 'Europe shops', where all kinds of European articles were sold.[22]

Next we come to a painting by James Baillie Fraser in 1819, *A View of the Scotch Church from the Gate of the Tank Square*. This shows the newly built St. Andrew's Church in the north-east corner of the Tank on the site of the demolished Old Court House. The large house on the right was the house of Dr. Hare. Two physicians of this name, uncle and nephew, have been mentioned by William Hickey. This could be the house of the younger Hare. The aqueduct built for supply of water for the natives is visible in the painting.

Frederick Fiebig in his painting *Tank Square from the Scotch Church in 1845* shows the changes in the area, assorted transport and the improved ornamentation of Lal Dighi.

We have a sketch of the north-eastern part of Lal Dighi by Colesworthy Grant in 1834. Grant was born at London on 25 October 1815. In 1832 young Colesworthy came to Calcutta and joined his brother Harry, who was carrying on business as a bookseller in a single-storey godown on the spot now occupied by Stephen Court. In place of the next building, British Library, we see a new sign 'The Hong Kong Tea Ware House' and 'C. Grant, Watch & Clock Maker'.

Meanwhile Colesworthy Grant had taken to painting. In 1833 he had begun contributing a series of lithographed portraits of Calcutta public characters to the *India Review* and the *Monthly Journal*. These portraits and others from the *Bengal Sporting Journal* came out as a book under the title of *Outline Portraits*; the dates for the individual portraits range from 1833 to 1850. He also issued a series of portraits of notable Indians, which he called *Oriental Heads*. He published *Rural Life in Bengal* in 1860, copiously illustrated by him. He founded the Calcutta Society for Prevention of Cruelty to Animals (CSPCA) in 1862. Grant was seen daily in the north-eastern corner of Lal Dighi helping animals to drink water from a fountain. After his death, his admirers erected an obelisk in his memory near the fountain, but today it must have disappeared somewhere, with the whole corner taken up by a public toilet complex.

In 1849, Grant accepted the position of Drawing Master in the Bengal Engineering College, Sibpore and Professorship of Drawing in the Civil Engineering Department of the Presidency College, Calcutta, a post from which he retired on pension four weeks before his death on 31 May 1880.[23]

Mrs. Christina Pringle, whom we have mentioned earlier, arrived in Calcutta in 1829, and wrote to her parents that 'In Calcutta there are no shops with their gay windows to tempt one, but just warerooms'.[24] But in another 40–50 years the road leading from the Old Court House became the most fashionable shopping area in town, with famous jewellers, clothiers, pharmacies, bookstores, shops selling musical equipments and others with their projecting and covered entrances standing shoulder to shoulder in this area.

On Old Court House Street, moving south along the western pavement, we come to No. 14, which had Octavius Steel & Co., and General Electric Co. (India) Ltd., advertising English-made Swan fans in 1915. No. 15 was occupied by Phelps & Co., Tailors. 16 & 16/1 were occupied by Lawrence & Mayo, Opticians, and Harnack & Co., selling trunks, suitcases, holdalls, etc. On this site now stands a high-rise housing the headquarters of the United Bank of India. Numbers 17 and 18 were residences, and No. 19 was the famous chemists' shop Bathgate & Co. They were one of the most prosperous chemists in Calcutta with branches in Camac Street and Ballygunge Circular Road. Old-timers will remember their sticky red hair oil which they had to use in their childhood.

Next we come to the entrance to Larkin's Lane, a small lane ending in Wellesley Place (Red Cross Place). The lane is marked in Wood's map of Calcutta of 1784. It was named after William Larkins, a leading citizen of Calcutta in his day, and an intimate friend of Warren Hastings. Larkins had some properties in this lane. American Express had an office in Larkin's Lane for a long time. Number 2 was and is still the address for one of the oldest jewellers of the town, Cooke & Kelvey. The original building has been replaced by a new mansion, housing a few offices including Housing and Development Finance Corporation (HDFC). Cooke & Kelvey has over the years developed into a major hire-purchase company, though it still retains its jewellers' concern. The last building on this stretch was James Montieth & Co., Saddlers and Harness Makers. Number 21 now houses the American Express Banking Division (they are the only ones to use a Hemanta Basu Sarani address— No. 21). The corner with Government Place North is the continuation of a Government House Staff facility. After Government Place North we come to the eastern part of the Governor's House and the Gateway. Opposite the eastern gate we cross the road and come to the Esplanade Mansions at the corner of Esplanade East and Government Place East. The site of the sprawling Esplanade Mansions was known for a long time as Scott Thomson's Corner, from the fact that Messrs. R. Scott Thomson & Co., the chemists, had carried on business there for a long time. They were located previously at 3, Council House Street from 1841 to 1843. There is a title deed dated 1 February 1788 recording that the house on this spot was leased out that date by Richard Johnson to Thomas Henry Davies, the successor in 1786 of Sir John Day, as Advocate General. Mr. Davies married Ann Baillie at St. John's Church, Calcutta on 3 April 1788. He died in Calcutta in 1792.

Figure 12: Government Place East

The eastern side of the road opposite the Governor's House was originally called Government Place East (part of which has now been absorbed into Hemanta Basu Sarani). Government Place East initially extended up to the corner with Waterloo Street. R. Scott Thomson occupied premises Number 15 with Tait's American Diamond Palace. Number 14 had the offices of H.T. Meyers and the establishment of Messrs Nash & Andrew. In 1896 S.C. Sen, photographer, 'By Appointment to Earl of Elgin', had a studio at 13/5; 13/4/1 was the premises of James Spence & Co.; and 13 to 13/4 was the large establishment of Francis, Harrison & Hathaway & Co., Clothiers; 12/1 was the premises of James Murray, Opticians (previously at 11, Dalhousie Square East, carrying on business as watchmakers, they shifted to Government Place East in 1899 as opticians). Number 12 was the premises of Harman & Co., Army, Navy and Diplomatic Tailors in 1885. Number 11 housed one of Calcutta's favourite restaurants, the Peliti's, and Davies Leech & Co., Tailors. This was also called White House. Federico Peliti established his restaurant in 1870, first at Chowringhee, and then moved to No. 11 much later; they used to advertise as 'Court Caterer and Confectioner, with Upstair Restaurant with Band' (1905). The premises Number 10 at the crossing with Waterloo Street and a few older buildings were demolished later in the nineteenth century for the new Ezra Mansions (now in a poor untended condition), that came to house several business houses like Brooke Bond & Co., Cuthbertson & Harper, Bootmakers, etc. (still existing). In some older books on Calcutta, Number 10 has been wrongly described as the residence of General Clavering and also as a temporary theatre. About the first there is no evidence, but for the second, this was housed in a building just across Waterloo Street.

Figure 13: Peliti's Restaurant, Government Place East. Photo Bourne & Shepherd

TEMPORARY THEATRE

The Calcutta Booksellers, W. Thacker & Co. and St. Andrew's Library (predecessors of Messrs. Thacker Spink & Co.) were located for many years in Lal Bazar but as the condition of the building deteriorated they shifted to Old Court House Street. The Directory of 1836 gives their address as 1, Old Court House Street. This premises has long been engulfed by the expanding Great Eastern Hotel. The booksellers were located on the upper floor, as an unexpected use was found for the lower floor in 1839. In the early morning of 31 May the Chowringhee Theatre established in 1813 at the corner of Theatre Road (Shakespeare Sarani) was totally gutted in a fire. Pending the erection of another theatre, it became necessary to secure a temporary accommodation. J. H. Stoqueler (of the *Englishman* fame) writes in his *Memories of a Journalist* (1873, p. 115), 'a long room beneath a bookseller's store was engaged'.

The temporary hall could accommodate 400 people. The first performance probably took place on 21 August 1839; and the play presented was *The Hunchback* by Sheridan Knowles, with Mrs. Esther Leach, Calcutta's 'star' actress of the time, as Julia.[25]

THE GREAT EASTERN HOTEL

The hotel occupies Numbers one, two and three, Old Court House Street. David Wilson, otherwise known as Dainty Davie, and owner of a confectionery in Cossaitolah (later Bentinck Street), opened the Auckland Hotel at 1, Old Court House Street in 1835. Soon the Indian hackney-carriage drivers came to call it 'Wilson Saheb Ka Hotel', and the name

Figure 14: The Great Eastern Hotel

Figure 15: Government Place East and Horse-drawn Tramcars, Photo Bourne & Shepherd

Wilson's Hotel stuck. Rabindranath Tagore uses the name in his autobiography. The *Calcutta Magazine* reported on 16 June 1862 that Messrs. D. Wilson & Company's firm assumed the title of the Great Eastern Hotel Company Limited with a capital of 15 lakhs in 6000 shares of Rs. 200 each, Mr. Wilson holding 1500 shares. Lord William Beresford, Military Secretary to three viceroys, lovingly called Lord Bill or Brassfoot Sahib, was a regular visitor in the early days. Lord Bill was a great race enthusiast. His mare Myall King won the Viceroy's Cup several times. In the 1880s, and probably for years previously, it was a custom to serve meals in the street to people who pulled up outside the hotel in *gharries*. A place was reserved near the entrance for Lewis, an advocate, who called every day in his palanquin where he was served a rupee tiffin-steak, or chop, bread and two vegetables, and of course a full peg. The name Great Eastern Hotel came into use only in 1865.

The original building had two storeys, the ground floor occupied by a number of shops, selling from trunks and suitcases to fashionable clothes, confectioneries, etc. The upper storey was used as a hotel accommodating 200 guests. The verandah that covers the pavement in front of the hotel was the work of Walter Macfarlane & Co. In 1883 one could enter the hotel through one entrance, buy a complete outfit, a wedding present, or seeds for the garden, have an excellent meal, a full peg for ten annas, and if the barmaid was agreeable, walk out at the other end engaged to be married.[26]

The Handbook of the Bengal Presidency with an Account of Calcutta City in 1882, written by Edward B. Eastwick in London, gives the charges for board and lodge in Great Eastern Hotel including carriage fare as Rs. 10 to 20 per day.

House Number 4 was the famous premises of Ranken & Co., fashionable tailors in the late nineteenth century. In 1895 H. Hobbs & Co., in Number 5, had a musical exchange advertising 'New Pianos for sale and hire'. Numbers 6 and 7 had the premises of Schroder Smidt & Co., Hamburg Fire Insurance Company and the Consulate of Guatemala.

The fine ornate building at Number 8 was the showroom of the famous jewellers, Hamilton & Co. The *maharajas* and the fashionable rich of the whole of India vied with each other to buy their latest creations. For their logo they had a small elephant. Mr. Snaith, the owner, had a sprawling bungalow with a hangar in Digha, by the sea near Contai. He used to go there in his de Havilland Puss Moth landing there on the hard seabeach. Hamilton & Co. has gone into oblivion and the beautiful ornate building has lost its splendour. Number 9 was the showroom of Baker & Catliff who had the largest number of toys east of Suez. They later changed premises and became clothiers. Harnack & Co., another clothier, occupied Numbers 10 & 10/1. Number ten and half was the office of Thomas Cook & Son, 'Originator of the European Tourist System, est. 1811'. They moved later to Number 9. Number 11 was shared by Favre Leuba, the 'Swiss Watchmakers and Jewellers,' and D. Macropolo, tobacconists. Number 12 was the showroom of F & C Osler, famous oil lamp and later electrical goods manufacturers. Number 13 was the Grosvenor House, housing the London Musical Depot., T.E. Bevan & Co., 'Importers of English pianos, gramophones, records, etc.' In 1905 they advertised having a large collection of Bengali records sung by Ram Das Dutta, Bedana Dassi, Hurrimottee Dassi and others.

Number 13/2 was the showroom of well-known firearms dealers, Manton & Co., at the corner of Mangoe Lane. The house has recently been demolished. I gather from Mr. Chamaria, the owner of Manton & Co. in the 1970s, that the company presented to the Victoria Memorial Hall two pistols supposed to have been used by Warren Hastings and Philip Francis at their duel.

Here we cross Mangoe Lane and enter Dalhousie Square East (B.B.D. Bagh East and now a part of Hemanta Basu Sarani). The road has on its west the eastern end of Lal Dighi. The whole eastern side of Lal Dighi is now a mini bus stand with a series of ugly green sheds in two rows.

CURRENCY BUILDING

At the corner of Mangoe Lane we come across Number 1, B.B.D. Bagh East, an ill-maintained lofty building in Italian architecture. The ground floor was once used as the office for Issue and Exchange of Government Paper Currency. The entrance has a very handsome gate, in three parts, of a fine florid design in wrought iron. The central hall is of grand proportions and is lit by skylights surmounting three large domes. Here were the exchange counters for notes, gold and silver and small change. The money was kept in a vault of massive masonry construction lined throughout with iron; an iron door six inches in thickness closed this vault, which was further protected by a second iron door and an inner iron grating. The rooms above are very massively and handsomely finished and are floored

Figure 16: The Currency Building. Photo Bourne & Shepherd

throughout with Italian marble up to the third storey. The building was originally erected in 1833 for the Agra and Masterman's Bank, but on the collapse of that institution (soon after completion) it was sold to the Government. The building is no longer in use. The Government of India, owner of the building, had started to demolish it, but at the request of the lovers of Heritage buildings in Calcutta, the Calcutta Municipal Corporation has stopped the demolition work.

Premises No. 3 were occupied in 1885 by Harold & Co., The Calcutta Musical Depot, who were selling pianos for Rs. 450 and harmoniums at the range of Rs. 35 to 500. Arlington & Co., Jewellers, were at No. 3E before moving to No. 5. The premises No. 4 have seen many changes. This is the plot East India Company sold in 1780 to Charles Weston, who sold it to the Barrettos in 1799. A building was erected nine years later. A double storey messuage tenement legal term for a dwelling house with outbuildings and land called Dwelling House was in the occupation of Messrs. Allport, Ashburner & Co. The Bengal Club, established in 1827, occupying Gordon's Building in Esplanade East, moved to this house during the early days of Charles Metcalfe's presidency. The Club finally moved to 33, Chowringhee Road in 1845. Number 4 was lovingly called the Club by contemporaries, long after the Club had moved to Chowringhee. But the ownership of the building changed. In 1836, it was sold for Rs. 82,000 by the assignees of the insolvent firm of Cruttenden, Mackillop and Co. to James William Macleod. A proposal of purchase of the 'Club House' was made in 1841 by Messrs. Jenkins Law & Co. to Thomas DeSouza & Co. In 1882 the premises were purchased by Sir Walter DeSouza for Rs. 1,80,000 and were sold by him a few years later for Rs. 3,50,000. After the Bengal Club vacated the house a shop called Bodelio's Emporium of Fashion carried on business. From 1880 Number 4 was the address of the well-known booksellers W. Newman & Co. When the building was demolished later, the company moved to the Great Eastern Hotel arcade. Number 6 was the Calcutta office of the *London Times* and Number 7 showroom of Anglo-Swiss Watch Company.

A young man of nineteen, an Armenian, whose family had settled in Ispahan in Iran, came to Calcutta in 1880. His was a fairytale rags to riches story. Starting business with a capital of Rs. 100, he became the biggest landholder of Calcutta and Darjeeling in 1892. He bought first the property belonging to an English lady at the corner of the Square and Lal Bazar, then housing the chemists Smith Stanistreet & Co. and Messrs. Black & Murray & Co. Next he bought No. 8 Dalhousie Square East, then occupied by Messrs. Rodda & Co. and Lewis Stewart. At the site he built the Stephen Building now called Stephen Court. Other well known business houses on this stretch included Dwarkin & Son; Paris Musical Depot, Branch Office (the main office at 8/2, Esplanade East is still there); D. Morrison & Co. Clothiers; Levetus & Co., offering Royal England cycles for Rs. 140 in 1905; Pistis & Pelikanos selling motorcycles in 1899; Uberoi selling sports goods in 1911; Bombay Sports Dept, West End Watch Co., and Singer Sewing Machine Co. offering table models in 1885 on hire purchase scheme at Rs. 10 per month.

DALHOUSIE SQUARE NORTH
(B.B.D. BAGH NORTH)

The first sight as we look northwards is St. Andrew's Church or the Scotch Kirk with its high steeple, built on the site of the Old Court House which was of great significance in Calcutta's past.

Plate 4: Thomas Daniell, views of Calcutta north side of the Tank Square, Writer's Building and the Old Court House 1786

THE OLD COURT HOUSE

The Old Court Hosue was probably initially a Charity School, then the Mayor's Court, a place for public meetings and entertainment, and finally the Supreme Court. Asiaticus, writing in 1802, traces its origin to the liberality of Robert Bourchier, second in Council at Fort William and Master Attendant of the Port in 1731, who gave it to the Company to be used as a Charity School. According to *Calcutta Review*, Bourchier built the house, made some additions in 1765 and gave it to the Company for 4000 Arcot rupees* per annum, to support a Charity School and for other benevolent purposes.[27] The Free School Society was established on 21 December 1789.

Another tradition connected it with the name of the Sikh millionaire, Omi Chand who bequeathed its rent to the charity fund which supported and educated English children in indigent circumstances. The Company rented a part of the newly built Charity School at

---

* Arcot rupees were minted in Arcot in South India and later also by the East India Company in the Madras mint.

the north-eastern corner of Lal Dighi. The Council wrote to London in 1729: 'Having set on foot a Charity School and for that purpose raised Rs. 23709 12 annas 3 p & appointed the President and Council for the time being to be Trustees'. There were eight boys on the foundation and forty other day-scholars, who were to be raised in the Protestant religion. The spacious building was obviously too large for the purpose of the school and was soon rented by the Company to be used as the Mayor's Court, which was established by the statute of 1727; and in Wills' Map of 1753, it figures under the name 'Court House'. For an excellent view of the house, we can refer to Thomas Daniell's *Views of 1786*, which shows a fine double-storeyed building with a portico running along its whole length and surmounted by a wide verandah. Of the upper floor, Stavorinus, the Dutch Admiral, who visited Calcutta in 1770, has left a description: 'Over the Court House are two handsome assembly rooms. In one of these are hung up the portraits of the King of France and of the late Queen, both life-size brought from Chandernagore by the British'. There was no mention of the Twelve Caesars which adorned the rooms. These were all transferred to the Government House when the house was demolished. The rooms were hired out at high expense for various purposes, as an Exchange for Merchants of the Settlement to meet, a Post Office, Quarter Sessions, Public Entertainments and all the General Meetings. The newly formed Grand Lodge of the Free Masons also had their meetings there. The newly formed Supreme Court met in this building from October 1774. Here was held, in the sweltering heat of June 1775, the infamous trial of Maharaja Nanda Kumar for forgery. Though the rent was increased to 800 sicca rupees* per month, no more space was available for the Court. So the Company in November 1780 rented a larger house at Esplanade Row for the Supreme Court. The Old Court House building was thereafter used solely as a place for entertainment, but the Company continued to pay the rent of 800 sicca rupees for the Charity School. The building was in such a bad condition that it was pulled down in 1792. Ultimately the land was handed over in 1818 to build the Scottish Church.

ST. ANDREW'S CHURCH

The church has two other popular names, viz. The Scotch Kirk and Lat Sahib Ka Girja. The last name probably has its origin in the fact that the foundation stone of the church was laid by Countess of Loudon and Moira, wife of the Governor General, Marquess of Hastings.

The church stands on the site of the Old Court House, directly facing the road leading to the Maidan. This elegant Grecian building is modelled on the Church of Scotland to which the church adhered. Standing in a very prominent position with its tall spire, it is a familiar sight of the city. On the north and south there are elegant porticos, with lofty

---

* Sicca rupees were coined during the Mughal and Nawabi rule and also used during East India Company's reign.

Doric pillars. It was opened on 8 March 1818. The total cost of the building came to 20,000 pounds. The first parish priest was the Reverend (later Doctor) Bryce.

There is an interesting story about the spire. Bishop Fanshawe Middleton, the first Bishop of Calcutta, believed that the Church of England had a monopoly on spires, not only in England but also in all British territorries and he asked the Company to refuse permission to St. Andrew's for the erection of a spire. When Rev. Bryce heard about this, he declared that he would not only have a steeple higher than the Cathedral Church of St. John's, but he would also place on the top of it a cock to crow over the Bishop, which came to pass accordingly. The Bishop Middleton was deeply mortified. The Government, allegedly to pacify the Bishop, directed that though the rest of the building might be repaired by the Public Works Department, the audacious bird would not be their responsibility. The bird is still there. There are several pictures of the chaplains and monuments inside the church. The church is well depicted in the paintings of James Baillie Fraser in 1819, Shaikh Muhammad Amir in 1828-30 and Sir Charles D'Oyly among others.

OLD COURT HOUSE CORNER AND OLD COURT HOUSE LANE

These two bore memories of the Old Court House. The Old Court Lane started from 1, Lyon's Range and went up to Radha Bazar Street; the Old Court House Corner starting from 21 Lal Bazar Street terminated near St. Andrew's Church. These two disappeared when the Brabourne Road (Biplabi Trailokya Maharaj Sarani, 1971) was constructed for a quicker approach to Howrah Station, and opened to traffic in 1950.

W. Thacker & Co. and St. Andrew's Library, predecessors of Thacker Spink & Co., was established in a house at the corner of Lal Bazar, immediately to the east of the church from which it was separated by Old Court House Corner. The address of the Library is given as Lal Bazar in 1827 and again in 1833. The site is now occupied by a large building named Norton's Building. One of James Baillie Fraser's views of St. Andrew's Church taken from Mission Row shows the old house, a two-storeyed building, seen prominently in the foreground to the right of the plate. At the corner of Old Court House Corner and Radha Bazar Street was the showroom of Benode Behary Dutt & Bros., Jewellers, at Number 7. Number 8 was a famous location in Calcutta, the premises of Steuart & Co., Coach Builders to the King. The business is believed to have started in 1775 under another name, before James Steuart arrived in Calcutta in 1783 and took over the business, the firm continuing under the old name for a long time. They were known to *hackney carriagewallas* as 'Buggy Steuarts'. The firm occupied a considerable area, the boundary of which has been given as: 'All that dwelling house and premises containing by a measurement two beegahs seventeen cottahs and thirteen chittacks or thereabouts situated and lying and being in Old Court House Corner and Radha Bazar and bounded on the south by Old Court House Corner, on the west by St. Andrew's churchyard and the house in the occupation of Shand Fairlie & Co. and on the east by native shops and Radha Bazar.'

Solvyns, the Flemish artist, during his sojourn in Calcutta, did some ornamentation work for Steuart & Co., and made some money. He painted and embellished several palanquins for the nobility, the first two ordered by Lord Cornwallis for the Mysore Princes and valued at Rs. 6 to 7,000. The ornamental paintings did Solvyns much credit—in single colour only on a gold ground. All the metal with feet, etc. were overlaid with silver and in some parts solid silver, the lining velvet with rich silver or gold embroidery and fringe. In 1874 a state *howdah* was made for King Edward VII; a state carriage for King George V in 1906; and another in 1911. On the occasion of the Coronation Durbar held by Lord Curzon in 1902, Steuart & Co. supplied a solid silver *howdah* for the Maharaja of Balrampur, and twenty-two *landaus* and eighteen *victorias* for the personal guests of the Viceroy. In 1907 Steuart & Co. moved to 3, Mangoe Lane. As the palanquins, phaetons and other lovely horse-drawn coaches were replaced by motor cars in Calcutta streets, Steuart & Co. switched over to sale and repair of motor cars and the manufacture of motor bodies. In 1930 they moved to a premises at the corner of Park Street and Free School Street.[28]

WRITERS' BUILDINGS

The whole of Dalhousie Square North (B.B.D. Bagh North) is covered by the Writers' Building, which began as a dwelling place for East India Company's writers, a part of Fort

Figure 17: The Writer's Building across Dalhousie Square before renovation

Figure 18: The Writer's Building after renovation.

William College and later the Bengal Secretariat, and after partition of India the West Bengal Secretariat.

In the early days of the Company, the only building on this stretch was St. Anne's Church built in 1716, at the site of the Rotunda of the Writers' Building. The rest of it was uninhabited wasteland. In October 1776, two parcels of land were granted to Thomas Lyon and in 1777 a range of buildings were erected in one parcel of the land but the land opposite on the northern side of the Lal Dighi was never built up. The original *pattah* for the transaction was discovered by Mr. R.C. Sterndale during his tenure of office as the Collector of Calcutta. Mr. Lyon actually was acting on behalf of Mr. Richard Barwell, member of the Council, when Warren Hastings was the Governor. The Writers' Building was the first building with three storeys in Calcutta. In 1780 Barwell leased out the range of buildings to the Company for the accommodation of its junior servants or those not receiving a salary of Rs. 300 per month. Mr. Philip Francis, another member of the Council, wrote in his diary of 29 February, 'Mr. Barwell's house taken for five years by his own rate at 31,700 current rupees per annum to be paid half-yearly in advance. Mr. Wheler and I declare we shall not sign the lease.'[29] A few days later—after this highly satisfactory deal—Mr. Barwell retired and Mr. Francis rose a step in seniority in the Council. For years the building was used for the purpose for which it was built, providing rent-free accommodation to the Company's junior servants. We can have a glance at the Building as it looked in 1786, from Thomas Daniell's *View of the north side of Lal Dighi*. At the far distance on the left are the remains of the Old Fort, Holwell Monument, the Writers' Buildings and a part of the Old Court House. James Baillie Fraser's *A View of Writers' Buildings in 1819* shows the dilapidated Holwell Monument in the foreground and the Buildings with thatched awnings jutting out on the western end. By this time the Old Court House had been demolished and St. Andrew's Church can be seen. In the meantime the College of Fort William had moved to the central portion of the Buildings. Maria Graham describes the 1810 season, 'The Writers' Buildings, to the north Government House, look like a shabby hospital, or poors-house; these contain apartments for the writers newly arrived from Britain, and who are students at the College of Fort William, which is in the centre of the buildings, and contains nothing but some lecture rooms.'[30]

But gradually the collegiate system of living was abandoned, and the nineteen set apartments drifted into the hands of merchants and private individuals. The Writers' Buildings, as we can see in the early pictures, was a large and long plain stuccoed building without any architectural beauty. In the hands of the merchants, the ground floors were mostly used as godowns and store rooms and quite a few shops.

In 1882, during the reign of Sir Ashley Eden as Lieutenant Governor of Bengal, the Writers' Buildings underwent transformation; a new facade, using the Corinthian order finished in the red brick styles of other Government buildings of the period, emerged. Baroque statuary were introduced at the top. A set of new blocks was added on the northern side in Lyons Range to house the Bengal Government. In 1883, the Rotunda portion was completed (at the old site of St. Anne's Church) at the western end of the building. In the same year the Bengal Legislative Council moved to the Rotunda and remained there until 1910, when it moved to the Durbar Hall of the Belvedere and three years later to the Council Chamber at the Government House, vacated by the Imperial Legislative Council, when the Capital shifted to Delhi in 1912.

Since that time the Writers' Buildings have not changed much. When the British left in 1947, with the partition of Bengal, this became the secretariat of the Government of West Bengal. Dr. B.C. Roy during his tenure as Chief Minister wanted to shift the Secretariat to Budge Budge in a new satellite township, but nothing came of it. The Writers' Buildings stand today as a symbol of power but the accommodation inside is cramped, in the vast dimly-lit halls, where a large number of men and women labour throughout the day in the most unhealthy conditions. For smooth and better functioning, modern office buildings are necessary and the Writers' Buildings can be transformed to a museum focusing on the City of Calcutta.

LYON'S RANGE

This street and some buildings were built by Thomas Lyon on instructions from Richard Barwell in 1780. He built a range of shops or boutiques for letting for the benefit of Barwell's children's trust fund. Originally this street started from the Old Court House Corner, ending in Clive Street in the west. The more common name used by locals was *Company Keranee Ka bareek ka oothar rasta* as has been mentioned in the *Bengal & Agra Guide* of 1850. The whole south side of the range is now taken up by extensions of Writers' Buildings for various departments of the state government. On the north, the range now starts from a new road, the Brabourne Road (Biplabi Trailokya Maharaj Sarani). The first house on the right was in the occupation of various Calcutta firms, like Macneill & Co. in 1877, and Hoare Miller & Co. in 1887. For a long time this company imported cotton piece goods and other merchandise and exported tea and jute, and managed railroads, navigation, etc. The Calcutta Steam Navigation Co. Ltd., managed by them, plied steamer services in various parts of Bengal, and competed with Indian entrants in navigation, often throwing them out of business by undercutting fares. One such sufferer was Jyotirindranath, elder brother of Rabindranath Tagore. Hoare Miller later moved to 38, Strand Road and now has its office at 5, Fairlie Place. Mackenzie Lyall and Co. was a later occupant of the first house on the right of Brabourne Road. In 1905 Numbers One and Two were occupied by the Exchange Gazette Office and Number 3 by the Exchange and Mackenzie Lyall & Co. All these buildings were demolished to make way for the modern office block, the Ilaco House. In 1905 Number 4 was occupied by some offices and the Consulate of the Netherlands. The building now called New Indian Assurance Building housed Lovelock and Lewes, the famous Chartered Accountants from the early years of the last century.

The company dates back to 1872, when William Adolphus Browne started practice in Calcutta as a Public Accountant, Auditor and Liquidator. In 1881, Arthur Samuel Lovelock was admitted as partner of W.A. Browne. The partnership was carried on in the name of Browne and Lovelock. The partnership prospered and subsequently John Herbert Lewes joined as partner in 1886. The firm's name became Browne, Lovelock and Lewes. In 1889 Browne retired from the Indian partnership and went back to London. Since then the firm is known as Lovelock and Lewes. In the beginning they had their office at 25 Mangoe Lane. The house, one of a few with treasure vaults, was owned by the Barretto family.[3]

Number 6 is a fine building in good repair, housing the office of Messrs. Turner Morrison and Co., who have wide interests in collieries, insurance, engineering goods, rope manufacturing and shipping. At one time Turner Morrison was basically a shipping company controlled from London by Asiatic Steam Navigation Company. Number 7 was occupied by some associates of Messrs. Turner Morrison & Co., viz. Vacuum Oil Co., Millars, Karri and Jarrah Co. Ltd. In 1928 the Calcutta Stock Exchange, once the busiest stock exchange in the East, started in this building. The office extends into the next lane, which was once called the New China Bazar Street, and was renamed Royal Exchange Place in 1914. The next building, Number 8, is a ramshackle mansion called Mitra Building, which houses several state government offices. As we head for the old Charnock Place (now a part of Netaji Subhas Road), the Eastern Railway Office with its ornamental panels stand on the west. As we turn right we come to the palatial Victorian building now housing Allahabad Bank.

TO INDIA EXCHANGE PLACE

The site of the Allahabad Bank building has historic associations. In 1775, a *pattah* on this site was granted to a large number of leading citizens of Calcutta, including the Governor General and Members of the Council and the Judiciary, for the establishment of a theatre, with a ballroom for grand occasions. The doorkeepers were Europeans, as it was felt that native people will not be able to manage the distinguished public. Mostly amateur actors and actresses performed on the stage, but extravagant costumes and sceneries soon left the theatre with a considerable loss of money, to the tune of 30,000 sicca rupees. Finally, Mr. Francis Rundell took over the entire management of the theatre, agreeing to give performances once a week during the winter season, and charging one gold *mohur* admission and eight sicca rupees for the pit. For some time the theatre did very well, but ultimately it closed down in 1808. The building was pulled down and the owners, the Tagore family, built a block of shops and named it the New China Bazar.

In 1870 Mr. Kirkman Finlay sent John Alexander Anderson from England to open the Calcutta branch of the James Finlay group. The Calcutta office started in the fine Victorian building at the site of the theatre. The group controlled at one time the largest number of tea gardens in India, but they had commenced business in Calcutta in imported piece goods, insurance and trade in rice, yarn, silk, salt, beer and wine. It was later named Finlay, Muir & Co. After Independence they entered into a collaboration with the Tatas. The Allahabad Bank, which had its office at 101/1 Clive Street, moved to this fine house owned by the Maharaja of Burdwan for the regional Headquarters. The next building is also a typical neo-classic Victorian building. The Chartered Bank obtained the Royal Charter in 1853 and the Indian branches were opened in 1857. They were located originally at 5, Council House Street. The Clive Street building was built in 1908. Tradition says that there was a neem tree at the site of the bank building. Under this tree share transactions were carried out. The Chartered Bank had its office on the ground floor and the upper floors were occupied by the well-known firm of Bird & Co. (recently extinct). Next we come to a thoroughfare leading to Brabourne Road to the east. It is a new road built by the newly-formed Calcutta Improvement Trust and was named Royal Exchange Place. One of the early enactments of the new Bengal Legislative Council was a measure passed in 1911, to provide for the improvement and expansion of the city of Calcutta, which authorized the creation of the Calcutta Improvement Trust.

The Trust's initial finance was drawn from the export duty on jute and jute manufactures. The Royal Exchange Place was renamed India Exchange Place on 24 August 1956. The road has mostly new buildings housing the offices of the Birlas, Kotharis and others, some of the leading players in the country's business scene. A little distance to our right we come to a side street leading to Lyon's Range, now incorporated in India Exchange Place. The Calcutta Stock Exchange Association was established on 15 June 1908. The first offices were situated at 2 New China Bazar Street, in a part of the house built by Mr. J.C. Galstaun.

Opposite the India Exchange Building, the headquarters of the Indian Chamber of Commerce, there is an old tortuous lane named Swallow Lane, full of shops selling glassware. The lane is also known as *China Bazar ka Glass Putti*.

Now we retrace our steps and come back to Netaji Subhas Road or the old Clive Street. With the rise in the East India Company's fortunes many Englishmen were attracted to India, particularly Calcutta. Calcutta with its rich hinterland and a modern port offered rich potential for quick money and longstanding profitability. From the middle of the nineteenth century they flocked to Calcutta and established import and export houses, trading in everything conceivable, and set up their business houses near the port and the seat of the Government along and around Clive Street and Clive Row.

CLIVE STREET
(NETAJI SUBHAS ROAD)

In the early days of the Company this was the road leading from the Old Fort to the great Indian bazar to the north, where stood the houses of the Burra Bazar Setts (the early settlers). Many of the East India Company's factors lived in the area, where Ross, Eyre, Jackson, Griffith and Williamson had their houses before the siege. In 1756, Robert Clive lived in the house earlier occupied by Griffith, said to have been a large house with a pediment north of the fort. In Thomas Daniell's *Views of 1786* of the East side of the Old Fort, Clive Street, the Theatre and the Holwell Monument, the house said to have been occupied by Clive can be seen a little north of the Theatre (now the Allahabad Bank Building at 2, N. S. Road). This house was later the residence of Philip Francis, member of the Council at the time of Warren Hastings. Francis writes in one of his letters: 'Here I live, master of the finest house in Bengal, with a hundred servants, a country house, and spacious gardens, horses and carriages, yet so perverse is my nature that the devil take me if I would not exchange the best dinner and the best company I ever saw in Bengal for a breakfast and claret at the Horn and let me choose my company'.

Francis left Calcutta in 1780 and in 1789 the house was occupied by Messrs. Paxton, Cockerell & Co.[32] The Royal Exchange came up on this site in the early twentieth century. Opposite the Royal Exchange is a small lane leading to Strand Road, Clive Ghat Street; on this site lived the grand old lady of Calcutta, the 'Begum' Johnson, remarkable for her influence and popularity in Calcutta society and her four marriages. At the age of thirteen she married Parry Purple Templer in 1744; her two children born out of this marriage died in their infancy, and her husband died in 1747-48. She married again, within a few months,

Figure 19: Sir Charles D'Oyly's View of Clive Street, 1835

Figure 20: The Same Area after 50 Years. Photo Johnston & Hoffmann

Figure 21: Clive Street 1910

James Altham of Calcutta, who died of small pox within a few days of marriage. She married on 24 November 1749 William Watts, Esq., Senior Member of the Council, by whom she had four children. In 1756, Watts was the chief of the Cossimbazar factory. Watts was not a wise man; instead of cultivating the friendship of the newly installed young Nawab, Siraj-ud-Daula, he incurred his wrath. When the Nawab wrote to him to demolish the new fortifications at Cossimbazar, Watts' reply was uncompromising and rather bold. An immediate advance on Cossimbazar resulted in the surrender of the English without firing a shot. Watts was in the palace at Murshidabad but Mrs. Watts and her three little children were taken prisoner and brought to Murshidabad and the Nawab placed them in the *zenanah* in the care of his grandmother (widow of Ali Verdi Khan) and mother. Is it believable that a Nawab who had the courtesy of putting Mrs. Watts and her children to his mother's and grandmother's care would incarcerate helpless European women in the so-called Black Hole? Mrs. Watts was shown every kindness and courtesy in the *zenanah* at Murshidabad and the old lady would regale listeners in her salon in Clive Street with her reminiscenses. In 1760 the Watts family left for England, where he died. Mrs. Frances Watts returned alone to Calcutta in 1769 to administer her husband's property. On June 1774 she married Reverend William Johnson, then Principal Chaplain of the Presidency of Fort William. She was now fifty. When Rev. Johnson left for England in 1788, she refused to go with her husband and remained in Calcutta, loved and respected as 'Begum' Johnson of Calcutta. On her death in 1812, the St. John's Church Cemetery which had been closed for the last forty years, was opened for her and the Funeral procession was led by the Governor General in his state coach, with all the Council members, judiciary and leading citizens of Calcutta following. Later, the Bengal Bonded Warehouse came up on the site of 'Begum' Johnson's house. The Calcutta Chamber of Commerce functioned from this house from 1853 onwards, until its successor, the Bengal Chamber of Commerce and Industries moved to the old building which later gave way to the new Royal Exchange building.

The Calcutta Corporation at its meeting held on 13 August 1947, took a unanimous decision to rename the entire length of Dalhousie Square West, Charnock Place and Clive Street up to Harrison Road as Netaji Subhas Road.

THE BENGAL CHAMBER OF COMMERCE AND INDUSTRY

The most impressive building in the business district of Calcutta is the Royal Exchange with its lofty portals and the office of the Bengal Chamber. There is a fading letter in the Meeting Room of the Chamber which is dated 19 December 1833 and bears the signature of twenty-five business firms, who in the following year, along with others became the founding members of The Calcutta Chamber of Commerce. Little is known about its early days, as there are no records prior to 1851, in which year it was more or less reconstituted. Housed in the Bengal Bonded Warehouse from 1853, it had by the middle of that year a total of 104 members, 80 local and 24 outstation, including those from Agra and Rangoon. *The Statesman* of September 1877 reported the introduction in the Bengal Legislative Council of a bill for levying a licence tax on trades and professions based upon Act VIII of that year. The licence tax was to apply to joint-stock and other companies, traders, artisans and professional persons. The Chamber supported the Government's move but the strongest objection came from the moneylenders. Gradually Income Tax came to be introduced on 1 April 1869. In 1893, the then President, Mr. James L. Mackay (later Lord Inchcape), acquired on the Chamber's behalf the premises of the Oriental Bank Corporation which was in course of liquidation. This was the site of Clive and Philip Francis's house. But the building was too small to accommodate the increasing activities of the Chamber; so a decision was taken in 1903, the Golden Jubilee Year, to build a new premises. The Jubilee Dinner was held at the Town Hall, Calcutta and the Viceroy, Lord Curzon, was the Chief Guest.

In 1914 the Chamber moved to temporary offices at 20 Strand Road and the demolition of the old building began. During the excavations at the site of the old Royal Exchange an interesting discovery was made, in the shape of two old wells each some 20 feet deep. They were in the northern part of the site and were filled up with lime concrete. The wells were estimated to be 150 years old and might have been there before Robert Clive lived at the site. Some presume that there was a *bustee* on the site for which the wells were sunk. The new building was inaugurated by the Governor of Bengal, Lord Ronaldshay, on 25 February 1918. The Bengal Chamber had its offices in the upper floors and the Royal Exchange (by an earlier permission of Queen Victoria) was used by traders for business transactions.

Figure 22: The Chartered Bank

Figure 23: The old building of the Bengal Chamber of Commerce
Photo courtesy Calcutta Historical Society

The Bengal Chamber of Commerce and Industry today is an effectively representative organization of a wide spectrum of trade and industry in eastern India. The primary aim of the Chamber is to protect and promote the interests of its members and to act as a central point of reference. It is recognized by the Government and opinion leaders who would refer to it for professional, balanced and responsible views on all economic matters. The Chamber communicates with other chambers of commerce and mercantile and public bodies throughout the world with a view to concerting promotional measures for the protection of trade, commerce and manufacturing. The Chamber also acts as an intermediary body between the Government and the interests it represents.

Some of the Presidents of the Chamber have left their mark in Indian public life. Mr. George Yule, younger brother of Andrew Yule, President in 1878-79, was member of the Indian National Congress and presided over the annual session held at Allahabad in 1888. The Hon. A.A. Apcar, President 1904-07, was a sports enthusiast, particularly in racing. He became the Senior Steward of the RCTC in 1887 and held that post for 22 years. Sir Paul Benthal, who headed Bird & Heilgers Group for a number of years, was President of the Chamber in 1950. He wrote a fascinating book on Trees in Calcutta.[34 & 35]

The next building on the old Clive Street, bearing Numbers 3 to 5, once housed the business premises of South British Insurance Co. According to Sanat Dhar, an old employee of the Bengal Chamber of Commerce, the property was bought by the Chamber for expansion, but later these plots were sold to Coal India, who has built a new office block. This is now No. 10, N.S. Road. The next building No. 12—in old days—used to be the office of Martin & Co. A young Bengali engineer, Rajendra Nath Mookherjee, started a construction business on his own in the later part of the nineteenth century. He successfuly completed the laying of a 40-inch water mains job from Palta water works to Calcutta. For further bigger projects he felt the need for collaboration with an English partner. He started a partnership firm on 50:50 basis with Mr. Thomas Acquin Martin, previously of Walsh Lovett & Co. Mr. Martin wanted the name of the firm to be Martin & Mookherjee, but Rajendra Nath declined; the company was simply called Martin & Co. Soon they received a big order, viz. the construction of the Allahabad Water Works Project, in competition with several European and Indian firms of repute. Rajendranath used to make very good estimates of a project and this gave them a large number of orders, beating other companies in open tenders. Styled as Engineers and Contractors, Martin & Co. were agents for Delhi-Ambala-Kalka Railway Co. Ltd., South Behar Railway Co. Ltd., Managing agents for Bengal Iron & Steel Co. Ltd., Iron & Steel Works and Collieries, Barakar, Delhi-Saharanpore Light Railway Ltd., Howrah-Amta and Howrah-Sheakhala Light Railway Co. Ltd. and several other companies. Martin was knighted. He died in 1906 and Rajendranath became the chief of this giant company. This building still stands, but shorn of its glory, in a poor state with it floors in a totally different architectural style, incongruously added to the still dignified old building, which now houses, along with several other offices, the West Bengal Development and Financial Corporation.

Next to the old Martin and Company building stands the gigantic block of an office complex known as Gillander House. The Gillanders Arbuthnot & Co. is one of the very few original founding members of the Bengal Chamber continuing under the same name. In 1905 they were known as bankers, merchants and agents. Their agency included Hooghly Mills Co., Hardwar-Dehra Doon Branch Railway, Darjeeling Himalayan Railway Co. Ltd., Nobel's Explosive Co. and others. The firm still exists, now their principal business given as: manufacturing loose-leaf binders, indices and sheets, conveyor belts; cultivation, manufacture and sale of tea; owning and managing real estate, acting as registrars, selling agents and agents; investing in other companies. Some of their huge blocks of offices are taken by different companies like G.E.C., Alsthom India Ltd., at one time one of the major electrical equipment manufacturers in India, who have now shifted their head office to Madras (Chennai), sold the G.E.C. House on Chittaranjan Avenue and are now tenants at D2 Gillander House. Voltas Ltd. (previously Volkart Brothers, a Swiss Company) has its Calcutta Office in Gillander House. Voltas, now owned by the Tatas, manufactures refrigerators, air conditioning machines, water coolers, etc.

Leaving the Gillander House we come to the Clive Street end of Clive Row, where we turn right and come to a building with a rounded front. This is now 14, N.S. Road, and houses Stanchart Bank on the ground floor. In 1905 it was 9, Clive Street and the business premises of Graham & Co. Graham & Co. used to be merchants, and agents for several major shipping lines and a number of marine insurance companies; and had branches in Bombay, Karachi and Rangoon.

The next building, Number 10 Clive Street, was the premises of the Indian headoffice of Messrs. Worthington Pump Co. Ltd. They were manufacturers of all classes of pumping machinery, air compressors, etc. They had agencies at Bombay, Madras, Karachi, Colombo, Rangoon and Singapore. The Company is now called Worthington Pumps India Ltd., with its headoffice located at 8, Acharya Jagadish Chandra Bose Road (old Lower Circular Road) and registered office at 4, Mangoe Lane (renamed Surendra Mohan Ghosh Sarani).

Other European concerns on this stretch were Blackwood, Blackwood & Co., Eugene Meiffre, G. Atherton & Co., and after crossing Canning Street one came upon F. W. Heilgers & Co.'s godowns. Up to Harrison Road (Mahatma Gandhi Road) the rest of the buildings were occupied by Indian business concerns. If we retrace our steps after crossing over to the western side of the street, just before we hit Canning Street we come upon the site of Jessop & Co.'s workshops and office. Jessop & Co. was engaged in the manufacture of boilers, roof and bridge work, railway rolling stock works, etc. Jessops used to be one of the major producers of railway rolling stock and goods wagons. Jessop & Co. is still there, at its premises at 63, N.S. Road, with factories at Dum Dum. Once a profitable company, it is now a 'sick' concern due to apathy from all sources.

Immediately on crossing Clive Ghat Street we come to the old premises No. 101, Clive Street, which used to be the office of Gladstone Wyllie & Co., import and export merchants.

The Duncan Brothers, Walter and William, established the famous firm of Duncan Brothers in the 1860s; and were pioneers in the tea and jute industries. They had their original offices at 21, Canning Street. The new building in Clive Street, the Duncan House, was erected in 1915. Not under British ownership any longer, Duncan & Co. is now owned by the Goenkas, who bought it after Independence. There are two companies at the Duncan House at 31, N. S. Road, viz. Duncan Brothers & Co. Ltd., rendering services including secretarial services to various companies, and Duncans Industries Ltd., their principal involvement being in cultivation, growing and manufacture, sale and export of tea, and manufacture and sale of fertilisers.

Next to Duncan House is 29, Netaji Subhas Road, bearing a board, with the inscription: 'North British Building—Property of Life Insurance Corporation of India'. In the ground floor there is a branch of ANZ Grindlays Bank. The old number was 101/1, Clive Street. The old building was occupied by the Allahabad Bank and Bird & Co.

The firm of Bird & Co. was formed in 1864, when Captain Sam Bird secured a 'coolie' contract at Allahabad from the East Indian Railway.

Sam's brother Paul joined him at Allahabad and by 1873 Bird & Co. was firmly established as Labour Contractor for E.I.R., with yet another labour contract—from the Eastern Bengal State Railway, for loading and unloading all goods between railway wagons and steamers, flats and country boats at the Goalunda and Goarie *ghats*. They were also given contract to run a bullock train service from Sahebgunje railway station to Darjeeling. This service was withdrawn after the opening of the Darjeeling Himalayan Railways in 1881.

In 1870 Bird & Co. came to Calcutta and took office premises at 25, Strand Road on a three year lease. Like other British firms in Calcutta, Bird & Co. too took on managing agencies for several industries like coal, jute, copper, tea, cement and sugar, notably coal and jute. The next generation saw Ernest Cable ensconced at 39, Strand Road in the late 1880s at the helm of affairs. The Company moved its office to 5, Clive Row, from where it operated from 1896 to 1901. It occupied 101/1, Clive Street from 1901 to 1909, and moved across the street to the newly built Chartered Bank building in 1908. F.W. Heilgers, a German company, that was previously at 136, Canning Street and was the chief rival of Bird & Co., in jute and coal, also moved to the Chartered Bank building at the same time. Bird expanded its agencies in other fields also, like Indian Patent Stone Co. Ltd., Bikaner and Dehra Dun Prospecting and Mining Co. Ltd., Fire, Marine and Life Insurance.

The great moment in the company's life came when it bought the F.W. Heilgers Company on 1 January 1917 under the Enemy Property Act. This coup was accomplished under great secrecy by Lord Cable in London. The German Company established in Calcutta in 1872 had only German partners and staff for a long time, before some British elements filtered in. In 1914 there were two German and one English partners. At the outbreak of the First World War, the foreign elements were expelled and the business carried on. They were managing agents for several notable companies like Titaghur Paper Mills. Co. Ltd., Naihati Jute Mills Co. Ltd., Kinnison Jute Mills Co. Ltd., several noted coalfields, insurance sectors, etc. After buying the rival's assets, Bird & Co. became the managing agents for a large chunk of jute and coal companies. The Bird & Heilgers group flourished under Lord Cable, Sir Edward Benthall and Sir Paul Benthall. It celebrated 100 years of its existence in 1964. Later the Bird & Heilgers group also disintegrated. While Heilgers went its own seperate way, Bird & Company's interests were taken over by the Government of India under a different name.

The next building, a fine old white structure at 25 Netaji Subhas Road, housed among others the Bengal Bonded Warehouse Association, an association falling under the category of a Trades Association, established in 1838. According to Mr. P. N. Roy, one of the present Directors, many old Calcutta firms had their birth in this old building at 102, Clive Street. The building caught fire on 1 January 1995, and all old records were destroyed.

Between the Bengal Bonded Warehouse Association and Balmer Lawrie, we find two new buildings, the Security House at 23B, and the multistoreyed Bank of India building at 23A Netaji Subhas Road. According to Mr. Russi Mody, former Managing Director of Tata Industries, the Tata concerns had their headoffice at Security House before the Tata Centre was built on the Chowringhee. Tata Airlines (Later Air India) also had its office at the Security House.

Balmer Lawrie & Co. had the last Victorian House built for its office at old 103 Clive Street (now 21 N.S. Road). At the close of the nineteenth century, it described itself as Merchants, Bankers, Army and General Agents, with considerable interest in tea and engineering. The Imperial Tobacco Company (now ITC Limited) collaborated with Balmer Lawrie in 1952 to set up Tribeni Tissues, an industry to produce tissue paper for cigarettes and packaging paper. Thirty-six years old now, Balmer Lawrie under Indian management has interest in manufacturing, trading and services.

Now we cross the street again and come to the eastern pavement of Clive Row which has been renamed Dr. Rajendra Prasad Sarani in 1983.

As we pass and leave behind the Gillander House, and continue northwards, we enter Clive Row and see a medley of modern office blocks and crumbling Victorian buildings. Number 4 houses Jardine Henderson Ltd., a pioneer British company. The first private merchant to play a pioneer's role in the growth of the tea industry was David Jardine of Jardine, Skinner & Co., who helped the first Government committee in procuring seeds, Chinese labour and other expertise through their associates operating in China, Jardine, Matheson & Co. In 1838 the first Indian-grown tea from Assam was marketed in England. 280 pounds were sold at prices ranging from 16 to 34 shillings per pound.[37] David Jardine first had Charles Skinner as partner to form a major partnership firm. Later George

Henderson & Co., another managing agency with interest in tea, jute coal and insurance, joined them to form the Jardine Henderson Group with a wide range of trading and manufacturing activities. Today under Indian management their principal business is tea, packaging and mining equipments. Birkmyre Bros., situated at 6, Clive Row, were jute manufacturers and merchants.

Number 8, the Yule House (1908), is the office of the famous Calcutta firm, Andrew Yule & Co. Andrew arrived in India in 1863 and began business as an importer of piece goods and agents for several insurance companies. His elder brother George and seventeen year old nephew David joined him in 1875. Ultimately the interests of the company extended to cotton, jute, newspapers (*The Englishman* and *The Statesman*). George Yule joined the Indian National Congress and presided over the Allahabad session of the Congress in 1888. In 1902, Andrew Yule were managing four jute mills, one cotton mill, fifteen tea companies, two flour mills, one oil mill, a small railway company, a jute press and a Zamindari Company.[38]

Thacker's Directory of 1868 gives Andrew Yule & Company's address as Number 6 Clive Row (subsequently renumbered 7), and this together with the adjoining buildings of 22 and 23 Canning Street, which were acquired in 1896 and 1897, was the headquarters of the company for a long time. In 1905 Sir David Yule purchased 8 Clive Row and erected the present building to which the firm moved in 1907. This site goes far back in history. The East India Company gave settlement of a plot of land at an annual rent of 'five rupees seven annas Pucca' on which a house known as 'Polly Bower's House' was later built. There is nothing to record who Polly Bowers was, but she was probably the widow of one of the innkeepers who were licensed by the company to keep victualling houses.

After Polly Bower's death, the property passed through many hands and was variously described. A deed of sale in 1868 describes it as 2 Clive Row, shortly before Clive Row was renumbered, and soon it became Number 8. Since his arrival in India in 1875 Sir David Yule lived in Garden Reach, but after the new office was built he moved over into a flat consisting of five rooms, which was constructed on a part of the roof over the main entrance.

In 1922 Sir David Yule received a Baronetcy, and assumed the title of Sir David Yule of Hugli River in the Province of Bengal.

The Andrew Yule & Company Limited has since been taken over by the Government of India, and its principal business is manufacturing and trading. Next to the Yule House there is a very old building now numbered Number 9 which can collapse any day. The old Number 9 on the north side of Clive Row was the Ernsthausen Ltd., German merchants and agents. They also acted as the Consul for Germany. There are two streets on the left, viz. Jackson Ghat Road and Canning Street. This was the beginning of the Indian business houses which went up to Burra Bazar. Canning Street was previously known as Murgihatta Street. The area was cleared in 1866 and a wide Canning Street replaced the Murgihatta. The Calcutta Corporation, at its meeting held on 25 March 1960, renamed the Canning

Street as Biplabi Rashbehari Basu Sarani, in memory of the famous revolutionary. The old Canning Street was mostly occupied by Indian establishments, but there were a few European ones too. No. 10 was Balmer Lawrie & Co's Machinery Showroom; at 21 was the office of Duncan Bros., and at 22 and 23 were the offices of Andrew Yule & Co. Numbers 102 to 104 were the offices of Voight & Co. and the Peruvian Consulate; 109 and 110 were the 'Shield of David' Jewish Synagogue. Just before Clive Street stood premises No. 136 housing F.W. Heilgers & Co. and Titagurh Paper Mills. Between Clive Street and Strand Road were the godowns of Robinson, Morrison & Co. and Hoare Miller & Co.

OLD CLIVE ROW

In the early days of the settlement, there were no roads, only narrow winding paths between houses, most of them leading from the riverbank and named after merchants using them. One such was Jackson Ghat Street, from which a small lane ran northwards. This lane was originally known as Barretto's Lane, later as Sackersteen Lane and finally Clive Row, but to be renamed as Dr. Rajendra Prasad Sarani after Independence.

Montague Massey, in his *Recollections of Calcutta*, gives an account of the area:

One of the very earliest street alterations and improvements that comes to my recollection was in Canning Street, just at the Junction of Clive Row, on the space of ground extending from the latter for some distance to the east, and north as far as the boundary wall of Andrew Yule & Co.'s offices, leaving but a narrow strip of a lane running parallel to the latter and affording access to China Bazar on the east and beyond. Earlier this space was occupied by a very mediaeval, ancient and old-fashioned building having a flagged, paved courtyard in front, surrounded by high brick walls. It divided Canning Street into two distinct sections, effectualy obstruction through communication between east and west, except for the narrow strip of passage. The place was then known as it is at the present day as Aloe Godown or Potato Bazar, and was in the occupation of George Henderson & Co. as an office. When it was pulled down, through communications were easier and new buildings were erected at the site.

PLACES OF WORSHIP AROUND THE AREA NEAR CLIVE STREET

The Armenian Church of St. Nazareth

Situated in Armenian Street, this is the oldest place of Christian worship in Calcutta, dating from 1724.

It is quite possible that the Armenians settled in Calcutta prior to Job Charnock, as presumed from the discovery of an old grave inside the church cemetery in 1895. The tombstone in Armenian language records that 'Rezabeebeh, the wife of the late charitable

Figure 24: The Armenian Church of St. Nazareth
Photo courtesy Calcutta Historical Society

Sookeas, departed this world to life eternal on the 21st day of Nakha in the year 15' of the new era of the Julpha which corresponds with 11 July 1630. The original chapel of 1724 stood about 100 yards away from the present church, which was used by the Armenians as a burying ground. Before the chapel of 1724 a church made of timber was used. As the number of Armenians increased, a masonry church was erected by voluntary subscription raised among the community under the auspices of Aga Nazar. In his name the church was called St. Nazareth. The steeple was added in 1734 by a generous merchant Hazarmall. In 1790 C. Arrakiel built the adjoining clergy house, the surrounding walls, and presented a clock for the steeple. Many of the distinguished early Armenian residents lie buried here.

The Roman Catholic Church

Originally in Portuguese Church Street, this church now stands in the present day Brabourne Road (renamed as Biplabi Trailokya Maharaj Sarani), built in 1950 by the Calcutta

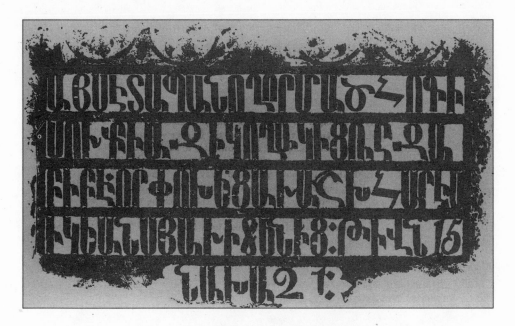

*Figure 25: The Epitaph of Rezabebe on the oldest Christian grave in Calcutta
Photo courtesy Calcutta Historical Society*

Improvement Trust. Shortly after the English settled here, they set up a market for fowls run by the Portuguese, hence the area was called Murghihatta. In 1710, a Mrs. Maria Tench built the first church building in brick. During the siege of 1756, both the Armenian and the Portuguese churches escaped destruction. Before the English could provide for a makeshift chapel in the Old Fort, this Murghihatta chapel was used by the English for church services. In 1796 the Portuguese community resolved to replace their old place of worship by a new one. Rs. 30,000 was available from the church revenues, another Rs. 60,000 were donated by the two brothers Joseph and Louis Barretto. The church is called the Cathedral of our Lady of the Rosary. The old Archiepiscopal Palace adjoins the Cathedral, which is chiefly used on grand occasions. In the churchyard lie buried many Vicar Generals and under the altar is interred Archbishop Paul Goethal (1833–1901), the first Archbishop of Calcutta. He had a vast library on India and was very knowledgeable about the history and culture of India.

The Jewish Synagogue, The Shield of David

This new synagogue was built by Mr. E.D.J. Ezra, in memory of his late father, well known to several generations of Anglo Indians as 'Daoud' Ezra. This was opened in 1884. Externally the building presents a fine frontage and spire. Inside, it is one of the best places of worship in Calcutta. The building is in Italian Renaissance style, measures 140 feet in length and

Figure 26: The Shield of David Synagogue. Photo courtesy Mr. Samuel Luddy

82 feet in width all over. The edifice contains an inscription: 'Elias David Joseph Ezra, the Father of the Jewish community who to orthodox principles united a heart susceptible of all that is good. This magnificent synagogue, Maghan David, was built at his sole expense on a site belonging to the old synagogue Neveh Shalom. He was born 20th February 1830, and died 3rd February 1880.'

A New Road in the Area

When the Calcutta Improvement Trust started building a new 100 feet wide road from the new Howrah Bridge Approach in Strand Road to St. Andrew's Church in Dalhousie Square North, necessary for the quick movement of traffic from Howrah station to central and south Calcutta, many old buildings, part of the busy China Bazar area, and a few old streets like the Old Court House Corner disappeared under the new road. The Calcutta Corporation in a Notification dated 10 April 1945 announced that the new road would be named after a former Governor of Bengal, Lord Brabourne (1937-38). The Brabourne Road was opened to traffic in July 1950. The road bifurcated at the Dalhousie Square end keeping St. Andrews Church in the middle as an island. Soon large office buildings began to appear on this wide street. The Life Insurance Corporation of India's skyscraper at the junction with Lyon's Range, the Tea Board Office and the United Commercial Bank Office stand out. If we turn at the Tea Board's Office and proceed left towards Chitpore Road (now Rabindra Sarani) we come to a part of Calcutta's old history. The market area called Teritti Bazar is actually Tiretta's Bazar. Edward Tiretta was an Italian, and had been an associate of the famous Jacques Casanova in Europe; but having made many countries 'too hot' for him to stay there, he arrived in Calcutta, in 1782. He was appointed Superintendent of Streets and Houses under the Municipal Committee, and Civil Architect to the Company. In India, he became in turns, respectable, versatile, wealthy and bankrupt. When the present Government House was being built Tiretta was supervising the works.

In 1781, we find Tiretta appealing to the Governor General, Warren Hastings, for permission to build a bazar at the plot of land in Lal Bazar called Bogden Garden. The Company records and correspondences show that there were then no permanent market places in Calcutta, vendors crowded on the roadside and even encroached on the road with their wares. Tiretta proposed to build at his own expense a *pucca* building divided in three different squares with shops and verandahs all round with a hall of halls in the middle for accommodation of vendors, three different sets for the sale of meat, fish and vegetables. Tiretta got what he wanted, he was given the plot of land for the bazar, and what came up was known as Tiretta's Bazar. But by 1788 he was in trouble, as evident from the *Calcutta Gazette* advertisement of a lottery, offering as first prize a large and spacious *pucka bazar* or market belonging to Mr. Tiretta situated in the north central part of the Town of Calcutta built by Count Edward Tiretta of Trevisa near Venice. His bankruptcy led to the public lottery and Charles Weston was the lucky winner. We find another mention of this bazar in the *Calcutta Gazette* dated 28 May 1827, when 'this valuable property was yesterday sold, by public Auction, to the Raja of Burdwan, at the price of three lacs and twenty-four thousand rupees'.[39]

Tiretta's young French wife, Angelica, died in 1796 at the age of 18 and was buried in the Portuguese cemetery in Calcutta. But after two years for reasons unknown Tiretta was asked to remove his wife's coffin from there. To bury his wife he bought a piece of land on Burial Ground Road (later Park Street) just opposite the South Park Street Cemetery, and Angelica's coffin was buried there. The new burial ground was open to all Roman Catholic Europeans and their immediate descendants dying in the settlement. The burial ground was called the North Park Street Cemetery. In the late 1970s the burial ground ceased to exist, giving way to the Assembly of God Church Hospital, Church, educational institution, etc.

LAL BAZAR

Leaving Brabourne Road and keeping St. Andrew's Church on the right we come to the crossing of Dalhousie Square North, Dalhousie Square East and Lal Bazar Street. This is one of the oldest roads in Calcutta. It has been recorded that Lal Mohan Seth, doyen of the Seth family, early settlers in Calcutta, used to observe Holi or *Dol Jatra* with great pomp and a temporary market was set up in the area for the sale of *abir*, the powdered colours used during the festival. This is one theory for the origin of the name of the road. Rev. James Long attributed the name of the road from the red coloured walls of the Old Mission Church. The road led from the Lal Dighi in the west ending at Baithakkhana and the Salt water marshes which in earlier days extended to the present Sealdah Railway Station.

During the early years of the Company, in 1710, a raised road was built from the east gate of the Old Fort William across Lal Bazar up to the Salt Lakes, the entire stretch four miles long.[40] Later the road was called the Great Bungalow Road. Sailors and soldiers called it the Flag Street, from the string of flags or coloured banners hung outside the taverns, eating houses and brothels. The Zamindar of Calcutta (later called Collector) had his *cutchery* next to the Old Play House near the Rope Walk, later Mission Row. The Play House was the only theatre in Calcutta before the siege of 1756. The Old Playhouse in Lal Bazar was one of the first places of social gathering in Calcutta, with mostly amateur actors performing. They are stated to have derived assistance from the famous English actor, David Garrick, who was sent two pipes of madeira in gratitude. During the siege of 1756, Nawab Siraj-ud-Daula's army formed an artillery point here to batter the fort. At No. 8, Lal Bazar Street, there was a very old single storey building, probably a tavern used by the theatre-lovers. At the end of the nineteenth century this was used as the Ralli Brothers' godowns.

Mr. Harisadhan Mukhopadhyay, in his Bengali book on Calcutta, quotes an advertisement published in the *Calcutta Gazette* of 14 November 1799, announcing that a Royal Bengal Tiger with two cubs have been brought from the Sunderbans and were for sale at Mr. Smith's premises at 230, Lal Bazar.

Besides the Harmonic there was another famous hotel in the area, called the London Hotel.

Across Chitpore Road on the Bow Bazar there is still a bar called The Cecil, which has two billiard tables on the ground floor and the upstairs balcony for ladies has fine old woodwork. The Parsi owner wants to keep it as such as a remembrance of the good old days.

A gun battery at the junction of Lal Bazar Street and Chitpore Road appears in a contemporary French map of Calcutta where it is described as 'Batarie de Lal Bazar'. It was located at the spot from 1742.

There was a house in the area opposite the present day Police Headquarters, called the Ambassador's House, which may have been for a time the residence of the Ambassador of Persia. Later the building was dilapidated and the Company used it as the common jail. At the centre of the enclosure there was a tank, where everyone bathed and washed clothes. European prisoners were generally permitted to erect small bamboo mat huts near the tank. The whole atmosphere was foul and poisonous, there were no jail allowances and no infirmary, and many died unattended. All executions and tortures were conducted here, before the jail was moved to a place south of Govindapore (the site of the Victoria Memorial Hall) in 1783.

In 1780, the East India Company appointed a Commissioner of Police for the administration of the city, the improvement of drainage and the disposal of fifth and rubbish. Hickey wrote in his memoirs that 'previous to the establishment of a regular police in Calcutta, it was customary for a judge to sit at chambers in Lal Bazar, for the purpose of transacting the daily business of the town, also of adjusting any little matters of dispute that might arise between natives not of sufficient magnitude in itself, or the parties too poor to enter into a legal contest. As the lowest order of people daily assembled there, it was commonly called Ragamuffin Hall.'[41] This was most probably situated at the north-east corner of the Police Headquarters, where prior to this building stood the magistrate's court. With the increase in custom, the street was filled with punch houses, low taverns run by Italians, Portuguese and Spanish. The most famous, however, was the Harmonic Tavern situated across the Chitpore Road, described as the handsomest house in Calcutta in that period. Mrs. Fay writes of it in 1780: 'I felt far more gratified when Mrs. Jackson procured me a ticket for the Harmonic, which was supported by a select number of gentlemen, who, each in alphabetical rotation, give a concert, ball and supper, during the cold season, I believe, once a fortnight.'[42]

There was an advertisement in the *Calcutta Gazette* dated 29 March 1787 for the sale of the old jail, describing it 'facing the Harmonic and next door to Messrs. Burrell and Gould's'. Francois Balthazar Solvyns made a coloured etching in 1799 painting the Lal Bazar from the junction of Chitpore Road looking west. On the left are the junction rooms of Burrell and Gould and later Taylor & Company. On the right is the Ragamuffin Hall.

James Baillie Fraser painted two pictures of Lal Bazar in 1819. The first he drew from the corner of Mission Row looking east. The centre is occupied by the house of John Palmer (a new building since the days of Solvyns). Opposite to it is the premises of the auctioneers, Taylor & Co.

The second drawn from the east, from Lower Circular Road, shows the Roman Catholic church of Our Lady of Doris, one of the Portuguese churches in Calcutta. John Palmer, called 'the Prince of Merchants' in Calcutta in the early part of the nineteenth century, was the son of the Secretary to the Governor General Warren Hastings. He was well known for his generosity, amiability and wealth. He held gala dinner entertainments for two Governor Generals. Palmer owned 16 ships all round the world, particularly to Mauritius, China, America, Java, Sydney and the Cape of Good Hope, carrying cotton, silk, coffee, tea, etc. The Bank of Bengal conducted banking in a small way, with most of the money transactions

Figure 27: John Palmer's House in Lal Bazar at the site of the present Police Headquarters
Photo Bourne & Shepherd

carried out by six great agency houses including Palmers. In 1830, however, the great house failed in the most disastrous way and drew down most of the old established agencies with it. Palmer & Company's loss was estimated at five million pounds. The aftermath however, was remarkable. Mr. Palmer enjoyed such public trust that in spite of the general panic, leading Indians came forward with offers of substantial assistance. Mr. Palmer survived the crash for six years, which he spent to re-establish his business. It is on record that the profits he made in his venture he passed on to those who had suffered from the crash. When he died on 22 January 1836, his coffin was followed to the North Park Street Cemetery by a large number of people of universal lineage.

His tombstone is simple, with the inscription, 'John Palmer, the Friend of the Poor'. There is a bust of John Palmer by Sir Francis Chantrey in the Town Hall, Calcutta. The Palmer family served in India for several generations.

The Government bought John Palmer's house in Lal Bazar in 1890 for the Police Headquarters. In 1915, Walter K. Firminger, the Arch Deacon of Calcutta, informed the Calcutta Historical Society that the old house of John Palmer was being demolished. The old building gave way for the new Calcutta Police Headquarters opened in 1919. It now houses the Police Commissioner's Office, the Central Control Room, the Central Lockup and various other police departments.

To the west of the Police Headquarters is an early landmark, a lane meandering north, the Radha Bazar Street. The origin of the name has been dealt with in the chapter on Lal Dighi. The street is now monopolized by wholesale and retail watch and clock-makers.

Some of the buildings opposite the Police Headquarters have Sir. R.N. Mukherjee Road numbers, including the new building housing Martin Burn, the Bikaner Building and the Mercantile Building. The last named building is menacingly fire-prone, having caught fire several times in the last few years. The electrical wirings of these old buildings are precariously intermeshed and may any day cause a giant conflagration which may burn down Lal Bazar, as most of the old houses in the neighbourhood have secret godowns of inflammable substances.

A LITTLE OF BOW BAZAR STREET

The Lal Bazar Street now ends at the junction of Chitpore Road, but in old days it continued up to the Salt Lakes. The name probably comes from the Bengali word 'Bahu' meaning plenty, and has nothing to do with 'Bou' or bride. The road was renamed Bepin Behari Ganguly Street in 1957 to commemorate a prominent nationalist leader who passed away in 1954.

The early English settlers and Eurasians resided in houses in the western part of the road.

The Hindu College (later Presidency College) was first started in a house on Bow Bazar Street. *The Calcutta Gazette* reports on 1 March 1824:

At about 4 p.m. yesterday, the fraternity of Free Masons, in and about Calcutta, met at the old Hindoo College, Bow Bazar for the purpose of laying the foundation stone of the new College. Each Lodge being opened by its respective officers Brother Patton arranged the procession, which about 5 o'clock began to move on towards the site of the new foundation in Potuldunga Square.

Each Lodge with its Tyler and Banner must have made an impressive show.

In the beginning of the twentieth century Whiteaway Laidlaw had its Furniture Department at 301-303 and workshops at 307 Bow Bazar Street. Number 309 housed a part of Balmer Lawrie & Co., John Dickson & Co., Macmillan & Co., and the Coroner's Court.

BENTINCK STREET

With the early English settlers came a large Indian populace to earn their living, and as people of many vocations settled in groups the areas assumed the names of the vocations. As the butchers selected this area, this was popularly known as Kassaitolla or Cossitola, the name appearing in all correspondences and books from the time. It was later named after Lord William Bentinck, Governor General of India from 1828 to 1835. Bentinck is remembered by Indians for at least two measures adopted during his reign, viz. suppression of *suttee* and *thugees*. And probably this is why he is the only Governor General who retains his name on a Calcutta street.

Reverend James Long describes Cossitolla as the road leading from Dhurrumtollah to Old Calcutta; in 1757 it was a mass of jungle; even as late as 1780 it was almost impassable for mud in the rains. In 1788 a Mr. Mackinnon advertised that he had established a school with 140 pupils. All the European chroniclers on Calcutta were sympathetic towards the religious Hindus, who had to pass along this only road to the Kalighat Temple, past the Cossitolla. In the late eighteenth century apart from Mr. Mackinnon's school there existed only a few buildings, viz. Mr. J. Trenholm's Tavern, Meredith Company's stables, Mr. John Palmer's Undertaking business, Mr. Oliphant, the coachmaker and the Union Tavern. The later-day premises of Llewellyn & Co. is said to have been used as a Government House during the time of the first Earl of Minto, Governor General from 1807 to 1813. The arches and pillars of the Throne Room, Council Chamber and Reception Room stood as they had been in the early part of the twentieth century. The house has since been demolished. Today Bentinck Street is a busy thoroughfare full of many Chinese shoe shops (though fastly dwindling in number), cycle stores, cinema halls, the new Income Tax Office Complex (Ayakar Bhavan) next to Paradise Cinema, and once the tallest building in Calcutta, the Tower House, near the junction with Chowringhee and Esplanade East. Opposite Paradise Cinema is the modern building housing the headquarters of the Calcutta Electric Supply Corporation—the Victoria House. Originally incorporated as the Indian Electric Company in 1897, it established the first generating station in Emambagh Lane; the actual supply began on 17 April 1899.

Numbers 60 and 61 once housed the famous furniture showroom of C. Lazarus & Co., billiard table manufacturers and cabinet makers. The Victoria House stands on a new road, Chowringhee Square, opened in 1935; this small street skirts the triangular plots in front of the Victoria House and across Central Avenue to the Statesman House. The newspaper, *The Statesman,* the Calcutta daily (published also from New Delhi), had a forerunner, the *Friend of India.* Their original office occupied the site of the present day Metro Cinema on Chowringhee Road. The Statesman House was completed in 1933-34 and *The Englishman* moved to this building from Hare Street before its closure. At one point of time both the newspapers were owned by Andrew Yule & Co.

Now retracing our steps north through Bentinck Street, we come to several old thoroughfares carrying memories of old Calcutta.

Waterloo Street

The first street on our left is Waterloo Street (renamed Jogesh Chandra Ghosh Street in 1965, after an eminent jurist), leading to Government Place East (Hemanta Basu Sarani).

The road was probably constructed in 1827-28, if we go by a letter published in the *Calcutta Gazette* on 17 January 1828:

> The road recently constructed through Dacres Lane, called Waterloo Street, has greatly added both to the beauty of the Government House, by opening its prospect, and to the convenience of the community, by affording a direct and speedy communication to the Cossitollah Street...and the salubrity of the vicinage has greatly secured.[44]

The street owes its name to the great victory of the English and allied forces over Napoleon Bonaparte at the battlefield of Waterloo on 18 June 1815. In the early days of the twentieth century the northern side had the Waterloo Street Police Station (24), the Adelphi and City Hotels. Some of the old establishments were later demolished to make way for the Bakery Department of the Great Eastern Hotel and the side entrance with a huge ornamental gateway. On the southern side from Government Place East is the premises of Cuthbertson & Harper, next is Dacres' Lane. Other notable occupants of the street were Dykes & Co., coach builders, Heatly & Gresham Ltd., Railway Engineers.

Dacres' Lane

It is a small winding lane leading to Esplanade East from 1 Waterloo Street; its entire length being one furlong. It was named after Philip Milner Dacres, Collector of Calcutta in 1773 and afterwards a member of the Council. When he went back to England in 1784, he sold his properties to one Henry Scott, comprising a dwelling house and ground (24 *cottahs*, 8 *chittacks*) bounded on the east by a house and ground, the property of Mrs. Robertson, on the west by a public lane leading from his own house towards the Esplanade. This street was once a fashionable locality, with Moore's Assembly Rooms, where the Europeans met for ball and festive occasions. The English citizens entertained Lord Minto at a farewell banquet here in December 1813.

Dacres' Lane had quite a number of boarding houses and lodges, and Francis, Harrison, Hathaway & Co., drapers and outfitters, had a small branch there. Number 6 was the office of the Chief Inspector of Explosives, Department of Mines. In 1982, the Calcutta Corporation changed the name of the lane to James Hickey Sarani. Hickey was editor of the first English newspaper in India, *Hickey's Bengal Gazette* or *Calcutta General Advertiser*, which appeared for the first time on 29 January 1780.

The lane is now crowded with cheap roadside eateries, both restaurants and kiosks dishing out excellent food at amazingly cheap prices.

British Indian Street

This old street dates back from before the siege of 1756, when it was known as Rana Modda or Ranee Moody Gully. Upjohn's map of 1784 records the name Rana Modda Gully. There is an opinion that it was called Rana Matta Gully after a fierce battle in this lane between the English soldiers and the Nawab Siraj-ud-Daula's army during the siege of Calcutta in 1756. The well-known Bengali playwright Girish Chandra Ghosh (1844–1912) has a song in his play *Prafulla*: '*Ranee Modinir Gali Saraber Dokan Khali*' (Ranee Moodini Lane is full of grog shops). At one time it was also known as Pilots' Row.

The name British Indian Street came from the establishment of the British Indian Association in 1851, the Association headquarters being housed in Number 18.

On 20 April 1843, an influential section of the educated middle class founded the Bengal British India Society, whose object was defined to be the collection and dissemination of information relating to the actual condition of the people of British India and to employ such other means of a peaceable and lawful character as may appear calculated to secure the welfare, extend the just rights, and advance the interests of all classes of fellow subjects. Four Bills were introduced by the Government of India in 1849 with a view to extend the jurisdiction of the East India Company's Criminal Courts over the British-born subjects who were then subject only to the Supreme Court in Calcutta. The violent agitation of the European community against these 'black acts' forced the Government to withdraw them. This came as a shock to the educated community in Bengal, who felt the need of a strong political association. The result was the amalgamation of the two contemporary political associations in Bengal into a new one named the British Indian Association founded on 29 October 1851,[45] with Debendra Nath Tagore as the founding Secretary. Many eminent Indians like Raja Digambar Mitra, Ramgopal Ghosh, Peary Chand Mitra, Jadulal Mullick and Harish Chandra Mukherjee were associated with it.

The Ranee Moody Gully extended from Bentinck Street ending at Old Court House Street, just north of Great Eastern Hotel. The street had a number of hotels, drapers and outfitters and residential houses. An advertisement gives the charges at W. Benton's Family Hotel, No. 12, Rannymoody Gully: Per Month Rs. 90; per fortnight Rs. 60; per week Rs. 35; per day Rs. 6; A Lady and Gentleman having two rooms and two separate tables Rs. 220, and no billiards or cards allowed in the establishment.[46] This street was renamed Abdul Hamid Sarani in 1965, to honour a brave soldier who fought gallantly against the Pakistan Army in the Indo-Pak War of 1965.

Barretto's Lane

This small winding lane links British Indian Street with Mangoe Lane. Non-descript though it is, it commemorates an eminent Portuguese family of yesteryears. This lane came into existence between 1785 and 1794 as it is shown in Upjohn's map of 1794.

Joseph Barretto was a man of great wealth and an eminent Persian scholar. He was largely instrumental in the erection of the Roman Catholic Cathedral (Portuguese Church); a tablet under the portico of its grand entrance perpetuates the memory of his munificence.

The Portuguese cemetery just beyond Sealdah station was purchased by him for Rs. 8,000 in 1785 for the use of the Roman Catholic community. Another member of the family, John Barretto bequeathed Rs. five lakh for distribution among religious and charitable institutions. The Barretto brothers set up a banking business with their office at 25 Mangoe Lane, the house with a vault. In the maps of 1792 and 1794 Barretto's Lane is described as Cross Street, while there is a Barretto's Lane, a private lane leading through No. 39 Strand Road with Armenian Ghat close by, named Barretto's Ghat. Joseph Barretto died in 1824 and the great banking firm of the Barrettos failed in 1827.[47]

Mangoe Lane

The street running from Rope Walk (Mission Row) to Bentinck Street in a winding fashion appears without a name in Will's map of 1753. Mangoe Lane gets its name only in Wood's map of 1784. The name probably originated from an abundance of mango trees in the locality. Today there are none.

The Barrettos' banking premises were situated at Number 25, the one with a vault. Initially the chartered accountants' firm of Lovelock & Lewes had its office in the upper flat, where there was a curious stunted door (studded with flat knobs) of which a writer had once said that it 'leads to nothing in particular, but when closed, hints at great possibilities.'[48] In the early twentieth century the firm shifted to 4, Lyons Range. This house was later occupied by Lyall, Marshall & Co. and Carlisle, Nephews & Co. The former was a firm of merchants and agents. They were managing agents for Carew & Co. Ltd., Powayan Steam Tramway Co. Ltd. and several tea estates. This was the corner house with Mission Row. In place of the old house we see today a new building, the offices of the Eastern Coalfields Ltd., bearing the Number 13, Rajendra Nath Mukherjee Road.

On the southern side, notable addresses from Dalhousie Square included Manton & Co. at No. 1 (the old building has recently been demolished to make way for a new block of offices). No. 2 was the International Ship Masters' Club; 2/1 the Ralli Bros. godowns; No. 3 Moran & Co., James Arbuthnot & Co., and Societe Pour Le Commerce De The. At Number 4 was the old premises of Williamson, Magor & Co. The same company occupies the site but in a new multistoreyed office block. The company served as agents for a number of tea gardens. Now the company's principal business includes cultivation, manufacture, sale and export of tea. At Number 5 was the office of D.T. Keymer & Co., noted contractors, merchants and agents. Later this building served as the office of Calcutta Tramways Co. Ltd. At Number 6 was the press of M/s. Thacker Spinks. In 1984 Mangoe Lane was renamed Surendra Mohan Ghosh Sarani.

A New Road Engulfing Mangoe Lane

In 1939, a new road constructed by Calcutta Improvement Trust took over portions of Mangoe Lane ending at Wellington Street. This 84 feet wide road facilitated the movement of traffic from around Dalhousie Square up to Wellington Street. The new road was named after Ganesh Chandra Chunder (1844–1914), a noted lawyer and social worker, and is known as Ganesh Chandra Avenue. A notable address on this road is the office of the Bengal National Chamber of Commerce and Industry, set up with the support and cooperation of some of the nationalist leaders of the time. It was established on 2 Feburary 1887 with Rai Buddree Das Mukkim Bahadur as Founder President. It has always propagated the need for the growth of industry, trade and commerce in the country and promoting the industrial development of West Bengal. The other notable address is that of the Hindu Family Annuity Fund started by Pandit Iswarchandra Vidyasagar for the benefit of Hindu widows.

ROPE WALK—MISSION ROW— RAJENDRA NATH MOOKHERJEE SARANI

On the eastern side of Lal Dighi the East India Company established a rope factory for their use, the narrow lane assuming the name Rope Walk. The Company forbade the building of any houses between it and Lal Dighi.

John Zacharia Kiernander and the Old Mission Church

On 14 April 1740 the Society for the Promotion of Christian Knowledge (SPCK) despatched to India on a pay of £50 a year a young Swedish graduate of the University of Halle—John Z. Kiernander. In 1758 Cuddalore, where he had settled as a missionary, was captured by the French, and at the invitation of Lord Clive, Kiernander with his wife arrived in Calcutta. In January 1759 he started a mission school with 49 students—7 Armenians, 15 Portuguese, 6 Bengalis and 20 English (from the Charity School). He was an exceptional character with a passion for things out of the ordinary. His wife Wendela died in May 1761, but *Asiaticus* goes on to record that 'the remembrance of all his former sorrows was obliterated in the silken embraces of opulent beauty: the tenth of February 1762 witnessed his union with Mrs. Anne Wolley.'[49]

In 1763 he obtained as a gift from the Council the former Collector's *cutchery* at Lal Bazar for the mission school. By 1766 his 189 parishioners included mostly former Catholics. Amazingly he converted no less than five Roman Catholic padres. Four years later the house gifted by the Company was taken back for official purposes. So Kiernander decided to build his own church and school. He built largely at his own expense, or as some would say, out of his second wife's fortune. The foundation stone of the Portuguese Protestant Church was laid in 1767. This was to be for the converts from the low caste Portuguese community. It was designed by a Dane, Martin Boutant de Mevell. The church under the name of 'Beth Tephillah' or House of Prayer was consecrated in December 1770. The cost was between 60,000 to 68,000 rupees. In the grounds behind the church Kiernander built in

1773, a Mission School, and later the Parsonage House between the school and the church. The church building was very different from the Old Mission Church today. It has been described to be a clumsy unplastered brick edifice, of small dimensions, hemmed in on every side by old houses, uncomfortable for its rude benches and the high society of Calcutta pronounced it utterly unsuitable for the reception of a European congregation.[50]

The reddish brickwork gave it the name Lal Girja among the Indians. Some historians went on to record that the reflection of the Lal Girja on the Great Tank gave the latter the name Lal Dighi.

Before the Daniells' arrival in 1786, the original church had been clothed in stone and had a spire. Like all other parsons Kiernander also speculated in property, but failing health and mismanagement of his financial affairs by his son drove him to financial ruin, compelling him to sell off his properties in Camac Street and Bhowanipore (later occupied by the London Missionary School and United Missionary Girls' High School). His school, the Mission Church and house were auctioned off. A close friend Charles Grant bought the property for Rs. 10,000 and was generous enough to allow the church services to continue.

The following year Kiernander was declared a bankrupt and he fled to the Dutch settlement in Chinsurah, where he remained until it was taken over by the English in 1795, when he returned to Calcutta and stayed on until his death. We will come back to Kiernander, when we visit the Presidency General Hospital, the site of which was his garden house. The Mission Church was considerably enlarged in 1835 with the addition of a south transept and the heightening of the spire which had to be taken down after the earthquake of 1897. The church still stands today dwarfed by the adjoining skyscrapers.

Number 8 was the house of General Sir John Clavering, colleague of Hastings and Francis in the Council. Clavering died in this house on 30 August 1777. Number 1 was the residence of Colonel the Honourable George Monson, Francis' second faithful supporter, who died at Hooghly in 1776. A few doors from the playhouse was the residence of Lady Russell. There used to be a club in Mission Row called Selby's, where the Company's factors used to ruin one another in gambling.

The Calcutta Gazette of 30 May 1787 carried news of a duel fought between Mr. Gibbon, an Attorney at Law and Mr. Arnot, one of the proprietors of the Calcutta Circulating Library, in which the former was killed on the spot. 'We understand that the quarrel originated in a gambling debt.' *The Gazette* on 5 July 1787 records that William Arnot was placed on his trial before the Supreme Court. On 3 July the jury brought in a verdict of 'Not Guilty'.

Shortly before his death on 8 October, 1784, William Johnson, a Calcutta coach-maker, wrote to his mother:

We have taken residence again in Calcutta in a house where a club called 'Selby's Club' was once kept, notorious to all gamblers. However as this may not lead you to the exact spot, it is southwards of the Mission, or Old Kiernander's Church, the next house in the same line to General Clavering's, which I know you recollect. To conclude, our house was built by Mr. Charles Child in 1775. It is an amazing large house.[51]

As the town grew, more businessmen arrived in Mission Row, residences receded and business took over.

In General Clavering's house in 8 Mission Row was the first office of the New Mart established by Robert Thomas and Charles Marten in partnership in 1851; the firm was successively known as Thomas, Marten & Co., R. Thomas & Co., and J. Thomas and Company. They were the first to auction tea in India on 27 December 1861. J. Thomas & Co., still in operation, takes pride in its indigo connection and calls its new multistoreyed office block The Nilhat House (Indigo Mart). Their principal business now is tea brokering and auctioning. The office has a new number: 11, R.N. Mukherjee Road.

At the beginning of twentieth century we find the following notable addresses in Mission Row—from Lal Bazar on the western side was Number 1, premises of jewellers Benode Behari Dutt; 1/1, D. Morrison's workshop; 1/2, W. New Man & Co.'s Caxton Press; 2/1, Office of the Board of Examiners, the last building being the back of the Paper Currency Office. On the eastern side from Mangoe Lane—7/4, Tea Sal Room; 8, J. Thomas & Company; 9, Carritt & Co. and Carritt, Moran & Co. (Carritt & Co. has been described as General Produce Brokers and the latter Tea Brokers. Carritt, Moran & Co. still continues at the same address as Tea Brokers); 10, Church Missionary Society; and 11, the Old Mission Church. Number 12, the last house, was the office of Begg, Dunlop & Co., mainly in tea and sugar business. This building later became the office of the Martin Burn Ltd. Sir Rajendra Nath Mookherjee, the doyen among Indian businessmen, was the Chairman of this big consortium. Sir Rajen started Martin & Co. in partnership with Mr. A. Martin (mentioned in the account of Clive Street). In 1927 he purchased their main business opponents, Burn & Co., by a single cheque, and the company came to be known as Martin Burn Limited. The greatest achievement of Sir Rajen was the establishment of the Indian Iron & Steel Company, in the third decade of the twentieth century, initially for the production of pig iron and heavy iron castings to cater to the needs of various industries.

The works were located near Asansol, a place now known as Burnpur. Once called the Heerapur works, it produced around 76,000 tons pig iron per annum, most of which were promptly sold to Japan. Simultaneously, the casting unit was set up at Kulti, approximately 12 miles up Grand Trunk Road from Asansol and came to be known as the Kulti Works. This unit consumed large quantities of pig iron when export to Japan was reduced. In the mid-thirties another subsidiary company called Steel Corporation of Bengal was set up adjacent to Burnpur, mainly to produce steel ingots; the two units virtually functioning as an integrated steel plant whose products matched international standards and fetched high prices in India and abroad. During the Second World War the IISCO became a key unit in the British war machine and the works underwent considerable expansion.

Earlier, Burn & Co., with its huge heavy engineering workshops engaged in steel casting, manufacturing and laying railway tracks, sleepers, pre-fabricated bridges,girders, etc., joined hands with its new masters, Martin & Co., leading to the coordinated engineering endeavour, the new Howrah Bridge, which was opened to traffic in 1943; its structure mainly fabricated by the Burn & Co. unit from steel mostly manufactured by IISCO.

The Victoria Memorial placement was the idea of Sir Rajen Mookherjee, whose estimates were accepted by the architect, Sir William Emmerson, and the foundation stone was laid by King George V. Martin and Burn built it in record time for the Memorial to be inaugurated in 1921 by the Prince of Wales (later King Edward VIII). Sir Rajen Mookherjee passed away on 15 May 1936.

The Calcutta Municipal Corporation changed the name of Mission Row and Mission Row Extension in August 1960 to Rajendra Nath Mukherjee Road to honour the great son of Bengal. The old office at Number 12 has since been replaced by a multi-storeyed office block and another office at 3B, Lal Bazar Street. At 9/1, next to Carritt, Moran & Co., a new skyscraper has come up, housing several Birla organizations.

References

1. Eastwick, Edward B. *Handbook of the Bengal Presidency with an Account of Calcutta City,* London 1882, p. 101.
2. *Bengal Past & Present,* vol. II, 1908, p. 55.
3. Ray, Nisith Ranjan & Mitra, Rathin. *Shashwata Kolkata* (Bengali), Calcutta 1988, p. 114.
4. Cotton, H.E.A. *Calcutta Old & New,* p. 416.
5. Ibid.
6. Nair, P.T. article in *Port of Calcutta 125 years,* Calcutta 1995, pp. 5–7.
7. Nair P.T. *A History of Calcutta Streets,* Calcutta 1987, p. 346.
8. Curzon, Lord. *British Government in India,* vol. I, pp. 31–32.
9. Nair P.T. *A History of Calcutta Streets,* p. 179.
10. *Calcutta 200 Years,* p. 74.
11. *Bengal Past & Present,* vol. VIII, p. 257.
12. Cotton, H.E.A. *Calcutta Old & New,* pp. 641–42.
13. Ghatak, Pranotosh. *Kolkatar Pathghat* (Bengali), Calcutta 1989, p. 71.
14. Cotton, H.E.A. *Calcutta Old & New,* pp. 644–45.
15. Nair, P.T. 'The Growth and Development of Old Calcutta,' in *Calcutta—The Living City,* Calcutta 1990, vol. I, p. 236.

16. *Bengal Past & Present*, vol. xlvii, 1934, p. 126.

17. Ibid. vol. xlviii, 1934, p. 28.

18. Ibid. vol. viii, 1914, p. 219.

19. *Calcutta—The Living City*, vol. i, pp. 107 & 130.

20. *Bengal Past & Present*, vol. i, 1907.

21. Cotton, H.E.A. *Calcutta Old & New*, pp. 271–72.

22. Losty, J.P. *Calcutta—City of Palaces*, pp. 56-57.

23. *Bengal Past & Present*, vol. xlv, 1933, p. 60.

24. Ibid. vol. iv, 1909, p. 461.

25. Ibid. vol. li, 1931.

26. *Calcutta 200 Years.* pp. 128-29.

27. *Calcutta Review*, Calcutta, vols. xiii & xiv, Jan-Dec. 1850, p. 447.

28. *Bengal Past & Present*, vol. 46, 1933.

29. Cotton, H.E.A. op. cit. Quoted on p. 270.

30. Losty, J.P. op. cit. Quoted on p. 85.

31. *History of Lovelock & Lewes 1877-1997*, Calcutta 1997.

32. Losty, J.P. *Calcutta—City of Palaces*, pp. 36 & 52.

33. Nair, P.T. *A History of Calcutta Streets*, p. 626.

34. Tyson, Geoffrey, *Bengal Chamber of Commerce & Industry, A Centenary Survey, 1853-1953*, Calcutta 1953.

35. Suhrawardy, Hasan. *Calcutta & Environs*, Calcutta, p. 48.

36. *Calcutta 200 Years*, p. 76.

37. Ibid. p. 70.

38. Ibid. p. 73.

39. Dasgupta, Anil Chandra, ed. *The Days of John Company—Selections from Calcutta Gazette 1824-32*, Calcutta 1959, p. 214.

40. Losty, J.P. op. cit. p. 23

41. Ibid. p. 86

42. Cotton H.E.A. op. cit. p. 275.

43. *Calcutta 200 Years*, p. 70.

44. Selections from *Calcutta Gazette*.

45. Majumdar, R.C. *Glimpses of Bengal in the Nineteenth Century*, Calcutta 1960, p. 84.

46. Raychowdhury, Ranabir, *Glimpses of Old Calcutta (1836-50)*, p. 1.

47. Cotton H.E.A. op. cit. p. 278.

48. *Lovelock & Lewes 125 Years*, Calcutta, p. 6.

49. Hyde, H.B. *Parochial Annals of Bengal*, Calcutta 1901, p. 123.

50. Cotton H.E.A. op. cit. p. 526.

51. *Bengal Past & Present*, vol. xxxv, 1928, p. 153.

Chapter Eight

Esplanade Row and its Environs

Government Place North

Starting from Government Place East, this road runs along the northern end of the Government House (Raj Bhavan) ending at the junction of Council House Street and Government Place West; the continuation once known as Hastings Street (now Kiran Shankar Roy Road). The entire stretch of Hastings Street and Government Place North once lay in the bed of the creek running from the river up to the Salt Lakes. Later the creek was filled up to create Hastings Street. Government Place is a comparatively new road created in 1803 after the construction of the new Government House on the site of the older Government House (Buckingham House) and the Council House. There was a road a little south of the new thoroughfare, called Wheler Place. Sir Edward Wheler was a member of the Supreme Council from 1777 to 1784. He laid the foundation stone of St. John's Church in 1784 while Warren Hastings was away from Calcutta. Wheler's house was situated at the site of the north-west wing of the present Government House. An advertisement in the Calcutta Gazette on 23 February 1786, offered for sale Wheler's House, which was described as commodious and elegant, built on 3 *bighas* and 14 *cottahs* of land, consisting of two halls, eight large chambers, four open verandahs, a grand staircase, and numerous out-houses, offices, etc. There was a theatre hall in Wheler Place, and a narrow lane called Corkscrew Lane leading from the Wheler Place and meandering northwards to the site of the present day Red Cross Place or old Wellesley Place, ending abruptly in the vicinity of Spence's Hotel. The entire Wheler Place with its buildings and the southern end of the Corkscrew Lane were demolished at the time of the construction of the Government House; a part of the grand staircase and the carriageway now occupying the site.

The entire southern side of the Government Place North is taken up by the northern boundary and the imposing Northern Gateway of the Government House. On the northern side there are the outhouses and staff quarters and the dispensary of the Government House. During Lord Curzon's reign, the fine stone structures of the Viceroy's stables were erected on both the corners of Government Place North and Wellesley Place. Now the right-hand building is used as quarters for the Secretary to the Governor of West Bengal as well as senior Government officers. The left-hand building is still used as the Governor's motor garage and staff quarters.

Before the time of Lord Curzon, the Government House kitchen was situated in a house in this street and food was carried in covered miniature palanquins. During Lord Curzon's tenure a kitchen was constructed inside the Government House.

An interesting painting of Government Place North by Zoynool Abdeen of Karryah dated about 1842 was reproduced in the *Bengal: Past & Present*, vol. 41, 1931, along with an article by Evan Cotton on 'A Famous Calcutta Firm—The History of Thacker Spink & Co.'

Evan Cotton writes, "Beginning on the right, we see the two houses, on either side of Wellesley Place, which has been transformed into the residence of the Private Secretary and the Military Secretary of the Governor of Bengal." The house on the extreme right bears two signboards: 'Boudet, Hairdesser, Perfumer' and '6/2, Hollway & Co., French and English Millinery Warehouse.' The house on the other side of Wellesley Place is inscribed: '6½ Madame Champenios, French and English Millinery'. The low building which comes next is the office of W. Thacker & Co., Army Agency, adjoining St. Andrew's Library, at the corner of Fancy Lane. Beyond it and bounded on the west by Council House Street, is a Government office; the words 'Office, 1st Fancy Lane' can be deciphered on a notice hung on the wall. On the opposite side of the road a glimpse can be had of Loudon Building, housing several offices; a building later demolished to make way for the Imperial Secretariat in the Government Place West. In the Calcutta Directory of 1842 it appears that the Government Office was the Secret and Political Department, 6 Government Place. In 1842 Thacker & Co. began their tenancy here which lasted until 1916.[1]

From Council House Street now, we see on the northern side a new multistoreyed office block at Number 4 called Delta House; one then crosses Fancy Lane to come to Number 5 which used to house Thacker & Spink & Co. The building now has some Government offices and the offices of the Red Cross, West Bengal, and the St. John's Ambulance.

Wellesley Place (Now Red Cross Place)

This new road was constructed from the north gate of the Government House to end at Dalhousie Square South. On the two corners with the Government Place North are the Viceroy's stable buildings, the imposing gateway visible to the west. In a long dimly-lit room under the gateway a group of Calcutta ladies meet from time to time. According to Mrs. Subhadra Roychowdhury, one of the participants, this has been the office of the Women's Coordinating Council since 1960, and the main purpose of the Council is social welfare. During the late nineteenth century Wellesley Place was also a fashionable shopping area, and shops with famous names occupied this street. We cross another opening of the

Fancy Lane and come to a building where Spence's Hotel, a famous landmark of Calcutta, was originally situated.

At the site of the Spence's Hotel (now defunct) was an old building, called Becher's Buildings, where F. Bennitt ran a hotel until 1847. A narrow lane called Becher's Place ran from Wellesley Place in a westerly direction to Fancy Lane. It was the first turning to the left from the Government Place North, and was later absorbed in Fancy Lane. In *Thacker's Directory* for 1866 Becher's Buildings are stated to commence from 1-1/2 Wellesley Place ending in Fancy Lane.

Spence's Hotel was originally located at Loudon Building on the then Council House Street, opposite Government House. The hotel was founded by Mr. John Spence, steward of the Town Hall. The earliest reference to the hotel occurs in the diary of Mary Ann Friend, wife of Capt. Curling Friend, who brought his ship to Calcutta in 1830.

Another reference is found in the *Diaries of Honoria Lawrence*, who arrived at Calcutta in August 1837 and put up at the Spence's.

Hotels are but of recent establishment in Calcutta. Hospitality in India...being a matter of necessity. But as the influx of visitors increased, the inhabitants must have felt the best hotel is Spence's, to which I went, and which is really a noble one. The sets of rooms so well arranged that parties do not interfere with one another, and the attendance is excellent...we got very nice apartments, a sitting room with two bedrooms and dressing rooms opening off it. But four pairs of lofty doors threw the whole pretty...nearly into one. Stranger still was it to see men act as chambermaids, making beds, arranging dressing tables etc. Colour and costume makes a wonderful difference in our notions. A black form does not give the idea of indelicacy and exposure, though nearly naked, and the white robed bearers going into a bedroom do not give the least of the feeling it would do to see footmen there.

John Spence seems to have severed his connections with the hotel in 1850. A reference to the demise of Mrs. Spence has been found in the pages of *Bengal Obituary:* 'Here lies the remains of Elizabeth, the wife of John Spence, who departed this life on the 15 September 1833, aged 33 years. This frail memorial is placed here by her husband, whom she sincerely loved.' Spence's had a good clientele, as it was in the centre of the white town and was famous for its service and food.

Before shifting to Wellesley Place (at the site of Becher's Buildings), the business was carried on for a short time at the site of the Ezra Mansions to the east of the Government House. Spence's became more popular at the new location. New annexe buildings were added in Fancy Lane.

A moving piece of Punjab history was played out at Spence's Hotel in 1861, when the old Maharani Juidan and her son Duleep Singh, separated by the East India Company, met for the first time in ten and half years in these premises on 16 January. 'Ships on the Hooghly river were full of Sikh troops returning from the second China War. When they heard rumours of Duleep's presence in the city, they flocked to shout old Khalsa war cries outside Spence's Hotel. Lord Canning was distinctly alarmed. He asked the Maharaja "as a favour" to leave Calcutta by the next available ship.'[2]

After the opening of the Suez Canal in 1866, journey to India from abroad became much easier and Calcutta hotel owners started to bring girls out to serve behind the bar. In leading European hotels they were engaged on contract for six months: some remained longer but comparatively few stayed beyond their time. One or two found a husband on board who took them off at Colombo or Madras and they failed to report at Calcutta. Others, perhaps more fortunate, married in Calcutta. One bright damsel attracted notice by putting in his place a fellow who thought he could shine with 'So you're the maid, are you?' He was told, 'I am, but I've had my chances.' Goldie Morrison, a big blonde Scot came to work in a Calcutta bank, fell in love with and married a pretty barmaid, in Spence's Hotel. Soon he was looking for a job as the Calcutta snobs would not have him.[3]

After the British left, the Spence's began to degenerate and ultimately disappeared from the Calcutta scene in the late 1970s. The next house, Number 5, was the old dispensary of the East India Company, hence the native name of the street, *Kompani–dawaikhana ka rasta*. Until a few years back Number 2 was occupied by the noted fire-arms dealer R.B. Rodda & Co., whose armoury was raided during the freedom movement by revolutionaries belonging to several organizations of Calcutta, Dhaka and Barisal on 26 August 1914. The raiders took away 50 Mauser pistols and a large amount of ammunitions, and distributed them among various revolutionary groups in Bengal. According to the Rowlatt Committee's report, the acquisitions from this historic raid sustained and intensified revolutionary activities in Bengal for years to come.

The last building on the western side before Dalhousie Square was the Viceroy's Body-guard Stables. This has since become a part of the Standard Insurance building. On the southern side is the Central Telegraph Office, which was built after filling up the 'Little Tank' used for water supply to the Europeans. The other buildings after the opening of Larkin's Lane are new office buildings.

Fancy Lane

Archdeadon Hyde traces the derivation of Fancy Lane to the *phansi* or gallows which he places in this locality in the early days when Calcutta was surrounded by palisades and the southern boundary was shut in by the creek which flowed along what later became Hastings Street.[4]

Archdeacon Hyde goes on to record that there was the third bridge over the creek near Fancy Lane but the palisades at this point swerved away from the natural boundary of the creek, so there must have been a tree in between. Fancy Lane today is a narrow lane opening out on three streets, the first opening from Government Place North, the second from Wellesley Place and the third from Council House Street. A conglomeration of the rear sides of buildings and some new office blocks, Fancy Lane with its three arms still exists, but with a different name. The Calcutta Municipal Corporation renamed it Pannalal Banerjee Lane in 1965.

Council House Street

The street derived its name from the Council House of the East India Company, who had rented it from Reza Khan in 1774. The Old Council House was pulled down in 1799-1800 to make way for the Government House. In the beginning the entire stretch from the southwest corner of Lal Dighi to Esplanade Row was called the Council House Street, but later, when the Imperial Secretariat was built to the west of the Government House, that portion was named Government Place West. Starting from Government Place North we come to the first building on the eastern side, Number 3, now the Remington House, headquarters of Remington Rand & Co. Towards the close of the nineteenth century this used to be the office of the Administrator General. The wine shop of John Petrino at 3/1 and other residential and office buildings later made way for the automobile showroom and workshop of Dewar & Co. Number 5 was the office of the Chartered Bank of India, Australia and China, before the new Chartered Bank building came up in Clive Street in 1908. This is now occupied by the West Bengal Industrial Development Corporation. Number 6 Council House Street today is a shabby double-storey unpretentious building, dark and gloomy, with a signboard describing it as the Distribution Cell of the Information and Cultural Affairs Department of the Government of West Bengal. When Calcutta was the Capital of India, this was the Office of Mr. J. Scott Portman, Private Secretary to the Viceroy in 1905. Adjacent to this building is the opening to Fancy Lane. Two other buildings on this side have banks and offices. The corner building, now occupied by Hong Kong Bank, was once the site of the Calcutta Exchange, College of Fort William, and later the Bengal Nagpur Railways godowns.

As we cross the road on the western side we come to a typical red brick Raj-era office building, which was built at the site of the old Foreign Office to house the Departments of Commerce and Industry.

ST. JOHN'S CHURCH

St. John's Church stands next to the Government building mentioned above, with its main entrance at the corner of Church House Street and Hastings Street (Kiran Shankar Roy Road). The original Parish Church of Bengal, it became the principal Cathedral with the advent of Bishop Middleton as the first Bishop of Calcutta in 1815, and remained so until the consecration of St. Paul's Cathedral in 1847. The church is situated between Hare Street on the north, Hastings Street in the south, Church Lane in the west and Council House Street in the east. Standing in the heart of the business district, the church is a rich repository of old memories and memorials, of Governors-General resplendent in their official regalia arriving in state coaches, the military on their horses, women in their quaint palanquins and Warren Hastings walking down from his wife's residence in Hastings Street.

Warren Hastings and the Reverend William Johnson (husband of 'Begum Johnson'), Chaplain from 1770, were the prime movers for the construction of the church. In March 1776, the Council had sent to London the Chaplain's petition for the building of a suitable place for worship. Several years passed and a site was selected. This was the old burial ground of the settlement, closed since 1767, where rose the mausoleum of Job Charnock, with the old powder magazine building and yard immediately to its east. The latter was actually auctioned by the Company in 1774 and was originally the property of Maharaja Nabakrishna Deb, who was persuaded in 1782 by Warren Hastings to sell it to him in his private capacity for Rs. 10,000. But the church was not built on this part of the ground at all. It was built entirely on the site of the old burial ground. About 35,000 rupees were collected from donations and a lottery produced another Rs. 36,800. Of the old mausoleums, only those of Charnock and Admiral Watson were left undisturbed, but the other graves were dug up and the remains taken away. Some headstones were laid round the periphery of the Charnock mausoleum. Lieutenant Agg of the Bengal Engineers was the architect. The foundation stone was laid on 6 April 1784 by Mr. Wheler, Senior Member of the Council, as the Governor General was away.

Building went on in a brisk manner. Sandstone from Chunar was brought for the steeple and blue marble from the ruins of Gaur for the flooring.[5] The building took three years to make. The ceremony of consecration was witnessed by Lord Cornwallis, who had brought with him the necessary legal instruments under the seal of the Archbishop of Canterbury. The date chosen was Sunday, 24 June 1787, being the nativity of St. John the Baptist.

Agg's design was that of a hall-church with a portico and main entrance at the east and a steeple at the west end. The altar at the east end was enclosed in an apse. The curious layout was probably necessitated by the requirement of the approach to the east, as the western part was cluttered with tombs and mausoleums, which by 1802 was in such a state of irreparable decay that they had to be removed.

William Hickey, the diarist, was present at the consecration ceremony. After a drinking session covering the entire night, he and a few friends decided to attend the consecration.

We accordingly remained pouring down claret until eight in the morning (Sunday)... At nine three carriages being announced ready, upon mustering the party no more could be prevailed upon to proceed than five...who all stepped into Mr. Keighley's coach and were rapidly conveyed to the church, the steps of which we were able to ascend by leaning upon and supporting each other. It may easily be believed that in such a state we sadly exposed ourselves, drawing the eyes and attention of the congregation upon us as well as that of the clergyman, who took occasion to introduce in his sermon a severe philippic against inebriety, against indelicate behaviour in a sacred place and Sabbath-breaking, and directing those parts of his discourse pointedly to the pew in which we sat. I have often since thought of that profligate scene with shame and contrition.[6]

The East India Company resolved to spend £ 1200 for a communion plate, an organ, bells, a clock, velvet for the pulpit, desk and communion table. Locally known as *Pathar-ka Girja*, the St. John's has a flat roof which measures 7,400 square feet and has a spire 174 feet high. The main entrance to the church was originally at the east end which was later closed although the portico and the steps still remain. In 1788 Thomas Daniell painted the church from the south-east and published it in his series *Views of Calcutta*. William Baillie drew another picture from the same spot in 1795.

The wide porticos on the north and the south were added in 1811, and during the same year the Doric pillars were changed to Corinthian ones. The Sacrarum, the Palanquin Slopes and Carriage Roads were later additions. An early account gives a feel of the place in those times:

If you were a person of fashion yet did not choose to go to church in your yellow chariot, you will arrive in a neat sedan-chair gleaming with black lacquer. You brought at least seven servants with you—four chair-bearers, two running footmen, with spears and one parasol bearer. If you had official rank, your silver mace would occupy the services of at least another runner. Alighting at the great eastern staircase of Chunar stone you ascended under the screen of your huge painted parasol to a tile-paved terrace beneath the eastern portico. Here a sentry with a firelock guarded the entrance. Passing him you found yourself in a narrow vestibule and at the back of a curved recess that enclosed the altar; to the right and left were staircases leading up to the doors of the galleries.[7]

The vestibule was torn down in 1811. Of the galleries the one in the west alone remains. It had once accommodated the singers, the organ and the Chaplain's family. In the middle of the northern gallery were the bowed-out pews of the Governor General and his Council: in the southern sat the judges of the Supreme Court. In 1901 the north and south galleries were removed to facilitate accommodation in the church and installation of electricity. On the wall above the western gallery now hangs the large painting of *The Last Supper* which the artist John Zoffany had himself presented to St. John's. Originally it had been placed over the altar. When the picture was originally hung Calcutta society was scandalized by Zoffany's indiscretion in introducing the features of important local persons in his picture.

It is said that the Greek priest Father Parthenio had sat for the figure of Jesus. According to tradition the auctioneer Tulloch who had been given to believe that he was sitting for St. John, went to law to avenge the insult of finding himself depicted as Judas Iscariot. The Police Magistrate, William Coates Blaquire, is supposed to have been the actual model for St. John in the picture.

The vestry room is full of history. The richly-chased communion plate is the gift of the East India Company, and has been in use for more than 200 years. In the original register may be seen the entry made by Chaplain Johnson of the marriage on 10 July 1777, of Miss Varle of Chandernagore and Mr. George Francis Grand, 'writer' in the Hon'ble Company's service, beginning the chequered life history of the 'Queen of Ganges, Queen of Seine,' who fascinated Junius in Calcutta and re-appeared in Paris as Talleyrand's princess. Immediately below, by the strangest of coincidences, is recorded the union on 8 August of Warren Hastings with Anna-Maria Apollonia Chapuzet, the beautiful Mrs. Imhoff. St. John's maintains the marriage records of William Makepeace Thackeray's father and grandfather. On a recent visit we were shown a Louis XV chair with faded satin upholstery bearing the Coat of Arms of the Company, and supposed to be the chair of Warren Hastings. The church contains many monuments of interest. The fine white marble cenotaph to the memory of Alexander Colvin is a work of great beauty—the handiwork of Westmacott. A bust of Lord Cornwallis stands in the stair leading to the west gallery. Among other memorials are inscriptions to John Mathias Turner, Third Bishop of Calcutta; Henry Lloyd Loring, the first Archdeacon of Calcutta; John Adam, Acting Governor General from January to August 1823 and many others. Within the chancel and behind the altar rails in the eastern end we find a plain marble slab on the ground with a single inscription 'T.F.M., D.D., Obiit VIII Julii 1822'. These words mark the last resting place of Thomas Fanshawe Middleton, first Bishop of Calcutta.

There are two more monuments in the church bearing the marks of the expert chisel of Richard Westmacott, R.A. The first is a marble monument in memory of George Cruttenden, Major in East India Company's Bengal Army, who died at Macao, 23 March 1822, aged 54 years. After retirement from the army he joined the firm of Cruttenden, Mackilop & Co. of Bankshall Street.

The other one, also of marble, was erected by public contribution to the memory of Michael Cheese, Surgeon of the Bengal Establishment and Garrison Surgeon of Fort William, who died on 14 January 1816.

Mention must be made of a marble tablet commemorating James Pattle of the Bengal Civil Service who died on 4 September 1845, aged 63 years, and also Adeline, his wife who died at sea, 11 November 1845. She was the daughter of Chevalier Antoine L'Etang, Knight of St. Louis, and a former page to Queen Marie Antoinette. The Pattles had seven beautiful daughters giving birth to a legend of sorts. 'You must know,' writes Mr. Frederick Leveson-Gower, a visitor to Calcutta in 1850, 'that wherever you go in India, you meet with some member of the Pattle family. Every other man has married, and every other woman has been a Miss Pattle.'[8]

During the incumbency of Chaplain H.B. Hyde, a museum was set up of pictures, records, etc. in the Vestry Room which still exists today for the benefit of those who would be interested in the ecclesiastical history of old Calcutta.

In the compound, the Charnock mausoleum stands in the north-west corner. Just before it is the tomb of Admiral Watson, which was originally elsewhere in the compound, but later shifted here. Close to the Admiral's tomb lies the grave of young Billy Speke, a midshipman, who was mortally wounded at the siege of Chandernagore, 24 March 1757. The cenotaph in St. John's Churchyard commemorating the officers who fell at Rampore on 26 October 1794 is thought to be based on Sir William Chambers' Temple of Aeolus, at Kew, England. It is perhaps the finest example of Neoclassical style in the city.[9] Inside there is a platform for some military trophy which was never erected. In 1895 an inscription giving the names of the officers was placed on the eastern side. Though the graveyard was closed in 1767, the gates were opened in 1812 for the famous Begum Johnson. According to her wish, she was buried here. Lord Minto, the Governor General, with his Members of the Council, the judges of the Supreme Court and other notables of the town, joined the funeral. In 1893 an archaeological find of great interest was made near the grave of Billy Speke, viz. the foundation stone of the Coil Dragon and Crouching Tiger Fort built in the Island of Chusan in 1651 AD. It is now in the Indian Museum at Calcutta.[10]

St. John's Church stands in desolate splendour now, with the garden taken over by tall unkempt grasses and weeds. There is a shallow footpath leading to the Charnock mausoleum, but the rest of the graveyard cannot be approached through the jungle of grass. The Church Lane gate has disappeared; there is a petrol pump on Church Lane built on a parcel of church-land. We could see another parcel of land bordering Church Lane near the Charnock mausoleum, barricaded by corrugated tin sheets, perhaps waiting to be sold off.

It is on record that the church was in the year 1903 placed, by Lord Curzon under the direct control of the Lieutenant-Governor of Bengal, and a fixed sum was set apart for its maintenance year in and year out.[11]

What is the present state of affairs? We have seen how an entire cemetery has disappeared from the face of Calcutta and land belonging to churches and missionary schools has been sold off in the recent years. Will the two hundred year-old church be grabbed by land-sharks?

Government Place West

This is a small stretch of road lined today by two large buildings, on the left the Government House and on the right the Imperial Secretariat and the Treasury Buildings. The road was

Figure 28: The newly erected Imperial Secretariat Building seen from the Government Place North

Figure 29: The Treasury Building at the southern end of the Imperial Secretariat

once a part of Council House Street, but the name was changed after the Imperial Secretariat Building was built in the late 1880s.

In the old days, before the present Government House (Raj Bhavan) was built, Esplanade Row was a straight road from Chand Paul Ghat to Dharamtolla Street. After the Treasury buildings stood the Council House and Buckingham House (Residence of the Governor General). The present Government House was constructed in 1803, after demolition of the previous houses on the same site. Esplanade Row West ends at the Treasury Buildings, and Esplanade East begins at the Esplanade Mansions.

The Treasury Building is the corner house with Government Place West and Esplanade Row.

William Hickey's description of the original Accountant General's Office or the Treasury Building runs:

The large house on the opposite corner with a colonnaded upper storey is a house used for public offices, built about 8 years ago by the Rev. Johnson, formerly inhabited by Sir Eyre Coote, then by Mr. Stables and lastly by General Sloper, upon whose return to Europe the Company purchased it for a lac of rupees which was less than the cost of the building.'

We have a view of the building in the painting by James Baillie Fraser, *A View of the Town Hall, 1819.* The painting shows the Town Hall, a house where William Hickey lived, and next to it the Treasury Buildings, a two-storey house; the first floor with a row of Doric columns. Lord Curzon writes that Lord Wellesley might have occupied a suite of rooms in the Treasury Buildings when the Government House was being built. From official accounts it is known that Lord Wellesley stayed there on the night of the Grand Ball in his new Government House on 26 January 1803.[12] Next to it were several residential houses. William Hickey lived in one of them when the landlord of his Esplanade Row house demolished the latter to have a new one constructed on the site. Next stood the Loudon Building, where Spence's Hotel was shifted for some time; there were other residences and offices in the building as well as the office and studio of the well-known photographers, Johnston & Hoffmann.

In the latter part of the 1880s, the Treasury Buildings and adjoining buildings up to the Hastings Street corner were demolished to make way for the impressive new building of the Accountant General's Office and Imperial Secretariat along the whole western side of the Government Place West and extending to a part of Hastings Street. The beautiful range of buildings has Italian Renaissance ornamentation and is reminiscent of the finest building activities of the hey days of the Raj.

The Government Place West had the following numbers:

1. Government House
2. Treasury Buildings
3. Legislative Department
4 to 4.7. Imperial Secretariat Buildings

The size and description of the building may be detailed. To give an idea of the size of the Treasury Building we have gathered details available in 1905.

The East Block runs from south to north, and all other blocks west of the east block run from east to west.

East Block

Treasury Buildings: Accountant General's Office, Press Room, Presidency Pay Department, Record Room, Finance Department, Library Section.

Gate to Government Place

Imperial Secretariat Buildings: Record Room, Home Department—Book Branch, Commerce Department.

Gate leading to Government Place

Record Room.

South Block

Treasury Buildings: Accountant General's Office

Middle Blocks

   I. Records
  II. Records, Pension Payment Department, Lobby, Waiting Room for Pensioners
 III. Records
  IV. (Facing the North Gate to Government Place): Records

North Block

Records
Gate leading to Hastings Street

First Floor
East Block

Comptroller General's Offices, Deputy Comptroller, India Treasuries, Public Works Department

South Block

Comptroller General's Offices

Middle Blocks

   I. Finance Department
  II. Offices of Comptroller, India Treasuries
 III. Secretaries and Deputy Secretaries and Assistant Secretaries of Home, Revenue and Agriculture Departments
 IV. Tiffin Room

North Block

Offices and residences

Second Floor
East Block

Offices of the Accountant General, Bengal; Public Relations Section, Deposit Section, Home Department—Establishment and Police Branches, Railway Board Departments of Revenue and Agriculture

South Block

Accountant General's Offices, Book Department, Resource Section, Budget Department, Examiner of local Fund Accounts

Middle Blocks

   I. Finance Department: Excise and Accounts Branches
  II. A.G. Bengal's Office—Copying Department, Finance Department—Expenditure Branch
 III. Railway Board, Office of the Examiner of Public Works Accounts, Passage to the Government Press

North Block

North Side: Department of Revenue and Agriculture—Despatch, Revenue and Forest Branches, Office of the Director General, Indian Medical Service, Home Department. Passage to the Government Press
South Side: Departments of Revenue and Agriculture, Cashier's Room, Home Department—Education, Judicial and Issue Branches.

Third Floor

Detached tin sheds occupied by the servants[13]

When the capital shifted from Calcutta to New Delhi in 1912, the office of The Accountant

General, Bengal, remained in the original Treasury Buildings, but the rest of the Imperial Secretariat came to be used by different Government of India offices from time to time. Before the Aaykar Bhavan (The Income Tax Headquarters) was built at Chowringhee Square, the Chief Commissioner and other Commissioners of Income Tax had their offices in these premises. There are still several offices of the Income Tax Department in this building including those of some Appellate Commissioners.

In the first floor there is a white marble statue of General Sir William Erskine Baker (of the Bengal Engineers), First Secretary in the Public Works Department of the Government of India, 1855-59. The Government Press originally situated adjacent to the building has since been shifted to Santragachhi, near Howrah, to make way for extensions.

The distinctive Raj era building with its Italian marble flooring now looks shabby inside. In some of the rooms one can see scaffoldings and wooden stakes supporting the roof. Heritage—yes, but no one prepared to foot the enormous bill for maintenance! At the northern end of the Imperial Secretariat, we come to Hastings Street once again, and move west. We can start through a small lane branching off from Hastings Street and ending in Hare Street just west of St. John's Church.

Church Lane

In Wells' map of 1753 this lane is shown as leading to the creek, which was crossed by a bridge at its crossing with Hastings Street. The name Church Lane appears for the first time in Wood's map of 1784. One would naturally assume that the name Church Lane came from its proximity to St. John's Church, which was consecrated in 1787. P. Thankappan Nair, however, is of the opinion that the name came from St. Anne's Church, which was destroyed in the siege of 1756. On the eastern side of the lane there is only one house, Number 7, as we enter from Hare Street. David Hare lived on this site and his garden extended up to the boundary wall of the church. In Lord Curzon's time a stone tablet marking the house was fixed on the wall. Later, there were several commercial establishments on this site. Now it forms a part of NICCO House, a commercial establishment. We could not find any stone tablet on the wall. The rest of the eastern side is covered by the western boundary wall of St. John's Church and a petrol pump at the crossing with Hastings Street.

On the western side from Hare Street, Number 1 Church Lane facing Hare Street had an old building which has recently been demolished to make way for a new office block. Number 2 is a very old house, which may fall down any day. Occupied by several offices now with a grand wooden staircase, Number 2 and Number 1 Church Lane were for a long time the head offices of the well-known Greek merchant firm of Ralli Brothers, established as merchants (export and import), later diversifying into shipping, insurance, agrochemicals, pharmaceuticals, fine chemicals, etc. Rallis India Limited is now situated at 16 Hare Street, with headquarters in Mumbai. The Tatas have taken over the management of the company.

The next building, Number 3, is at present the Stationery Office, Government of India. The building, usual red brick, is built on the site of the office of the Superintendent of Stamps and Stationery. This also functioned as a mint, before the new one in Strand Road was built. The original mint was in the Old Fort. The next old Number 5 was for some time the Calcutta Collectorate. The Ganges flowed just west of these buildings. The new Number 6 is a branch of ANZ Grindlays Bank, probably the site of Moran & Co., until 1870 (before they moved to 3 Mangoe Lane), holding indigo sales at their premises, the advertisement describing the location as the 'Old Mint Mart'. Calcutta's first post office was established in a house at the corner of Church Lane and Hastings Street. Later the post office shifted to a house in Old Post Office Street, opposite the High Court.

Mrs. Eliza Fay lived in this house during her sojourn in Calcutta. Mrs. Fay's *Original Letters from India* was published in 1817, describing Calcutta in the 1780s. Her vitriolic pen vividly describes Calcutta during the days of Warren Hastings.

Now we retrace our steps to the crossroads, the junction of Government Place West, Council House Street, Government Place North and Hastings Street, and carry on towards the west along the latter.

Hastings Street

The street was named after the first Governor-General of Bengal, Warren Hastings, 1772-85. After Independence the street had a new name, Kiran Shankar Roy Road. Kiran Shankar Roy, born in 1891, was a notable public figure in Bengal. As a member of the Indian National Congress, he joined the freedom movement under Deshbandhu Chittaranjan Das. He died in 1949, when he was Home Minister in Dr. B.C. Roy's cabinet.

The first building on the south side is the continuation of the Imperial Secretariat and Government of India Publications Sales Counter. The next building Number 7A (old Number 7) was the town house of Mrs. Marian Imhoff, the second wife of Warren Hastings.

Marian's first husband was Karl von Imhoff, a German Baron who had married Anna Maria Apollonia Chapuzet de St. Valentine. While travelling to India by sea on the *Duke of Grafton*, they met Warren Hastings who was proceeding to Madras as a Member of the Council. During the long voyage a strong friendship sprang up between Mrs. Imhoff and Hastings. According to the story generally believed, arrangement was made soon after the arrival of the trio at Madras and institution of divorce proceedings began. Baron Imhoff came down to Calcutta, but Mrs. Imhoff stayed back in Madras as the guest of Warren Hastings. Imhoff was doing well in Calcutta as an artist, so his wife joined him in October 1771. Hastings came to Calcutta as Governor-General in February 1772. Baron Imhoff was sent back to England in 1773, but the lady stayed back. After marrying his beloved Marian on 8 August 1777, Warren Hastings rarely used his official residence at Buckingham House.

He would always stay at his wife's house. They loved the countryside and had houses at Alipore and Sukhchar. A stone tablet has been fixed on the walls of the present building recalling the fact of Hastings' residence in the building. The building has since been modernized and the present red brick appearance may not be that old. But there were a few relics of the past in the form of ancient *punkah* frames painted in crimson and gold which the later occupants of the building, Messrs. Burn Ltd., donated to the Victoria Memorial Hall, along with a few pieces of furniture. Burn & Co., eminent builders and main competitors to Martin & Co., had their office in the first floor. Sir Rajen Mookherjee bought the firm with a single cheque in 1972 and the famous firm Martin Burn Limited was born.

History has left the building now, with a second floor built later without any architectural continuity with the rest of the building. Minor offices and law book stalls now occupy the building. Mr. Subir Burman, owner of the New Law Book Stall located in the ground floor, took me around when I visited it recently, maintaining that the building was the original from the day of Hastings. He showed me a round tower at the back of the building from which, according to him, Hastings used to hurl his enemies down to their death. According to him the building belongs to the family of Raja Rajendra Lal Mullick and a stone tablet on the front says that the building belongs to Jitendra Mullick Trust.

Number Six was the office of R. Cambray & Co., law booksellers, who also specialized in the sale of rare books on Calcutta, and their advertisements were a regular feature in the Bengal Past & Present.

Old Post Office Street

To maintain continuity we would now enter the left hand street, a short one meeting Esplanade Row West. To the natives it is *Poorana Dak Ghar ka Rasta*, the name derived from the post office which was located opposite the present High Court. Two other names have been attributed—Ali Baba Lane, probably conceived by the lawyers, and Bond Street. In the beginning when Calcutta was expanding and moving away from Lal Dighi in 1757, this area was once a fashionable residential area.

The new Supreme Court started functioning (at the site of the present High Court) and the judges and lawyers wanted to live near the court house. A house on the western side of the street was until 1825 the residence of Sir Francis Macnaghten, acting Chief Justice; later taken over by Advocate-General John Pearson and gradually turned into consultation chambers for the attorneys and lawyers. On the western side the High Court building was extended with a walking gallery, to accommodate the Sheriff's Office.

Returning to Hastings Street (now Kiran Shankar Roy Road) and moving west we come to the junction with Strand Road. On the left a couple of old buildings were demolished to construct the Metropolitan Magistrate's Court and the huge block of the

New West Bengal Secretariat extending on to the Strand Road, at the site of the old Somerset Buildings, in which there were the offices of the Officer Commanding Station Supply, Principal Medical Officer and the Agent for the Government Consignments.

Then we come to a huge building complex, nearly finished, superbly designed to gell perfectly with British Calcutta. This will be the office complex of the State Bank of India. On this site stood the Bank of Bengal, a heritage building quietly demolished to allow for the new structure.

THE BANK OF BENGAL

The agency houses in Calcutta played a pioneering role in establishing the European banking system in Bengal. Alexander & Company started the Bank of Hindostan in 1770, the first European Bank in India. It was for all practical purposes a counting house of the company. It crashed in 1832. The Calcutta Bank started by Palmer & Company failed in 1829 with the failure of the parent company.[14]

The East India Company formed a Provincial Bank of Calcutta on 1 May 1806. This became the Bank of Bengal on 2 January 1809 when the original charter was granted by the Governor General Lord Minto, and the directors held their first meeting. To obviate any chance of the Bank falling into the hands of a clique of shareholders it was provided that not more than a lakh of stock should be held by any single shareholder. At the same time a limitation of advances to the Government was set at rupees five lakh. This restriction was probably borrowed from the Constitution of the Bank of England. The Bank of Bengal

Figure 30: The Bank of Bengal, Strand Road

was functioning well when its premises were erected in 1825 at Strand Road at a cost of Rs. 61,500.

We can have some idea of the Bank's state of affairs from the advertisements in the *Calcutta Gazette*.

12 January 1826
Bank of Bengal January 5, 1826

The proprietors of the Bank of Bengal are hereby informed, that the thirty-fourth Halfyear's Dividend will be paid at the Bank, tomorrow at the rate of Sicca Rupees 655 for each share.
Published by the order of the Directors.

C.T. Glass
Secretary

Thursday 11 January 1827
Government Advertisement

To save trouble, Notice is hereby given that no other Banknotes, than those of the Bank of Bengal are receivable at the General Post Office.

Colin Shakespear
Post Master General

Bank of Bengal
January 7, 1839

The proprietors of the Bank of Bengal are hereby informed that the fortysecond half-year dividend is payable at the Bank at the rate of Rs. 450 for each share.

J.A. Dorin
Secretary & Treasurer

In 1866 there was a great economic crisis, when no less than six banks in Calcutta closed down. The Bank of Bengal came proudly through the year, and with profits so large that the directors ordered a bonus of one month's pay granted to the staff.

In 1900, Numbers 1 & 2 Strand Road, and 1 Esplanade Row West were acquired under the Land Acquisition Act and large extensions were made to the famous building. The Bank of Bengal merged with other Presidency Banks under the Act of 1920 to form the Imperial Bank of India.

On 1 July 1955, the Imperial Bank of India became the State Bank of India and the old Bank of Bengal building became its local head office.

Strand Road

During the siege of 1756, the Strand had been under the riverbed. As the river receded towards the west, land was reclaimed and in 1823 work on a New Strand began. Only the Chand Paul Ghat has not changed its position. Close to it in 1820 was a house occupied by a Mr. Tyler and to the north of the house was a grove of trees, 'The beautiful trees of the Respondentia'. The Respondentia Walk, the ancient haunt 'of those fond of moonlight rambles, and the children with their train of servants as no horses were allowed to go in it' was swallowed up in the Strand. Southwards the Strand Road carried up to Garden Reach and northwards went up to the Nimtolla Ghat.[15]

Ghats on the Strand

Along the Port Commissioners Railway (Now Circular Railway) and godowns are some *ghats* or landing stages which are part of the history of Calcutta.

Colvin's Ghat

Situated opposite Hastings Street, it was once known as *Goodee Ghat*, or the place for collecting country boats that were hauled up in the old days on the banks of the creek which ran along Hastings Street to the Salt Water Lakes on the east.

Chand Paul Ghat

Situated to the west of the High Court, where the Esplanade Row West meets the river, it derives its name from one Chandra Nath Paul or Chandan Paul, who kept a grocery shop in the vicinity 'for the refreshment of pedestrians and boatmen' in days when the maidan was a dense forest interspersed with a few weavers' sheds, and the river was scarcely frequented. The *ghat* was in existence in 1774 on the southern boundary of 'Dhee Calcutta'. This was the port where India welcomed and bid adieu to its rulers. It was here that Governors-General, Commanders in Chief, Judges of the High Court, Bishops, Members of the Supreme Council and all who were entitled to the honours of a salute from the ramparts of the Fort William, first set foot in the metropolis. The most famous of these landings was on 19 October 1774, when Philip Francis and his companions counted one by one the guns which boomed from the fort, and found to their mortification that they did not exceed seventeen, whereas the expected number was nineteen. According to Alexander Mackrabie, Francis' brother-in-law and secretary:

Exactly at noon, a comfortable season for establishing the etiquette of precedency, the whole party are disposed in three boats, and both courts safely landed at the capital of their jurisdiction. The procession to the Governor's house beggars all description: the heat, the confusion, not an attempt at regularity. No guards, no person to receive or show the way, no state. But surely Mr. Hastings might have put on a ruffled shirt. The ceremony of introduction gone through, the audience broke up, and we changed the scene though not the climate. At two, the whole party, increased by this time to one hundred and fifty, met again at the Governor's house to dine. In such a company little order can be expected. We ate and drank and endeavoured at Society, but even wine in ale glasses can not remove suspicion.[16]

The relationship between Francis and Hastings thus began on a sour note and they remained sworn enemies, their animosity culminating in a duel in 1780. On the same date landed the new Judges of the Supreme Court and the Chief Justice, Impey, who, as he contemplated the bare legs and feet of the multitude who crowded to witness their advent, exclaimed to his colleagues, "See brother, the wretched victims of tyranny. The Crown Court was not surely established before it was needed. I trust it will not have in operation six months before we shall see all these poor creatures comfortably clothed in shoes and stockings."[17]

The old *ghat* was later removed to make way for a new embankment and the Port Commissioners' railway. An elaborate landing stage came to be erected a few yards further south. But the pomp and splendour of the arrival and departure of dignitaries moved to Howrah Railway Station after the rail services began. The Chand Paul Ghat and Outram Ghat are still very much in use for ferry steamer services across the river. Next to the old boathouse of Calcutta Rowing Club (shifted to Dhakuria Lakes in 1928) is Babu Ghat, a Doric colonnade headed by the following inscription:

> The Right Hon'ble Lord William Cavendish Bentinck, Governor-General of India, with a view to encourage public munificence to works of public utility, has been pleased to determine that this Ghat erected by Baboo Rajchunder Doss in 1838, shall hereafter be called Baboo Rajchunder Doss's Ghat.

Baboo Rajchunder Doss was the husband of Rani Rashmoni. Babu Ghat still continues to be one of the major bathing *ghats* on the Ganga. Opposite Eden Gardens there is the Outram Ghat, very much in use for ferry and pleasure boat services.

The Strand opposite the new Fort William has its share of landmarks, including The Gwalior Monument, a brick structure faced with Jaipur marble, and crowned by a metal dome manufactured by Jessop & Co., out of guns taken from the enemy. At the centre of the upper storey is a bronze sarcophagus, on the top of which are inscribed the names of officers, non-commissioned officers and soldiers of His Majesty's and the East India

Company's services, who fell in the victorious actions of Maharajpore and Panniar on 29 December 1843.

Further south is the wooden landing stage known as Man of War Jetty where the naval vessels cast their moorings.

The last ghat on the Strand is Prinsep's Ghat, erected in honour of James Prinsep, one of the noblest and most versatile of the early English settlers in Bengal, by his fellow citizens. His services to the Asiatic Society were of great importance and included the decipherment of the ancient alphabets of India. Prinsep's Ghat with its Doric columns is a fine building and was intended to supersede the Chand Paul Ghat as the ceremonial place of arrival for the Governors-General. King George V, during his ceremonial visit to Calcutta in 1911, arrived at the Howrah Station, but crossed the river in a steam launch and landed at Prinsep's Ghat. Now the river has receded from the ghat, which is no longer in use. Barricaded behind a tin pallisade, the ghat can scarcely be seen, with the approaches of the newly erected Vidyasagar Setu, commonly called the second Hooghly Bridge, looming over it. Now we can come back along the Strand towards the north, where the Maidan ends and old Calcutta comes into view. Our first stop will be the once famous Eden Gardens.

EDEN GARDENS

There are records to prove that the Gardens came into being from the Governor-General Lord Auckland's desire to create a circus and garden at the north-western corner of Esplanade. In a letter to the Civil Architect, Capt. Fitzgerald, who was entrusted with the execution of the project, we find a sum of Company Rupees 6,000 sanctioned for the project.

Figure 31: The Burmese Pagoda, Eden Gardens

Figure 32: The Bandstand, Eden Gardens

Thus a pleasure ground with an oblong tank in its centre was laid out on a site generally resorted to for riding and recreations. Initially named 'Auckland Circus Gardens', it was bounded on the south-west by the Respondentia Walk; on the east by the Calcutta Gate Road and on the north by the Esplanade Row.

The inception of the garden is usually attributed to the Misses Emily and Fanny Eden, sisters of the Governor-General Lord Auckland, but the whole project was ordered by Lord Auckland himself. Searches were made in the Imperial and Bengal Government records to determine when and under what circumstances the name Auckland Circus Garden was changed to Eden Gardens. The name Eden Gardens first appears in Capt. R. Smyth's *Plan of Calcutta* showing the latest improvements in the Maidan and Esplanade West as existing in 1854.

In 1856 the Burmese Pagoda was added to the Gardens. This Pagoda has an interesting history. It was built in 1852 in Prome by Ma Kin, wife of Moung Honon, Governor of Prome. It was constructed by Moung Hune and ten other carpenters, who completed it in three months' time. The woodwork cost Rs. 1400 or 1500. Within the Pagoda there was an image of Gautama Buddha with its forehead set with precious stones and it cost another thousand rupees. The Pagoda belongs to the class of buildings called Tazoungs or Thein Tazoungs, used by Buddhist priests for worship but also, and perhaps chiefly, by Puzins or neophytes on the occasion of their consecration to the monastic life.

It was Lord Dalhousie, who on his visit to Prome in 1853, decided on the removal of the Tazoung to Calcutta; and it was dismantled by his order and shipped to Calcutta reaching there on 29 September 1854. It was handed over to Lieutenant Blair of the Madras Artillery. There was a difference of opinion about a suitable site for the Pagoda to be re-erected. So the Pagoda was left with Lt. Blair in the Arsenals of the Fort William. On the eve of his departure on 22 Feburary 1856, Lord Dalhousie wrote in a minute:

> Before I go I would propose to ask the Lieutenant Governor whether there is any objection to the erection of the building in the Auckland Gardens. If it is resolved to set it up, workmen for the purpose had better be got, indeed they must be got from Rangoon; as well as some one to superintend the work. Communication with the Court Major, Phagu, will readily procure all that is required.'

The Lieutenant Governor in Council having no objection to the erection of the ornamental building in the Auckland Gardens, it was set up by a dozen Burmese artificers under the direct supervision and guidance of Lieutenant Blair, and they took three months to complete the work. The cost of the project was Rs. 6,000. The Pagoda bears an inscription: 'The above specimen of Burmese ornamental architecture was removed from the city of Prome in the months of August and September 1854, and re-constructed on this site in the months of October, November and December 1856.'

In 1865 a detailed scheme for the enlargement and improvement of the Gardens was drawn up by Captain S.T. Trevor, R.E., Garrison Engineer, and approved by the Government of India. The work was completed during the years 1865-71. The Gardens were considerably extended eastward beyond the Calcutta Cricket Club ground by the removal of the old road, which running from the High Court to the Calcutta Gate of the Fort, then formed the western boundary of the present cricket ground. A broad turfed ride for equestrians was made after the scheme of Capt. Trevor, its course being diverted to the north of the Gardens so as to pass immediately to the north of the Pagoda block and then in a north-easterly direction round the cricket ground up to the Band Stand, the triangular space enclosed between the ride, the Strand and the Auckland Road being reserved for the Gardens.[17]

Towards the close of the nineteenth century the evening stroll at the Eden Gardens was reserved for the Calcutta Elite, and, if not in uniform, one had to assume a top hat and frockcoat in order to mingle there with the high and mighty. The advent of the twentieth century saw the Indians also enjoying the Gardens and listening to the military band playing in the bandstand. The gardens were well laid out, the oblong tank could be used for the purpose of pleasure boating and to the east was the famous Eden Gardens cricket ground known throughout the world for its lush green. Old-timers would remember the tall trees surrounding the cricket ground that cast their friendly shadow on the stands, and the afternoon breeze from the river that came through them to cool down the spectators scorched in the mid-day sun.

Figure 33: The Bengal Council House 1931
Photo courtesy Calcutta Historical Society

The Calcutta Cricket Club formed in 1825/26 prepared the ground, set a fence round it and built a fine makeshift pavillion along the south-western part of the cricket ground. As the whole Maidan is under the control of the military authorities, they would not allow any *pucca* structures in the Maidan area. Eventually the Cricket Association of Bengal was formed and they took over the management and control of the ground. The Eden Gardens was a popular venue for Cricket Test Matches between India and visiting cricket teams. The cricket ground was renamed Ranji Stadium after Prince Ranjitsingh, a famous cricketer. The first block of the stadium came up in 1950/51 and gradually the whole stadium was built up. The beautiful tall trees were felled. The B. C. Roy Club House replaced the quaint pavillion, and the old dreamy atmosphere is now completely gone. Several other structures have by now eaten into the Eden Gardens. Most of these are architecturally drab and in the typical style of PWD buildings all over the country. They include the Akashvani Bhavan that houses the offices and studios of the Calcutta station of All India Radio, to the north-east of the cricket ground; and the Netaji Indoor Stadium and Khudiram Anushilan Kendra at the western end of the ground.

The road north of the Eden Gardens is called Auckland Road, after the Governor-General who was the creator of the Eden Gardens.

There are only two buildings in the street. The first, diagonally opposite the Akashvani, is the West Bengal Legislative Assembly House, now called the Bidhan Sabha. The new

Bengal Legislative Council House was inaugurated by Sir Stanley Jackson, Governor of Bengal. The Bengal Legislative Council was first set up as a separate entity in 1862 and appears to have sat in a room of what was then the Government of India Legislative Department, close to the Town Hall.

On completion of the Rotunda built by Sir Ashley Eden at the western end of the Writers' Buildings, the Bengal Legislative Council moved there in 1883. The Rotunda remained its home till 1910 when it moved first to Belvedere and then three years later to the Council Chamber of the Government House vacated by the Imperial Legislative Council on the removal of the capital to Delhi. The Council had only 12 members in 1862, all of them nominated, of whom half were officials; but by 1913 had a body of fifty with an elected majority. The reform of 1921 led to a reconstitution of the Council. Then the upper storey of the Town Hall had to be rented for its sessions till the completion of the new building.[18]

The other building on this road is on the western side opposite the Netaji Indoor Stadium. This is a new large building at 10A Auckland Road, serving as the headquarters of the West Bengal Telecommunications Circle. Now we are back on the Strand Road opposite Babu Ghat.

In the vicinity of the new Telecommunications building was the headquarters of the Calcutta Volunteer Rifles with the motto 'Defence not Defiance'. For many years the headquarters was located at 6 Lindsay Street; later at 4 Humayun Place. About the year 1887 Lieutenant Frank W. Chatterton became the commandant. He did not approve of the Humayun Place accommodation and obtained permission from the Government for a new building, to be only a wooden structure.

During construction everybody could see what was going on, but the brickwork was covered with plaster, and painted, to resemble boards. Officially it was a temporary wooden hut, removable at any time.

On 1 April 1889, Lord Lansdowne formally declared the building open and inspected the inside of the building. While walking downstairs he happened to put his hand on one of a line of hat pegs which with some inches of plaster came away with great ease showing bright red brickwork underneath. The Viceroy looked surprised after what he had said about a wooden structure.[19]

On the banks of the river just north of the Babu Ghat was the Club and boathouse of the Calcutta Rowing Club, founded 1858. The first boat races in Calcutta have been traced back to 25 July 1813, when seven sailing boats competed on the Hooghly. On 4 June next year, there were several rowing matches, with boats of several kinds participating. The crowded state of the river was the complaint of W. H. Carey in 1882. The Calcutta Rowing Club moved to the newly dug Dhakuria Lakes (Rabindra Sarobar) in 1928.[20]

The membership of the Club was for many years restricted to Europeans only. This prompted Indians to establish a rowing club only for Indians The Lake Club in 1932. The

Club Constitution to this day bars Europeans from permanent membership, though the Calcutta Rowing Club opened its doors to Indians well after Independence.

The next building on the Strand before Esplanade Row West is the Calcutta Swimming Club, yet another example of an exclusively European establishment until the 1970s, when a Marxist State Minister forcibly entered the Club and commanded them to allow Indian members. The forerunner of the Club, the Calcutta Swimming Bath, was opened in 1887.

Esplanade Row West

When the construction of the new Fort William was started in 1757 an Esplanade was formed out of the jungle surrounding the new Fort, extending northward to a new road, Esplanade Row, extending from Chand Paul Ghat to Dharamtalla and called *Chand Paul Ghat ka Samna Rasta*. The area grew rapidly and had soon become a fashionable residential area.

In 1761 many old buildings were pulled down in the Esplanade and an amount of Rs. 5,727 was given out as compensation.[21] In May 1780 Mrs. Fay wrote, 'Esplanade Row seems to be composed of palaces; the whole range, except what is taken up by the Government and Council Houses, is occupied by the principal gentlemen in the settlement.'[22]

Esplanade Row: Late Eighteenth Century

THE NEW COURT HOUSE

This dignified building with an open colonnade along its south facade was leased by the Council from Archibald Keir in 1773 for government offices and again in November 1780 as the new Court House. Here, after additions and alterations, the Supreme Court met for the first time on 2 January 1782; and Hickey, on his return from England in 1783, found 'it being a noble pile of buildings, close to the edge of the river at Chandpaul Ghat, and in which Sir Elijah (Impey), with his family resided.' Impey had by then given up his residence at the site of the present day Loreto House.[23]

The new Court House was the place of activity of Sir William Jones, who came out as a judge in 1783. Every afternoon scholars would assemble in his chamber for studies in oriental subjects. Jones used to walk all the way to the Court from his residence at Garden Reach.

William Hickey notes in his diary:

The present Court House is the private property of Mr. Kear (Keir), to whom the Company pays a rent of near four thousand pounds sterling a year. The court is held at the east end, the judge's bench is in a recess under the dome (on the extreme right).

This house is delightfully situated upon the banks of the river, and quite open to the southward (the prevailing wind in this country). It is upon the Esplanade about a mile from the Fort.

Behind the Court were the residences of Sir Elija Impey and later Sir Robert Chambers, the Chief Justice after Impey. Mr. Justice Hyde resided in a house where later the Town Hall was built. He took this house on rent on his arrival in 1774, and had paid rent to the amount of fifteen thousand pounds. Next lived advocate William Dunkin, who was a great friend of William Hickey. Between his house and the Accountant General's office was the first residence of William Hickey. Hickey writes:

I found the house delightfully situated upon the Esplanade, open to the southward and eastward, and commanding an extensive view both up and down the river, to which it was close. The only reasonable objection that could be made was its being *cutcha*, that is built with mud instead of mortar... . For this house we agreed to pay three hundred sicca rupees per month' (vol. II, pp. 133–34).

Hickey writes again:

In the month of July (1784) a house upon the Esplanade, the best and most airy situation in Calcutta, becoming vacant, I had the good fortune to procure it and immediately took possession. The building itself was very old and in a decayed state, but the beauty of the view from it, and its vicinity to the Court House made it a most desirable residence for me (vol. III, p. 236).

But the house was so dilapidated that Hickey decided to move elsewhere; the landlord agreed to pull it down and build a new house and offered a set of rooms to Hickey. Hickey moved temporarily to a house in Council House Street. The new house was ready in 1790. Hickey was back:

In March 1790 my new mansion being finished and very handsome I removed into it. I furnished it in such a style as gained universal approbation and acquired me the reputation of possessing great taste. The principal apartments were ornamented with some immense looking-glasses, also with a number of beautiful pictures and prints, forming altogether a choice and valuable collection. The expense was enormous, but as I looked only to pleasant times, having no idea I should ever be able to lay up a fortune, I was indifferent about the prices of things purchasing every article I felt any inclination for. When completed my house was pronounced to be the most elegantly fitted up of any in Calcutta and in fact there was no one like it. Some of my facetious acquaintances christened it "Hickey's picture and print warehouse" (vol. III, pp. 357–58).

Hickey was an attorney, and, living near the Court House, he became popular in Calcutta society. He writes, 'Notwithstanding I lived so dissipated a life in point of drinking and late hours, no man laboured harder. I was always at my desk before seven in the mornings, and with break of half an hour for breakfast, never ceased work until dinner, after which, unless upon emergencies, I never took pen in hand.'

It was time for Hickey to move once again:

I resolved to look for another residence, and in March following 1794 closed with Sir Robert Chambers, the Chief Justice, for his elegant mansion built by Thomas Lyon, out of the very best materials. It had to me, as an officer of the Court, the great advantage of being situated immediately behind the Court House, with which it had a door of communication, so that I could at any time when my presence was required either in Court or in the Sheriff's office to be there in two minutes from my apartment. This capital house was certainly one of the best in Calcutta, I took on lease for five years at four hundred and fifty sicca rupees a month' (vól. IV, pp. 115–117).

Hickey lived in this house behind the Supreme Court until he left for England in 1808. There was an advertisement in the Calcutta Gazette of Thursday, 24 December 1807:

Valuable property to be sold by Public Auction
By TULLOH & COMPANY
On Monday the 25th January 1808
At his house adjoining the Supreme Court
The Truly Elegant Property of
WILLIAM HICKEY ESQ.
Returning to Europe

The items included valuable household ware, furnitures, collections and his buggy and horses, palanquins, etc. The auction was later postponed until 8 February 1808.

With the departure of Hickey, Calcutta lost a very colourful character, who had made quite good use of his camera obscura and drawn sketches of Calcutta.

THE COUNCIL HOUSE

The new Council House was built across the road from the Treasury Buildings (in the Raj Bhavan compound). It was designed by Colonel Fortnom, the Civil Architect. It was a building of two storeys occupying three sides of a quadrangle. This new Council House was also used as the Governor's residence, before Buckingham House was rented. Warren

Hastings lived in this house for a number of years and in a Council Minute he states that 'it was the habitation of former Governors,' from which it is not possible to draw any other conclusion than that it was occupied by Clive, Verelst and Cartier.[24] The building lasted from 1765 to 1800, when it was demolished to make way for the present Government House. It has been depicted in the maps of Mark Wood (1784) and Upjohn (1794), and is illustrated in the coloured drawings of Daniell (1788) and Baillie (1794). It was in a private room of this house, that in August 1780, Philip Francis, after a meeting of the Council, drew Hastings aside, and handed to him the written challenge which resulted in the famous duel between them a few days later. This building had a remarkable resemblance in shape and appearance to the Factory or Government House in Old Fort William.

When Lord Wellesley decided, on his own authority, in 1798 to demolish the Council House and to purchase and pull down the adjoining Government House, he acted upon reasons which, as regards to the former, he subsequently explained in his reply of 1806 to the censure of the Court of Directors in 1805. In paragraphs 143 and 144 he declared that the

Council House did not afford the necessary accommodation for the meeting of the Council and for the public officers attached to the Government, exposing the members of the Government and the public officers immediately attached to it, to serious personal inconvenience, and subjecting the transaction of the public business to material obstruction.

Figure 34: The Buckingham House
Photo courtesy Calcutta Historical Society

(He went on to say) That the Council House was an old and extremely decayed building, and that for the long period of time which had elapsed since the principal part of the Council House had been erected, from the various alterations which it had undergone, and from the bad quality of materials of which it had in general been constructed, the building was actually in danger of falling, and that the expense of reconstructing the Council House, even on the same confined scale would have subjected the Company to a charge of Sicca Rupees 1,20,000 or £ 15,000, an expense which must have been incurred in the course of a few years. The expense alone of repairing the Council House would have been Sicca Rupees 43, 243 or £5,405.[25]

BUCKINGHAM HOUSE

This was a large building immediately to the east of the Council House. The house belonged to Mohammed Reza Khan, Nawab of Chitpore, who bought it from a European for Sicca Rupees 1,20,000. During the tenure of Warren Hastings, the Company rented it from the Nawab at Rs. 1,000 per month for the residence of the Governor-General.

The ground plan of this house shows a building covering three sides of a quadrangle. Its external appearance was that of a two-storeyed mansion, the rooms of which were protected from the sun on the southern side by an arched verandah on the ground floor and a closed one above. From either side of it there projected towards the Esplanade two long one-storeyed wings or arms, presumably containing offices or quarters of the staff, and enclosing between them a courtyard of fair size, shut off from the Maidan by a low wall with pillars and railings upon it, and pierced by two tall pillared gateways.

The flat roof of the mansion had a white plastered balustrade with urns on the skyline, and a single projecting room, probably a sleeping chamber, in a tower or belvedere, with a sloping roof. Between this house and the Council House next door was a garden thickly planted with trees. The house has been depicted by Thomas Daniell in a painting in 1788. This house was taken on rent by the Company not earlier than 1773, but they had made use of it before 1773. We are indebted to Admiral J. B. Stavorinus, who accompanied the Dutch Governor at Chinsurah making a state visit to Calcutta in 1770, for the information 'that it was a very handsome building, provided with many and roomy apartments, all furnished in the European style, and hung with damasked silk.'[26]

In June 1779, two years after his marriage to Baroness Imhoff, Hastings is found complaining about this new Government House, of having to use it for his own accommodation and that of his family, and for Government business, and the Council therefore proposing to rent a house owned by the late Colonel Fortnom on a one year lease for Sicca Rupees 1200 per month. This was the house at 7 Hastings Street.[27]

The French traveller, M de Grandpré, who came to Calcutta in 1789. while Lord Cornwallis was the Governor-General, wrote of the residence of the latter:

The Governor of the English Settlements East of the Cape of Good Hope resides in Calcutta...As there is no palace yet built for him, he lives in a house in Esplanade, opposite the citadel. The house is handsome, but by no means equal to what it ought to be for a personage of so much importance. Many private individuals in this town have houses as good: and if the Governor were disposed to any extraordinary luxury, he must curb his inclination for want of the necessary accommodation of room. The house of the Governor of Pondicherry is much more magnificent.[28]

The Buckingham House was finally purchased from the son of the Late Nawab Reza Khan, Nawab Dilawar Jang, only to be pulled down in 1798.

Esplanade Row West: Nineteenth Century and Later

THE HIGH COURT

The New Court House, which housed the Supreme Court, along with three residential buildings, was demolished to make way for one of the most impressive buildings of the city—The High Court.

Figure 35: The High Court, Calcutta

In 1771, the Directors of the Company told the Government of Bengal that it was their intention to stand forth as Dewan, and, by the agency of the Company's servants, to take upon themselves the entire care of the management of the revenues. This led to transference not only of the financial but also of the judicial control from Murshidabad to Calcutta. The two principal Mahomedan courts at the time were:

The Sudder Dewani Adaulat for justice in civil concerns, and
The Sudder Nizamat Adaulat, the criminal court.

In 1772, during Hastings' tenure, it was arranged that the former court should be presided over by the Governor-General and Council, assisted by learned native lawyers. The proceedings of the criminal court were to be conducted by a judge appointed by the Nawab himself. In 1790 Lord Cornwallis persuaded the Nawab to surrender his rights of appointing criminal court judges throughout the province.

In 1774, by the Charter of 26th March, a Court of Chancery and a Court of the King's Bench were established, consisting of a Chief Justice and three Puisne Judges. The jurisdiction of this body was confined within the limits of the city of Calcutta.

In 1780, the Chief Justice Sir Elijah Impey was made the sole Judge of the Sudder Dewani Adaulat, thus taking the place of Governor-General and Council. Two years later, the Governor-General and Council again assumed charge of the civil court of appeal, Lord Wellesley objecting to the combination of judicial with legislative and executive functions; and introducing a regulation that the Sudder Dewani and Nizamat Adaulats should be selected from the covenanted servants of the Company, not being members of the Supreme Council.

In 1862, after many changes, the Supreme Court was united with the Sudder Dewani Adaulat, and the Calcutta High Court was born. The design was made by the Government Architect, Walter Granville. The design in florid Gothic style was generally inspired by the Clothes Hall or Town Hall at Ypres, Belgium.

The main entrance is through the handsome central tower on the south side which leads into the magnificent quadrangle. Facing the Maidan is a beautiful row of pillars running along the lower storey. The capitals of the colonnade are of Caen stone beautifully sculptured, each one having a different design. The tower is 180 feet high, and is fifteen feet higher than the Ochterlony Monument, but the massiveness of the building conceals its real height. Entering beneath the tower we find a grand staircase and Chantrey's statue of Sir Edward Hyde East (Chief Justice, 1813–1822), one of the founders of the Hindoo College. The first floor contains seven courts, the Judges' and the Bar Libraries, and sundry offices. On the upper floor are the offices of the Advocate General, the Legal Remembrancer, etc.[29]

There are some valuable paintings in the Judges' Library, including portraits of Sir Robert Chambers, Chief Justice; Sir Lawrence Peel, Chief Justice (by Grant); Sir Edward Ryan, Chief Justice (by Martin Grant). Portraits of Sir Elijah Impey, Chief Justice (by John Zoffany) and Sir Henry Russell, Chief Justice (by George Chinnery) adorned the Principal Court, Appellate Side. In the second Branch Court, Appellate Side, east of the principal staircase there is a painting of the Hon'ble Sambhu Nath Pandit, who was the first Indian to sit on the Bench of the High Court.

The Principal Court, Original Side, had a fine portrait of Sir Elijah Impey by Tilly Kettle, sent to the Dhaka High Court after Partition. But there is a fine portrait by George Chinnery of Sir Frank Workman Macnaghten, Puisne Judge.

The Judges' Library has the portrait of an interesting man, Mr. Binny Trevor, ICS, Judge of the Sudder Dewani Adaulat from 1856 to 1862 and a Puisne Judge of the High Court from 1862 to 1867. He was one of the Judges named in the Charter by which the High Court at Fort William was constituted in 1862. In the Great Rent Case, which was heard by the whole Bench of fifteen Judges, he boldly differed from the Chief Justice and carried the day. As a poet describes:

Then first his judgement Trevorus
Read out in language clear,
And such a silence then was kept
A pin's drop you might hear.
At length when all grew weary
And sleep proclaimed her reign,
Great Trevorus thought it was time enough
To close his lengthen'd strain.
And this is how the learned Judge
The Rent Case did decide:
He settled that a tenant
Who twelve years should abide
Upon his landlord's right
To share the rent, and landlord
Should get it as he might.[30]

P.B. Chakravarti was the first Indian to become a permanent Chief Justice of the Calcutta High Court. He had joined the High Court as a Puisne Judge in April 1945. Notable Indians who have served the High Court as Puisne Judges in the colonial period include Sambhu Nath Pandit (1863–67), Dwaraka Nath Mitter (1867–74), Ramesh Chandra Mitter (1874–1890), Sir Chunder Madhab Ghosh (1885–1907), Sir Gooroodas Banerji (1888–1904), Sir Ashutosh Mukherjee (1904–1924) and Sir Ashutosh Chaudhuri (1912–1920). Many eminent lawyers have attained fame and prosperity in the court rooms and many a legal battle have been won or lost here.

The High Court has two sides, the Original Side and the Appellate Side. The Original Side deals with original cases and the Appellate Side with appeals from the districts, as also from the City Civil Court. Under the present Advocates Act 1961, all branches of the legal profession have been unified, but in the city of Calcutta, the dual system has been retained.

THE BAR LIBRARY CLUB

This is a club of the Barristers of the High Court. It has a large room full of open shelves of enormous proportions with thousands of leather-bound books and a gallery of portraits of past giants like Deshbandhu Chittaranjan Das, W.C. Bonnerjee, Deshapriya Jatindramohan Sengupta and Abdul Rasul, among others. There is a smaller room of the Library (once the rendezvous of elders, and still known as the 'House of Lords'), containing some rare books and more portraits.

The first Barrister to be enrolled in the Supreme Court at Calcutta was Thomas Ferrer who joined on 22 October 1774, the date of its inauguration. He was the only Barrister available to defend Maharaja Nandakumar.

> The Bar Library Club is both a library and a club. As a club it has been like the Inns of Court in England, a centre of goodfellowship. The Club is a refuge where rivals meet and shake hands after bitter fights in Court. It is the privilege of each member to mix, on equal terms, with every other member, however big in earning, deep in learning, venerable in age or great in pretensions.

The Library is one of the best Law Libraries in India. Among its rare collections are: (i) A Quarto volume containing 40 Charters granted to the East India Compamy from 1601 to 1761; and (ii) Manuscript Notebooks and reports in the handwriting of Mr. Justice John Hyde (1774–96).

During his long term of office as a Puisne Judge of the Supreme Court, Mr. Justice Hyde kept notes of cases that came up before him. Frequently he had differences with his Chief, Sir Elijah Impey. Rarely did he miss an opportunity of including, in his notes, interesting points of law and administration, together with his own comments on men and matters. His notebooks are really a gold mine of historical evidence. Unfortunately, the part of his notebooks covering the trial of Maharaja Nanda Kumar has disappeared mysteriously.[31]

HIGH COURT BAR ASSOCIATION

This was formerly known as the Sudder Court Bar Library. The last sitting of the Sudder Dewani Adaulat took place on 30 June 1862. After the amalgamation of the former Court and the Supreme Court to form the new High Court, forty members of the Sudder Court Bar Library formed a new Association which they called Vakeels' Association. The native *vakeels* received high praise for their legal acumen from the then Chief Justice, Sir Barnes Peacock. The High Court Bar Library at that time was called Barristers' Library, with its membership open only to Europeans. So when Michael Madhusudan Dutta joined the Calcutta High Court as a Barrister, he was denied membership of the exclusive Club and could be a member only of the Vakeels' Association.

Dr. Rajendra Prasad, the first President of India, joined the Calcutta High Court as a *vakeel* in August 1911. Two members of the Association, Dr. Naresh Chandra Sengupta and Dr. Radha Benode Pal, attained international repute.

On 14 August 1928, Ramdayal Dey moved that the Vakeels' Association should be named 'Bar Association', to which two amendments were moved, one for 'Advocates' and the other for 'Advocates Association'. The amendments were lost and the Vakeels' Association became the High Court Bar Association in 1928.

THE INCORPORATED LAW SOCIETY OF CALCUTTA

The Law Society, and its members, the solicitors and attorneys-at-Law of the Calcutta High Court have a distinguished history.

Old documents from 1851 record a proposal mooted by the attorneys of the Supreme Court for construction of suitable rooms to be used as the Attorneys' Library and accommodation rooms. Once it was sanctioned, the first Attorneys' Library was constructed with funds raised by the attorneys amongst themselves.

Before the present Law Society came into existence, the attorneys of the city had an association known as the Calcutta Attorneys' Association. On 20 March 1908 the Association met at the Attorneys' Library to consider the advisability of forming an Incorporated Law Society of Calcutta, which found approval among members and the Incorporated Law Society of Calcutta was incorporated on 6 June 1908. Now housed in the High Court buildings, this association is an important and integral part of the legal system.

With the manifold increase of work in the High Court after Independence, annexe buildings have been added, merging and mixing well with the old architectural beauty. Shaded corridors or bridges connect the annexe with the old building.

THE TOWN HALL

The first Town Hall of Calcutta was in the Old Court House, where the social gatherings, balls, etc. were held. That building was demolished in 1792.

Figure 36: The Town Hall

The British inhabitants of Calcutta resolved in two meetings held in 1793 and 1804, to erect marble statues of the Marquises Cornwallis and Wellesley in some prominent part of the Town of Calcutta.

The committee appointed to carry out the resolutions of the meeting in 1804 suggested to the Government, the necessity of constructing a Town Hall for the reception of the statues, out of funds to be raised by public lotteries. The suggestion was approved by the Government.

The first Town Hall Lottery had a total number of 5,600 tickets at 60 sicca rupees each, of which 1,331 carried prizes amounting to rupees three lakh, and 3,699 were blanks. The second lottery was arranged in 1805 and advertised 'under the sanction and patronage of His Excellency the Most Hon'ble the Governor General in Council. This lottery was for five lakh sicca rupees. The public on this occasion were informed that

> as the profits arising from the present lottery will be inadequate to the purpose of completing the public edifice proposed to be constructed a lottery will be offered annually to the public, under the same sanction and superintendence until the requisite funds shall have been provided.

That this promise was kept is proved by the discovery of the plates of the third and fourth Town Hall Lottery tickets.[32]

Sufficient funds for the commencement of the building were available in 1806, plans and estimates were sanctioned the next year, and Colonel J. Garstin, the Chief Engineer, was entrusted with the construction. The construction started on 1 December 1807 and was completed on 22 March 1814, when it was placed under the charge of a Committee of Management, called the Town Hall Committee, and one Mr. William Hastie was appointed steward. The total cost came to rupees seven lakh, which was quite high for the period.

It is a fine building, built in the Doric style of architecture with steps leading to a grand portico on the south. Here stood Richard Westmacott's beautiful statue of Warren Hastings, which was later removed to the Victoria Memorial Hall.

The carriage entrance is to the north under a lofty covered portico. The building consists of two storeys, and was originally used for public meetings, receptions, balls and concerts that generally took place on the upper floor, which is boarded with teak with a 30 feet high ceiling. The great saloon which runs end to end of the upper floor of the building is 172 feet in length and 65 feet in width, and is divided into a centre room and two aisles by a double row of pillars. At the western end there is a raised wooden balcony with a flight of stairs. On the south front there are two corner rooms 43 feet by 21 feet, and a central one 82 feet by 30 feet, the latter situated immediately over the portico. These rooms were utilized as card and supper rooms. For many years the central room was used for the meetings of the Corporation of Calcutta until the opening in 1905 of the Municipal Council Chamber in the new offices at Corporation Street (Surendra Nath Banerjee Road).

The large hall on the lower floor is paved with marble and rises to a height of 23 feet. It was very rarely used. At the western end stood Bacon's fine statue of Lord Cornwallis, later removed to Victoria Memorial Hall. The western part of the room was sometimes used as the Municipal Magistrate's Court. As we stand in the vestibule of the northern entrance in front we see the seated marble statue of Maharaja Rama Nath Tagore, C.S.I., brother of Prince Dwaraka Nath Tagore, beautifully sculpted by E.E. Geflowski in 1880. To the right there is the bust of John Palmer, the 'Merchant Prince,' and on the left a bust of Mr. Charles Beckett Greenlaw. On both sides rise grand double staircases leading to the upper floor.

Towards the beginning of 1815 it was apprehended that the building was unsafe due to the great spring in the boarded floor of the upper floor caused by the beams having been placed at considerable distance from each other. A Committee of Engineers, appointed to inspect the building, suggested a remedial plan; but as it involved a considerable expense, which the Government was unable to meet. Nothing was done until 1818, when it was found that several pillars on the upper floor had sufferred damage consequence of their having been built of inferior materials. Accordingly, the building was put in thorough repair in 1818-19, the pillars in question were re-erected and additional beams introduced under the boarded floor. The expense of re-erecting the pillars was borne by Garstin according to the original agreement.

In 1866 the Town Hall was passed over to the late Justices of the Peace to be kept in trust for the public; and later, when Calcutta Corporation was founded, the building passed on to their hands.

The Town Hall appears in its full glory in the 1819 coloured aquatint painted by James Baillie Fraser, *A View of the Town Hall*, published in *Fraser's Views of Calcutta and its Environs*, London 1826-27. It is also depicted by Shaykh Muhammad Amir in his watercolour, *Government House and Esplanade Row from the Course, 1828-30.*

When the new High Court building was being erected, some of the courts were held at the Town Hall. On the morning of 30 September 1871, Mr. John Paxton Norman, one of the Judges of the High Court, who was officiating as the Chief Justice, was mortally wounded by a fanatic as he was ascending the steps of the northern portico of the Town Hall. He was placed in a palanquin and carried into the premises of Messrs. Thacker Spink & Co. in Government Place North, where he was laid on a table in the partners' back room. Doctors attended to him immediately, but the injuries received were fatal. Mr. Norman died shortly after midnight on the same day. Even when the firm moved to Esplanade East, the same table was kept there on the upper floor and one could see bloodstains on it which would simply not go.[33]

The Town Hall had no colour bar like some clubs and associations. It was open to all. Europeans mixed with Indians. Prince Dwarka Nath Tagore, his brother, Maharaja Rama Nath Tagore, Babu Ram Gopal Ghosh, Keshub Chunder Sen, Naba Gopal Mitra, Surendra Nath Banerjee, Mancherjee Rustomjee, the first Indian Sheriff in 1874, all added glitter to the Town Hall.

On 27 August 1891, the Sheriff of Calcutta, Mr. Muhammad Farooque Shah called a meeting at the Town Hall to condole the death of Pandit Iswar Chandra Vidyasagar. The Lieutenant Governor of Bengal, Sir Charles A. Elliot presided over the meeting. Among the notables were Maharaja Jatindra Mohan Tagore, Mr. Doorga Churn Law, Sir C. Patterson, Lord Chief Justice of Bengal, and others. The upstairs hall was overcrowded.[34]

Three years later a meeting was convened to condole the death of Bankim Chandra Chatterjee. In 1895, Sir Jagadish Chandra Bose held a demonstration of his invention in which he transmitted wireless (radio) waves through the solid wall. The waves knocked out a heavy-weight ringing bell and exploded a mine in a closed room. One of the spectators was the Lt. Governor of Bengal. This was a year before Signor Marconi announced his invention to the world, in London on 2 June 1896.[35]

In 1905 a meeting was held here to protest against the Partition of Bengal. In 1913 Rabindranath Tagore was accorded a public reception when he became a Nobel Laureate. Such is the history of the Town Hall at Calcutta. Numerous statues, busts, fine oil paintings of both British and Indians adorned the Hall. According to a reliable source some of the pictures put up in the Town Hall have been donated to the Victoria Memorial Hall, but others were allowed to wither in shreds, beyond the scope of restoration.

After Independence the Town Hall fell into disuse. The British were gone with their festive balls, concerts, farewell dinners. The new leaders of the country preferred open spaces to address the public rather than a closed hall. Various municipal offices and godowns took over the edifice, while the rest of the area was claimed by the staff for residence. The historic Town Hall was soon falling apart from official apathy.

In 1980 the Calcutta Corporation decided to demolish the Town Hall and erect a multi-storeyed office complex in its place. Calcutta lovers formed a Save Town Hall Committee. Their agitation and rising public opinion against demolition forced the Corporation to back out. But not for long; in 1987, the Calcutta Corporation decided to erect a seven-storey commercial complex on the northern lawns of the Town Hall. It was public opinion again that compelled the Government to take a decision in 1989 that the Town Hall would be preserved, and a Committee was formed with the Chief Minister of the state as the chairman.

A unique step was taken to create a fund for restoration. No Lottery Committee was possible, so 24 remarkable oil paintings by the well-known Bengali artist Bikash Bhattacharya were auctioned at the Victoria Memorial Hall, Calcutta, in January 1992. Rupees one crore and fifteen lakh were collected. A Homage Trust was formed. Some industrialists like the Gujarat Ambuja group came forward with more support.

On 14 April 1998, the restored Town Hall was handed over to the Calcutta Corporation. On 15 August 1998, the Town Hall was again opened to the public with an exhibition of paintings by members of the Tagore family. The road in front, i.e. part of the Esplanade Row West, has been decorated with old ornamental street lamps, letter boxes, troughs to contain drinking water for horses, to create an atmosphere.

The future use of the Hall is still uncertain. But this will remain as a great instance where public opinion prevented the government from destroying part of Heritage Calcutta.

Between the exit gate of the Hall and the Treasury Buildings there is a blind lane leading to an old building, which could be one of the houses where William Hickey lived. The building is now used as the Currency Office, Government of India.

As we walk past the Treasury Buildings and the Accountant General's Office, on our left is the short stretch of the Government Place West. The Esplanade Row West ends here abruptly, blocked by the huge compound of the Government House or today's Raj Bhavan, which stands on the site of the old Council House and the old tenanted Government House, the Buckingham House.

References

1. *Bengal, Past & Present*, vol. 41, 1931.
2. Campbell, Christy. *The Maharaja's Box*, London 2000, p. 119.
3. Cotton, H.E.A. op. cit. p. 268.
4. Hobbs, Major Harry. 'Calcutta Barmaids,' in *Bengal, Past & Present*, vol. 59, 1904.
5. Hyde, H.B. *Parochial Annals of Bengal*, Calcutta 1901.
6. Quoted in J.P. Losty. op. cit. p. 181.
7. Hyde, H.B. *Parochial Annals of Bengal*, pp. 109–10.
8. Cotton, H.E.A. op. cit. pp. 416–17.
9. Lahiri Chowdhury, Dhritikanta. 'Trends in Calcutta Architecture, 1690–1903', in *Calcutta—The Living City*, vol. I, p. 166.
10. Suhrawardy, Hassan. *Calcutta & Environs*, p. 84.
11. Firminger, Walter K. *Thacker's Guide to Calcutta*, Calcutta 1906, p. 139.
12. Curzon, Lord. *British Government in India*, vol. I, p. 27.
13. *McCluskie's Calcutta Directory & Guide 1906*, Calcutta 1906, p. 626.
14. *Calcutta 200 Years*, p. 63.
15. Firminger. op. cit. pp. 161–62.
16. Quoted in Losty. op. cit. p. 62.
17. 'The Eden Garden,' in *Bengal Past & Present*, vol. 27, 1924.
18. *Bengal Past & Present*, vol. XLI, 1931, p. 2.
19. Ibid. vol. LXV, 1945, p. 10.
20. *Calcutta 200 Years*, p. 144.
21. *Bengal Past & Present*, vol. XLIII, 1932 p. 128.
22. Quoted in Losty. op. cit. pp. 44–45.
23. Losty. op. cit. p. 61.
24. Curzon. op. cit. vol. I, p. 10.
25. Ibid. p. 34.
26. Quoted in Losty. op. cit. p. 58.
27. Losty. op. cit. p. 59.
28. Quoted in Curzon. op. cit. vol. I, p. 18.
29. Firminger, W.K. *Thacker's Guide*, pp. 41–42.
30. Cotton, H.E.A. op. cit. p. 579.
31. Cf. Anil Chandra Ganguly, in *The High Court at Calcutta: Centenary Souvenir, 1862–1962*, pp. 69–71.
32. Dunbar, Roberts. 'The Town Hall Lotteries,' in *Bengal Past & Present*, 1.1. 1907.
33. *Bengal Past & Present*, vol. 41, 1931.
34. From the 'Diary of Hemendra Prasad Ghosh,' in *Bengal Past & Present*, vol. CVI, 1987, p. 85.
35. Mitra, Rathin. *Calcutta Then and Now*, Calcutta, p. 67.

Chapter Nine

The Government House, Calcutta

The Government House (Raj Bhavan today) owes its existence to Marquis Wellesley, Governor-General (1798-1805), who assumed office on 17 May and went into occupation of the Government House, known as Buckingham House, described in the previous chapter.

Lord Wellesley was dissatisfied not only with the state of disrepair in which he found the building but also with the meagre accommodation provided. Within a month he had decided to build a more suitable residence and is credited with having declared that India should be ruled from a Palace and not from a Counting House; with the ideas of a Prince, not with those of a retail dealer in muslin and indigo. Without consulting or even informing

Figure 37: The Government House, North Front

the Court of Directors in England of what he was doing, he proceeded at once to put his plan into execution and called on Captain Wyatt (an Engineer Officer and nephew of the well-known English architect James Wyatt) and Edward Tirretta, East India Company's Civil Architect, to prepare plans for the building. Capt. Wyatt's design was preferred and accordingly he is the architect responsible for the Government House. The Chief Engineer, Major General Cameron, was then instructed to furnish an estimate of the cost which he put at £66,150 which was accepted and the work was put in hand forthwith.[1]

The Buckingham House with its gardens were purchased from Nawab Dilawar Jang for £13,450. William Hickey writes:

Not only the site of the old Government House, but taking in the Council House and about sixteen other private mansions, many of them not having been erected about five years, the whole of which were pulled down, the ground upon which they had stood being cleared away to create a superb open square area, in the middle of which his meditated palace was to stand.[2]

The total cost of the land came up to £71,437.

There was no ceremonial laying of a foundation stone as the Governor-General was away at Madras leading the campaign against Tipu Sultan. The first brick was laid on 5 February 1799 by one of the supervisors.

The House was completed on 18 January 1803, although its construction had been sufficiently advanced to permit official parties and levees being held in it from April 1802 onwards. As a matter of fact, Lord Wellesley took up his residence in it many months before the last artisan was out of the house.

The cost of the building was £87,790 and £18,560 was spent on furniture and plate, so that with the £71,437 spent on acquiring the land on which it stood, the total cost was about £178,000 in addition to which £3,433 was spent to lay two new streets (Government Place North and Wellesley Place).[3] With the building of the new Government House came quite a few changes. The Esplanade Row running straight from Chand Paul Ghat to Dhurrumtollah was cut into two as the southern compound of the building extended further south of the street, thus the Esplanade Row became Esplanade Row West and the Esplanade East. The Wheler Place behind the Buckingham House and the Council House, with all its buildings, disappeared under the northern block and the carriageway. The design of the Government House is a variation on the plan of Keddleston Hall in Derbyshire which was built for Lord Scarsdale, the great-great-grandfather of Lord Curzon of Keddleston, in the years 1759-1770 by the well-known architect Robert Adam. The design was remarkably suitable with a few alterations for a tropical climate.

The scheme of a great central pile with curving corridors radiating from its four angles to detached wings, each constituting a house in itself, was admirably adapted to a climate where every breath of air from whatever quarter must be seized. It resembles Keddleston Hall in the broad external features of shape, design and orientation, in the extreme dimensions from east to west, in the concentration of the main state rooms in the middle pile, in the placing of a great marble hall supported by columns and in the superimposition of a dome above the southern facade, but the two houses differ radically both in material and arrangement. Keddleston was built mainly of sandstone and partly of brick, while the Government House is built entirely of brick covered over with white plaster. They differ also in completeness of construction, for only two of the projecting wings have been finished at Keddleston, while Government House has all four. Government House also has a semi-circular projecting portico and colonnade on the south front and spacious verandâhs there to get more air.[4]

Before we proceed on a tour of the great building, let us go back to the beginning. A drawing of the new Government House from the south-east was made by James Moffat in early 1802, as we do not see the four great ceremonial gateways, based on Adam's archways at Syon House, that were already in place by April. The building is not yet complete and there are no perimeter fences.

When the Government House was being built Lord Wellesley resided at the Government House in the new Fort William. Wellesley was jubilant when his vision took shape in record time. On 4 May 1802, the anniversary of the fall of Seringapattam, he gave a breakfast to seven hundred of the principal ladies and gentlemen of the settlement and on this occasion, the great apartments of the new Government House were opened for the first time.

On 26 January 1803, a grand gala entertainment was held at the Government House. Though Lord Wellesley was supposed to have been residing at the Treasury Buildings at that time, on that evening he rode in state from the Fort William to the Government House. The ramparts of the Fort, the shipping in the river and the Esplanade were all brilliantly illuminated. Lord Valentia, who arrived in Calcutta on the same day and attended the ball, has left a vivid account in his *Voyages and Travels*:

At the upper end of the largest room was placed a very rich Persian carpet, and in the centre of that, a *musnad* of crimson and gold, formerly composing part of the ornaments of Tipoo Sultan's throne. On this was a rich chair and stool of state for Lord Wellesley; on each side, three chairs for the members of the Council and Judges. Down to the door on both sides of the room were seats for the ladies, in which they were placed according to the strict rules of precedency, which is here regulated by the seniority of the husband in the Company's service... . The room was not sufficiently lighted up, yet still the effect was beautiful. The row of *chunam* pillars, which supported each side, together with the rest of the room, were of a shining white, that gave a contrast to the different dresses of the company... . About 800 people were present, who found sufficient room at supper, in the marble hall below, thence they were summoned about one o'clock to the different verandahs to see the fireworks and illuminations. The side of the citadel facing the palace was covered with a blaze of light.... . The rockets were superior to any I have ever beheld. They were discharged from mortars on the ramparts of the citadel. The colours, also, of several of the pieces were excellent; and the merit of singularity, at least, might be attributed to a battle between two elephants of fire, which by rollers were driven against each other.[5]

The Grand Entrance with its great ceremonial stairway faces north with its large gravelled carriageway. Lord Ellenborough (1842-44) set up on a plinth in front of the Grand Staircase the huge iron gun mounted on a winged dragon with red glass eyes and scaled convolutions of the tail ending in a forked point. Around the plinth are ten iron guns with embossed Chinese inscriptions planted upright in the ground. The inscription on the plinth reads:

Edward, Lord Ellenborough, Governor General of India in Council, erected this trophy of guns taken from the Chinese, in commemoration of the peace dictated under the walls of Nankin by the Naval and Military forces of England and India under the command of Vice-Admiral Sir William Parker and of Lieutenant-General Sir Hugh Gough (1842).

THE CENTRAL PILE

The Ground Floor

The Public Entrance is in the north under the Grand Staircase, and the Private Entrance is at the southern end. The Public, after entering through the entrance, pass a portico and enter the North Hall to come to the Central Hall, which was paved with grey marble by Lord Curzon. The Private entree guests similarly come through the South Hall into the Central Hall. Four staircases lead to the upper floors. During a large banquet or ball the entire central hall was used as a cloak room.

The First Floor

The Grand Staircase leads into the Breakfast Room or small Dining Room. The Breakfast Room once had a full-length painting of Earl Amherst, Governor-General (1823-28), on its walls. Lord Amherst was a great stickler for rules, pomp and ceremony and never moved from one room of Government House to another without a long train of mace-bearers preceding him: when riding on the Maidan with his wife it was a rule that she would never advance beyond his horse's quarters. We are indebted to their daughter, Lady Sarah Elizabeth, for the set of fine drawings she made of the Government House from different angles. The Amhersts also started the first flower garden in the compound.

The Marble Hall

We come to the Marble Hall through the Breakfast Room. It consists of a central nave separated by pillars from the side aisles in the style of a Roman atrium. It has always been used as the State Dining Room; in case of a large attendance the tables being extended to the Breakfast Room. It was also used for sittings of the Governor-General's Legislative Council when a large attendance was anticipated. Perhaps the most famous of such occasions was when the Ilbert Bill was discussed during the Viceroyalty of Lord Ripon in January 1884. Like the other State Rooms on this floor this is paved with grey marble and lit with lustre chandeliers. It is on record that these chandeliers were the property of Col. Claude Martin in his palace at Lucknow. They were bought in an auction and since then adorn the Government House. Mrs. Vijayalakshmi Pandit, sister of India's first Prime Minister Jawaharlal Nehru, was once the guest of Dr. Harendra Coomar Mukherjee, Governor of West Bengal. She admired the chandeliers and politely enquired whether they could be removed to the official residence of the Prime Minister at New Delhi.   Dr. Mukherjee did not agree and Mrs. Pandit did not broach the subject again.

When the house was first built the pillars were covered with the exquisite *chunam* or plaster said to have been made of burnt shells, for which India had been long famous, and looked like burnished ivory. In the passage of time the *chunam* decayed and the pillars were painted. When Lord Mayo came in 1809 he found all the pillars painted black and the teak doors white. Lord Mayo took the matter up in earnest; *chunam* workers were brought in from Madras and pillars on this floor and the upper floor were renovated.

When Lord Curzon took over as Viceroy he found them again in great decay, but the art of *chunam* work had in the meantime perished. Artificers from different parts of India were brought in to do the renovation.

Along the east and west walls of the Marble Hall are ranged more than life-size marble busts of the Twelve Caesars. Lord Curzon found them 'reposed upon the most hideous painted wooden pedestals, out of all proportion to the size of the bust'.[7] Curzon installed new pedestals made of the best Indian marble.

There are spacious *verandahs* on each side of the Marble Hall which Lord Curzon says were not part of the original building but were added afterwards. The west one was used as a service pantry and the east one for playing of the band on festive occasions. The south portion of the east *verandah* was screened off by Lord Curzon as he found it a very cool and convenient lounge for coffee and cigarettes after lunch.

The Throne Room

Leading from the south end of the Marble Hall is the Throne Room. Till the middle of the nineteenth century the throne was placed and levees were held in the Ball Room on the second floor. Lord Wellesley used the Throne Room for distribution of prizes to the students of the College of Fort William as well as the Hindoo College.

Figure 38: The Government House, Throne Room

It was again Lord Curzon who brought the Throne Room back to its full glory, where Princes were received, addresses were presented, levees* and drawing rooms were held and where guests assembled in order to be presented before large banquets. He also used it for *durbars*. King George V held a Levee, an Investiture and a Court in this room in 1911, and the then Prince of Wales, later King Edward VIII, a Levee in 1921.

Now the Governors of West Bengal are sworn in this room. At the west end of the room is a red lacquer *taktaposh*, i.e. ceremonial seat, which belonged to Theebaw, the last King of Burma. Under the Throne canopy is a four-legged sofa with silver lion arms which was brought from Belvedere and is said to have belonged to Warren Hastings.

There is a State seat made of gold in Oriental design known as Tipu Sultan's throne. Again we have to rely upon Lord Curzon's meticulous research to get to the truth. He found four brass rings at the four corners at the bottom, and suggested that it could very well be an elephant seat or *howdah* or the main part of a sedan chair used by Tipu Sultan. In this room there are also two great silver chairs of State, said to have been made by Messrs. Hamilton & Co., Calcutta under the orders of Lord Northbrook. Now to a sad ceremony that took place in the Throne Room. On 8 February 1872, the Viceroy Lord Mayo was stabbed to death by the hand of a Pathan convict at Port Blair, Andaman Islands. Ten days later his body reached Calcutta, and lay in State for two days on 19 and 20 February in the Throne Room.

---

* Levee is an archaic word used in those times and means an assembly of visitors/guests at a formal reception given by a sovereign or his representative.

Figure 39: The Government House, Ball Room

The Second Floor

The Southern Drawing Room, just above the Throne Room, was furnished lavishly by Lord Wellesley who placed some handsome mirrors on the wall. But Miss Emily Eden (sister of Lord Auckland), who found that they had all lost their quicksilver, sold them off in an auction in 1841 and was surprised to receive £400 for them. With this sum, she set about gilding the Ball Room. The room was properly furnished during the short-lived reign of Lord Mayo (1869-72) in preparation for the visit to Calcutta in 1870-71 of Queen Victoria's second Son, His Royal Highness the Duke of Edinburgh, the first member of the Royal Family to visit India.

History was recreated in the Central Ball Room, when on 26 January 1903, Lord Curzon gave a fancy dress ball to commemorate its opening with great revelry exactly one hundred years ago, and participants were dressed in the typical costumes of 1803. The costume worn by Lord Curzon was a replica of that worn by Lord Wellesley and is now in the Victoria Memorial Hall. From 1803 to about 1863 this room was used as the Throne Room where *durbars*, levees, receptions, investitures took place.

Like the Marble Hall and the other public rooms, it is lit by a large number of cut-glass chandeliers. A good many of them were taken away to New Delhi with the shifting of the Capital, and only one of the original bought from General Claude Martin still remains.

The North Ball Room was a minor Ball Room, scarcely a room.

Each wing of the Government House is a complete building going up to three storeys.

The south-western wing has always been marked for the domestic and official use of the Governor-General, though it was surrendered for illustrious visitors like the then Prince of Wales (later King George V) and his Consort during their visit in 1905-06 and again when they came to Calcutta as King and Queen in 1911-12. The big room on the first floor looking on to the garden was throughout the work and study room of the Governor-General with the room for the ADC in waiting and a waiting room for the visitors on one side; and rooms for his private secretary, assistant private secretary and a typist (when typewriters came into vogue) on the other.

The upper floor contained the bedrooms of the Viceroy and his family. Lord Curzon furnished a very pretty sitting room for his wife (to save the ten league march to the south-east wing, where the sitting rooms are). He was also responsible for the introduction of an electric lift into this wing. The beautiful ornamented lift still works.

The ground floor contained a number of rooms for the European servants.

The first floor of the south-east wing has two sets of drawing rooms that had been named pink, blue, green and brown, probably according to the colour of the new furnishings. These were used by the family of the Governor-General on ordinary occasions or to meet visitors. The second floor has a set of bedrooms. One suite was specially prepared and furnished for the King Edward VII, when he came to India as Prince of Wales in 1876. A special bathroom was constructed for his use. In the ground are the sleeping quarters of the ADCs.

The ground floor of the north-west wing is occupied by the Military Secretary's Department. The upper floors are the principal guest chambers. Lord Curzon found the earlier arrangement utterly inadequate and took the place apart. The north-west wing as it now stands owes its dispensation to Lord Curzon. The suite on the first floor has been known as the Prince of Wales' Suite since it was specially prepared and occupied by the Prince of Wales (later King Edward VIII) in 1921.

The ground floor of the north-east wing has the ADC's room and other facilities. On the first floor was the Council Chamber, where the Governor-General used to preside over the Executive, and later, the Legislative Council. After the shifting of the Capital, the Governor in the British days used it to preside over meetings too large to be held in the Study and for private film shows; a billiard room was also added at some stage.

It was in this Council Chamber that each new Viceroy was sworn in. The upper floor was used as guest rooms. Winston Churchill, who almost became an ADC to Lord Curzon, stayed as his guest in one of the rooms and wrote his book on the Omdurman campaign in 1899.

When the building was constructed there was a dome on the southern side of the Central Pile with a figurine of Britannia at the top. The figurine was destroyed by lightning in 1838 and never replaced. The dome as we see it today was set up during the reign of Lord Elgin with a coronal and gallery at the summit.

Lord Curzon was responsible for many changes and the general ornamentation of the Government House. He broke the monotonous level of the parapet, unrelieved by a single ornament, by placing upon it a number of urns six feet tall at regular intervals.

As can be seen from the painting by James Moffat, there was initially only a bare field in front of the Government House, without any hint of a garden. Three Viceroys, Lords Mayo (1869), Northbrook (1872) and Lytton (1876), were the architects of the beautiful garden and trees in the compound. Simm's survey of 1850 estimates the area of the Government House and compound as more than 75 bighas (25 acres). Later surveys show the area to be larger, over 81 bighas (27 acres).

The Gateways

Originally there were four great external gateways (two on the east and two on the west) consisting of masonry arches surmounted by sculptured lions and sphinxes (the lions on the main or central arch and the sphinxes on the lower side arches). The gates look incongruous in comparison with the low railings at the side in the paintings of James Baillie Fraser (1819). When the gates were first erected the lions and sphinxes were not there, but were added shortly afterwards by a local artist named Wollaston. The sphinxes were made of clay and the lions of wood. Much later brick and plaster figures replaced the original ones.[8]

In preparation for the visit of King George V and Queen Mary in 1911, Lord Hardinge put up new large wrought iron gates with the Royal Cypher in the centre at the South and North Entrances with new pillars made of Surajpur stone. Before that the northern gate had been confined to domestic use. Though the Government House was a large affair with a vast compound, it did not have provision to accommodate a large staff. Premises for offices and servants' quarters were acquired from time to time as need arose, in a haphazard manner, mainly in the network of streets which existed in the early twentieth century between Government Place and Dalhousie Square. The area eventually came to accommodate the residences of the Private Secretary and Military Secretary; the Viceroy's stables and coach houses; the quarters of the steward, chef and native servants; the stables and quarters of the bodyguards; the Private Secretary's office and Press; the dispensary and the kitchen. All the food that was eaten in the Government House had to be carried nearly two hundred yards in *doolies* or boxes carried on poles on the shoulders of men. The space in the stable yard was so limited that every time the big carriages were used they had to be dragged out by coolies into the compound of the Government House and the horses harnessed to them in front of the main entrance.

In 1905 Lord Curzon took the initiative to acquire a large area outside the compound to the north of Government House, to provide for a range of buildings to house all the staff who did not actually live in the house. Lord Curzon drew up a plan to acquire the whole of Wellesley Place for the accommodation of the staff and other buildings connected with the Government House. But he had to resign and go back to England before he could complete the project. When it was known that the Capital would be transferred to Delhi the building programme was abandoned.

The days of glory for the Government House, Calcutta, from which the whole of India and Burma was ruled were suddenly over. The Capital of India was transferred to Delhi. The Viceroy left with many of the treasures accumulated in the premises, paintings, statuary, lustres, etc. The Government House was designated to be the residence and office of the Governor of Bengal. Since the Government House was built in 1803 and before it was abandoned in 1912 it was occupied by twenty-four Governors General of India, on an average of a little more than four years each. Some of them were among the foremost men of their time. Within its walls great decisions were taken, momentous scenes enacted, important movements born.

When the news of the transfer of Capital to Delhi reached Curzon in England, he was beset with anger. He remarked that the transfer of Capital was a stupendous folly and would entail a huge wastage of money.

Independence came to India on 15 August 1947. The Governor of the newly created state of West Bengal (after partition of India), Sri C. Rajagopalachari entered the Government House exactly at 8 a.m. and hoisted the National Flag. A large number of people had gathered outside the Government House to witness this historic occasion. Suddenly they broke through the security cordon and entered the compound and rushed up the grand staircase, destroying in their trail marble statuary, paintings and several objects symbolic of British Rule. Under the circumstances the outgoing Governor Sir Frederick Burrows left without the usual farewell ceremony, unnoticed and unwanted by the crowd.

After Independence there was a proposal to shift the Imperial Library (now National Library) to the Government House, which has enough space and to move the Governor to Belvedere. But the Governor did not agree, so the library shifted to Belvedere. Now named Raj Bhavan, the Government House still stands, as the residence of the Governor (now called Rajyapal) of a partitioned state, gradually losing importance in the country's economy and industry.

One of the Governors sold off antique furniture in an auction. Suddenly it was found that the twelve Caesars adorning the Marble Hall had disappeared into thin air, nobody knew or cared to know what happened. Some fifteen or sixteen years later another Governor found them in the Fort William and arranged for their restoration in the Marble Hall. Encroachments by the State Government have been another danger. Quarters for the ministers (including the Chief) were built along the western boundary. Apathy and neglect was the order of the day.

A hundred years after Lord Curzon West Bengal has a new Governor who has a keen interest in the Government House. Mr. Viren J. Shah is opening closed cupboards and stores to bring out old paintings and objects reminiscent of the Raj, renovating them and placing them where they were before. Years of apathy and neglect are gone. In 2003 the Government House will celebrate its bi-centenary. The Government House has seen three remarkable men, the creator, Lord Wellesley in 1803, Lord Curzon in 1903, who celebrated the Centenary with great pomp and Mr. Viren J. Shah who is eagerly looking forward to the Bi centennial in 2003.

References

1. Symons, N.V.H. *The Story of Government House,* Calcutta 1935, pp. 102-103.
2. Quoted in J.P. Losty, *Calcutta, City of Palaces,* Calcutta 1990, p. 71.
3. Symons. op. cit. 103-105.
4. Ibid. pp. 1 & 2.
5. Quoted in J.P. Losty. op. cit. pp. 75-76.
6. Das, Ramen. *Lat Bhavan theke Raj Bhavan* (Bengali), Calcutta 1933, p. 43.
7. Lord Curzon, *British Government in India,* vol. I, p. 100.
8. Symons. op. cit. pp. 63-64.

Chapter Ten

Esplanade East to Park Street

Esplanade East

Now we come to the eastern part of the former Esplanade Row, interrupted in the middle by the Government House. The south side was a part of the Maidan, with the part opposite to the Government House a plot of open ground cut through by untidy paths and covered with rubbish extending from the Esplanade to the Ochterlony Monument and containing the Dharamtollah Tank. Under the orders of Lord Curzon the tank was filled up and the entire area was converted into a beautiful public garden which came to be called the Curzon Gardens. There was another tank on the eastern side, which was filled up to make way for the Esplanade Tramway Terminus. After Independence the Curzon Gardens was renamed Surendranath Park after Sir Surendra Nath Banerjea, an eminent nationalist leader, with a statue of Banerjea installed in the southern part of the park. The well laid out garden was then allowed to perish and overgrown shrubs now harbour the largest cluster of giant rats in town. No gentleman or lady can visit the park to enjoy the evening air as the garden is dark and a favourite haunt of unsocial elements.

Now the state government has installed a *Bhasha Shaheed Smarak Stambha*, a Memorial for those who have laid down their lives for the Bengali language. This is in memory of the martyrs of the language movements in Dhaka, Bangladesh, and Silchar, India. This marble memorial surrounded by water augurs a rejuvenation of the park.

The Esplanade East leading to Dharmatala Street (now Lenin Sarani) has been renamed Sidho-Kanhu Dahar, to commemorate two Santal rebels against the British. For many years Number One was known as Scott Thomson's Corner, from the Medical Hall run by them; next to it was the office premises of Morrison & Cottle, the saddlers. Both these buildings gave way for the extensive Esplanade Mansions constructed by Sir David Ezra in the early part of this century. Number Three was the site of an old building which housed the old Mountain's Family Hotel during the Mutiny. Later, the site was long known as Number One Chowringhee and was acquired by Mr. R. N. Mathewson, the United States Consul General, on a long lease of 30 or 40 years. The Palace Hotel was situated on the ground floor. The old building was demolished and a new three storey building came up as the

Figure 40: Thacker Spink & Co. Photo Bourne & Shepherd

premises of the famous publisher Thacker Spink & Co., who moved here from Government Place North in 1916.

Mr. William Thacker died in London on 2 January 1872. His nephew Mr. William Spink was now the head of the firm. During his residence in Calcutta he served as Master of the Trades Association (1851) and was also a member of the Calcutta Corporation and of the Bengal Legislative Council (1876). His elder son Mr. Thomas William Spink came out to Calcutta in 1882, to become Master of the Trades Association in 1896 and 1897; was appointed a Port Commissioner (1899-1901), and was a member of the Bengal Legislative Council (1898-1900). Busteed's *Echoes from Old Calcutta* (1882) and Rudyard Kipling's *Plain Tales from the Hills* (December 1887) are two of the major Thacker Spink publications from his regime. The *Thacker's Guide & Directory* was published every year. *Thacker's Guide to Calcutta* by Walter K. Firminger was yet another significant title. The intelligentsia of the city, including Rabindranath Tagore, loved to visit their bookshop to browse through the books. Thacker Spink & Company ultimately closed down in the 1970s.

Number Four housed Walter Lock & Company, Electrical Engineers, iron and metal merchants, motor and automobile experts, importers of ironmongery, cycles and sporting goods and sole agents for Elkington's silver and EPNS goods. This firm is also extinct now. At numbers five and six now stands the imposing building originally known as the Military Department, Commissariat and Foreign Office, Government of India. Previously, at this site stood a four-storey building called Cordon's Building. The Bengal Club was established in 1827 and by July the same year, the Club took on rent the ground and first floors of this building. The monthly rent was Rs. 800 and the Club was able to provide public rooms as well as bedrooms for members at the moderate rate of Rs. 4 per week. The first Steward of the Club was Thomas Payne, whose culinary skills were well known. He was also permitted to conduct an ice manufacturing business of his own, as the following notice was published in 1831:

> Ice—Thomas Payne (Bengal Club House) will continue to supply Families with Ice during the Hot Season and Rains at the following rates:
> Ice for cooling wine, etc., at 8 annas per seer, creams of all kinds at 1-8-0 rupee mould (coolpee).
> N.B. The Ice will be delivered from a Godown next to the Club House in Mission Row(a) from 6 to 7 o'clock in the morning and at the same hour in the evening.
> It is requested that orders for the Ice may be sent the day previous.[1]

In early 1830 the Club moved to 4 Dalhousie Square East. Mr. Montague Massey in his *Recollections of Calcutta—For over half a century* gives an interesting story:

> There used to stand on the site of the Military and Foreign Secretariat a long one-storeyed tenement which went by the name of 'The Belatee Bungalow', the proprietors being two brothers of the name of Payne. They sold provisions of all sorts and did a

Figure 41: Curzon Garden and the Imperial Military Office

very lucrative trade. There was only one other shop of this kind in Calcutta, the Great Eastern Hotel.[2]

The old buildings were demolished and the new building of the Military Department and Foreign Office was constructed in 1909. The imposing three storey building had six Corinthian pillars supporting a large pediment over the main gateway. The building has Italian style ornamentation with two loggias at both ends of the building. The Foreign Office moved here from the old Council House building at the corner of Hare Street, when the old building there was demolished to make way for a new one. But in 1912 the Capital moved to Delhi and the Government of India building became vacant. The Metcalfe Hall was found to have an acute shortage of space for storing books of the Imperial Library. So the Imperial Library moved here in 1923. During the Second World War the books were shifted to Jabakusum House on Central (Chittaranjan) Avenue for safe-keeping. After the end of the war, the books again returned to the Esplanade East house. Again shortage of space necessitated another move, now to the Belvedere Palace at Alipore under a new name, National Library, in 1953. But the Newspaper section stayed back at Esplanade East. Other parts of the building are still being used by some Government of India offices.

Number eight was the office premises of Mackintosh, Burn & Co., well-known firm of architects, builders, surveyors and contractors of yesteryears. Number nine was the office and showroom of the firm of T.E. Thomson & Co. Ltd., hardware and metal merchants, electrical engineers, wholesale and retail ironmongers, engineers, contractors, founders and smiths, importers of agricultural and engineering machinery and tools. T.E. Thomson no longer exits; Mackintosh, Burn Ltd. has since moved its head office to Gillanders House in Netaji Subhas Road.

The famous departmental stores, Whiteaway, Laidlaw & Co. was established and continued for some time in this street before moving on to the palatial building in Chowringhee.

Numbers ten and eleven were occupied by Peliti's before they shifted to Government Place East and their premises were taken over by Trocadero Restaurant. Some old buildings disappeared and modern ones were raised on this stretch but the general picture is shabby and dowdy. The Sidho Kanhu Dahar could be called the Street of Protest for every other day, processions converge on this street, protesting against government policies, on the way to Writers' Buildings, but finding their way barred near the Curzon Park by a posse of armed policemen, sit down on the street, fiery speeches are made, slogans rend the air and the traffic around the area goes berserk. When the crowd gets restive the police resort to firing tear-gas shells, *lathi* charge and more often than not firing from rifles and service pistols to disperse the crowd. Probably more people have died from police firing in Independent India than in the British era on this street.

At the intersection of Esplanade East, Chowringhee Square, Bentinck Street and Dharmatala (Lenin Sarani), on our right starts Chowringhee Road (now renamed Jawaharlal Nehru Road).

Plate 5: Thomas Daniell, Views of Calcutta, Houses on the Chowringhee Road, 1787

Plate 6: The same scene a few years later. The small pond has now been extended and beautification done by a Benares banker.

CHOWRINGHEE ROAD

This is the old road leading to the temple of Kali at Kalighat. To its right stretched a tiger-infested deep jungle, haunted by notorious dacoits. Holwell described it as the 'Road leading to Collegott'. Chourangey was one of the 38 'towns' listed in Surman's Embassy to Delhi in 1714.

But there are others who claim that 'the original name of Chowringhee is Cherangi in all the early records'.[3] For Mr. A. K. Ray, "and finally it is to the goddess Kali herself, called 'Cherangi' from the legend of her origin by being cut up with Vishnu's disc, that they trace the name of Chowringhee." He goes on to write that "there is no tangible evidence that Chorangee Swami ever came to Calcutta and lived in its jungle as an ascetic and gave his name to the village as some writers have stated." Other historians including H.E.A. Cotton trace the name back to the Hindustani term for 'the Square'.[4]

When the new Fort William was being built starting in 1757, the jungle east of the fort from Esplanade Row in the north to Marhatta Ditch in the south was cleared and a grassy plain two miles long was created to provide the artillery with an open line of fire in case of an attack. Thus was created the lungs of the city, The Maidan. Large and lofty garden houses were built by the Europeans for residence in Cherangi. The newly built houses in Cherangi gave Calcutta the title 'The City of Palaces'.

We have a first glimpse of the houses on the Cherangi Road from a painting by Thomas Daniell, titled *House on the Cheringhee Road, Looking North, Calcutta in 1787*. William Hickey identified the buildings and named their owners as in 1789. The view was taken from the Manohar Dass Tarag or Collinga Tank looking north towards Esplanade Row. Hickey comments, "This is a view of part of Calcutta called Cheringhee; the whole has been built within the last twelve years; it extends a mile and half further than this view, and all noble houses."[5] The nearest house belonged to the estate of the Late Charles Short. The wide house with a pediment was owned by Capt. Collins, the Military Storekeeper, and lived in by Col. Murray. The two tall narrow houses in the centre were owned by Col. Wood, the one occupied by Mr. Dawson, the other empty.

The air was so good in Cherangi that "the Government sanctioned the hire of a house in an airy part of Cherangi for the accommodation of sick officers who came to the Presidency for the benefit of their health".[6]

The architecture in the beginning was undecorated Tuscan or Ionic to be followed by pure Grecian in the nineteenth century. The affluent Europeans gradually moved to other areas to build their palaces for living, away from the Chowringhee, mainly to the south, south-east, the suburbs of Ballygunge and Alipore. In Mark Wood's map of 1784 and Upjohn's map of 1792-93 the area behind the main road is shown as Collinga and Talpooker. The area of today's Park Street is described as Chourangi and the area south was Dhee Birjee. These areas were covered by *bustees* where the native people who worked for the

Europeans lived. These were the Colinga, Colvin's Bustee, Bamun Bustee, Bhediapara, Kashiabagan etc.

From the last quarter of the nineteenth century the character of Chowringhee Road up to Park Street began to change, as it gradually grew into the most fashionable shopping and recreation centre of the city. Large emporia, departmental stores, hotels, bars, restaurants, theatres and later cinema halls appeared on this stretch. The lofty palaces were either modified or demolished to make way for new buildings. As the humid weather and heavy monsoon rains took their toll of the old buildings there was no one prepared to bear the enormous costs for repair.

The big industrial houses were the last to come to Chowringhee. The Imperial Tobacco Company shifted its office from 5 Fairlie Place to Chowringhee in 1928.

With all the changes that have overtaken Chowringhee, one can still weave together the story of Heritage Chowringhee.

Number 1 Chowringhee Road is a very old ramshackle building, part of which has simply withered away with no attempt of repair. The building carries a sign board, 'The Chowringhee Hotel', and the ground floor is occupied by various shops. In the heydey of the British Raj it was the Bristol Hotel, one of the best in Calcutta, run by Mrs. P. Magre in 1897. Earlier still it was known as the Hotel D'Europe; its proprietress, Mrs. Scott of the Park Hotel, Darjeeling, formerly known as Madame Feinberg, who was highly respected and greatly esteemed by the older generations of Calcutta.

Figure 42: Bristol Hotel, Chowringhee
Photo Johnston & Hoffmann

Number 3 is now occupied by the Metro Cinema Hall, once one of the most elegant cinema halls in Calcutta showing mainly Metro Goldwyn Mayer's movies. Calcutta's elite once thronged to the hall. One still remembers a particularly tall door-keeper at the gate to ensure that no unruly element entered its portals. Those days are gone. The old MGM classics have given way to films loaded with sex and violence in Hindi or other languages and the clientele has completely changed.

On this site stood the building of the earlier *Statesman* office. The founder of *The Statesman*, Mr. Robert Knight, came to Calcutta in 1872, with some experience in journalism in Bombay, and started *The Indian Economist*. But the indefatigable Knight, keen to launch a group of journals, sold shares to 24 merchants to start the *Indian Statesman*. Late in 1875, he bought the *Friend of India*, founded by the illustrious William Carey in 1817, for Rs. 30,000 and brought it from Serampore to Calcutta. The *Friend of India* continued as an independent weekly until 1883 with which the weekly overseas edition of the *Statesman* was incorporated. After that it was the *Friend of India* which was incorporated with *The Statesman* and for some decades the paper was simply headed *The Statesman and Friend of India*.[7] The paper was published from this office until 1933-34 when it shifted to its present office in Chowringhee Square.

Whiteaway, Laidlaw and Company, the famous departmental stores, was probably founded in 1882 and was first situated at 7 Esplanade East, as evident from the following insertion in *The Statesman* dated 15 July 1885, 'To sub-let: premises no. 7, Esplanade Row East presently occupied by Whiteaway, Laidlaw & Company for remainder of Lease, two years from September, or for shorter period apply to Mackintosh, Burn and Company.' From this address the firm moved to the three-storey palatial building at 5 and 6 Chowringhee Road on 5 August 1885.[5]

In the Directories of 1906, the firm is stated to be occupying 4, 5, 6 Chowringhee Road and adjoining 145 to 147 Corporation Street (S.N. Banerjea Road of today) and 301 Bow Bazar Street where the furniture department was. The partners were R. Laidlaw, London, M. Wilkinson and A. Forward, Calcutta, E. Copplestone, Bombay, A.W. Prior, Calcutta and W.M. Turner, Rangoon.

In this palatial building, which is still a Calcutta landmark, the Company had a large stock of wares, including cycles to men's and ladies' outfits, shoes to children's toys which could be bought for cash or on hire purchase. The firm closed down a few years after Independence. The building is now the property of the Life Insurance Corporation of India and called the Metropolitan Building, badly in need of urgent repairs and a facelift. Just behind it on Corporation Street (S.N. Banerjea Road) is the once famous studio of Messrs. Bourne and Shepherd, the well-known photographers. Their large archival collection of photographs of old Calcutta and India in the days of the Raj was destroyed in a midnight fire some time back.

Opposite this part of the Chowringhee are the Esplanade Metro (underground transit system) Station and the Esplanade Tram Terminus. As we cross the S.N. Banerjea Road (previously known as Corporation Street, earlier still as Jaun Bazar Street) and come to the other side, the first building on our left is No. 7, an old building, almost falling down, but still carrying the nameplates of the famous dentists, Dr. Smith Brothers. In 1905 Number 8 was the studio of Bourne & Shepherd.

The site now occupied by Peerless Quality Inn was once occupied by The Continental Hotel, one of the best hotels in its time. Distinguished guests who have stayed here include Mark Twain and Winston Churchill. The hotel was set up in the middle of 1895 by Messrs. Boscolo Brothers, who announced in *The Statesman* of 14 July 1895, that 'they have built extensive premises at No. 9, Chowringhee' which were 'in every way suited to the requirements of a First Class Hotel, where they will continue to cater for the public as heretofore, under the style and title of the Hotel Continental.' In 1899, the hotel was

Figure 43: The Metropolitan Building, originally built by the Whiteaway and Laidlaws Departmental Stores. Sketch Rathin Mitra

overhauled and expanded. An announcement on 15 September 1899, said: 'patrons, constituents, and the Public generally are hereby informed that the extensive additions and alterations which have been in progress for the last few months are now complete.' The claim was also made that the refurbished premises 'now form the most Recherche and Comfortable Residence for families and Bachelors in Calcutta'. Further expansion and alterations were carried out in 1904; F.A. Boscolo, the managing proprietor, stating in *The Statesman* of 6 October 1904: 'The extensions and alterations to the Continental Hotel at 9, Chowringhee Road have been completed, special attention is being paid to the improvements of the new Private Tiffin Rooms, to ensure comfort to visitors, entrance to which is from 10, Chowringhee.' The advertisement added that Guest Nights were Wednesdays and Saturdays 'When the Italian Orchestra will be in attendance during dinner hours.' The address of the hotel had by then expanded to 9, 10, 11 and 12 Chowringhee with a branch at 3 Royd Street.[9]

A 1915 advertisement in *The Statesman* announces 'Special Hot Weather Rates from 1st February.' The hotel had a branch in Darjeeling, the Grand Hotel, Drum Druid, Darjeeling.[10] The Hotel Contimental went out of business and was replaced first by the Ritz Continental and more recently by the Peerless Quality Inn.

The Chowringhee Place is now a thoroughfare leading to the Calcutta Municipal Corporation Offices, but at the turn of the century it was a cul de sac with houses bearing Chowringhee numbers. Thus 10, 11 and 12 were extensions of the Continental Hotel. Number 10 was once occupied by a Colonel Searle, who was well known in Calcutta society as the father of two very pretty daughters. The next house was the premises of Cartner and Newson, manufacturers of jams, pickles and Indian condiments. The next large house at 13 was an extension of Mrs. Monk's Boarding House, replaced by Mr. Aratoon Stephen with The Empire Theatre, when he built the Grand Hotel at the site of the Theatre Royal which was completely gutted in 1911. The Empire Theatre built in the neo-classical style is today a cinema hall, The Roxy.

THE STORY OF THE GRAND HOTEL

At Number 13 stood the mansion of Colonel Grand, who won the plot in a lottery. Mrs. Annie Monk, a stout Irish lady, came to Calcutta to make her pile in 1870. She established a boarding house at Colonel Grand's house at No. 13, which obviously flourished for she soon expanded her business to the neighbouring houses at Numbers 14 and 15 at first, and later to Numbers 16 and 17 Chowringhee.

At Number 16 was the Theatre Royal, once a famous theatre hall that drew big crowds. *The Englishman* reports that in *Hudson's Surprise Party*, Miss Ivy Scott used to bring the house down with her song 'I do love you'.[11] On the ground floor was a billiard saloon, bar and lounge for the convenience of people attending the theatre. Numbers 16 and 17 were

Figure 44: Grand Hotel, Chowringhee

once occupied by an institution called the Calcutta Club, and were connected with each other by a plank bridge. The members of the club were merchants, brokers, public service men and sundry. After the club was wound up, the houses were let out as residential flats and boarding houses, and at one time No. 16 was converted into the Royal Hotel by Mr. Jack Andrews, former proprietor of the old Spence's Hotel; they were finally acquired by Mrs. Monk.[12] There was also an open air skating rink run as a private club.

In 1880-81, Aratoon Stephen, a young man of twenty, of Armenian descent arrived at the city from New Julfa in Ishpahan with barely hundred rupees in his pocket. He started with a barrow of wares, which he pushed up and down the Chowringhee. One day he entered the showroom of J. Boseck & Co. and asked for a job. He had an unusual gift, the knowledge of precious stones and the craft of jewellery, which he had learnt in his native land. Under Boseck's watchful eyes, Stephen learnt all the tricks of the trade. Gradually he hoarded up some money and waited for the right opportunity. Fortune came his way in 1894, when he bought the Theatre Royal at 16 Chowringhee Road. The theatre, with all the glamour of its regal name, was not doing well and during an amateur performance of Shakespeare's *Much Ado About Nothing*, a horse had fallen through the worm-eaten stage, to be extricated only the following day. The Theatre Royal was burnt down at midnight on 2 January 1911. Mr. Stephen was fully insured, so he did not lose money. From the ashes of the burnt out theatre, rose a great hotel, whose name would spread all over the world.

Stephen named it the Grand Hotel. Soon he acquired No. 17, bought Mrs. Monk's original boarding house at No. 13, and then the rest of Mrs. Monk's property, and a new premises at No. 18, Chowringhee Road. The whole length from Corporation Palace to Humayun Place became one edifice, the Grand Hotel. The street where he once pushed his barrow for a living bowed to him after only thirty years. The hotel was two storeys high with rooms so cleverly positioned that a gentle breeze wafted through them. Aratoon Stephen soon added one more storey, putting up a third floor, and added a sweep of verandah overlooking the Maidan. Electricity was added in 1914 and soon a hydraulic lift was installed. He built a hotel in Darjeeling, the famed Mount Everest, which also did brisk business. Aratoon Stephen died in 1927 and was buried in the Armenian Church compound in Calcutta. His son-in-law took charge of the Grand. But disaster struck in 1937, when the plumbing gave way and the sewage seeped into the drinking water. First typhoid and then enteric fever swept through the hotel, killing six people. Several other occupants, including Stephen's widow, fell seriously ill. Panic drove away the customers and the huge gates of the hotel were dragged shut in 1937. The Grand Hotel was closed, the property was entrusted to a mercantile bank for lease or sale.

Here begins the story of another young man, born in 1898 in a village in west Punjab (now in Pakistan), a college drop-out, arriving in Shimla to sit for a test for a government job. He failed the test, but found himself in front of the Cecil Hotel, Shimla, looking for a job. The gatekeeper would not let him in, so he waited for the manager to come out. Impressed by this young man's smart appearance, well ironed suit, neatly tied cravat and shining shoes, he asked him to meet him the next week.

The Manager, Mr. Grove, looked at the smart young man, Mohan Singh Oberoi, gave him a typing and shorthand test and appointed him as a guest clerk at the monthly salary of Rs. 60. After some time Grove left the job to run a confectionery shop and a new manager Ernest Clarke took over. He was very pleased with the hardworking Sikh. One day, Clarke entered his office and asked, 'I have rented the Carlton Hotel. Would you like to come with me?' Oberoi joined Clarke and became a man for all jobs in the hotel. When Clarke went on home leave after four years, Oberoi was left in charge. He worked so hard that the profits doubled. When Clarke returned, he was amazed. Soon he proposed that he would go back to England and offered Oberoi the first option for his shares, but the latter did not have the Rs. 25,000 which was the price. He asked if he could have some time to get the money. Out of trust Mr. Clarke proposed that the money could be sent in instalments to his England address. The entire amount was repaid in five years. Thus Mohan Singh Oberoi became the owner of a 50-room hotel in Shimla. Carlton Hotel was renamed Clarke's and did good business.

One day Mohan Singh bumped into a friend at Delhi Railway station and learned that the Grand Hotel with 500 rooms was up for sale. He lost no time even to inform his family, and boarded a train to Calcutta. The year was 1938. Soon he was standing before the magnificent hotel, as Aratoon Stephen stood before Mrs. Monk's boarding house fifty years ago. Probably the same gleam appeared in their eyes, and the same desire in their hearts: this will be mine! Oberoi immediately contacted the mercantile bank that had been appointed the liquidator of the estate of Aratoon Stephen by his son-in-law.

The bank manager offered to lease the hotel to Oberoi for Rs.10,000 per month, but raised the question of paying goodwill. With good humour, but making it quite clear that he was not joking, Oberoi countered, "What good will? It's bad will. In fact you should be reducing the rent." The banker laughed, and did. The deal was signed. The Grand became Oberoi Grand, for the time being on lease. The only condition imposed by the bank was that the manager should be a European. He immediately remembered Mr. D. W. Grove, the man who had given him his first job at Cecil Hotel at Shimla. Grove was delighted at the offer, which made him not only the General Manager but also Managing Director with Oberoi as Chairman. The Oberoi Grand was nursed back to its past grandeur. In the past sixty years they have never had to look back.[13]

Over the last sixty years many changes have taken place at the Grand; the old entrance has been closed and a new imposing gateway built in the style of Raj era architecture. Underground parking facilities are a new feature. Once the nightly meeting place of the rich and famous, the two night clubs, Prince's and Scherezade, are no more, the nouveaux riches prefer the disco at the Pink Elephant. Renovations are going on in the front rooms overlooking the Maidan. Calcutta loves the Grand, of course those who can afford it. The Grand Hotel Arcade on Chowringhee has many fashionable shops, selling everything from shoes to jewellery.

Humayun Place

This is a short thoroughfare leading from Chowringhee ending in front of New Market (Sir Stuart Hogg Market). Schalch's map of Calcutta (1825) shows Hydra Bagan and Upjohn's map of 1794 marks the Fenwick's Bazar in its place. The property seems to have belonged to the Nizam of Hyderabad, and Humayun was probably the personal name of one of the Nizams. Montague Massey describes it as

> greatly changed from what it used to be. Some time in the very early days it was occupied principally by boarding houses of a second class type, and amongst them was one situated at the top at the left hand corner, which has since been pulled down and another building erected on the site, in which young assistants in offices on not so large a salary used to get comfortable quarters with homelike surroundings at a very moderate figure. It was as far as I remember run by a widow whose husband had left her rather badly off, and she took much interest in, and carefully mothered her young charges, amongst others a son of her own who was in the Bank of Bengal. On the

opposite side an old house has been renovated and faced with iron railings which has much improved its general appearance.[14]

In the 1880s the headquarters of the Calcutta Volunteer Rifles was situated at 4 Humayun Place before it moved on to its new building on Strand Road.

Today the left side is occupied by a number of shops and a newly-built sprawling shopping arcade. On the right we see the New Empire Theatre, once used as a theatre hall, but now, with its next door neighbour The Lighthouse, used only for screening of films. There is a corridor on the first floor level between the two theatres. Over these tower the slowly decaying building complex, the Humayun Court. Coming back to the Chowringhee, we see another fine arcade, covering 18/6 and 18/7, which only 25 years back used to be one of Calcutta's favourite confectioners, restaurant and night club, the Firpo's. Their large tea lounge, laid out under a *shamiana* on the first floor terrace, with the evening breeze from the river wafting in, was a pleasure to sit in. When the Firpo's closed down, both the floors were taken over by a wide assortment of shops, turning the old hotel into a modern shopping complex, the Firpo's Market. Before the Firpo's came up, the site had been occupied by yet another famous Calcutta restaurant, Castellazzo's.

The next plot of land up to Lindsay Street and a part of the latter was the property of the Gubbay family, one of the eminent Jewish settlers of the nineteenth century. This entire land was bought by W. Leslie & Co. who built a three-storey house at 19 Chowringhee Road. Now the ground floor of this building is occupied by Austin Distributors, a car seller. Next stood the Picture Palace, which later became Tiger Cinema, and wound up recently to make way for a shopping complex.

Lindsay Street

Now renamed Nellie Sengupta Sarani, this street starts from 22 Chowringhee Road and ends in Free School Street. This was shown as Fenwick's Bazar Street in the map of Mark Wood (1784) and as Fenwick's Street in Upjohn's map of 1794. The name Lindsay Street appears in the *Bengal and Agra Guide* of 1850. As Cotton describes it, 'Beyond Sudder Street and leading to the Municipal Market is Lindsay Street. The eponymous hero of the Street in all probability is the Hon'ble Robert Lindsay (1754–1836), whose adventurous career in the Company's service may be found related by himself in the *Lives of the Lindsays*. His house in the locality is thus advertised for sale in the *Calcutta Gazette* of September 27, 1804:

> The house at Chowringhee, belonging to the Hon'ble Robert Lindsay, at present occupied by William Trower Esq., on leave for twelve months from the 5 July last at Rs. 250 a month and the taxes.
> Lindsay was the second son of the Earl of Balcarres, and was sent out as a writer to India by Henry Dundas, Lord Melville. He landed in Calcutta in September 1772, and after spending some years at Dacca, succeeded William Holland as Collector of Sylhet

in 1777... . In Lindsay's day the supply of elephants for the Company's troops yielded a good profit, and the bag of tigers were plentiful, for he was able to account for sixty or seventy yearly, upon all of which the Company allowed liberal rewards. But he devised other methods of money making in addition. "Thrown on his own resources he assumed by turns, as circumstances minister to occasion, the character of soldier, magistrate, political agent, elephant-catcher, tiger-hunter, ship- builder, lime manufacturer, physician and surgeon." The revenue, he found, was collected in cowries. A fleet of armed boats was maintained to convey the annual accumulation of 700 million of these little shells to Dacca "at a loss of no less than 10 per cent, exclusive of depredations on the passage down." Lindsay conceived the idea of remitting the value of cowries in limestone, for which he held the contract, and keeping the revenues of Sylhet. Lindsay also launched a ship-building trade from the timber of the Sylhet forests after some Crusoesque experiences as he failed to get his craft down the river owing to their large size. He wrote an account of his enterprise to his mother, Lady Balcarres, who wrote back: "Your talents in this line I do not dispute but I have one favour to ask of you, which is that you will not come home in a ship of your own building!" Lindsay followed his mother's advice, leaving India in 1787; the purchase of the baronetcy of Leuchar in Fife having established him as a landed proprietor while still in the Company's service: and lived for nearly fifty years in enjoyment of "the large fortune he had amassed."[15]

Nellie Sengupta was born in 1886 in Cambridge, England and married Jatindra Mohan Sengupta in 1909. When Jatindra Mohan left his legal practice and joined the freedom movement in 1921, Nellie followed her husband. She was arrested by the police while addressing a public meeting in Esplanade East. She was elected a member of the Bengal Legislative Assembly in 1940 and 1946. She died on 23 October 1973 at the age of 87. Lindsay Street was renamed Nellie Sengupta Sarani in her memory on 22 July 1978.

Opposite Lindsay Street, on the eastern fringe of the Maidan is a large tank with four pavilions at four corners and with a railing all round. This is the Manohar Das Tank. The *Calcutta Gazette* of 30 May 1793 records, 'Monohur Doss, the great Benares banker, has commenced a very useful and extensive work for an individual. The large tank which is now digging on the Chowringhee Road, three hundred and fifty feet in length and two hundred and twentyfive feet in breadth, is, we understand, at his expense.' In the course of the digging operation stumps of Sundri trees were found, establishing once and for all that the maidan was a part of the Sunderban jungle many years back. The tank dried up while the underground railway system was being built, but now it has been re-excavated to its old glory.

In 1877 the General Post Office was situated in Chowringhee at the corner of Lindsay Street, causing considerable inconvenience. Instructions were given that year to the

Superintending Engineer to survey and report upon the practicability of accommodating all the public offices and departments of the Government in Writers' Buildings or in Loudon Building or in both.[16]

In the early twentieth century Numbers One to Five Lindsay Street belonged to the family of Butto Kristo Paul, eminent Bengali chemist. The ground floor of Number 2 was a branch of the Great Eastern Hotel. At Number 6 was a Calcutta Police Outpost and Detective Department. Number 6/6 was the Aligarh Dairy Farm of Edward Keventer and Number 7 was the Opera House (now Globe Cinema). The old Opera House was a wooden structure and a well-known theatre hall. It was here that Charles Mathews on New Year's night, 1876, played the part of Adonis Evergreen in his own comedy, *My Awful Dad*, before the Prince of Wales (later King Edward the Seventh). On that occasion, says Mr. E.W. Madge in an excellent article on the theatres of Calcutta, 'with the view, no doubt of reserving a place for Indian Noblemen, the following prices of admission were used: upper tier boxes, six seats Rs. 1000: lower tier boxes, six seats Rs. 500: stalls Rs. 50 each.'[17] The wooden Opera House was demolished in the nineteenth century and the new structure and adjoining shops were built within a short distance of the Fenwick's Building.

Next to the Opera House lies a short lane leading to Sudder Street, called Madge's Lane, named after a well-known East Indian family who at one time owned landed property where the New Market and Opera House stood. James Madge, who was head assistant in the office of the Chief Engineer, Bengal, was one of those who signed the farewell address to Lord Minto in 1813. Mr. W. C. Madge was Secretary to the European and Anglo-Indian Defence Association, and his son E. W. Madge was Superintendent of the Reading Room of the Imperial Library in 1906. In 1905, Madge's Lane had only three houses, of which No. 3 was the Vine Villa, a Church of England Zenana Mission.

The rest of the buildings on Lindsay Street on the south side up to Free School Street were either shops or residential buildings. At No. 9 Pundit P. Saraswati, Ph.D., Astrologer, had his offices in 1905. On the northern side before the New Market were the premises of Mr. Gubbay and some members of the Apcar family.

SIR STUART HOGG MARKET OR NEW MARKET

The site of the New Market was once occupied by a dirty old bazar called Fenwick's Bazar with filthy lanes and filthier surroundings. The newly formed Calcutta Corporation decided in 1866 to build a proper clean marketplace for the European inhabitants of Calcutta. The old Fenwick's Bazar was demolished and gradually the new market took shape. It occupies three sides of a quadrangle and was completed on 1 January 1874. It was named after Sir Stuart Hogg, who was the Chairman of the Justices of Peace in Calcutta from 1866 to 1876, Chairman of the Calcutta Corporation and Commissioner of Police, Calcutta. It has been described as the largest market in the world under one roof. The entrance is on Lindsay

Figure 45: New Market

Figure 46: Christmas Morning in the New Market

Street. The main entrance has a fine carriage porch and a clock tower on the eastern end. 'It has been said that the Clock Tower was shipped from Huddersfield to Calcutta, brick by brick.'[18] The market is set out and arranged in groups or ranges for different merchandise. The meat, fish and poultry ranges are in the extreme eastern part. A fire on the night of 11 December 1985 had destroyed a large part of the northern part of the market. This part has recently been built as a separate block three storeys high.

At the corner of Lindsay Street and Chowringhee Road there used to be a post office which is no longer there.

As we continue south towards Park Street along Chowringhee Road, we find a very old building with two floors, set back from the main road; this was definitely a residential building later occupied by Partridge & Co., Chemists and Druggists, with their address, Number 20 Chowringhee. The next house was the office premises and studio of photographers Johnston and Hoffmann, who moved here when the Loudon Building was demolished. Next is the double-storeyed building of the Bible Society. Next is the six storeys high Youngmen's Christian Association building. Mr. Montague Massey reminisces:

> On this particular spot many of my readers will doubtless recollect that Mr. W.T. Woods, one of Calcutta's earliest and most successful dentists, had his surgery and residence for a great number of years, and laid the foundation of the fortune with which he returned to England early in the present century.[19]

The Y.M.C.A. Building at 25 Chowringhee Road was completed in 1902. A meeting was held in August 1899 at the Dalhousie Institute, where the Lieutenant Governor of Bengal presided. Mr. Campbell White, the Y.M.C.A. General Secretary, estimated that the total cost of the site and building would be Rs. 200,000. After its completion, the first meeting— a lecture by the Reverend A.H. Bowman on 'Alcohol, Science, and Christianity'—was held in the hall of the new building on 6 November 1902. The Y.M.C.A. building has a few shops on the ground floor, behind which is a swimming pool. Upper storeys have halls, indoor sports facilities, offices and residential rooms.[20]

The next building at the corner of Chowringhee Road and Sudder Street at 26 Chowringhee Road is still known as the old Samuel Fitze Building (six storeys high), after Samuel Fitze, the well-known tailoring and departmental stores that occupied this building till a few years back. On this site stood a double-storeyed building of the old colonial bungalow type with a carriage porch on the main road which 'had always had the reputation of being haunted, and no one would go near the place for years, and it was gradually falling into decay, when one day to the surprise of everybody some native appeared on the scene and occupied it.'[21] The 'native' in question was probably Baboo Hem Chunder Goswami, Zeminder of Serampore, who has been shown as the owner of the building in 1905 in McCluskie's *Calcutta Directory & Guide* of 1906.

SUDDER STREET

As we turn left we come to Sudder Street connecting Chowringhee Road with Free School Street. This is an old thoroughfare, as it appears as Ford Street in Wood's map of 1784. Then the name changed to Speke Street, after Peter Speke, member of the Supreme Council, 1789–1801. He built a house in 1790 in the street and the extensive grounds went up to Kyd Street. The tank Jhinjree Talao or the Sieve Tank was Speke's private property, around which he erected a high perforated wall. Speke's house was later let out and ultimately sold to the Government to hold sessions of the Sudder Dewani Adaulat, which gave its name to the street. After some time the Sudder Dewani Adaulat shifted to a house west of the Presidency General Hospital, and the old building came to house the Government Observatory which started in 1836.

Though historic, the street had a dubious reputation throughout the twentieth century. Montague Massey describes it as

> an extremely dull and most uninteresting street, entirely lacking in all the essential elements that go towards making a place look bright and cheerful. I really forget what it was like before the Indian Museum was erected, but this did not apparently have the effect of adding to its attractions. The Wesleyan Chapel, School and Parsonage have been built in my day on the site of what, as far as I remember, were ordinary dwelling

Figure 47: Sudder Street

houses. There does not appear to be even much traffic of any sort passing through the street during the day.[21]

In a Letter to the Editor of *the Statesman*, Calcutta, published on 6 March 1897 (reproduced in *The Statesman 100 Years Ago*), we find the resident of No. 12 Sudder Street writing of insanitary bustees on Cowie's Lane near the junction with Sudder Street, with the bustee adjoining No. 12 with a privy just under the windows of these premises; and complaining of the constant odours from it that are anything but welcome or conducive to health as any medical officer can testify. 'Here is the hot weather upon us, and we are obliged to keep all our shutters closed, and it is useless, from past experience, to appeal to the Municipal executive about it.'

But Sudder Street has always enjoyed favour and patronage from foreigners, its cheap boarding houses and ramshackle eateries appearing in the tourist guide books abroad. During the Second World War this area was frequented by English and American troops for an evening of pleasure. Sudder Street turned into a red-light area around this time. After the war came the overlanders, travelling in buses and cars all over the east, seeking refuge in Sudder Street. The seventies brought the 'hippies', seeking *charas* and *ganja* and other addictive drugs.

They have been replaced since by the 'backpackers', men and women of every nationality travelling around the world with a rucksack on their back. Sudder Street has offered temporary homes to poor travellers from all over the world for more than a century now.

As we enter the street from the north we come to the Sudder Street Church, formerly known as the Wesleyan Methodist Church at 14/2. The church was built in 1866, as a place of worship for both civilians and military personnel, by the tireless efforts of Rev. James Broadbent and H.G. Highfield. It was an 'only whites church'. During the Second World War the army personnel came to this church to attend services. This church is now a part of the Church of Northern India.

The Wesleyan School stood next to it in a very fine single-storey building looking like a parsonage. Today it is Mrs. Williams' Nursery School. After the school is the entrance to Madge Lane.

Between Madge Lane and Hartford Lane were mainly old colonial residential houses, which were taken over by the Jewish family of the Cohens in the 1930s. No. 13A, which is now Fairlawn Hotel, has a long history. According to a hotel pamphlet, the land on which it stands was first purchased by a European, Mr. Ford, from Sheikh Ramjan and Bhonay on 27 May 1781 more than two hundred years ago. The area of the land is 2 *bighas* 8 *cottahs* and 7 *chhitacks* and in those days was valued at Rs. 1552-2-0. The street was at that time named after him and continued on until Sudder Court was established years later.

He must have had the main building constructed soon afterwards as it passed to a Mr. George Chisholm in 1801, it being noted that a 'pukka' building had been built by Mr. Ford. Chisholm died in 1812, when it passed into the hands of Captain Sir James Mount, later to Sir George Mount through the 1830s, and back to a Chisholm in the 1840s, 50s and 60s. Sir David Ezra inherited it on 7 December 1873 and it stayed in Jewish hands until fairly recent years. Kyd Street and Sudder Street housed many influential Jewish families in the 1890s when that community had extensive trading interests from Bengal to Hong Kong and China.

> In the 20th century it has operated as a guest house, run for many years by two English spinsters, the Misses Clark and Barratt, and from 1936 by my wife's parents and by us. During the Second World War it was requisitioned for Canadian Air Force personnel and for two years became 'Canada House'. Melvyn Douglas, then a Canadian Air Force major, occupied our room during that time.
>
> *Signed E.F. Smith*

E.F. Smith actually married the daughter of the house and since then they have been running the Fairlawn Hotel in the old house, older than Mr. Speke's house described earlier.

Next to the hotel are Numbers 12 and 11 Sudder Street; both once properties of the wealthy Jewish Jacob family. Number 12 has been taken over by the Institute of Cost Accountants in a new multistoreyed building, but Number 11 is still in the possession of the Jacob family, a fine colonial building in its own compound; and a Jacob still lives there.

Across Hartford Lane is Calcutta's historic Number 10 Sudder Street, once a fine colonial house fronted by a wide *verandah* with Doric columns supporting a pediment. During 1881-82 this house was taken on rent by Rabindranath Tagore's immediate elder brother Jyotirindranath and his wife Kadambari. Rabindranath was very fond of this couple and often stayed with them in this house. During one of his stays, one early morning he stood at the *verandah* and looked towards the garden in the compound of the Free School. The rays of the early morning sun and a gentle breeze played among the leaves of the flowering trees in the garden; looking at them the poet had a vision spurred on by the Muses. He rushed indoors and wrote one of his famous poems, *Nirjharer Swapnabhanga* ('Awakening of the Fountain'). The Tagores moved back to their ancestral home in Jorasanko in north Calcutta and the Muses abandoned this house, which was taken on rent by the Salvation Army and the Scottish Masonic Lodge among others. Somebody placed a marble plaque on the walls of the building commemorating the stay and the composition of the poem, in Bengali and English, hidden away in a dark corner away from the public eye. The ground floor considerably altered gives an impression of the old house, but the upper floors have been demolished and a new structure built, housing a hotel, Hotel Plaza.

On the opposite side was old Number 5, the residence of a Muslim nobleman, Nawab Aziz Ahmed, CIE, Bar-at-Law. On this side up to Chowringhee Lane is the backpackers' paradise, with hotels cafes, and cheap eateries occupying this stretch.

Chowringhee Lane, a small street, connecting Sudder Street with Kyd Street, shot to fame with the film *36, Chowringhee Lane*, directed by Aparna Sen. A non-descript residential area, it has only two notable addresses, No. 11, the residence of Maharaja H. L. Roy of Rangpur, and No. 4, the British India Marine Service Club in the 1930s.

Back to Sudder Street we move on to Number 2, Lockwood House. In 1905 it was a residential building, later transformed to the Red Shield Guest House of the Salvation Army.

The Naval and Military League began work in India in 1895, and later that year the corps was established in Calcutta as part of the recently formed Armed Civil, Military and Naval Union. It was announced in *India's Cry* (September 1901) 'that three leaguers have come to stay and they had quite a miniature Soldiers' Home.' The same magazine in July 1902 carries the information that the Soldiers' Home has moved from Dharamtolla Street to 5, Sudder Street. *The War Cry* (Simla, April 1910) announced that the Civil, Naval and Military Home had moved to 10 Sudder Street.

The Home moved to its present site (according to *The War Cry*, Simla, July 1913) at 2, Sudder Street, described as more suitable premises and occupying a commanding position next to the Museum. Improvements, we are told, had been carried out at a cost of Rs. 1200. The new home consisted of a double-storeyed building; with a large refreshment room downstairs, with bar and reading room, a well-stocked library, office and dormitories for furloughmen; and officers' quarters, the Salvation Hall (seating 100 persons), a reception room and other rooms for temporary and permanent accommodation, in the upper floor.

The Red Shield Guest House is still there, providing perhaps the cheapest dormitory accommodation in the city. Number 1 was at one time the Office of the Reporter on Economic Products, later taken over by the Indian Museum.

Before we come back to Chowringhee we find a gate on our left and a three-storeyed house in red brick, housing the Botanical Survey of India on the ground floor and the upper floors serving for extension galleries of the Indian Museum, approached by a bridge from the main building. Inside the compound we find the old Speke's House, which is the second oldest house in Chowringhee, now used as the office of the Director, Indian Museum, and other offices.

The two centuries old building has been preserved in excellent repair. Behind Speke's House is another red brick India Government building which is now the property of the Indian Museum. Most probably this had once been erected for the Bengal Secretariat. In 1897 this was leased out to the Geological Survey of India, who still occupy the building as their office. I am grateful to Mr. Sidney Kitson, IPS (Retired), who lives in Sudder Street and had been collecting material on the street for an article. He kindly gave me his collection of newspaper cuttings, correspondence with the Salvation Army and other papers.

Here we leave Sudder Street and come back to Chowringhee.

THE INDIAN MUSEUM

The Indian Museum stands on Chowringhee Road between Sudder Street and the United Service Club (now defunct, the premises occupied by the Geological Survey of India). It was built on the site of the Old High School which in 1863 was transferred to Darjeeling (and is now known as St. Paul's High School), and a part of the house of Mr. Speke.

It was erected from the designs of Mr. Walter B. Granville, the Government Architect, and was opened to the public in 1875. The frontage on Chowringhee is over 300 feet, while the depth facing Sudder Street covers 270 feet. The facade has two storeys of great height, in the Italian style of architecture; the two projecting wings and the central portico set on elegant Corinthian columns. A broad flight of steps leads to a lobby, which opens on other sides into a room eighty feet by thirty. Three series of arches lead to a double staircase of very fine proportions ascending to the right and left. Beyond the foot of the staircase the lobby opens on to a grass-covered quadrangle, 180 feet by 105 feet, surrounded by an array of tropical plants.

Figure 48: Speke's House
Sketch courtesy Rathin Mitra

Around this along the inner side of the building runs a piazza or arcade. The piers of the arches are decorated on the side facing the quadrangle with columns in the Roman Doric style on the ground floor, and the Italian Ionic on the first floor.

Initially the Museum was set up by the Asiatic Society of Bengal in about 1814. In 1866 an Act was passed by the Governor-General of India in Council providing for the establishment of a Public Museum in Calcutta,

> to be devoted in part to collections illustrative of Indian Archaeology and of the several branches of Natural History, and in part to preservation and exhibition of other objects of interest, whether historical or physical, in part to the records and offices of the Geological Survey of India and in part to the fit accommodation of the Asiatic Society of Bengal, and to the reception of their Library, Manuscripts, Coins, Busts, Pictures, Engravings and other property.[22]

The Act provided for the erection of a building for this purpose and constituted a body of trustees. It also provided that all expenses and salaries connected with the Indian Museum could be defrayed by the Government of India.

The provision in the Act for the accommodation of the Asiatic Society of Bengal in the new building was not carried out. In 1876, when the extent of the large number of objects had been meticulously observed, the trustees could see that the Asiatic Society could not be provided with space in the new building, and they were requested to relinquish their claim. A new Act was accordingly passed.

In 1874 Lt. Governor George Campbell established a museum in Hastings Street containing mainly specimens of ordinary products of Bengal, e.g. agricultural, minerals, forest, wastes and other curious objects. These objects were transferred as an annexe to the Calcutta International Exhibition in 1883, held at Sudder Street in an open field behind the main Museum.

After the closure of the Exhibition these Bengal Government exhibits along with other exhibits of the same nature collected by the Government of India came to form part of the exhibit of the Indian Museum.

The Indian Museum today stands tall and elegant, with one more storey added, one of the five most eminent museums in the world. It is called Jadughar in the local parlance and attracts the ordinary and the discerning equally. While the Victoria Memorial Hall was being built, the collected exhibits were on display here. New buildings have since been added to the rear including the Asutosh Centenary Hall with its lecture theatre and exhibition gallery. The ancient tank extending up to Kyd Street has been partly filled up for another building.

THE GOVERNMENT ART COLLEGE

This is situated in a building at 28 Chowringhee Road, adjoining the Museum. Its predecessor, The Calcutta School of Industrial Art, was founded in 1854 by an Association of gentlemen under the name of The Society for the Promotion of Industrial Art. The society held its sessions at the residence of Hodgson Pratt. The object of the society was stated to be to form schools for East Indian and native students for instruction in: (*a*) elementary drawing, drawing from models, and natural objects, and architectural drawing; (*b*) etching and engraving in wood, metal and stone; (*c*) modelling including pottery.[23] The first teacher was a Frenchman, M. Rigaud, who was followed in 1860 by Mr. Garrick. In 1864 the school came under the charge of the Government of Bengal. The well-known teacher, Mr. E.B. Havell, joined in 1896; it was under his guidance that a new trend in Indian painting was born. The School holds an Annual Art Exhibition, which still draws a large number of people. Eminent Indian artists who have served the institution as principals include Abanindra Nath Tagore, Mukul Dey and Chintamani Kar.

KYD STREET (DR. M. ISHAQUE ROAD)

Popularly known as *Jhanjhree Talao ka Rasta* and shown as Chowringhee Tank Street in Wood's map of 1784, this street runs from Chowringhee Road to Free School Street. The *Jhanjhree talao*, literally a sieve tank, can be seen in Sir Charles D'Oyly's painting of the Sudder Board of Revenue from Kyd Street of 1835. The sieve or the water gate was installed to prevent trespassers from drawing water from the tank. The street probably commemorates a distinguished Englishman, Lieutenant Colonel Robert Kyd, Military Secretary to the Government of Bengal, a distinguished botanist, who had his residence at the site of today's Chowringhee Mansions at 30 Chowringhee Road. Col. Kyd persuaded the East India Company to establish the Botanical Gardens at Shibpore on the opposite bank of the river from Garden Reach, in 1786. Until his death in 1793 he was the honorary Superintendent of the Gardens. His sons, James and Alexander Kyd, built a ship-building firm at the dockyard started by Col. Henry Watson in 1780. Kidderpore seems to be named after James Kyd.

According to Kathleen Blechynden, Kyd Street was named after Robert Kyd's son General Alexander Kyd.[24] In Independent India the street was renamed after Dr. M. Ishaque (1898-1969), Founder General Secretary of the Iran Society. He was an eminent Arabic and Persian scholar and taught at the Calcutta University from 1927 to 1960. Due to the efforts of Dr. Ishaque, the Iran Society could buy the premises at 12 Kyd Street, a palatial building with compound and outhouses, which had originally belonged to James Barwell, son of Richard Barwell, member of the Council in the time of Warren Hastings.

The numbering of houses on Kyd Street starts from the southern side. The narrow lane was widened when the Chowringhee Mansions and the new United Service Club came to be built, particularly on the Chowringhee end, and pavements were laid.

Number 1 was previously the Residential Chambers of the United Service Club inside the compound of the old club building. This has been replaced by a huge pile of residential flats called the Palace Court, its gateway made of magnificent wrought iron. From 1903, Number 2 was the official residence of the Commissioner of Police and a few other senior officers. The Calcutta Directory of 1906 identifies its resident as Mr. F.L. Halliday, M.V.O., the Commissioner of Police. The house had a huge compound, now the site of a number of concrete high-rises, including a hostel for Members of the Legislative Assembly of West Bengal.

Number 3 used to be the residence of Lady and Sir David Ezra, the doyen of the Jewish settlers in Calcutta. Sir David was respected throughout the country. He was knighted in June 1927 by King George V. He was Director, Reserve Bank of India, several jute mills, coal companies, flour mills, Steel Corporation, Assam Steamship Co. Ltd., Port Shipping Co. Ltd., Howrah Oil Mills and the vast Ezra estates. He was the Sheriff of Calcutta in 1925-26, a member of the Managing Committee of the Alipore Zoological Gardens and Bengal Veterinary College, and a prominent member of Royal Calcutta Turf Club. His palatial home at Kyd Street had a miniature zoo with prize zebras, birds of paradise, golden turkeys, swans from the King's swannery, tortoises and many rare birds whose plumage lent a galaxy of colour to his home. He was a patron of stamp collecting, particularly air mails. The first Air Mail Stamp Exhibition in Calcutta sponsored by the Air Mail Society of India was held at his residence in1934. He died at the age of 76 after sustaining a fatal fall during his morning walk.[25]

THE UNITED SERVICE CLUB

Very little is known about the early history of the club. It was founded in 1845 somewhere in Esplanade under the name of Bengal Military Club, which became Bengal United Service Club in 1853. The first President of the Club was Col. Finch. Membership of the club was confined to Commissioned Officers of the Army and the Navy, Barrister-Judges of the High Court, members of the Indian Civil Service and all Government Chaplains. The old club house stood at the site of today's Chowringhee Mansions at 30 Chowringhee Road and extended some distance into Kyd Street. The nondescript club house was enclosed with a low brick wall skirting the Chowringhee. The club left 30 Chowringhee in 1904-05 to 29 Chowringhee Road, where a handsome club building was built by Messrs. Mackintosh Burn & Co. over the site of a house, which had once been the residence of John Palmer, 'the Prince of Merchants'. This house has been described as a one-storeyed structure like a pavilion with a crescent shape, supported by pillars with a verandah encircling the whole of the outer portion facing the Chowringhee. At a later period the building was remodelled and used as the residence of the Commissioner of Police, who shifted to Kyd Street in 1903. It was perhaps the only British Club in Calcutta which never admitted Indian members

Figure 49: The Old United Service Club Building
Photo courtesy Johnston & Hoffmann

Figure 50: The United Service Club

and disappeared from the face of Calcutta after Independence. The building now houses the Geological Survey of India.

After Independence, the more prosperous Jews mostly migrated to Israel, USA and Canada. The vast Ezra estates and business passed into other hands. Number 3 Kyd Street was taken over by the Government of India. Sir David Ezra's palatial residence now houses the Central Drug Laboratory, with some new buildings erected in the compound to be occupied by the Central Food Laboratory and the Central Serological Laboratory.

Numbers 4 to 9/3 on the southern side were mostly residential houses. Montague Massey describes the changes in the Free School Street end:

> New buildings have taken the place of old and antiquated ones. I well recollect there was for some time a house on the left hand side which was occupied by the assistants of the old Oriental Bank, all of whom I knew very well, and it went by the name of the Oriental Bank chummery. They subsequently removed to one of the Panch Kotee houses in Rawdon Street, where they used to give dances and other entertainments. The house next to their old one in Kyd Street suddenly collapsed one day and was reduced to a heap of rubbish, but fortunately no one was hurt.[26]

On the northern side from Free School Street stood the buildings described above. Number 12 is the old colonial building now occupied by the Iran Society. Number 13 was the office of the Executive Engineer, Public Works Department, Northern Drainage and Embankment Division. Number 14, an old house still standing in its old state, was in the early 1900s the Consulate General of Italy. After this we come to a gate leading to the Sieve Tank. In 1835 Sir Charles D'Oyly painted a picture from this gate showing the Sieve Tank in the foreground and one of the most interesting buildings which used to be the Sudder Dewany Adaulat. As we enter the gate we find a grey house on the right occupied by the Geological Survey of India. The tank does not have the sieve any more and half of it on the furthest side in the north has been filled up to erect extensions of the Indian Museum, The Ashutosh Centenary Hall, etc. There is another gate further west which used to be the entrance to the Government Art School; this is now closed, probably not opened in a decade as one gathers from looking at the pile of garbage inside. The quarters of the Principal of the Art School are on the bank of the tank. When Mukul Dey was the Principal, Rabindranath Tagore would often stay here and enjoy the scenery which inspired some of his poems. The Calcutta Directory shows Number 16 Kyd Street as the residence of Mr. E.B. Havell, the first Principal of the Art School.

Here we leave Kyd Street and come to another historic site on Chowringhee Road, Number 30, the Chowringhee Mansions of today. The site was in the occupation of many famous persons and institutions. We have already noted that Lt. Col. Robert Kyd used to live here.

Dr. Thomas Fanshawe Middleton, the first Bishop of Calcutta, arrived in the city on 28 November 1814. His first residence or Episcopal Palace was in Council House Street in a building next to the present day Hong Kong Bank. The accommodation in this palace was not enough, so he shifted 'to a better house in Chowringhee'. The new palace was probably the large building situated at the north-western corner of Park Street and

Chowringhee, the present site of the Chowringhee Mansions. It had an enclosed *verandah* forty feet long by thirteen feet wide which adjoined the Bishop's library and at the other end of it was the Bishop's Dressing Room.[27]

Dr. Simon Nicholson, who was Lord Dalhousie's physician, lived in a house on this site, probably the same house described above. From 1820 to 1855 he was the most eminent physician in Calcutta. The avenue leading across the Maidan (the Mayo Road, now Guru Nanak Sarani) is said to have been laid to enable him to have direct access from his house to the Government House. A portrait of Dr. Nicholson hangs in the Asiatic Society. Later the old United Service Club building came up on the same site.

References

1. Pankridge, H.R. *A Short History of the Bengal Club 1827–1927*, pp. 20-21.

2. Massey, Montague. *Recollections of Old Calcutta*, p. 8.

3. Wilson, C.R. *Early Annals*, vol. II, p. 173.

4. Cotton, H.E.A. *Calcutta Old and New*, Revised Edition, p. 230.

5. Quoted in *Calcutta—the City of Palaces*, p. 63.

6. Carey, William. *The Good Old Days of John Company*, vol. I, p. 270.

7. *Hundred Years of the Statesman 1875–1975*, p. 19.

8. Raychowdhury, Ranabir. *Early Calcutta Advertisements 1875–1925*, p. 452.

9. Ibid. p. 513.

10. Ibid. p. 509.

11. *The Englishman*, 20 December 1898 to 6 January 1899.

12. Massey. op. cit.

13. Karkaria, Bachi J. *To a Grand Design*, Calcutta 1988. The saga of the Grand Hotel has been mainly taken from this book.

14. Massey. op. cit. pp. 99–100.

15. Cotton. op. cit. pp. 246–47.

16. *Bengal Past & Present*, vol. 36, 1928, 'Editor's Note Book,' p. 57.

17. Cotton. op. cit. pp. 247-48.

18. Mitra, Rathin. *Calcutta Then and Now*, p. 39.

19. Massey. op. cit. p. 101.

20. Raychowdhury, Ranabir. *Early Calcutta Advertisements*, p. 624.

21. Massey. op. cit. p. 102.

22. Cotton. op. cit. p. 759.

23. Ibid. pp. 761–62.

24. Blechynden. op. cit. p. 172.

25. Abraham, Isaac S. *Origin and History of the Calcutta Jews,* Calcutta 1969, pp. 68–69.

26. Massey. op. cit. p. 103.

27. Birney, W.S. 'Episcopal Palaces in Bengal,' *Bengal Past & Present,* vol. LXIII, 1943, p. 18.

Chapter Eleven

From Burying Ground Road to Park Street

The old burial ground (in what was later St. John's Church) was full and closed in 1767. On 25 August of the same year a new burial ground was opened near the Marhatta Ditch, at the end of the road which began from Esplanade opposite the New Fort William and continued south-east past the garden house of Governor Vansittart up to the Ditch. The road was for a while called Burying Ground Road. The local name was *Badamtala*, from the large number of almond trees in the area. After the opening of the new cemetery it assumed the name *Gorsthan Ka Rasta* (*Bengal & Agra Directory* 1850). The area was desolate and infested with dacoits, compelling people to form a group before going out in the direction. It was considered so far out of town that palanquin bearers would charge double fare for the destination. It was so far for the Chaplain to come there from the church that he was allowed a separate palanquin allowance of Rs. 30 per month. With the high mortality rate, this cemetery too was rapidly filling up; so a new one on the north side of the road was opened in 1785. The vast new Lower Circular Road Cemetery was opened in 1840. The road was once called the Vansittart Avenue before the new name Park Street came into use, probably originating from the Deer Park in Vansittart's garden house (today's Loreto House).

After the Chowringhee area became a prime residential part of the town, people ventured to buy land in the Burying Ground Road to build their own houses. Except for a few institutions like the Asiatic Society, it was mostly residential quarters like Middleton Street and Harrington Street. The Hall & Anderson was perhaps the first shop (a huge departmental store) in Park Street. Other shopping establishments, restaurants, night clubs, car showrooms and large mansions followed to make the area a fashionable shopping and entertainment centre.

In the *Calcutta Directory* of 1906 we find the houses numbered from the south side, after the Hall and Anderson building, which was on 31 Chowringhee Road. The numbers continued on the north side from Lower Circular Road ending at number 57, the last house on the Chowringhee side housing the Asiatic Society and the Staunton Chess Club.

If one enters Park Steet today from the Chowringhee end, the first complex of buildings on the left is occupied by the Asiatic Society. The new multistoreyed building on the grounds adjacent to the old building and forming part of its compound stands most probably on the site of a riding school opened by Chevalier Antoine Pierre de L'Etang, a French emigre (supposed to have been a page to the unfortunate French Queen Marie Antoinette) who came to Calcutta in 1796 from Pondicherry. The school, which had also facilities for fencing and billiards, was quite popular for a time.

THE ASIATIC SOCIETY

The Asiatic Society of Bengal (originally known as the Asiatick Society) was founded by Sir William Jones, then Chief Justice of the Supreme Court, on 15 January 1784. This is one of the oldest institutions of its kind in the world. Hastings, the then Governor General, was the first Patron. "The bounds of its investigations," says the founder in his first discourse, "will be the geographical limits of Asia, and within these limits its inquiries will be extended to whatever is performed by man or produced by nature." Originally its meetings were held in the Grand Jury Room of the Supreme Court. A library was also started in the same room.

The old Park Street building was erected in 1804, to which additions and alterations were made in 1836 and 1850 to accommodate the growing library and collections.

Figure 51: William Wood, the junction of Chowringhee and Park Street and the Asiatic Society Building in 1830

To the original name of Asiatick Society, the words 'of Bengal' were added by James Prinsep in 1832 on the title page of the journal in order to distinguish it from the Royal Asiatic Society of Great Britain and Ireland, which is an entirely separate and distinct body.[1]

Since the foundation of the society its academic activities have been uninterrupted. Its first publication had the title of *Asiatic Researches*. They extend over 20 volumes issued between 1799 and 1839. As the *Journal of the Asiatic Society of Bengal*, it has since continued for a long time.

From 1829 Indians could join the society. Another department which has greatly added to the renown of the old society is the Bibliotheca Indica. When the College of Fort William closed down its library, its printed books and manuscripts were transferred to the society, along with the Government collection of manuscripts. The bulk of the Arabic and Persian manuscripts of Tipu Sultan's library brought down from Mysore were also transferred to the society library.

The Museum of the society up to 1866 contained a large collection of zoological and ethnological specimens, besides many archaeological relics and statues of great value, nearly all of which were presents made to the society by its members. The society was however unable to provide space and funds to maintain the ever increasing collection, and offered the Museum to the Government in 1865 on condition that the society will receive free accommodation in the Indian Museum, which was then taking shape in the adjoining Chowringhee. Ultimately, the Indian Museum was born with a shortage of space, so the Asiatic Society had to relinquish its demand.

The society however retained its collections of valuable coins, copper *sanads*, portraits and pictures and busts, and its large library. Many of the important paintings have been lent to the Victoria Memorial Hall for display.

Today, the Asiatic Society of Bengal, despite its multistoreyed new wing, is beset with many problems. The library has acute shortage of space. Rare books and manuscripts are dumped on the floors of Metcalfe Hall. There is great governmental apathy. Instead of increasing the fund allocation, the Government of India has recently halved it. Many rare original paintings just lie on the floor gathering dust, 'there is no space to keep them'. These include oil paintings by artists like Peter Paul Rubens, Guido Reni (*Cleopatra*), Sir Joshua Reynolds (*Cupid Asleep on a Cloud* and *Young William Jones*), Canaletti, Nicholas Roerich, George Chinnery, Thomas and William Daniell (*Ghat of Benares*). Notable portraits include those of Raja Radha Kanta Deb by F.R. Say, Sir William Jones, James Prinsep, Sir Asutosh Mukherjee, Sir U.N. Brahmachari, Sir P.C. Ray. Some rare books are preserved well, among them are *Kubjikamata Mantra* of the seventh century, many Buddhist manuscripts, a rare Asoka edict in Prakrit and Sanskrit written in Brahmi script dating back to 250 BC. There are many printed rare books of which the oldest is a book printed in Venice in 1497.[2]

The Asiatic Society needs funds from the Government and other agencies, and needs better administration, initiative and concern to preserve its treasures for posterity.

The society building once had a chess club, the Staunton Chess Club, and the Photographic Society of India had its headquarters in the basement.

Past a few shops and restaurants we come to the exit gate of the Park Hotel and an adjoining garden before the A.P.J. House, pushed slightly to the rear. At the site of the garden there was once a large mansion called Park House, with several shops on the ground floor; the other floors were residential. Park House was rebuilt on a portion of the compound and the site of the stables and coachhouse of the old 56 Park Street, at one time occupied by J. Thomas, senior partner of the old firm of R. Thomas & Co. Next we come to the grand arcade in which we find Trinca's Restaurant, Oxford Book Store-Gallery and the Kwality Restaurant, and between them the entrance to Park Hotel, one of Calcutta's five-star hotels.

FREEMASONS' HALL

Since 1904 the headquarters of Freemasonry in Bengal has been housed at 54 Park Street (new number 19). Its earliest meeting place was at the Old Court House. In 1786 it moved to a house prepared for its reception by a firm of auctioneers, Messrs. Gould and Burrell, over their place of business in Lal Bazar. From 1840 to 1904 the Masonic headquarters were at 55 Bentinck Street. In the Banqueting Hall there was an interesting portrait of the Marquess of Hastings, who was the first and only 'Grand Master of all India'.[3]

Freemasonry in Bengal has an ancient and honourable record. Its earliest District Grand Master, George Pomfret, assumed office in 1728 and the lodge 'Star in the East' is the oldest of any lodges outside the United Kingdom and dates from 1740. Many of the Governors, Governors General and high officials were members of the lodge and we find foundation stone-laying and inaugural ceremonies being conducted according to Masonic rites. The building in Park Street is set back from the main road in its own compound, away from the hustle and bustle of a busy street. There are a number of portraits in the Banquet Hall, among Indians are the likes of Maharaja Sir Nripendra Narayan Bhoop Bahadur of Cooch Behar, Prosunno Coomar Dutt, who was the first Hindu initiated into Freemasonry and Deputy District Grand Master of Bengal in 1890-91.

Coming out of the gate we see another gate on the left leading to the sprawling residential block, the Karnani Mansions, with its huge parking lot. The main building stands on the Free School Street. On the Park Street front there is a double-storeyed building which houses several shops and restaurants, including the well-known Olympia, rendezvous of the literati and the Bohemians, the Moulin Rouge and the Blue Fox, where the connoisseurs of Calcutta gathered in the sixties and early seventies to hear Pam Crain sing with Louis Bank's orchestra. At the corner of Park Street and Free School Street was the Park Street Police Station. But the rest of the site of Karnani Mansions from Freemasons'

Hall was occupied by the building and grounds of the Girls' Department of Doveton College. Opposite it on Free School Street was the Doveton College for boys, which has since given way to the Park Mansions.

The founder of the college, Capt. John Doveton, once in the Nizam of Hyderabad's Army, inherited a large fortune after the death of his uncle. He passed away in London in 1853. A Eurasian by birth, he bequeathed his fortune of nearly £50,000 for the education of his community. This sum was equally divided between the Parental Academy of Calcutta (renamed Doveton College) and the Doveton Protestant College which was soon after founded at Madras. The Parental Academic Institution was established by John William Ricketts on 1 March 1823. The object was to impart good education to the poor Christians of the city. After the Doveton endowment the name was changed and the institution turned to a college affiliated to the University of Calcutta. An Infant and Juvenile Department and a separate section for girls followed. But the institutions closed or were merged with other bodies in the early twentieth century.

On our left we find a long street starting from Park Street and ending in Lenin Sarani to the north.

Free School Street

The street draws its name from the Free School established here in 1789-90. The Calcutta Corporation renamed it Mirza Ghalib Street in 1969, the centenary of the death of Mirza Asadullah Khan who used the *nom de plume* Ghalib, and was a Mughal nobleman and master of Urdu and Persian poetry.

The area was a bamboo jungle in 1780 and people were afraid to venture into it at night. Even when the Free School was shifted in 1789, the rest of the area remained a mass of jungle, some ponds and a few dwelling houses.

Today the street is busy, and crammed with offices, shops, schools and colleges, some Government offices, the Fire Brigade, shops, eating houses, cheap lodges, and allegedly a popular haunt for sex workers. On the western side we find only one notable address, Number 39.

According to tradition the novelist William Makepeace Thackeray was born on 18 July 1811 in a house at 39 Free School Street. His father, Richmond Thackeray, was at the time Secretary to the Board of Revenue; about six months later he was appointed Collector of the 24 Parganas. Number 39 today houses the Armenian College and the Armenian Philanthropic Academy.

THE ARMENIAN COLLEGE

The first school for Armenian children in Calcutta was started by a commandant named Margar in his house. The first regular Armenian School was started in 1798 by Aratoon

Kaloos. The Armenian Philanthropic Academy was established in 1821 at 358 Old China Bazar Street, to be amalgamated with Aratoon Kaloos's school in 1825. This is probably the second oldest existing institution, the first being the Free School. In 1883, the college shifted to its final haven at 39 Free School Street, where a three-storeyed house with a large compound was purchased for Rs. 48,000.[4]

Today there are hardly 100 Armenians left in Calcutta. The college has a desolate look. Gone are tycoons like Sir A.A. Apcar, Aratoon Stephen and J.C. Galstaun. The Armenian Club was once a force to reckon with in Indian hockey. The community has not thrown up any hockey star recently. Only some faces are seen in rugby games. Young students are brought in from outside India, mostly from Iran, as the college has rich endowments for education. The students, forced to live a cloistered life, are not allowed to mix with outsiders.

A short-lived German Musical Club was established close by on 2 April 1872 to offer to the German community of Calcutta a place of recreation, where 'German Music, Gymnastics, Theatricals and Amenities of Social Life' were made available.

Up to Lindsay Street there were shops and residential houses mostly inhabited by Eurasians. But at the Sudder Street Corner there was a Young Women's Christian Association Home for some time.

The area from the Lindsay Street crossing up to Lenin Sarani was known as Jan Bazar.

THE CALCUTTA FREE SCHOOL

We have already referred to the Charity School run by the Vestry north of Lal Dighi till a part of the school building was taken on rent by the East India Company to use as a Court House, the 'Old Court House'. On St. Thomas's Day, 21 December 1789 the Vestry called a public meeting inviting a few other gentlemen and the Governor General for the formation of a school for Christian children born to poor parents. The Free School Society of Bengal was formed, of which the governing body was to be the select Vestry and six other gentlemen then elected with the Governor General as Patron, the Church wardens being perpetual treasurers of the funds.

The Free School however did not commence work before 12 January 1790. A proposal to unite its establishment with that of the Charity School was in the air and this was actually carried out next month on 28 February. The Vestry and the Governors took on two years' lease a large house with six *bighas* and six *cottahs* of land, belonging to Mr. Charles Weston at 8 Mission Row, where General Clavering used to live (later the premises of J. Thomas & Co). On 1 April 1790 there were seventeen boys and twelve girls in the Free School establishment and by the end of the year the number grew to fifty and thirty, respectively.[5]

The Vestry was looking for a permanent habitation for the school and in 1793 a property, consisting of a house and a considerable plot of land near Jan Bazar, was purchased by the

Governors of the Charities from Mr. Louis Barretto. The house is said to have been the residence of Mr. Justice Le Maistre who came out with Sir Eliah Impey and was one of the Judges in the trial of Maharaja Nandakumar. The value of this garden house at Jan Bazar was estimated in 1802 at Sicca Rupees 87, 869-8-5. This was the site of the Free School opposite and running further south of Lindsay Street. In 1795 school buildings were erected upon it, and all the children on the rolls, 70 of the Charity and about 78 of the Free School, were moved into them; day scholars were also now taken in and taught gratis; in 1796 their number was nearly sixty.[6]

At Easter 1802, the Vestry resolved that as the school was too full of Portuguese and Bengali children keeping out European children, in future none but children of European parentage should be admitted, and that the total number of boys and girls in the school was not to exceed 250.

In 1833 a church called St. Thomas's Church was erected in the school compound, mainly through the efforts of Bishop Turner. The foundation stone was laid by Lady William Bentinck on 13 April 1830, and on 2 February 1833 it was consecrated by Bishop Wilson.

Free School had to part with some of its land when in the early 1920s the Free School Street Fire Station was built. The Free School went out of existence during the Second World War and has since been replaced by another school (not free), St. Thomas's. A further plot of land was taken away from the school after Independence, when the West Bengal Government's Food Department office block was built (a hideous one too).

At the site of the present Dunlop India, one can locate G. Isaia & Co., confectioners, at 42 Free School Street, north of the point where it meets Royd Street. They were a company of Italian chocolate manufacturers and caterers. Later they moved further north and opened a restaurant called Isaias, which was a popular haunt for the local Anglo-Indians, with a live band for dancing that continued till the early hours of the morning. After the exodus of these people from India after Independence, Isaias became a joint for visiting seamen and prostitutes, with brawls and fistcuffs as part of the daily routine, till the restaurant ultimately closed down.

DUNLOP (INDIA) LTD.

John Boyd Dunlop's leisure time experiments gave birth to the first pneumatic tyre in England and the first pneumatic bicycle tyre arrived in India in 1898. The company sent their manager for India Mr. Huet in November 1898 to open the Indian branch at Bombay. Mr. R.J.C. Park took over as the new manager on 1 January 1899 and a new office was opened at Apollo Street. The Dunlop House at 57/B Free School Street (at the site of G. Isaia & Co., at old Number 42) was built in 1928. This was still a branch office. With immaculate foresight the Dunlop Rubber Company decided to build a factory, about

36 miles away from Calcutta, and the head office was consequently transferred to Calcutta in 1935. The factory was erected at Sahaganj, a village in Hooghly, which being situated on the banks of the river Hooghly was well served by river, road and rail transport. The factory started production in July 1936.

With 1200 workers the factory started producing tyres for different transport requirements. With the beginning of the Second World War in 1939, production was at full swing.

After the end of the war came Independence and Dunlop India emerged as one of India's major producers of car tyres. They even started producing aircraft tyres, but other competitors entered the market and it became necessary to modernize production equipments to compete with the new entrants. But it failed to do so and the company was soon running at a loss. The Chhabrias, one of those groups of non-resident Indians who have emerged in the last twenty years, with money power to buy into and control sick Indian industries, took advantage of its crisis and took over Dunlop (India) Ltd. They did not inject new money in the coffers, but made away with whatever little was still there. The huge Sahaganj complex grinded to a halt, leaving hundreds of workers starving and driving several to suicide. Dunlop has started production again in the new millennium. South of the Dunlop House is a street leading east to Wellesley Street. Royd Street is named after Sir John Royd, Puisne Judge of the Supreme Court from 1787 to 1816. He died in 1816 at the age of 65 years and is buried in the South Park Street Cemetery. He was also a Vice-President of the Asiatic Society during his sojourn in Calcutta. He used to live in the corner building of Free School Street and Park Street, 41 Free School Street. This later became the boys' section of the Doveton College. Montague Massey writes that there was quite a bit of waterlogging there after a heavy shower. When he was going to office 'after three days and nights of heavy rain,' he found quite a lake at the Doveton College compound and a tall form rose from the water: a master of the college taking his students for a bath and romping in three to four feet deep water. After the closure of the Doveton College, the old premises were pulled down and in 1910 came up the present Park Mansions, one of the earliest residential mansions on Park Street, with several shops on the ground floor.

We come to Park Street again and continue eastward along the northern pavement. From Free School Street up to Wellesley Street (Rafi Ahmed Kidwai Road) most of the buildings are new, but there are narrow pathways leading to some very old colonial houses in a precarious condition. Old Number 52/4 was occupied by the Bengal Landholders' Association and the United Bengal Club. Both organizations had the same set of office-bearers in 1905: President—Maharaja Suryyakanta Acharyya Chowdhury of Mymensingh, and Hony. Secretaries—Raja Pramada Nath Ray of Dighapatia and A. Chowdhury, Bar-at-Law. Eligibility rules limited membership of Bengal United Club to men of position, rank and education among natives of India, chiefly landholders of Bengal. Elections were by ballot and subscriptions, residents paying Rs. 50 and non-residents Rs. 5 only.

We find a fine ornamented one-storeyed structure on Park Street, now occupied by an auctioner's firm. It once housed V. Morello & Co., manufacturing confectioners and caterers of yesteryears. The present Park Street Post Office is a new building, but a lane next to it leads to a very old Calcutta institution (though not on this site)—the Jewish Girls School.

THE JEWISH GIRLS SCHOOL

Initially, the Christian Missionaries started the education of Jewish children by setting up a free Christian Hebrew Mission School. By subscription from benefactors the first Jewish educational institution was formed in 1881 under the name of The Jewish Girls and Infants School. The very next year the Ezra Benevolent Institution was founded to impart education to the poor Jewish children in Hebrew, religious knowledge and general subjects.

The Jewish Girls and Infants School opened an independent section for boys and came to be known as the Jewish Boys and Girls School. In 1885, this section was merged with the girls' school and the institution was called simply The Jewish Girls School. The school was situated at 8 Pollock Street.[7]

In 1956 the school shifted to its Park Street premises. A huge iron gate leads to a sprawling campus. Mr. Sam Luddy, one of the very few Jews who decided to stay back in Calcutta, remembers his cousin Miss Ramah Luddy who was the Principal of this school for thirty years, before retiring in 1963. But, by the mid-seventies there were hardly any Jewish children left in Calcutta to attend the institution. The school opened its gates to other communities. Mr. David Nahoum is the only Jew in the school committee.

Opposite Camac Street, we find the towering spank new Park Plaza, a multistoreyed shopping and office complex. In our younger days here was the garage and motor car showroom of M/s Walford's. It was always a wonder to watch the latest shining motor cars displayed in their first floor showroom.

Crossing the Wellesley Street we come to another surviving colonial house with a large compound: the garden has long disappeared. A part or parts of the large building have simply disintegrated from years of neglect. There is a litigation on the property; the West Bengal Government wants to take over the site and build a new hotel. The owners of the property are the Nawab Nazims of Murshidabad, descendants of Mir Jafar.

The old Number 46 Park Street housed a famous club for Europeans, The New Club. Earlier still this house was used as the seminary of William Meadows Farrell and afterwards occupied by the Surveyor-General's office.

The New Club was established in 1884 and immediately gained popularity. There was great demand for residential quarters and the club took on lease a building at 52/1 Park Street for the purpose. The library was excellent. Amusements included lawn tennis, billiards, smoking concerts, house dinners, dances etc.[8] In 1905 we find the club open to all gentlemen received in general society. Entrance fees were Rs. 64, subscriptions for residents Rs. 8 per month and for non-residents Rs. 16 per annum. Mr. Arthur Preston was the President and Mr. C.A. Graham Managing Member. Further east the old Number 41 was the residence of Mr. S.P. Sinha (later Lord Sinha of Raipur).

The houses up to Park Lane, mostly residential, have mostly given way to modern skyscrapers, with only a very few in dilapidated condition.

THE PARK STREET CEMETERIES

Three of these on the northern side of the street have all disappeared due to land-grabbers.

The first of the three was the Tiretta's or the French Cemetery, described earlier in this volume. A short distance further on, past McLeod Street, was the Mission Cemetery, where the chief object of interest was the large blue monument marking the family vault of John

Figure 52: The Tomb of Hindoo Stuart in South Park Street Cemetery
Photo courtesy Calcutta Historical Society

Zachariah Kiernander, the first Protestant missionary in Bengal, the vault containing the remains of the missionary and his two wives.

There was another cemetery on the north side, viz. the Scottish Cemetery, which contained the grave of Richmond Thackeray, father of the famous novelist.

These cemeteries have by now given way to modern buildings. The Assembly of God Church is the largest building complex at this end of Park Street with its school and hospital, next to the modern multistoreyed building of Berger Paints. As we cross the road near its junction with Lower Circular Road (now Acharya Jagadish Chandra Bose Road) we come to the southern side of the road, where the South Park Street Cemetery was opened in 1767, giving the road itself the name Burying Ground Road, later changed to Park Steet. This cemetery still exists. An early account by Sophia Goldborne from 1785 reads:

> Obelisks, pagodas, etc. are erected at great expence; and the whole spot is surrounded by as well-turned a walk as those you traverse in Kensington Gardens, ornamented with a double row of aromatic trees, which afford a solemn and beautiful shade: in a word not old Windsor Churchyard with all its cypress and yews is the smallest degree comparable to them: and I quitted them with unspeakable reluctance. There is no difference between these two grounds, but in the expence of the monuments, which denote that persons of large fortune are there intered and vice versa: whence in order to preserve this difference in the appearance, the first rank pay five hundred rupees, the second three for opening the ground; and they are disjoined merely by a broad road... Funerals are indeed solemn and affecting things at Calcutta, no hearses being here introduced, or hired mourners employed: for, as it often happens in the gay circles, that a friend is dined with one day and the next in eternity—the feelings are interested, the sensations awful, and the mental question, for the period of interment at least, which will be tomorrow's victim? The departed one, of whatever rank is carried on men's shoulders...and a procession of gentlemen equally numerous and respectable from the extent of genteel connexions, follows.[9]

The South Park Street Cemetery was opened on 25 August 1767, for the reception of the body of Mr. John Wood, a writer in the Custom House, whose tomb was later levelled to make way for the western crossroad. Numbers of tablets from monuments similarly removed have been collected and inserted in the walls of the little house at the entrance. On the right hand is the grave of Samuel Oldham (1788), the undertaker, who first brought to Calcutta the Gaur stone from which many of the slabs here were cut. His initials S.O. Fecit are to be seen on many a Bengal tombstone. A fluted pillar commemorates Rose Aylmer, who died in 1800. Among a large number of pyramids and obelisks stands the whitewashed monument to Sir William Jones (1794) with an epitaph written by himself: 'Here was deposited the mortal part of a man who feared God, but not Death, who thought none below him but the base and unjust, none above him but the wise and virtuous.'

Among distinguished civilians, Richard Becher and Edward Wheler are interred here. The stately monument to Lucia (1772), the young wife of Robert Palk, who as the Judge of the Court of Cutcherry first committed Maharaja Nandakumar for forgery, inspired the famous and imaginative idyll to 'Lucia' in the last chapter of Rudyard Kipling's *City of Dreadful Night*.

> The tender pity she would oft betray,
> Shall be with interest at her shrine returned
> Connubial love connubial tears repay,
> And Lucia lov'd shall still be Lucia mourned.[10]

Here lies the East Indian poet Henry Louis Vivian Derozio, who died in 1831 at the age of twentytwo.

Probably the most remarkable monument of the lot was built in the form of a Hindu temple erected over the remains of Major General Charles Stuart, better known as 'Hindoo Stuart' from his conformity to Hindu customs and ideas. In 1828, he died at his residence at Wood Street. The largest pyramid has been attributed by Busteed to that of Elizabeth Jane Barwell, the young bride of Richard Barwell, member of the Council during the reign of Warren Hastings. Another contemporary member of the Council, Sir John Clavering, is also buried here (1777). Judges Lemaistre, Hyde (1796), Sir John Royd, who gave the name to Royd Street are buried here. Among the military, the most prominent burial was that of Colonel Thomas Deane Pearse (1789), 'Father of the Bengal Artillery'. Chaplains of the calibre of David Brown, the first Provost of the College of Fort William, Thomas Yate and Christian Diemer have their last resting place in the same cemetery.

The South Park Street Cemetery was closed in 1840, when the new Lower Circular Road Cemetery was opened within a stone's throw. The former has a large number, almost a 'jungle' of monuments to the young and the old, the noble and the poor, aristocrats and commoners who died so far away from their country.

Today most of these monuments are crumbling from disrepair, vandalism and neglect. High walls have been erected to keep the vandals out. But according to reports anti-socials and drug addicts take over the domain of the dead at night for their nightly chores.

Leaving the cemetery, we come to a road leading south, named Rawdon Street after the Marquis of Hastings, Governor General of India from 1813 to 1823, who was created Earl of Rawdon in 1916. The street was residential except for the last two buildings at its junction with Lower Circular Road which house the La Martiniere Girls' School on the east and the Boys' School on the west. The most interesting structures on the street were the Panchkotee houses, five houses of similar design on the eastern side. These were the residential Auckland Houses between Theatre Road and Auckland Square bearing numbers 16, 16/1, 16/2 and 16/3 to 16/5. These have since disappeared. The street is now renamed as Sarojini Naidu Sarani since 1971. Sarojini, called 'Nightingale of India', was a poet and a politician who took part in the Freedom Movement, and died in 1949.

Moving along Park Street by the south side, further west after Rawdon Street are mainly shops and residences. The only remarkable house was the old Number 22 which was the residence of the Raja Bahadur of Nashipur. Then we come to another road leading south, parallel to Rawdon Street—initially known as Loudoun Street named after Lady Hastings, wife of the Marquis of Hastings, who by her birthright was the Countess of Loudoun. Gradually the second 'u' in the name of the street disappeared. This was again a fashionable residential area. The Maharaja of Tripura had a house in 1905 near Park Street at the old Number 20 at the crossing with Short Street. Gradually the old houses are giving way to new ones. The Commissioner of Police, Calcutta, now resides at Number 2. Locally this street was once known as *Short Bazar-ka paschim-rasta*.

In 1967 the road was renamed after Dr. U.N. Brahmachari, an eminent physician, who lived in a palatial building on this street. Dr. Brahmachari invented the drug Urea Stibamine as cure for the deadly disease *Kala Azar*. He was a Fellow of the Royal Society of Medicine and the Royal Society of Tropical Medicine. He was knighted in 1934.

There are a few more streets south of Park Street, mainly residential, that deserve brief descriptions.

Short Street

Short Street running from Rawdon Street opposite the South Park Street Cemetery and ending in Camac Street, was named after Charles Short, a businessman and owner of large properties in Calcutta. He was the owner of several parcels of land in the vicinity of the street and of a bazar named after him. He died on 2 July 1785.

Robinson Street

This short street begins from Loudon Street and ends in Rawdon Street. According to H.E.A. Cotton, this was named after Charles Knowles Robinson, Police Magistrate of Calcutta and architect of the Metcalfe Hall and other public buildings.[11] But according to other sources it is named after Reverend John Robinson, who was a translator at the High Court.

Outram Street

This short thoroughfare, beginning at Short Street and ending at Theatre Road, is named after Lt. General Sir James Outram, who was a gallant soldier. At a later date the spacious Outram Club was established in the neighbourhood.

Hungerford Street

Starting from Short Street and ending at Lower Circular Road, it was named after the Governor-General, the Marquis of Hastings, who was also Baron of Hungerford. This has been renamed as Picasso Bithi by the Calcutta Corporation in 1982 in honour of the Spanish-born artist, Pablo Picasso.

Moira Street

This is another street in Calcutta named after the Governor-General, the Marquis of Hastings, who was also Earl of Moira. This begins at Loudon Street and ends at Hungerford Street.

Albert Road

Albert Road begins at Hungerford Street and ends at Camac Street. According to P.T. Nair, the road was originally known as Dalhousie Street, but was later renamed Albert Street in honour of Queen Victoria's husband, the Prince Consort, Prince Albert of Saxe-Coburg Gotha, a princely state in Germany. He was married to the reigning Queen Victoria in London on 10 February 1840. He died at Windsor Castle on 14 December 1861.

Park Street between Loudon Street and Wood Street

The corner building Number 36 now houses the Seventh Day Adventist School and the church of the same name. In 1905 the house was Number 14 and was the residence of Mr. H.M. Percival, Professor of English at Presidency College, Calcutta. The next complex of buildings now the Headquarters of the Deputy Commissioner (South) of Calcutta Police has grown around an old building inside a compound. Over the gateway and other parts are residential quarters of senior police officers.

Now Number 34, it bore the Number 13 in 1905, when it was owned by Mr. Hem Chandra Goswami. The Goswamis were landlords of Serampore and owned extensive properties in Calcutta. According to Mr. Dipak Lahiri, a descendant of the Goswamis, Hemchandra's grandfather Raghu Ram Goswami was a business partner of John Palmer, 'The Prince of Merchants'; and amassed large wealth that he wisely invested in landed property.

Number 32 (old Number 12) is the Roman Catholic Archbishop's House. A double-storeyed building, with a sombre design, it lacks the grandeur of the Protestant Bishop's House on Chowringhee. It had once been the site of the residence of Mrs. Esther Leach, the 'Star Actress' of Calcutta. While appearing in a play being staged at the newly built Sans Souci Theatre next door (site of St. Xavier's College), on the evening of November 1843, as she was waiting for her cue, her dress caught fire from an oil lamp, one of a row placed on the floor. She rushed on to the stage, calling for help, was instantly thrown down and the flames extinguished; but she was already severely burnt. She was carried to her home next door and she ultimately breathed her last on 18 November, at the age of 34. She was buried in the Bhowanipore Military Cemetery.

From Sans Souci Theatre to St. Xavier's College

Too many Calcutta theatres were burnt down in the nineteenth century and one of them, the Chowringhee Theatre, at the corner of Chowringhee and Theatre Road, was destroyed in 1839. Soon Mrs. Esther Leach aided by Mr. J. Stocqueler of *the Englishman,* started collecting funds for a new theatre. In May 1840, the Sans Souci Theatre was ready at 10, Park Street (new Number 30). It was a fine building with an imposing portico. The formal opening took place on 8 March 1841, under the patronage and immediate presence of the Governor General and his suite. Sheridan Knowles' play *The Wife* was enacted, and Mrs. Leach, who played the role of Mariana, recited a metrical prologue written for the occasion by Sir John William Kaye. Her company comprised both amateurs and professionals. Among the former were Mr. H.W. Torrens, a versatile Bengal Civilian, and his son-in-law, Mr. James Hume, afterwards a Magistrate in Calcutta. Mr. Stocqueler hired some actors from England. One of them, Mr. Barry, had a capricious voice which was given to deserting him at the critical moment, often leaving him to end up in a dumb show. After the tragic death of Mrs. Leach, the Sans Souci was hired out to a French company, but it never ran well, so the doors closed on 24 April 1844.

The first St. Xavier's College was founded on 1 June 1835 in Portuguese Church Street by English Jesuits, the number of pupils being 80–100. Three years later the college was

Figure 53: St. Xavier's College, Park Street, a picture postcard with a
postage stamp postmarked on the first day of issue 12.4.1985

removed to a rented house at 3 Park Street, and in January 1841 to 22 Chowringhee Road, when the number of students was about 300. In 1843, at the insistence of Babu Moti Lal Seal, the Indian philanthropist, the Jesuit Fathers took over the management of the Seal's College at 60 Coloottola Street. This however proved disastrous and led to the closing down of the institution and their leaving India.

After the departure of the Jesuits St. John's College at Entally, founded by Archbishop Carew in 1844, became the centre of Catholic education in Calcutta. In September 1849 the derelict Sans Souci Theatre and the adjoining land were bought by the Archbishop on behalf of the Roman Catholic community for Rs. 27,500. The college however was not a success and, on the death of Archbishop Carew, it closed its doors in 1855. Carew's successor, Archbishop Oliffe, anxious to save Catholic education in Calcutta, tried to persuade the English Jesuits to come back to the city to open the college. Proving unsuccessful he approached the Belgian Jesuits who readily agreed and landed in India on 28 November 1859. The present St. Xavier's College opened its doors on 16 January 1860. The property at 10 Park Street was made over to the Society of Jesus.

In 1862 the college was affiliated to the University of Calcutta. In February 1868, No. 11 Park Street, with the adjoining grounds, was acquired, and by 1869 the number of students rose to 500. In 1875, an observatory was erected at the cost of Rs. 28,000. The Crohan Building to house the school classes was completed in 1915 at a cost of Rs. 1,06,000. The magnificent old facade of the Sans Souci Theatre was ultimately demolished in 1831 and in its place now stands the modern four-storeyed structure.

Immediately after the college, moving towards Chowringhee we come to a large old building inside a high-walled compound. The building, Numbers 13, 14 and 15 Wood Street, houses the Survey of India Office, Photographic and Lithographic Office and the Mathematical Instruments Office.

The Survey of India is an old organization that moved to Park Street from Dalhousie Square. At first it was located near the Park Street and Chowringhee Road junction. The Wood Street buildings came up in 1888-89. The building at the corner was the Mathematical Instruments Office, which after Independence shifted to Jadavpur as National Instruments. The middle building is the Photographic and Lithographic section and the last one is the office of the Surveyor General; and the Deputy Surveyor General's Office, Eastern India. The buildings are massive and conform to the red brick designs of the late nineteenth century.

Other than surveying the office was also involved in a memorable task, viz. producing the first postage stamps of India. Lord Dalhousie, then Governor-General of India, expressed the desire that stamps should be issued in simple designs with the British Coat of Arms and the Queen's head as motifs. The job was first entrusted to Col. Forbes, Superintendent of the Royal Mint at Calcutta in 1853. Col. Forbes made several experiments with the Wyon portrait of Queen Victoria, but the project failed. In came Capt. H.L. Thuillier, the Deputy

Surveyor General, in charge of the Lithographic Department of the Survey of India in Calcutta. The Captain submitted rough sketches drawn on transfer papers for different values of the stamps on 22 February 1854. The designs were approved and they were engraved at the Lithographic Press by the master craftsman Muneerooddin. The stamps of the denominations of half anna, one anna, two annas and four annas made their appearance after August 1854.

Wood Street connecting Park Street to Theatre Road

A portion of Wood Street near the Theatre Road end is called Upper Wood Street. This is a direct continuation of Wellesley Street (Rafi Ahmed Kidwai Road) to Theatre Road (Shakespeare Sarani). According to H.E.A. Cotton, Wood Street was named after Mr. Henry Wood, who, on 13 July 1848, brought to the notice of the Lottery Committee, 'the inadequate manner in which the establishment entertained for the purpose performs its duty in removing the filth'—a complaint which persists after the lapse of all these years.[12]

P.T. Nair however ascribes the name of the road to the memory of Lt. Col. Mark Wood, whose plan of Calcutta executed in 1784 and 1785 was the basis of much work on Calcutta. The area was a part of Baman Bustee, as the road was described as *Baman Bustee ka Rasta* in the *Bengal & Agra Guide* of 1805.[13] As described in the section on the South Park Street Cemetery, Colonel Stuart, popularly known as 'Hindoo Stuart', lived in a house at the corner of Theatre Road and Wood Street. Montague Massey tells us that the Calcutta Amateur Theatrical Society or CATS formed by a group of young men staged their plays in a building on the site of the building of the Saturday Club at 7 Wood Street. There were no actresses, young men acting the role of girls. Massey used to play the leading lady.

The Saturday Club was founded in August 1878, mainly through the initiative of Mr. Justice Louis Jackson. The finest feature of the club is its spacious tennis courts. This 'Europeans only' club was patronized mainly by young people just arrived from England and the business community called 'Boxwallahs'. After Independence the club opened its doors to Indians.

The Calcutta Corporation renamed Wood Street and parts of Upper Wood Street as Martin Luther King Sarani on 20 January 1986. Reverend Martin Luther King was a crusader of civil rights for blacks in the United States. His non-violent movement forced the US Congress to pass the Civil Rights Act in 1964, authorizing the Federal Government to enforce de-segregation of public accommodation and outlawing discrimination in publicly owned facilities as well as in employment. He won the Nobel Peace Prize in 1964. He was killed by a white sniper's bullet on 4 April 1968.[14]

Park Street

We come back to Park Street and proceed west from Wood Street. On our left is a well-kept garden called until the other day Allen Gardens. This was known for many years as the three-cornered tank, the banks of which were both high and precipitous, and a constant source of danger to children playing in the garden. When the Corporation filled it up, they mixed along with earth and rubbish, ashes from incinerators, then in use for the filling up operation. This gave rise to such an obnoxious and foul smell that all buildings in the vicinity were evacuated. One of the houses facing the new garden to the south was at the time in the occupation of a lady who took in boarders, all of whom left at once. She claimed compensation from the Corporation of the sum of Rs. 30,000 for the loss and damage she had sustained, and they paid it to her. She had to close the house for several months.

When the new Fort William was built, the residents of Gobindapore were given land elsewhere in the city; the rich went to Bara Bazar and Pathuriaghata area, but the poor got accommodation in bustees south of Park Street, spawning the Baman Bustee, Colvin's Bustee, Duncan's Bustee, Kashiabagan, etc. But as the town expanded, the Europeans shifted to these areas for residence and the *bustees* were gradually razed and the poor inhabitants moved to other pastures.

From the Allen Gardens we see a broad road leading south, ending at Lower Circular Road, hitting the later day Galstaun Park or Nizam Palace. The Road was called Camac Street.

Camac Street

Once popularly known as *Duncan Bustee ka rasta*, it was later named after William Camac, a wealthy merchant in the days of Cornwallis and Wellesley, who 'owned a large number of houses in the locality a century and quarter ago'. In the *Calcutta Gazette* of 6 March 1788, he advertises one of them for sale in the following terms: For sale, that small upper roomed garden house with about five biggas of land, on the road leading from Chowringhee to the burial ground, which formerly belonged to the Moravians. It is very private from the number of trees on the ground, and having lately received considerable additions and repairs, is well adapted for a black family. William Camac, according to the Directory of 1785, was a judge of Tipperah, and subsequently of Dacca. The name of Camac is well known in the Indian Civil and Military Services. Major Jacob Camac defeated Scindia in 1781 and retired in the following year with the rank of Colonel. Burges Camac was aide-de-camp to Lord Wellesley in 1804, and in Dodwell and Miles may be seen the names of two other Camacs, George and Turner. The road does not appear in Wood's map of 1784, and although it is shown in Upjohn's map, it bears no name. With the demolition of the *bustees* in Theatre Road it became 'one of the pleasantest streets in the English quarter'.[15]

In the early twentieth century there were several boarding houses on the east side. In the old Number 25, at the crossing with Short Street where the Vardaan Market is now situated, lived the Hon. C.G.H. Allen, ICS, Chairman of Calcutta Corporation. The mosque near Theatre Road was already there. After the crossing with Theatre Road, Number 19 was the residence of the Hon. Sir A.T. Arundel, KCSI, ICS, member of the Viceroy's Council. The old house with a large compound was demolished only recently. The other houses were mostly residential, except Number 14, next to Victoria Terrace, which was Mrs. Drew's Boarding Establishment.

On the western side the old Number 11 was the residence of J.C. Galstaun, before the Galstaun Park across the road was built. The Old Number 9 was the residence of the Hon. Sir Denzil Ibbetson, CIE, KCSI, Member of the Governor-General's Council. Number 6 was the residence of Mr. R.L. Ross, Under Secretary to the Government of Bengal. Presumably this building belonged to the Bengal Government as the resident on the ground floor was Miss Cornelia Sorabjee, legal adviser to *purdah* ladies under Court of Wards.

Number 5 too was in the possession of the Government for a spell. Residents during the period included Mr. W.S. Marris, ICS, Deputy Secretary, Home Department, Government of India, and Mr. L. Robertson, ICS, Under Secretary to the Government of India, Revenue and Agriculture Departments. The last building on the stretch stood at the junction with Theatre Road. In 1905 there were no buildings up to Harrington Street. Now we see a palatial building on the corner plot, built by Sir Rajen Mookherjee of Martin & Co. and later of Martin Burn Ltd. Between Harrington Street and Middleton Street there was only one house shown in early records, Number 4, which was the residence of Mr. C.J. Stevenson-Moore, ICS, Inspector General of Police. The house, with a large compound, has recently been demolished by the West Bengal Government for a new construction. Number 3 was one of Mrs. Monk's many boarding houses in the area.

In 1905, Number 2 was the residence of A.T. Apcar, Bar-at-Law, Calcutta High Court. Mr. Aratoon Stephen, the owner of the Grand Hotel, bought the property from Mr. A.T. Apcar's mother, Mrs. Matilda Thomas Apcar, for his own residence. He was a great collector of antiques and specialized in rare Oriental China. Lord Kitchener of Khartoum, another great collector of China, when he was Commander in Chief in India, used to visit Stephen's house to see and admire any new acquisition. Stephen Wilkinson, the architect of Stemphen's Mount Everest Hotel in Darjeeling recalled:

During one of my visits 'K of K' called and as usual we all proceeded to the room containing the collection. Among the exhibits was a small vase having a tubular stem and a bulbous base which 'K-of-K' greatly coveted, but the owner would not part with it at any price.

While examining the piece the stem unfortunately came in two, and the great "K" (Kitchener) was left standing aghast with a piece in each hand, apologizing for the accident, and offering to make good, as far as possible, the damage. Of course Stephen made light of the matter until after the departure of 'K' when there was much lamentation and not a little blaspheming during which he asked me 'what was to be done about his precious piece'.

I suggested that it would be a good idea to have the stem joined and the fracture covered with a gold band, stating that 'this vase was accidentally broken by His Excellency Lord Kitchener of Khartoum, etc.' giving the date of the occurrence. This was done by a local jeweller, and so effectively, that the vase was given a more prominent place in the collection than before, and for all I know still occupies this position at No. 2 Camac Street, Calcutta to this day.

Family members of Aratoon Stephen vouch for this story. But the vase is no longer at 2 Camac Street. It is in England, in the house of one of Stephen's five daughters, Burma.[16]

Aratoon Stephen breathed his last in this house on 14 May 1927. Gradually the family migrated from India. Only one of his granddaughters, Mrs. Irene Harris, still lived in the city until 1988. The house is still there, a place with a large portico falling into disrepair, but the old grandeur lingers. After crossing Middleton Row we come to No. 1/1, which was the Camac Street Branch of the chemists, Bathgate & Co. The corner building, No. 1, was Mrs. Pell's Boarding House and the Belgian Consulate. Over the years Camac Street has changed; many of the old garden houses are gone, their place taken over by modern office blocks, residential flats, shops, etc. One of the old houses, Number 6, a very fine Victorian bungalow, has been well maintained and is now occupied by the West Bengal State Planning Board.

The name of the street has changed too. In 1982 it acquired a new name Abanindranath Tagore Sarani. Nephew of the poet Rabindranath Tagore, Abanindranath is rightly called the Father of Modern Indian Art. Born at Jorasanko, the ancestral home of Rabindranath, on 7 August 1871, Abanindranath was a great-grandson of prince Dwarkanath Tagore. He got his training in painting from some British and Italian painters of repute. He gave up painting in the European style at the age of 29, and under the influence of Principal E.B. Havell, the renowned English artist, established the Calcutta School of Painting. He was for some time Vice-Principal of the Government School of Arts, working with Principal Havell. Besides his famous paintings he wrote several books for children. His lectures on art as Bagiswari Professor of Indian Fine Arts at the Calcutta University are of great value.[17]

As we come back to Park Street and proceed westward along the southern pavement the first building on the left (old No. 7) was once a residential house, which later became No. 26 and showroom of Refrigerators (India) Ltd. Next to it there was a large plot No. 24, which now houses a market, called Park Centre. No. 26A, once the showroom of Allen Berry & Co. Ltd., famous dealers of motor cars, is now the site of Waldorf Restaurant. The old No. 6 was a historic house at one time as the residence of Sir John Peter Grant, Lt. Governor of Bengal, 1859-62. Grant exerted his influence to procure the purchase of this large mansion as the official residence of the Lieutenant Governors of Bengal, but without success, the mansion at Alipore, Belvedere, being selected in preference.[18] The house was later purchased by Mr. W.C. Bonnerjee, Advocate, Calcutta High Court, and the first President of the Indian National Congress in 1885. The house was later renumbered as 24.

At 24A the Calcutta Light Horse Club was established in 1909. The history of the Calcutta Light Horse stretches back to the reign of Lord Clive. In 1759 Clive hurriedly enlisted local merchants and other Europeans to help repel an invasion by 700 Dutch troops with 800 Malayan mercenaries on the then new settlement (Calcutta). The Dutch party sailed up the Hooghly in seven large ships, landed by sheer weight of numbers, and began to advance steadily on Calcutta.

Clive concealed his men behind a ravine, and as the invaders paused, wondering how best to cross this, the Volunteer Cavalry charged them on their horses. The Dutch and the Malays fled in surprise and confusion. The Calcutta merchants had greatly relished this taste of military life, and kept the association alive through successive units—The Mounted Company of the Calcutta Voluntary Rifle Corps, the Calcutta Volunteer Guards, the Calcutta Volunteer Lancers, and finally, the Calcutta Light Horse.[19]

Generations of merchants, accountants and other Europeans joined the Calcutta Light Horse, which gradually relegated military activities to a secondary position, and made social and sporting interests into the priorities. Everyone was expected to attend a fortnight's annual summer camp, and a certain number of evening parades during the year. These were loosely defined. An evening in the clubhouse bar could often be dignified in the Regimental Ledger as parade. Young men in business or profession just out of Britain, would join for several reasons; first, they could live cheaply at the club's residential rooms; secondly, to become acquainted with congenial people of the same age; and thirdly for the incentive from the Government of India, a Horse Allowance of Rs. 32 per month. The greatest attraction of the Light Horse was friendship and fun. Everyone joined as a Trooper, whatever their position in society or office may be, all promotions were by popular vote. Parties and paper chases were regular activities.

Volunteers from Calcutta Light Horse fought in the First World War with distinction. When the Second World War was declared, all the young members joined up. The middle-aged ones felt let down, they also wanted to do something during the war. An opportunity came when four German ships and one Italian were interned in Goa, a Portuguese territory. Portugal was neutral, but the ships were sending radio signals to U-boats in the Indian Ocean about the Allied shipping, and the U-boats merrily sank most of them. It was necessary to silence these ships. As Portugal was neutral, the British Army could not mount an offensive. The task fell upon the Calcutta Light Horse. These middle-aged men with the help of the Calcutta Scottish sailed in an ancient Hooper barge and sank these ships. No official accolade or a medal came their way, but they had done their duty. After Independence, the Calcutta Light Horse was disbanded and the Calcutta Light Horse Club vanished into thin air.

The old Number 5 (new Number 22) was the residence and office of the Estate Agents, E.T. McCluskie, who used to publish the very useful *Calcutta Directory & Guide*. He was also the promoter of the beautiful township on the Chhotanagpur Hills in Bihar, McCluskie Ganj.

Number 4 at the corner of Park Street and Middleton Row, an old residential house, has given way to a large mansion with fine shops on the ground floor. The lane to our left is full of history and nostalgia. Once a narrow pathway leading to the Deer Park, lined with almond trees, it became known as Middleton Row and has been now renamed Sir William Jones Sarani.

THE PARK—LORETO HOUSE

In the early days of the settlement, there was only one house, that of William Frankland with a large park stretching from Camac Street to Chowringhee Road and to the south beyond Middleton Street. In a map of Calcutta drawn in 1742, the house is shown with a circular tank in front. The garden and the house standing in it came to the possession of William Frankland by 1749. This is the house which was destined to be the Loreto House School and College after 1842.

Mr. Frankland was the sixth Member of the Council at Calcutta at that time. Lord Curzon placed an inscription in the premises: 'This House was the Garden House of

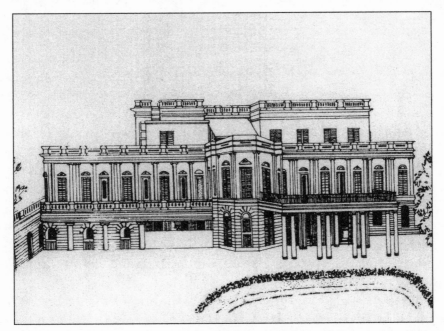

Figure 54: Loreto House, the old building dating back to Eliza Impey, in 1842
Sketch courtesy Loreto House

Mr. Henry Vansittart, Governor of Bengal 1760-64'. It was occupied by Sir Elijah Impey, the first Chief Justice of the Supreme Court, Calcutta, 1774-82, and also by Bishop Heber for a few months in 1824.

The Bengal Public Consultations of 5 January 1761 show:

> There being no garden house for the refreshment of the Governor when the matter of business will permit him to retire, and we being convinced that the Honourable Company will have no objection to so reasonable an indulgence.
> Agreed we purchase the garden house formerly belonging to Mr. Frankland for that use, at the price of 10,000 Arcot Rupees which we esteem is very well worth.

On 19 February 1762, the Court replied:

> Most certainly the purchasing of Mr. Frankland's house for, as you mention, the refreshment of the Governor when the multiplicity of business will permit him to leave the town, at the expense of the Company's (Arcot) Rupees 10,000 is, notwithstanding your allegation to the contrary, a superfluous charge, and must as in reason it ought be borne by the Governor at his own private expense, this is the more necessary and reasonable since the noble appointment settled upon the Governor by our directions last season which are intended to take in all the expenses he may be put to on the Company's account.

The verbiage of the Court's reply is part of a letter from Bengal dated 16 January 1761. A general letter from Bengal to the Court dated 30 October 1762 shows that Vansittart paid the money for the garden house and for the cost of the outhouses built since.

In a room at the south-west corner of the old house, which became the Senior Cambridge Classroom or the Third Parlour, was a pane of glass inscribed 'George Vansittart Jr. Born June 1768'. Since glass panes were a rarity at that time, this may be the oldest pane of glass in the city. After the demolition of the old school building, the pane has been carefully preserved. On 1 November 1769 Henry Vansittart sold the house to George Vansittart for Rs. 41,000.

The next occupant of this famous house was Sir Elijah Impey, Chief Justice of the Supreme Court, 1774-82. Lady Impey joined her husband in 1777. A water colour by Shaykh Zain-al-Din done in 1780 shows Lady Impey with her servants (numbering 17) in a large and lofty room.

Reverend James Long has given an elaborate account of the garden house: 'It was surrounded by a fine wall, a large tank was in front, a guard of *sipahis* were allowed to patrol about the house and the grounds at night, and occasionally firing their guns and muskets to keep off the dacoits.' It is said that in Sir Elijah's days palanquin-bearers wanted double fares for going so far beyond the town limits as the old garden house then was. And the servants returning to Calcutta would go in gangs leaving their good clothes behind for fear of being stripped by dacoits on the way.

After the departure of Impey, the house passed through the hands of several owners in a few years. First it was sold to Lt. Col. Henry Watson, Chief Engineer of the Presidency, and Henry Halsey on 1 August 1782, for Rs. 80,000. They sold the house only nineteen days later to Charles Scott. The property then consisted of 819 bighas of ground. This was again sold to John Dyrnley on 12 August 1784 for Rs. 83,156. On 1 March the following year this was sold to John Bristow for £7,750. In February 1806 John Bristow's heir John Charles Bristow sold it to Samuel Middleton of the Bengal Civil Service, who acted for a while as the Police Magistrate and after whom Middleton Row was named. By this time it is said that the grounds of the property had reduced considerably in area and measured only 43 *bighas*, 9 *cottas* and 8 *chhataks*.

On 30 August 1811 Sam Middleton sold it to John Palmer, the Prince of Merchants, and others, and the latter party sold the property to William Leycester on 22 August 1822. The Anglican Bishop Heber lived in the house for a few months in 1824. This is how Heber describes the house: "We are established in a house so large as to quite exceed all our ideas of comfort. I feel almost lost in a dining room sixty-seven feet long, a drawing room of the same dimensions and study supported by arcades, and though low in proportion to its size forty-five feet square.' The Bishop left this palace on 15 June 1824 and on his return resided at the new Episcopal Palace at 5 Russell Street.

In October 1835 the property was purchased by Col. Duncan Macleod and others and finally sold to Messrs. John Lackersteen & Bros. in June 1841 for the Community of the Loreto House.[20]

LORETO HOUSE

Mary Ward (1585–1645) founded the Institute of The Blessed Virgin Mary and introduced a new way of life for religious women. By 1840 a Catholic school for girls was thought of. In September 1840, Dr. Bakhaus, the Military Chaplain of Hazaribagh, was going to Rome on business of the Vicarate. He was entrusted with the task of finding nuns of the Holy Order to start a school in Calcutta. He first approached the Ursulines, but they had to decline, as they had used up their funds to establish a new convent at South Carolina. Next he went to the Loreto Abbey at Rathfarnham near Dublin. He went to see Mother Mary Teresa Ball. The Mother agreed.

The Catholic Archbishop Carew procured the house in Middleton Row (then No. 5). He describes it as a "noble building, spacious, airy, splendid three-storey mansion well adapted for the residence of our future nuns, and for the purposes of a seminary (boarding school). It stands on 7 *bighas* (2½ acres) of ground, well laid out with choice trees and shrubberies. The purchase money is Rs. 40,000".[21]

Twelve young nuns, their average age only eighteen, sailed for Calcutta in the vessel *Scotia* under the charge of Mother Mary Delphine Hart, who was only twenty-three. After four months they arrived at Calcutta. The Honourable Misses Eden, sisters of the Governor General Lord Auckland, were among the large number of people assembled at the landing *ghat* to welcome them. They were taken to the Cathedral where the Archbishop Carew led the formal reception. The Cathedral was the Portuguese Church at Murgihatta.

The young ladies finally arrived at Middleton Row and swept up the stairs of the grand old historic house.

They gazed with admiration at the great hall with its massive pillars, moulded capitals, and garlanded arches. It seemed too large for a community room, and much too grandly furnished, in the lavish early Victorian style. Between the tall grooved pillars, curtained recesses were arranged as the nun's cells.

To the nuns, they looked more like boudoirs, with their cushioned armchairs, embroidered counterpanes, and strangest of all, in each cell, a demure little lady's maid—an *ayah*, *salaaming* their astonished mistresses!

Preparations for the establishment of the school went ahead in a brisk manner; the syllabus was 'writing, arithmetic, grammar, geography, chronology, history, French, and plain and fancy needlework'. The fees for boarders were Rs. 25 per month and for day scholars, Rs. 12 including tiffin.

On 10 January 1842, Loreto House opened its doors to the first sixty young girls, as pupils. The same morning, classes began for the orphans at the Cathedral. The College section began in 1912.

From the very beginning, the Loreto House was a popular school in Calcutta. Not only Christians, but Hindus and Muslims of aristocratic background attended the school. The young ladies of the Tagore family attended this school, the first being Rabindranath Tagore's niece, Indira Devi Choudhurani. Later Rabindranath's young wife was also admitted here for studies.

Begum Shaista Ikramullah (née Suhrawardy), daughter of Sir Hassan Suhrawardy, claims in a book, to be the first Muslim student of Loreto House. Her father decided to send her to the Loreto House, one of the best English schools in Calcutta, despite the protests of the womenfolk of the house. This was in 1927. Born in an aristocratic Muslim family, she had to observe *purdah* in school also; with the Mother Superior's permission, her car was allowed up to the Entrance Hall, while other girls had to disembark at the gate, lest she came across a 'man', may be one of the menial staff of the school! She was allowed to eat in the parlour.

She studied at Loreto House for five years and expressed high praise for the teachers, particularly Mother Joseph Agatha.[22]

When the school needed more space, No. 8 Middleton Row was purchased for extension. The numbers have since been changed to 7 and 7/1. Other schools of the Loreto Order were opened in Calcutta and the first Loreto Convent in Darjeeling in 1847. Generations of Sisters devoted to God and education have served the institution. Little girls joined the nursery section and, under the loving care of the teachers, left school as accomplished young ladies.

The old school building was often described as the oldest existing house in Calcutta, where a Governor had once resided. But it had to be demolished in 1958 to make way for the new school building, modern, spacious and with every facility in a large compound. There are three gates on Middleton Row and one large one on Middleton Street to the south.

Adjacent to the school is the St. Thomas' Church, with one gate opening on Middleton Row and the other in the Loreto School compound.

ST. THOMAS'S CHURCH

This Roman Catholic Church was erected after filling up the round tank in front of Sir Elijah Impey's house. Construction started in 1841. The church is very popular and the speciality is its Sunday service. Millions visited this church in September 1997, when Mother Teresa's mortal remains lay in state in this church to enable people to pay their last respects.

Now we may take a tour of this short lane, previously known as Badamtolla, and Vansittart Avenue, and later as Middleton Row, after Samuel Middleton, President, Board of Trade, Fort William, and once owner of the site of the old house, where Loreto House now stands.

Middleton Row has since been renamed as Sir William Jones Sarani in 1982.

On the east side from the Park Street end was No. 11, 'The Palms', Mrs. Monk's Boarding House (one of the many in the area). The Prince Mansion stands at the site now. The next, viz. No. 10, was Mrs. Ashworth's Boarding House where the Asiatic Mansions are located now. The rest up to Camac Street had fine residences with gardens, now mostly replaced by modern buildings.

To the south and west side from the Camac Street end No. 8 is an old residential house. Numbers 7 and 7/1 are the Loreto House and St. Thomas's Church. Next to the main gate of the Loreto House we find a blind alley ending in a gateway. The gateway has a sign: 'Royal Calcutta Turf Club—5 & 6, Middleton Row'. Previously No. 6 was a residential house and No. 5 was Mrs. Blake's Boarding House. Presumably, the Club bought both Numbers 5 and 6, which are still there inside the compound with Middleton Row numbers. But it is strange how the club was allowed to acquire part of the public road, a part of Middleton Row, leading to these houses. On the west side in 1905 was the palace of the Maharani of Mayurbhanj, which later became Birkmyre Hostel Club. The remaining houses up to Park Street were residential houses, where two High Court Judges used to reside.

Number 1 today is the Gallway House (YWCA Hostel), for which the foundation stone was laid by the Countess of Lytton in 1925. Like the YMCA, its women's section, the Young Women's Christian Association, is very popular in Calcutta. The Calcutta section was founded in 1879 with the purpose of bringing women and girls into a world-wide fellowship—'to help them to find a definite purpose in life, to be honest and fearless in their thinking, to attain the fullest appreciation of the joys of friendship, service and beauty, and to interpret by radiant living the love of God as revealed in Jesus Christ.'[23]

Now as we come back once again to Park Street and proceed along the southern pavement, we come to 18 Park Street, with the famous Flury's Swiss Confectionery and Tearoom on the ground floor (old No. 3), part of a large block of building erected by the Armenian tycoon Aratoon Stephen, and still known as Stephen Court. The next site, covering Numbers 12 to 16 (old Numbers 2 & 2/1), was built over by another Armenian giant, Mr. J.C. Galstaun. This is a large building with several blocks of flats, named Galstaun Mansions by the owner, and extending to the next street, Russell Street. The present owners changed the name to Queen's Mansion in honour of the visit to Calcutta of Queen Elizabeth II of Great Britain. The old Bengal Club at one time occupied some flats in this mansion as residential accommodation for its members. The ground floor is occupied by fashionable shops, restaurants, etc. and the covered portico provides a shade for window-shoppers.

Russell Street

As we turn from the north-western corner of the Queen's Mansion on Park Street, we come to a road leading south to Middleton Street. This was named Russell Street, after the fourth Chief Justice of the Supreme Court, Calcutta. He succeeded Sir William Dunkin as Puisne Judge in 1797 and became Chief Justice in 1806. Sir Henry Russell initially resided in a portion of the court house in Esplanade Row, but later shifted to Chowringhee. This was on Russell Street, on the site of the present southern wing of the Queen's Mansion (old Galstaun). This house was built in 1798 and his niece, Rose Aylmer, died in this house in 1800.[24]

Mr. P.T. Nair believes that Russell's house was situated at the premises Nos. 12 and 13, now belonging to the Royal Calcutta Turf Club, and he had purchased the house from Mr. Nemy Churn Mullick.[25]

Sir Henry was a friend and patron of William Hickey, who alludes frequently to him in his memoirs. But he was also the only Chief Justice of Bengal after whom a ship built in Calcutta was called. The *Calcutta Monthly Journal* reported:

> On Tuesday last (January 17 1809), a magnificent merchant vessel named the *Russell* of 990 tons burthen was launched from Mr. Smith's dockyard amid the acclamation of a multitude of spectators. The Lord Chief Justice honoured the ceremony with his presence and performed the office of naming the ship.

A later report said:

> Sir Henry Russell on March 3 gave an entertainment on board the new ship, *Russell*, he was received with a salute of 17 guns on his arrival at 2 p.m. The *Russell* made her maiden voyage to Canton, and sailed with a number of other ships, under convoy of HMS *Victor* on May 7.[26]

On the eastern side, the house at the corner of Park Street bore the old No. 14/1, which was R. Scott Thomson's Branch Pharmacy. The next two houses were residential, and are now a part of the southern wing of the Queen's Mansion. No. 12 had a funny name 'The Unceremonias Golightly Hall' and No. 11 was the Hon. A.A. Apcar's residence. The rest of the houses on this side were either residential or lodging houses.

Apcar & Company was a prosperous Armenian concern with interests in shipping, collieries at Churunpore and Sitarampore, and foundries in Shibpore. A. Apcar was a patron of racing, President of Bengal Club for several terms and either president or patron of several sporting organizations during his time.

THE ROYAL CALCUTTA TURF CLUB

The Club popularly known as RCTC was founded a little more than 150 years ago in 1847, though horse racing was popular even before that and races were run at a place called Akra near Garden Reach.

Racing moved to the Calcutta Maidan in 1809.

Figure 55: Sir. A.A. Apcar's House in Russell Street, now the Royal Calcutta Turf Club
Photo courtesy RCTC

The Club was formed at a meeting on 22 February 1847 of the 'gentlemen interested in the turf' with Mr. J.P. Mckilligan in the chair. Mr. W.F. Fergusson read a paper proposing among other things 'the formation of a permanent association to regulate all matters concerned with Racing and to protect the interests of the Turf'. The meeting was held at the race stands at the Maidan. Thus the Calcutta Turf Club came into being with 'thirty-six original members and any remaining members of the old Bengal Jockey Club'.[27]

About 1888-9 the club acquired premises for an office and some sort of club facilities at 29 Chowringhee Road (on the Kyd Street corner). But they had to leave the premises as the Government requisitioned it. By April 1893 the club was at 33 Theatre Road, where it remained until 27 February 1920, when they moved to the present Club House and Offices which had been bought a few years after Sir A.A. Apcar's death.[28] After Apcar's death his house at 11 Russell Street was acquired by Mr. J.C. Galstaun, from whom the club bought the property, at the same time 9 Russell Street was bought. 5 Middleton Row was bought two months later. The club paid Rs. 2,30,000 for each. After protracted negotiations 6 Middleton Row was bought for Rs. 2,50,000 a year later. The last property to be acquired was 10 Russell Street. Later the walls between the properties were pulled down and the whole turned into one big premises with two entrances on Russell Street and one on Middleton Row. Fifty years later 9 and 10 Russell Street have been sold, one of them now housing the Meghalaya House complex.

The Club House and the office block is an imposing two storey house with beautiful columns supporting the roof on the first floor. Much has changed, but the memories remain, of Viceroys, Maharajas, Kings and Queens, the horses, owners, jockeys and trainers and also the punters, some celebrating their jackpot win, the losers drinking to the dregs to drown their sorrows.

Now we pass on to the western side of the street. The first address we find in the directories of 1905 and 1934 is 5 Russell Street, which must have had a large compound. The house was historic, as the Bishop's Place from 1825 to 1849. The imposing gateway (in ruins) is the only memory left. The Government rented this house from Mr. James Pattle, Member of the Board of Revenue, for the official residence of the Bishop of Calcutta, at a rental of Rs. 600 per month on a lease for eleven years, dating from 1 January 1826. It was a large structure built in the Grecian style of architecture with a long, deep, colonnade to each storey on the southern front to protect it from the sun, and each *verandah* fitted with green blinds made of cane. The rooms were of noble size and proportion, the largest being the dining room, a double cube, nearly eighty feet long with the windows fitted with venetian blinds. The entrance to the house was from a spacious covered portico, under which carriages drove in. It is quite probable that at this period the building also had a gateway in Chowringhee, as there were no other buildings around it, such as we see today.

This property originally belonged to Colonel Mark Wood, who sold it to John Ubric Collins, who in turn later sold it to Russick Lall Dutt. In December 1823 Mr. Dutt died at

Benares and his son Woodoy Chand Dutt agreed to sell the property to Mr. James Pattle on 30 January 1824, for the sum of Rs. 95,000, and received Rs. 250 as earnest money. Disputes however arose. But finally, the matter was settled on a further payment of Rs. 5000, making the total purchase price Rs. one lakh.

The release was an indenture between Woodoy Chand Dutt on the one part and James Pattle, Esq., C.S., and Richard Chicheley Plowden, C.S., on the other part. Mr. Plowden appears to have been trustee for James Pattle. This house was described as:

All that Messuage Tenement or Dwelling House, late of one Russick Lall Dutt, but now of the said Woodoy Chand Dutt together with the land or ground to the same belonging and therewith occupied and enjoyed, formerly the property of Colonel Mark Wood and afterwards of John Ubric Collins Esq. and situate and being in Dhee Birjee and Chowkerbar otherwise now called Chowringhee...containing by estimation 12 *bighas*...and bounded on the north by landed property formerly also of the said Mark Wood but now or late of Colonel Thomas Wood on the south by landed property formerly of or belonging to Charles Short Esq. but now in the occupation of Major Higgins, on the east by the Public Road there leading north & south and now called Russell Street and on the west by the great Public Road there called Chowringhee Road.

During 1826 Archdeacon Corrie, the first Bishop of Madras, occupied the palace and considering it unsafe, he reported the matter to the Government, who appointed a committee of engineers, consisting of Col. C. Mouat, Capt. Edward Garstin and Lieut. N. Forbes to examine the house. Their report dated 13 November stated that the building was quite safe and that the walls were adequate to support the superincumbent weight of the third floor. The house however was thoroughly repaired during 1827 for the occupation of Bishop James.

Bishop Turner, who occupied it at a later date, desired to change his residence during 1830, but was informed that this could not be done as the house had been taken on a lease for the period of the Charter. On 7 June 1831 he again wrote to the Government about the condition of the house, enclosing a report from Mr. Parker, an architect, who had carefully examined the building and pronounced the north and south walls of the principal hall as unsafe. This led to extensive repairs and the house was not ready for occupation again, until the middle of November 1831. Bishop Turner unfortunately had died on 7 July 1831.

Bishop Wilson, who arrived in Calcutta on 5 November 1832, also lived in the Russell Street Palace and continued to do so, even after the expiry of the lease on 1 January 1837. In the meantime, Mr. James Pattle had sold the property to the Honourable East India Company on 30 June 1838 for the sum of Rs. 75,000. Twelve years later, Bishop Wilson, on 23 March 1849, expressed his intentions for changing his residence to a building nearer his

Figure 56: The Hall & Anderson Building
Photo courtesy Bourne & Shepherd

Cathedral, and during June of the following year, he removed to the present palace at 51 Chowringhee Road opposite the Cathedral.[29]

In 1905, No. 5 Russell Street was occupied by Phelps & Co. and the Phelps family and Mr. Justice Woodroffe; later this house was occupied by the YMCA Press, *Youngmen of India* Journal and the YMCA Book Depot. No. 4 was at one time Office of the Executive Engineer, PWD. Some old buildings were demolished to make way for the new ITC Centre, housing several offices of the India Tobacco Company and other concerns. Numbers 1, 1/1 and 2 were once the Bengal Club Chambers. Now this portion houses

Plate 7: The New Spanking ITC Centre, Courtesy ITC Ltd.

the Bengal Club House.

Now we come again to Park Street and proceed westward along the southern pavement. The old houses were No. 1 Bengal Club Chambers, C 1 Telegraph Office, B 1 Edward Art Gallery, and A 1 Park Street Post Office. Later these buildings were demolished and became extensions of the departmental stores, Messrs. Hall & Anderson, acquiring new Numbers, 2, 4 & 6. The original address of Hall & Anderson was Nos. 31 & 31/1 Chowringhee Road. At one time the Survey of India office was situated here. According to Montague Massey, Hall & Anderson was the first departmental store in this region. The site was an old tumbledown godown, in the occupation of some French people of the name of Dollet, who sold French wines, brandy, and condiments.[30]

The original partners were P.N. Hall and William Anderson, with branch establishments at Mussoorie and Darjeeling. According to their advertisement they were twentytwo shops in one. It was indeed a pleasure to shop at their premises. Among the giant departmental stores, they were probably the last to close their business. Their premises have been taken over by two large banks and other offices and shops.

Now we come back to Chowringhee again and proceed south.

References

1. *Bengal Past & Present*, vol. LII, 1936, p. 49.
2. Chatterjee, Dr. Gautam, in *The Week*, 27 Sept. 1998, p. 63.
3. Firminger, W.K. *Thacker's Guide*, p. 85.
4. Seth, M.J. *Armenians in India*, p. 481.
5. *Parochial Annals of Bengal*, p. 239.
6. Ibid. p. 241.
7. Abraham Isaac S. *Origin and History of Calcutta Jews*, Calcutta 1969, pp. 68-69.
8. Cotton, H.E.A. *Calcutta Old and New*, Revised Edition, p. 230.
9. Losty, J.P., *Calcutta, City of Palaces*, London 1990, p. 15.
10. Cotton. op. cit. p. 466-67.
11. Ibid. p. 237.
12. Ibid. p. 238.
13. Nair, P.T. *A History of Calcutta Streets*, p. 909.
14. Ibid. p. 566.
15. Cotton. op. cit. pp. 237-38.
16. Karkaria, Bachi J. *To a Grand Design*, pp. 21-23.
17. Nair, P.T. *A History of Calcutta Streets*. pp. 119-20.
18. Cotton. op. cit. p. 235.
19. Leasor, James. *The Boarding Party*, London 1978, pp. 33-34.

20. *Bengal Past & Present*, vol. LXIII, 1943, p. 22.

21. *Loreto House, Calcutta 1842-1992*: from the article by Mother Mary Colmcille.

22. Ikramullah, Begum Shaista S. *From Purdah to Parliament*, London 1963, pp. 31-37.

23. Barry, John. *Calcutta Illustrated*, p. 77.

24. Ibid. p. 29.

25. Nair, P.T. *A History of Calcutta Streets*, p. 147.

26. *Bengal Past & Present*, vol. XXXVII, 1929, p. 164.

27. Firth, W.G.C. *The RCTC*, Calcutta 1976, p. 26.

28. Ibid. p. 78.

29. Birney W.S., in *Bengal Past & Present*, vol. LXXX, 1943.

30. Massey, Montague. op. cit. pp. 103-4.

Chapter Twelve

Chowringhee Road from Park Street to Lower Circular Road

After passing the old Hall & Anderson building we come to a new modern building, the Global Trust Bank at No. 32. There was once

> one of the handsomest houses in Chowringhee of three storeys on the site. It was however so badly knocked about by the earthquake of 1897 that it was considered unsafe, and would have had to be pulled down and re-built; but rather than do this, Mr. Meyer, the owner, made an arrangement with Kellner & Co., whose premises at that time were in Bankshall Street, to build to their own plan a thoroughly up to date place which would embrace on an extensive scale all the necessary requirements for their very large and expanding business, including residential quarters for their senior partner. That this has been successfully accomplished I have recently had ocular demonstration, and I have no hesitation in saying it is a marvel of perfection down to its very smallest details.[1]

Next was a two-storey building where the travel agents, Trade Wings, were located for many years. It has recently been demolished and some construction is going on.

THE BENGAL CLUB

Number 33 Chowringhee is an important address, once the site of a house owned by Babu Kaliprasanna Sinha, a learned young man belonging to a family of wealthy zamindars at Calcutta, and a well-known writer, best known for his prose translation of the *Mahabharata* and *Hutom Penchar Naksha*, a sparklingly satiric view of social life in Calcutta. He died at the young age of 29. Thomas Babington Macaulay stayed in this house during his residence in the city from 1834 to 1838 as Law Member of the Supreme Council. Here he wrote for *The Edinburgh* some of his famous essays and sent them to be set in type at the Englishman Press. In India Macaulay's name will always be linked with the decision taken in 1835 to adopt English as the medium of higher instruction. He was President of a Committee of

Figure 57: William Wood, Chowringhee Road, south of the junction with Park Street
The house on the left was owned by Babu Kaliprasanna Singha, 1830.

Figure 58: The Bengal Club (old building on the Chowrighee)

Public Instruction evenly divided on the question whether education should aim at developing Indian culture on its own lines or at giving as many students as possible the opportunity to drink at the spring of western learning. Macaulay threw all his weight on the side of the 'Westerners', and his views carried the day with the Government. A torrent of controversial ink has flowed unceasingly ever since, and there are those who attribute the greater part of India's ills to the policy that Macaulay so vigorously supported.

His views are well expressed in a letter of 1838:

'Our English schools are flourishing wonderfully. We find it difficult—indeed, in some places, impossible—to provide instruction for all who want it. At the single town of Hooghly fourteen hundred boys are learning English. The effect of this education is prodigious. No Hindoo who had received an English education ever remains sincerely attached to his religion. Some continue to profess it as a matter of policy, but many profess themselves pure deists, and some embrace Christianity. It is my firm belief that if our plans of education are followed up, there will not be a single idolator among the respectable classes in Bengal thirty years hence. And this will be effected without any efforts to proselytise, without the smallest interference with religious liberty, merely by natural operation of knowledge and reflection. I heartily rejoice in the prospect. (*Life & Letters of Lord Macaulay*, vol. I, p. 498).[2]

Perhaps the most lasting monument to Macaulay's abilities is the Indian Penal Code, the first draft of which appeared in 1837. It did not actually become law until 1860 after revision by Sir Barnes Peacock; retaining substantially Macaulay's original scheme.

Macaulay liked his house in Calcutta and called it the best. He wrote:

I have a very pretty garden not unlike our little grass plot at Clapham but larger. It consists of a fine sheet of turf, with a gravel walk round it, and flower-beds scattered over it. It looks beautiful just now after the rains, and I hear it keeps its verdure during a great part of the year. A flight of steps leads down from my library into the garden and it is so well shaded that you may walk in it till ten o'clock in the morning.[3]

But he did not enjoy the Calcutta weather: "We are annually baked four months, boiled four more, and allowed the remaining four to become cool in if we can. Insects and undertakers are the only living creatures which seem to enjoy the climate."

In 1845 the Bengal Club moved to this house from Tank Square. With the redoubtable Sir James Outram as President in 1860, the club enjoyed a popularity that drove every European of any importance to seek membership. There was great festivity in 1887 to celebrate the golden jubilee of Queen Victoria's reign, with every house in Chowringhee from the Dharmatala Street crossing to the Bengal Club illuminated.

The lease of the house was renewed in 1875 and 1895 for twenty years each time, but the necessity of a larger space was felt. Plans were afoot to acquire a new site to the south-west of the junction of Camac Street and Theatre Road. There was a suggestion that the site No. 41 Chowringhee, later to become the Army & Navy Stores, should be purchased, but neither of the projects materialized. The site at 33 Chowringhee was purchased in 1907 for five and a half lakh of rupees and in the same year a registered company was formed. A competition for the design of the new building was held in which Mr. Vincent Esch, a well-known Calcutta architect, was successful. The contract for the actual work, which was begun in 1908, was entrusted to the Bengal Stone Company, with Mr. Esch as consulting architect.

At the request of the Corporation a tablet was placed upon the west wall of the house bearing the inscription:

In the House which formerly stood on this site, and was dismantled in 1908, resided Thomas Babington Macaulay, Law Member of the Supreme Council 1834-38.

During the building of the new clubhouse the Bengal United Service Club invited Bengal Club members to use their facilities. The new premises were formally opened on 17 November 1911, when an afternoon 'At Home' was given to which ladies were invited. On the same evening there was an inaugural dinner too.[4]

The Bengal Club premises was a fine example of the newly emerging Edwardian architecture, finely ornamented with a central cupola and turrets at four corners. When completed, it was the finest building standing on Chowringhee. It had three storeys; the general area facilities were excellent with cosy residential rooms.

In 1927 the club purchased the adjoining No. 34 Chowringhee Road, the grounds of which extended from Chowringhee to Russell Street. Residential rooms were built on the Chowringhee side and the club was extended up to the Russell Street side. There was a great demand for residential rooms, so a few flats were taken on lease at the Galstaun Mansion.

After Independence in 1947, there was a general exodus of Europeans from Calcutta, and the Committee considered on more than one occasion opening the gates to Indian members. But it took another twelve years and further dwindling of the club funds before this was done.

In an Extraordinary General Meeting in 1959, an overwhelming majority of members voted conclusively in favour of admission of Indian nationals to membership. Among the first batch of Indian members were D.P.M. Kanga and V.V. Parekh, who later became Presidents of the Club.

In February 1969, National and Grindlays Bank Limited made an offer for the purchase of the Chowringhee half of the club, and at an extraordinary general meeting held on

2 June 1969, the members approved the sale. A few more proposals were agreed upon for the future of the club, viz. *(i)* to adapt the Russell Street premises to requirements; *(ii)* to rent or buy an old building elsewhere and ultimately sell the Russell Street premises also; *(iii)* rent a floor in an air-conditioned building; and ultimately *(iv)* pull down the Russell Street building and build a two-storey club building on the site.

Ultimately, work started at the Russell Street site for the new club building in July 1969.

A Dinner Dance was held on 2 February 1970 to celebrate the relinquishing of the premises at No. 33 Chowringhee Road. As part of the colourful ceremony, the keys of the premises were handed over to the General Manager of National and Grindlays Bank.[5]

The fine building was demolished. The Club library containing a considerable stock of rare books could not be accommodated in its entirety in the new wing. About 7,500 rare books had to be sold. Mr. Chandra Sekhar Rudra, an ardent reader of hunting stories, bought his famous collection of *shikar* books from Bengal Club.

Though the National and Grindlays Bank bought the site for its own building, it had to sell it to the Government of India who were looking for a suitable site for the underground railway headquarters (the Metro Rail). Mr. Benoy K. Chatterjee, who was one of the main contractors for the Metro Railway, took charge of the construction of the Metro Bhavan and at the site just to the south of it built a 24-storey commercial building called Chatterjee International Centre. The Overseas Branch of the State Bank of India occupies the ground and several other floors of the tallest building in the town.

The only sign of the Bengal Club that remains on the Chowringhee is a gateway leading to the club just south of the Chatterjee International Centre.

THE METRO RAILWAY

After the partition of India, a large number of refugees took shelter in and around Calcutta, the roads were congested, and the public transport system was overburdened. The idea of an underground railway system to ease the transport problem was envisaged by the then Chief Minister of West Bengal, Dr. Bidhan Chandra Roy. He invited an advisory team from the *Compagnie du Chemin de Fer Metropolitan de Paris*, but their suggestion was not implemented. Many other reports followed, but finally the D'Costa Report of the Metropolitan Transport Team of the Planning Commission in 1968 was accepted. It was on the basis of this report that the Metropolitan Transport Project (Railways) was set up in 1969 under the Ministry of Railways, Government of India, to undertake a techno-economic feasibility study for the Calcutta Metro. The MTP (R)—renamed 'Metro Railway' in 1978— identified the Dum Dum-Tollygunge alignment as the most useful one for Calcutta's first underground railway, and submitted a very comprehensive report in 1972.[6] Construction was sanctioned in June 1972 and the Prime Minister of India, Mrs. Indira Gandhi, laid the foundation stone in December. The construction of the Tollygunge-Esplanade section took seven years to complete. In the Chowringhee it runs west of the road along the eastern fringe of the Maidan. The first run from Esplanade to Bhowanipore took place in October 1984, to be extended further south to Tollygunge in April 1986. A few years later the Dum Dum-Belgacchia service was introduced, and then the service through the Chittaranjan Avenue section was completed. Now the Metro Railway runs the full stretch from Dum Dum to Tollygunge. Calcutta is the first city in India to have an undergound railway system and the Calcuttans take great pride in it. But to ease the traffic problem, other routes to Garia in the south and Howrah Station across the river are urgently needed.

THE ICI HOUSE

After crossing the gate of the Bengal Club on Chowringhee we come to a five-storey building of modern design with the ICI logo on the top. The house was built in 1953, on the site of an old residential house.

Brunner, Mond & Company (India) Ltd., ICI's trading subsidiary in India, set up a trading office in Calcutta in 1923. But upon the formation of the giant chemical combine of ICI (Imperial Chemical Industries), the group floated in 1937 the Alkali and Chemical Corporation of India to commence production of caustic/chlorine,[7] leading to the setting up of a giant plant at Rishra near Calcutta. ICI India pioneered the use of synthetic nitrogenous fertilizers in India. Other ICI products included dyes, pharmaceuticals (during the Second World War, the anti-malarial Paludrine was a must for all soldiers going to fight in the jungle), industrial explosives, heavy chemicals, paints, etc. They were the first to introduce polythene and perspex. The rest of the buildings on this stretch of Chowringhee in the old days were mostly residential right up to Middleton Street.

No. 35 has now three buildings. Next to the ICI House there is a two-storey building, the ground floor once occupied by Japan Airlines, who left it to a travel agency, when they withdrew service through Calcutta and went to more lucrative pastures.

Next stands the seventeen-storey Kailash Apartment building. The next one is a four storey building with a branch of the State Bank of Travancore on the ground floor. When Orient Airways was formed before the partition of India, it had its office here. After partition the Orient Airways became Pakistan International Airlines (PIA). I still remember the large queues in front of the office immediately before and after Partition waiting to buy tickets to a safer haven. The PIA office functioned here until the 1965 Indo-Pak-War.

No. 36 has become an automobile showroom.

VIRGINIA HOUSE

The Imperial Tobacco Company was the first corporate giant to move out of the Dalhousie Square area. On 24 August 1926, the company celebrated its sixteenth birthday by taking a

Figure 59: The Virginia House
Photo courtesy ITC

board decision to purchase the old dilapidated building standing for a century at 37 Chowringhee for the sum of Rs. 3,10,000 and to erect an office there when the site was cleared. Virginia House was ready by 1928.[8]

The beginning of the Imperial Tobacco Company in Calcutta is quite interesting.

Indians had been smoking tobacco for ages, but in the form of *hookahs* or *gargaras* or the hubble bubble. Many of the Englishmen in India picked up the Indian style of smoking. But times were changing, and the early years of the twentieth century brought in the new fangled cigarette and the Imperial Tobacco to India, who began with an office in Bombay and a factory in Moonghyr. But the first persons to come to Calcutta to promote cigarettes were Mr. Jellicoe and Mr. Page, who made their way from London to Calcutta in 1906. They were both representatives of the British American Tobacco Company (BAT) and the purpose of their visit was to find an agent to establish W.D. & H.O. Wills' brands, and more particularly Scissors in India. With the appoinment of a wholesaler as their Sole Agent, it was felt, trade in cigarettes between England and India could proceed smoothly. But none of the Canning Street or Clive Street merchants were really interested.[9]

The one person who probably foresaw a great future for the white incarnate of the *biri*, so popular in India, was Bukhs Elahi, a minor employee of one of the agencies in the business district in Calcutta. Having no money himself, he prevailed upon a familiar courtesan to lend him money, to avail himself of the BAT offer, and in due course was appointed Sole Agent for W.D. & H.O. Wills in India. The business was a great success and Buksh Elahi prospered and married the courtesan. Imperial Tobacco's first office in Calcutta was in a ramshackle house in Radha Bazar Lane, from where it shifted to 5 Fairlie Place in 1926 and to Chowringhee in 1928. The company are still there.

This is a five-storey building, a part of which was let out to Lloyds Bank in the early years.

A whole history of advertising has grown around the cigarette in India, from the cartoon for Scissors, which soon became the common man's brand, with the caption 'You do not know what you are missing' in Bengali to the more elitist Made for Each other campaign for Wills more recently. As the taste for cigarettes spread, ITC had to open new factories all over the country. The partition of India brought in many changes, but ITC had to wait till 1968 for the first Indian Chairman of the Company, Mr. A.N. Haksar. In 1970 the company changed its name to India Tobacco Company. The ITC has since diversified into other fields, like hotels and marine products. Though the company has prestigious hotels in other parts of India, it is yet to build one in Calcutta.

Today ITC's principal business includes tobacco and cigarettes, paper, packaging and printing, hotels, agricultural business, financial services, information systems and international trading. The company employs over 20,000 employees, and has factories at Calcutta, Moonghyr, Bangalore, Saharanpore, Tiruvattur, Mantralayam and Bhadrachalam.

In 1934, No. 38 Chowringhee was the New Club Chambers, providing residential accommodation for the members of the club.

A five-storey building that has come up recently houses the American Centre. Its previous incarnation was USIS, or United States Information Service, which started in the ground floor of the Whiteaway Laidlaw building facing S.N. Banerjea Road, with an excellent library, information service and an auditorium.

No. 39 in the old days was the Office of the Telegraph Accounts, later a residential building that eventually gave way to a nine-storey office-cum-residential block, Himalaya House.

No. 40 is a modern eight-storey building called Ispat Bhawan, the office of SAIL, Steel Authority of India Limited, a Public Sector company.

ARMY & NAVY STORES

This was situated at 41 Chowringhee Road. The Bengal Club had once thought of buying this site for erection of a new club house in 1895 and

Figure 60: The Army & Navy Stores, Chowringhee

had even gone the length of having plans and estimates prepared, but for some reason the negotiations fell through and the idea was abandoned. As far as I recollect, the price was very moderate, some Rs. 2,50,000 or Rs. 3,00,000. I think the main objection to the scheme was based on sentimental grounds disliking the idea of forsaking the old place... . [10]

Soon after a very fine building came up on the site consisting of three storeys. This was one of the great departmental stores in Calcutta, the Army & Navy Stores. It is a fine building, built in the late Victorian style and could be mistaken for a Government structure of the same period. It is a large building where one could once buy everything under one roof at a cheaper rate. They had their own whiskey: the Army & Navy Scotch Whiskey was a favourite of Calcutta. After Independence the establishment did not last long. The present owners have given it a new name Kanak Buildings, which is occupied by ANZ Grindlays and many other offices; with the British Airways occupying a large space on the Middleton Street side of the building.

Middleton Street

Next to the old Army & Navy Stores, Middleton Street leads east from the Chowringhee Road. The names of both Middleton Street and Middleton Row are attributed by some to

Dr. Thomas Fanshawe Middleton who was a member of the Civil Service and owned considerable property in the neighbourhood and who flourished in the time of Cornwallis and Wellesley.[11]

The Calcutta Corporation had once planned to rename the street as Anandi Lal Poddar Sarani, but according to Dr. Samaresh Gooptu, one of the residents, all residents sent in objection letters to the Corporation resenting the change, hence the old name was retained. In the old directories the street had a native name, viz. *Poorana Bukhshee-khana-ka-rasta*. As we walk along the northern side of the pavement from the Chowringhee end and pass the British Airways office and come to the end of the building, on our left is Russell Street. As we cross Russell Street the first building on our left, No. 10 Middleton Street, was once Mrs. Walter's Boarding Establishment. The old No. 9 gave way to a large mansion now called Middleton Mansions with new numbers Nos. 9 and 9/1. Next is the compound and southern gate of the Loreto House. New multistoreyed mansions have replaced most old buildings in the vicinity.

From Camac Street the first house on the southern pavement was No. 7, residence of the Honourable Mr. Justice R. Harrington, Bar-at-Law, Puisne Judge of Calcutta High Court in 1905. In *Thacker's Directory* of 1934 No. 7 has been shown as the residence of Dr. D.N. Gooptu and Rai Saheb F.N. Gooptu. F.N. Gooptu's name was once famous in India as the pioneer in the manufacture of 'Deer' brand pencils and fountain pens, with his factory in Beliaghata.

According to Amaresh Gooptu, a resident of Middleton Street and a descendant of the famous Gooptu family, one of their ancestors was D. Gupta, well-known for his anti-malarial and other medicines. D. Gupta resided in Gupta Lane, a small alley of only 9 houses. Mr. Gupta bought extensive properties in the Chowringhee area, including the Tower House and the corner house of Esplanade East and Bentinck Street. His son, Gopal Chandra Gupta, bought an old house at No. 5 Middleton Street in the 1890s. There were many Indians who owned landed properties in the White Town but none used to take residence in the area. Gopal Chandra decided to live in the newly acquired house, causing great consternation among the European residents, who resented an Indian daring to come to live among the *Burra Sahibs*!

The old building was demolished and a fine new mansion with a large garden and a clock tower was erected at No. 5 by Mackintosh & Burn for Gopal Chandra. When the tower was damaged and a crack appeared in the building, the firm repaired the whole thing without charging Gopal Chandra. According to Mr. Gooptu all the houses on the southern side of the street up to Little Russell Street belong to the Gooptus, with some of the property leased out, but never sold. The old No. 5 had been leased out to the Kotharis' medical centre, a plan later abandoned and the lessee for it accordingly changed.

Montague Massey describes No. 4: 'that two new houses have been built in the compound of old No. 4; cannot say that this is any improvement, and it has involved the sacrifice of one of the most attractive compounds in the street'.[12]

Across Little Russell Street was the old No. 3, once Mrs. Hiller's Boarding Establishment. In 1934 the ground floor was being used as the Methodist Episcopal Church and the other two top floors as residential flats. The National Insurance Company's office has come up on this site, but a part of a very old wall can still be seen on the Little Russell Street corner. Numbers 1 and 2B were once the palace of the Maharajadhiraj of Darbhanga, a native state in Bihar. It was a fine building inside a large compound. The fine wrought iron gates had the Darbhanga Coat of Arms. The palace has since been demolished and the twelve-storey Jeevan Deep building has come up on the site.

It is time to retrace our steps and come back to the street mentioned before, the Little Russell Street.

Little Russell Street

Like Russell Street this too was named after Sir Henry Russell, Chief Justice of Bengal. This street leads from Middleton Street southwards cutting across Harrington Street and ends in Theatre Road.

According to Massey:

> In the old days there were only three houses numbered 1, 2, 3. No. 1 was demolished in a far-off time and the present numbers 5 and 6 were built on its site. No. 4 was then No. 2, No. 8 is built...on the grounds of old 2, Harrington Street, and No. 1 and No. 2 in the compound of the old No. 3, which latter house has been greatly enlarged and improved, and was once known as the Officers' Hospital.[13]

The street is now mainly residential with some old houses with compounds, and several new houses with the Kenilworth Hotel on the western side from Middleton Street, occupying the site of Mrs. Hiller's Boarding Establishment (No. 3 Middleton Street); and the New Kenilworth Hotel on the eastern side near Theatre Road, which had all along been used as a boarding house, first as Mrs. A. Palmer's and later as 'Kingsleigh', or the King's Boarding House.

Now we come back to Chowringhee Road and proceed south. This segment of Chowringhee Road is part of the history of Calcutta's urban development as the first piece of pavement built in Calcutta in 1858 over the open drains.

After the Jeevan Deep building, there rises a seventeen-storey high-rise built by the Life Insurance Corporation of India on the grounds of the Darbhanga palace (No. 41/1). No. 42, now under demolition, was a Calcutta landmark known as the PAN AM building, as the Pan-American Airways had its office here for a long time, serving later as the office of Delta Airlines (under GSA).

In the 1860s it was the residence of Sir Joseph Fayrer, then Professor of Surgery, Medical College Hospitals, Calcutta. Later in the early 1900s it was a residential building with the French Consulate on the ground floor. In 1934 the building was known as 'Minoo Mahal', still a residential building.

In No. 43 lived Sir Comer Petheram, Chief Justice of Bengal from 1886 to 1896.

In 1964 there came up yet another city landmark on the site, viz. the Tata Centre, seventeen storeys high, housing the offices of the Tata business empire.

Harrington Street

This is a street leading from Chowringhee, from beside Tata Centre to Camac Street. In the early nineteenth century this was known as Graham Street, after a prominent local resident, Thomas Graham. Graham had a house on the southern side of the road with a large compound nearer to Chowringhee. The local name was *Elliot Talao ka samna rasta*, as the Elliot tank was situated on the eastern fringe of the Maidan opposite to the street. According to William Hickey, Thomas Graham was an old servant of the Company who expected a seat on the Supreme Council, and at the same time a partner in a great mercantile firm (with John Mowbray, Robert Graham and William Skirrow) which failed in 1790. Graham himself seems to have survived the firm's bankruptcy quite well, and continued in his career, becoming in due course a member of the Supreme Council. He did not however continue long in the station, the Court of Directors removing him from the idea that

> his commercial engagements and consequent connections with many of the principal black people, to some of whom, it was notorious, he stood largely indebted, might induce an improper bias in mind... But the worthy Cheesemongers of Leadenhall Street were never very remarkable either for their sagacity or even consistency;

as was proved when they placed him at the Board of Revenue upon turning him out of the Supreme Council, thereby putting him in a situation of all others the most objectionable, from the weight and influence it afforded him.[14]

During the visit of Lord Valentia to the city he brought with him Henry Salt as his secretary and draughtsman. His drawings were used to illustrate Valentia's book, as well as Salt's own *Twenty-four Views of 1809*. The Valentia party stayed at the house of Thomas Graham, a view of which from the house towards Fort William and the Maidan was published by Salt, for which a preliminary wash drawing survives. A map in a field survey book of 1809-11 in the National Library, Calcutta, by C.G. Nicholls, identifies this street as Graham Street.[15] The Graham House was a fine double-storey house with a large compound and garden off Chowringhee.

The street was later renamed Harrington Street after John Herbert Harrington, once a judge of the Sudder Dewani Adalat and later a member of the Supreme Council, and a prominent resident of the locality in the 1820s. In 1823 he became the Agent of the Governor-General in Delhi and President, Board of Trade. He was also Professor of Law and President of the College Council of the College of Fort William. Author of the book *Analysis of the Laws and Regulations,* he was one of the founders of the Calcutta School Book Society established in 1827.

After leaving the Tata Centre we come to the old No. 13, once the residence of several ICS officers, and now the Rajgarhia House. No. 12 was the residence of A.N. Sassoon, of E.D. Sassoon & Co. of 2 and 3 Clive Row, a famous Jewish firm in old Calcutta. The main activity of the Sassoon family was in Bombay. The house, since renovated, looks every inch a colonial house.

Here we cross Little Russell Street. The last two houses on the northern side, Numbers 9 and 8 were Mrs. Monk's Boarding Houses. Both the houses were later demolished and J.C. Galstaun built Harrington Mansions on the site.

The first house on the southern side from the Camac Street end is No. 7, a mansion conceived and built by Sir Rajendranath Mukherjee. Lady Ranu Mukherjee, wife of his son Sir Biren, was the sole occupant of this house till she passed away a year ago. Lady Ranu, in her adolescence and youth, was close to Rabindranath Tagore, who addressed several poems and letters to her. Later in life, she became a great patron of the visual arts, and set up the Academy of Fine Arts, a fine institution, now in decay. Incidentally, both Harrington Mansions and the Mookherjee house were designed by Ted Thornton, a well-known Calcutta architect. Number 6 is a new set of buildings, housing the Harrington Nursing Home, an X-Ray Clinic, and other establishments. Next is the large compound of the United States Consulate in Calcutta. No. 4 was once a famous address, the residence of Sir Richard Garth, Chief Justice of Bengal from 1875 to 1886. In 1905 it was the residence of the Hon'ble Mr. L. Hare, CSI, CIE, ICS, Member of the Board of Revenue. No. 3 had its share of glory too; Bishop Heber stayed here for a short span, after his stay on arrival at the Government House in Fort William. But he did not like the house in Harrington Street, for it was too small for his family and his books, and too far from St. John's Cathedral and the Free School.[16] This is an old mansion with a decaying colonial gateway. In the 1930s it was called Birnam House, harbouring among others Mrs. E. Clark's Boarding Establishment.

Here we cross Little Russell Street again and come to the old No. 2, probably a part of Thomas Graham's house. Massey writes:

It consisted of an old fashioned, long, straggling two-storeyed building, situated in the centre of a large ill-kempt compound. It was run as a boarding house, together with several other establishments of a similar kind, by a lady of the name of Mrs. Box, who was well known at that time, and who held the same sort of position in Calcutta as did Mrs. Monk at a later period... . The houses Nos. 2, 2/1 and 8, Little Russell Street were built in the old compound of No. 2.[17]

During this century No. 2/2 was mostly residential, with a Doctor's clinic. No. 2/1 still exists today, under the name of 'Holmcroft'. Once a guest house, King's Boarding House, it retains intact three tall floors with a beautiful ornamented old lift, which reminds one of the one installed at the Government House by Lord Curzon. Some framed posters with labels like 'Visit Europe' or 'Versailles' remind us of the old days. Later it became St. Vincent's Nursing Home run and managed by an order of nuns. In 1973 it became St. Mary's Nursing Home under the supervision of Dr. A.K. Deb. A small bit of the decaying garden has survived with some marble statuary and wrought iron garden seats from the old days. New buildings cover parts of the compound. No. 2, a residential building, reached from the street by a driveway has given way to a multistoreyed residence-cum-office complex. No. 1 belongs to the Paikpara Raj family. The Hon. Kumar Arun Chandra Singha was a prominent resident in the 1930s. The house had a large garden. This was later leased out to the British Deputy High Commission. After the expiry of the lease they were allowed to build a new complex in the garden west of the former house. The old house was demolished and a giant shopping complex is coming up at the site.

In spite of his good deeds and love for Calcutta, John Herbert Harrington could not avoid the axe of the frenetically active Renaming Committee of the Calcutta Corporation. In 1969 it was named Ho Chi Minh Sarani, to honour the veteran Communist leader and later President of the Democratic Republic of Vietnam.

Back to Chowringhee

No. 44 at the corner of Harrington Street was for a long time the residence of the wealthy Armenians, J.G. and A.G. Apcar. J.G. Apcar, Bar-at-Law, had a busy legal practice; Mis Amy Apcar, a descendant, lived here for a long time. The old house has been demolished, leaving an ugly unfinished structure in its place.

In the old No. 45 lived Harry Evan Augustus Cotton, better known as H.E.A. Cotton or just Evan Cotton. He was a Bar-at-Law and practised at the Calcutta High Court. He was the son of Sir Henry Cotton, who presided over the 1904 session of the Indian National Congress at Bombay. Evan was born at Midnapore, Bengal in 1868, when his father was posted there. Educated in England, he joined the Calcutta Bar in 1893 and practised there for thirteen years. He loved Calcutta and carried out valuable research work on the history of the city. His book *Calcutta Old and New—A Historical and Descriptive Handbook to the City* was first published in 1909. He was editor of *Bengal Past & Present,* the journal of the Calcutta Historical Society, and his research articles as well as the column 'Editor's Note Book' remain a source of useful information. Like his father he was also close to the Indian National Congress.

The old building at No. 46 has been demolished to accommodate one of the earliest high rises in Calcutta, the Everest House, twenty-one stories high. The next spot which had also been a part of No. 46, later renumbered 46/1, was for a long time the showroom of the Chowringhee Motor Stores; it has been lying vacant for a long time.

Theatre Road to Shakespeare Sarani

This was once a part of the extensive *bustee* in Dhee Birjee. It appears in Upjohn's map of 1792-93 as a road without a name. The building of the Chowringhee Theatre that came up in 1813 gave the street its name that remained unchanged until 1964. Over the years it became one of the popular residential areas for the Europeans. The road originally ended at Lower Circular Road, but in 1934 it was extended across the road to end at the Park Circus Five Point Junction.

The numbers in the road have changed many times. Initially it began with No. 1 on the south side, the site of the Chowringhee Theatre, continuing up to Lower Circular Road and progressing on the north side ending on Chowringhee Road at No. 50. Now the even numbers are on the south side and the odds on the north.

Along the north side we come to a multistoreyed office complex with the Air-Conditioned Market on the ground and two basements. Earlier this was No. 29 Theatre Road, the address of the first office of the East Indian Railway from around 1854. Before moving to Russell Street the Royal Calcutta Turf Club was here for a while, the number then 49. Once the RCTC had left, the premises were taken for a short time by the Constitution Club.

The premises No. 48 (now No. 3) at the corner with Little Russell Street was bought in 1893 by Sir C.C. Ghose, a Judge at the Calcutta High Court. The house had a large compound extending into Little Russell Street. The house in the old days was always rented out to Europeans. All that remains is a 10 *cottah* piece of land which Justice Ghose had gifted to his daughter, where her descendants now live. The rest of the property on Little Russell Street side houses Larsen & Toubro. On the Theatre Road front a new building houses the Hong Kong Bank on the ground floor. Across the street we come to a set of new houses ending on Camac Street, the old Numbers 47, 46 and 45 'are built on what was, at one time, part of the compound at 5, Harrington Street, owned and occupied by Mr. George McNan, the boundary wall of which formerly extended to Theatre Road'.[18] No. 47/1 is now No. 5 and belongs to the family of the late Mr. N.C. Chatterjee, Bar-at-Law, now leased out to the British Council Division of the British Deputy High Commission. No. 47 once belonged to the wealthy Jewish family of A. Curlender, a partner in S. Curlender & Co., 8, Old Court House Corner, proprietors of the Bengal Bone Mills, Dhapa Fertilizer Works, Aligarh Manure Factory and Agra Manure Works. But the Curlender house in Theatre Road was famous for its garden and lush lawn, where the world came to see a dream lawn. Once we pass the huge new complex of the Nagaland House and the Astor Hotel, an old Victorian house with a lawn, we reach the site of the old Theatre Road Post Office. The corner building housed a branch of the chemists Smith Stanistreet & Co., which later became O.N. Mukherjee's, which has been closed for some years.

Across Camac Street the corner house was A.D. Kyrillo's Boarding House, now replaced by a high rise with ANZ Grindlays Bank on the street level. Between Wood Street and Hungerford Street looms the blank white southern wall of the Saturday Club; and during a night game of tennis the whole area is flooded with light. No. 38 in the beginning of the twentieth century was the Guest House of H.H. Nawab Salimullah Bahadur of Dacca, later the site of the famous Three Hundred Club.

> The Committee of the Saturday Club had reprimanded Allan Lockhart for giving a party for the ladies of a theatrical touring company. It was an unwise move. Allan's rejoinder—after giving the committee a typical trenchant reply—was to start a social club which set out to provide everything that the Saturday Club did not. In particular it would admit Indians. Success was immediate. The three hundred sponsors that gave the club its name were found at once from senior Indian and European businessmen. The club became the haunt of the sprightlier members of the princely families, the small but expanding number of Indian business executives with European tastes in entertainment, Central Europeans, Americans, and a slightly raffish band of bachelors, Indian and British... . Boris Lissanevich, a cabaret dancer and ex-Cadet of the Russian Imperial Navy, was an inspired choice for Secretary. The chef, the pianist, the violin player, the cuisine too were Russian. Boeuf Stroganof, Chicken Kiev, exotic forms of vodka, cosmopolitan membership, small tables and shaded lights; the changes from the Saturday Club, with its atmosphere of a well-lit gymnasium, could not have been more complete. The Three Hundred flourished. During the war, it was a welcome oasis in a squalid city and for the Army a rest from a world of damp uniforms and anti-malarial mepacrine... . The building that housed it was an architectural extravagance called 'Philip's Folly'. It abounded in alcoves and recesses, where there were tables where people could dine quietly a deux, whether there was a crowd on the dance floor or whether—as was more usual in the early part of the evening—it was simply empty.[19]

The Three Hundred Club is no more. The building that stood vacant for a long time has since been demolished for a new one. The old Number 36 was before the First World War, the Imperial and Royal Austro-Hungarian Consulate General. This house later became the residence of the Nawab Bahadur of Dacca. The rest up to Lower Circular Road was residential; a handful of the old houses still in existence.

On the south side from Lower Circular Road up to the junction with Pretoria Street was *bustee* land around shallow insanitary tanks. The land was reclaimed gradually and residential houses came up. After demolition of some of the old houses, there came up the Kala Mandir, one of Calcutta's finest theatres, with two auditoriums, a large one thousand plus seater above and a basement playhouse below. The Swiss Club was established in 1924, with a lovely bowling green, which does not exist any more. The club has changed its name, it is now the International Club; some of the old Swiss furniture and trophies are all that remain of the heritage. The old Number 22 was yet another house owned by H.H. Nawab Salimullah. The new No. 22 was the residence of H. Holmwood, CIE, ICS, District and Sessions Judge. This house later became the 'Unceremonial Golightly Hall'.

Here we cross Rawdon Street. No. 21 was the Italian Consulate General. Next were two old houses where senior officers of the Government and High Court Judges used to live. These have been demolished to make way for the new building of the Bharatiya Bhasha Parishad (Indian Languages Institute), a private cultural body. Just before the crossing with Loudon Street there was an old tank, which has been filled up and a garden has been laid. Now known as Macpherson Square, it bears the name of Sir William Macpherson, ICS, Judge of the Calcutta High Court from 1885 to 1900.

After Loudon Street one can see a two-storeyed house, now an office of the Enforcement Branch of the Calcutta Police. Once this was the residence of the Raja of Nazargunje, Bihar. Numbers 14 and 15 at the crossing with Upper Wood Street and Hungerford Street was the Hathwa House, residence of the Maharaja of Hathwa, another princely state in Bihar. Up to Camac Street all the old houses have been demolished and new high-rises have come up. Across Camac Street Numbers 10 and 9 were Mrs. Lord's Boarding Houses. In the 1930s the corner house, No. 12, was the residence of the Hon. Mr. Justice Dwarkanath Mitter, M.A., D.L., Judge, Calcutta High Court. No. 11 had several shops, No. 10 housed the Girls' Friendly Society, Hostel and Club. At the corner with Pretoria Street was the old No. 9, a residential house, which since 1938 has been the Metropolitan Nursing Home, one of the oldest in Calcutta. After Pretoria Street, a range of old houses, new numbers 16 and 16A, were demolished to be replaced by a ramshackle building called B.K. Market, a shopping complex.

> Old No. 5 on the south side, from time immemorial, has had an undefinable, sinister, and uncanny reputation. What it is no one can exactly say, but it is sufficiently significant to keep people from occupying it. At one time it seemed as if the owners were going to allow it gradually to tumble to pieces, but this year they have apparently awakened up and have built an entirely new facade and enlarged it on a considerable scale, which must have entailed a very heavy outlay, but so far unfortunately for no purpose. If all I hear is correct it has already been let twice, but the would-be tenants cannot get a single servant to venture near the place.[20]

The old No. 5 is probably the old building with an iron gate, and unkempt garden opposite the Hindusthan Lever House. The other houses before Elysium Row are the old Number 4 (new No. 8), now occupied by Shri Aurobindo Bhawan, a typical Victorian English house inside a compound; and the old No. 3 (new No. 6) which is now the State Bank of India's Guest House.

Next we come to the road on the left leading to Lower Circular Road. This was called *Poorana Nachghar ka Poorab Rasta* in the old directories. The Elysium Row at one time had many distinguished residents. No. 17 on the east side, the first house from Theatre Road, was the residence of Lord Sinha of Raipur. Later the Sinhas shifted to No. 7 on the same side of the road, just before Lower Circular Road, where they still live. No. 4 in 1905 was occupied by the Maharaja of Nepal.

No. 13 was the German Club, and No. 6 on the west side was the office and residence of the Consul General for Persia. No. 13 later became the office of the CID, the Intelligence Branch of the Calcutta Police. This was the infamous office where young Indian revolutionaries were brought in for interrogation and torture.

Now there are two educational institutions on the street, viz. Sakhawat Memorial Girls' High School and the Shri Shikshayatan school and college. The Intelligence Branch is still there and on the western side there is a big camp of the Border Security Force.

The Calcutta Corporation, vide notification dated 14 November 1929, renamed Elysium Row as Lord Sinha Road, though not without objections. Satyendra Prasanna Sinha, the first Indian to serve in the Governor General's Executive Council (1909), was knighted in 1914, and made a KCSI in 1926. Lord Sinha was an active member of the Indian National Congress from 1896 to 1919, presiding over the Bombay Session of the Congress in 1915. He was raised to the peerage in 1919 as Baron Sinha of Raipur.[21]

Coming back to Theatre Road, we come to the new No. 4, a huge apartment house called Embassy with the Government of India Tourist Bureau on the ground floor. This was once the old No. 2, a residential house. The old No. 1 was the site of the Chowringhee Theatre founded in 1813.

CHOWRINGHEE THEATRE

For representations of the Theatre we are indebted to two contemporary artists, firstly William Wood, with his lithograph of 1830, *Chowringhee Road and the Theatre*, a plate from his *A Series of Twentyeight Panoramic Views of Calcutta*, published in London in 1833; and to William Prinsep with his *Interior of the Chowringhee Theatre of 1835*, pencil and pen-and-ink, now in the India Office Library, London.

From the first picture it is obvious that the Theatre was set within a very spacious compound bounded on the east by the present Lord Sinha Road. The building had deep *verandahs*, *chunammed* pillars, and boarded floors, and was surmounted by a wooden dome. It was more than a theatre, for Calcutta's elite would gather here every evening for gossip and drinks, whether there was a performance on the bills or not. The female roles were played by professional actresses, but those of the men by amateurs. William Prinsep, the artist, was one of them. As he recalls in his memoirs:

Figure 61: Willam Wood—The Chowringhee Road and the Theatre 1830

Being myself particularly fond of everything connected with the stage, I was soon enrolled among the dramatis personae, and hard at work in leisure hours in painting scenes and devising costumes, which being made entirely by native tailors had to be most particularly designed. From that time until the Chowringhee Theatre met the fate of all theatres and was totally destroyed by fire, I was more or less connected with Parker in the stage management as well as the performances, my line being of course comic and in musical representations.... The theatre was a proprietary one, each member, comprising nearly all of our society having of course free entrance, and therefore the money taken at the door for performances only once a fortnight never covered the expenses and we were consequently obliged to have frequent recourse to house benefits which deprived the proprietors of their free entrances.[22]

In 1836 Prinsep was engaged in remodelling the theatre, particularly the ill-contrived stage and scenic arrangements, while a new roof was put on the whole building. The theatre had accommodation for 800 persons in the boxes and about 200 in the pit.

Here Mrs. Esther Leach, the leading beauty of the Calcutta stage, made her bow as Lady Teazle on 27 July 1826. She was then barely seventeen, and for many years she continued to be the idol of the theatre-going public. In the early morning of the last day of May 1839, the Chowringhee Theatre was completely destroyed by a devastating fire. The wooden dome blazed fiercely and the conflagration was visible from the remotest part of the town. In an hour the entire building was gutted. It was never rebuilt.

A house was later erected on the site and was the residence of Sir William Markby, a judge of the Calcutta High Court from 1866 to 1877. It then became a prosperous boarding house. In 1905 this was called Bedford House, Mrs. M. Campbell's Boarding House. H.E.A. Cotton had a flat there. In the 1950s there was a three storey house on the site with residential as well as office accommodation. The house was falling into decay. Recently, it has been completely renovated and is called Sahara Sadan, belonging to the Sahara Group of Industries including an airline. Here ends the old Theatre Road, in native terms *Poorana Nauchghar ka Rasta*.

On 25 April 1964, the Calcutta Corporation renamed Theatre Road as Shakespeare Sarani, to pay homage to William Shakespeare on his 400th birth anniversary.

Now we are back to Chowringhee for the final stretch to Lower Circular Road.

On the east side Numbers 47 to 50 were called Ballard's Buildings, which were residential premises. At the site of this old building now stands a new shopping complex called Victoria Plaza, a petrol pump and the new Air-India office.

BISHOP'S PALACE

In 1849 Bishop Wilson expressed his desire to change his residence from the palace at Russell Street to somewhere closer to the new Cathedral, St. Paul's. In 1850 the Bishop moved to the present palace at 51, Chowringhee Road, once the property of Mr. Wilberforce Bird, BCS, Senior Member of the Council, from whom the Bishop purchased it for Rs. 55,000 in exchange for the palace in Russell Street, which still remained his property. It was not until the Bishop's death that the Russell Street house was sold in 1863 by the executors of his will to His Highness Prince Golam Mohammed. The Bishop spent a sum of Rs. 24,000 on improving the Chowringhee Palace before he occupied it. The house has not changed since. This is now the residence of the Metropolitan in India.

It is a fine house with a spacious verandah running round its west and southern sides. Close to the gateway there is a massive Chinese Bell. The following is a translation of the inscription.

BELL AT LIMBO AND PLACED IN THE SAINT'S CHURCH

With joy and gladness we place this bell in the Church, so that the sound of the peals may not only be heard close by but afar.

The saints have their dwelling place everywhere.

If you believe, you will follow God's way and will find easy access to Him. On hearing the sound of the bell, you will be brought to a recollection of your sins.

Even the dead on hearing the sound of the bell, will ascend to heaven. We on this earth are burning in fire, on hearing the sound of this bell, will escape out of its heat to a cooler place.

Those who believe in God shall all become saints.

Chan Lung (Viceroy of) Thai-Chin in his 4th year, on a lucky day in November made this bell. The fourth year of Chan-Lung is said to be 1720 AD.[23]

The next two buildings, 52 and 53, were residential ones. No. 54, once the Chinese Ambassador's house and office, was demolished to make way for Birla Mansions. No. 55 was the Office of the Protector of Emigrants in the early twentieth century before it gave way to King Edward's Court, a huge block of buildings with a large garden in front. This building had a number of beautiful residential rooms with lofty ceilings and deep *verandahs* to the west that are still there though the garden is no longer there. It is now being built over for an office complex. No. 55 1/2 was the Horse Menage and Riding School of R.A. Turnbull. This disappeared later and was probably absorbed in the building next door. Numbers 56 to 58 were old buildings, now replaced by newer non-descript ones. And with that we are at Lower Circular Road. The Chowringhee Road continues still further up to the crossing of Elgin Road. But this stretch is mostly in the Indian quarters.

Since 1964, Chowringhee Road has a new name, Jawaharlal Nehru Road, after Jawaharlal Nehru (1889-1964), first Prime Minister of Independent India until his death in 1964. It is ironic that this historic road is named after one who called Calcutta 'The Nightmare City'. In the British days Calcutta was the second city of the Empire, but during Nehru's reign business and industry were deliberately taken away from the state, and Calcutta and a partitioned Bengal came to be fleeced for the benefit of the new states that came into being.

References

1. Massey, Montague. *Recollections of Old Calcutta*, p. 106.

2. Firminger, W.K. *Thacker's Guide*, p. 81.

3. *Bengal Club*, p. 35.

4. Ibid. pp. 50-51.

5. Ibid. pp. 122-24.

6. Ray, Tathagata. 'The Calcutta Metro', in *The Living City*, vol. II, pp. 157-58.

7. *Calcutta 200 years*, p. 176.

8. Basu, Champaka. *Challenges and Changes : The ITC Story 1910-1985*, Calcutta 1988, p. 75.

9. Ibid. p. 13.

10. Massey. op. cit. p. 107.

11. Cotton, H.E.A. *Calcutta Old and New*, Calcutta 1980, p. 107.

12. Massey. op. cit. p. 108.

13. Ibid. p. 112.

14. Losty, J.P., *Calcutta, City of Palaces,* London 1990, p. 15.

15. Ibid. p. 76.

16. Cotton. op. cit. p. 231.

17. Massey. op. cit. pp. 108-09.

18. Ibid. p. 118.

19. Jenkins, Sir Owen, in Laura Sykes (ed.), *Calcutta Through British Eyes 1690-1986,* Calcutta 1992, p. 79.

20. Massey. op. cit. p. 111.

21. Nair P.T. *A History of Calcutta Streets,* pp. 521-22.

22. Quoted in Losty. op. cit. pp. 100-01.

23. Firminger, W.K. op. cit. p. 79.

References

1. Massey, Montague. Recollections of Old Calcutta, p. 106.

2. Firminger, W.K. Thacker's Guide, p. 81.

3. Bengal Club, p. 35.

4. Ibid. pp. 50-51.

5. Ibid. pp. 122-24.

6. Ray, Tathagata. 'The Calcutta Metro', in The Living City, vol. ii, pp. 157-58.

7. Calcutta 200 years, p. 176.

8. Basu, Champaka. Challenges and Changes : The ITC Story 1910-1985, Calcutta 1988, p. 75.

9. Ibid. p. 13.

10. Massey. op. cit. p. 107.

11. Cotton, H.E.A. Calcutta Old and New, Calcutta 1980, p. 107.

Chapter Thirteen

Lower Circular Road

The Circular Road, stretching along and covering the unfinished Marhatta Ditch, became the longest street in the city; from Shyambazar in the north to the Sealdah Railway station it was known as Upper Circular Road, now renamed Acharya Prafulla Chandra Road. From Sealdah to Kidderpore and now up to the approaches of Vidyasagar Setu, the new bridge across the Ganga, it is the Lower Circular Road, renamed Acharya Jagadishchandra Bose Road. The road came into being after filling up the Marhatta Ditch.

From Chowringhee Road to Beck Bagan and the Ballygunge Circular Road crossing, there were large *bustees*, such as Colvin's, Baman, Kassiah Bagan, etc. The white town gradually moved closer, but still it was considered quite infra dig to reside in this part of the town. It is only in the late nineteenth century that considerable improvements were carried out, the *bustees* were razed, and Lansdowne Road, previously known as *Peepul Puttee Rasta*, was widened and newly laid out.

The Circular Road was for a time also called *Bahar Sarak* or the outer road by the Indians.

Lower Circular Road (Eastern Part)

We shall now move through the part of the road up to the point where Ballygunge Circular Road and Beck Bagan Row meet the Lower Circular Road.

We are moving east along the northern side of of the road; the buildings we now see up to the Elysium Row were once part of the premises No. 58, Chowringhee. Between Pretoria Street and Camac Street was the huge property known as Colvin's Bazar with two tanks extending up to Theatre Road, as evident in the map drawn by Major L.P. Schalch and Capt. T. Prinsep for the Lottery Committee in 1832. St. Joseph's Home and the Little Sisters of the Poor now occupy what was once Colvin's Bazar. In about 1882 one Mr. Asphar, a wealthy Catholic merchant of the city, saw the wonderful work of the Little Sisters of the Poor in Europe and conceived a plan of opening an establishment of these Sisters in Calcutta. He got the help of the Roman Catholic Archbishop of Calcutta, Paul Goethalls. On 30

November 1882 the first batch of six Sisters of the Poor landed at Calcutta, and these were further strengthened by the arrival of two more next year.

The Little Sisters of the Poor is a religious order belonging to the Roman Catholic Church; they take the three vows of Poverty, Chastity and Obedience, and to these they add Hospitality. They devote their lives to the care of the aged poor exclusively. The first home for the aged poor started in a house directly opposite St. James' Church. In 1887 the present site at 2 Lower Circular Road was purchased, but the new building could only commence in 1898 when the Maharajah of Darbhanga donated Rs. 10,000 towards the building fund. The old premises, completed in 1901, had two separate buildings, one for the men and the other for the women. There were spacious dormitories, sitting rooms, wide *verandahs* and a garden for the inmates to enjoy fresh air, a chapel and a sick room. The Home was open to all classes and creeds, and all the inmates were treated alike. There was accommodation for about 200 inmates.

Recently, the old buildings have been demolished and a fine new building one has taken their place. St. Joseph's Home still takes care of the aged people of Calcutta. Only a portion of the old building has been preserved at the Camac Street corner. Here we cross the Camac Street and proceed further east.

According to the Plan of the City drawn by L.P. Schalch and Captain Thomas Prinsep for the Lottery Committee in 1825-32, the entire area from Camac Street with the Theatre Road as northern boundary was 'Bhamun Bustee' with a large tank in the middle, that later became the Victoria Square. A new road was laid to lead to the tank, and called Dalhousie Street for a short time, before it was renamed in honour of the reigning British Queen Victoria in 1874. Gorky Sadan, the Cultural Centre of the Russian Federation, stands at the corner of Victoria Terrace facing one of the oldest Nursing Homes in Calcutta, Park Nursing Home, managed and run by three generations of Dr. Chatterjees.

Dr. Subir Chatterjee, one of the owners of the Park Nursing Home (now Park Clinic), recalls:

> On a winter day in December 1937, I had my first glimpse of 4 Victoria Terrace. My parents said that we would live in the first floor of this two-storeyed building and the ground floor would house Park Nursing Home. My father was running this Nursing Home at 83 Park Street since 1934; it then had 5 beds and would now have 8. The premises had been taken on lease from Raja Janaki Nath Ray of Bhagyakul from 1 January 1938.
>
> However our first patient arrived a day prior to this. He was seriously ill and was admitted under the care of Dr. Bidhan Chandra Roy and Dr. Kumud Sankar Ray; his name was recorded as Dr. S.C. Chatterjee, the same as my father's. However his full name was Sarat Chandra, not Susil Chandra. I was told that he was a world famous

novelist and would not enter any of the existing institutions of the city as these were run by the British... .

Sarat Chandra was operated upon by Dr. Lalit Mohan Banerji for advanced cancer and he passed away on 16 January 1938.[1]

Many distinguished patients have been treated here and the Nursing Home is one of the best in the city. In 1949 the family vacated the upper floor and the entire house was used for patients. In 1977 the Park Children's Centre was opened and ultimately the Chatterjees bought the premises and started dreaming about a modern hospital to take shape. In 1998 a seven-storeyed structure was completed at the corner of Victoria Terrace and A.J.C. Bose Road, as the first phase of the dream project—The Park Clinic.

The next address in the old directories is No. 5, the palace of Harihar Prasad Singh of Dumraon. There are now two buildings on the site. Here we cross Hungerford Street and come to another large tank extending up to Loudon Street, shown clearly in the Plan of Schalch and Prinsep. This was later enlarged and beautified and given the name of Minto Square. In Independent India, this acquired a new name, Bhagat Singh Udyan (Garden) in memory of Bhagat Singh, a noted revolutionary in the freedom movement hanged by the British.

Between Loudon Street and Rawdon Street lies the large compound of the La Martiniere for Boys and beyond Rawdon Street and before Auckland Mansions is the premises of La Martiniere for Girls.

THE LA MARTINIERE SCHOOLS

These institutions together with similar ones in Lucknow and Lyons (France) were founded from the funds left by General Claude Martin. Martin was born in Lyons in 1735 and came to India as a soldier in the French Army in 1752, and fought under Count Lally. Later, in recognition of his outstanding abilities, he was given a commission in the army of the East India Company. He rose to the rank of Major General. He amassed a princely fortune and died in Lucknow on 13 September 1800. He bequeathed Rs. 200,000 to be devoted to the establishment of a school for the Christian inhabitants of Calcutta; and a further sum of Rs. 150,000 'to add to the permanency of the school'.[2]

The building completed in 1835 was constructed by J.P. Parker from the design of J.H. Rattray at a cost of £23,000. It is a structure of two storeys, and is surmounted by a large dome. In the centre of the building is a chapel, and on either side ample accommodation for teachers and students. There are two porticos, south and north, communicating with the chapel. The building stands on a ground covering over seven acres. An additional block containing an Assembly Hall with galleries, spacious airy classrooms, a library and Chemistry and Physics laboratories, was completed in 1915. The grounds today do not

Figure 62: La Martiniere School

have seven acres, as the School authorities have sold off or leased out a part of the grounds, one on Lower Circular Road and another on Rawdon Street for office complexes.

Across the Rawdon Street is the Girls' section. A perfectly plain structure devoid of any architectural beauty, this building stands in a compound of over four acres. Though established for the Christian poor, the school authorities soon forgot their vow, as the following report in the *Calcutta Review* of 1850 bears out.

> The La Martiniere, founded 1st March 1836 from the funds left by Major General Claude Martin is a richly endowed institution—the most wealthy in Calcutta. There is an anomaly in its constitution; it has effected a compromise between Popery, Church of England and Presbyterianism. It is a charitable institution, but the charity is expected not so much to the low and ragged poor, as to the rich and respectable poor, of whom there are hundreds in Calcutta.[3]

The school buildings still stand in an aura of heritage, with the plaster peeling away, particularly in the Girls' section where the ground floor classrooms are dark and gloomy.

After the school there stood the old No. 6, which before the First World War was the Consulate General for Germany. In 1905 the Consul General was Count A. Von Quadt Wykrat-Ismy. Here we leave the rest of the Lower Circular Road going north towards

Sealdah Station and cross the road at the Beck Bagan-Ballygunge Circular Road crossing. Just before the crossing No. 224 is Bishop's College, dwarfed by the multistoreyed building built in a part of its compound.

BISHOP'S COLLEGE

The college was established by the Society for the Propagation of the Gospel at the urgent request of Bishop Middleton, who laid the foundation stone on 15 December 1820. It was founded for the purpose of (i) instructing native and other youths in the doctrine and discipline of Christ's Church, with a view to their becoming preachers, catechists or school masters; (ii) extending the benefits of education generally; (iii) translating the scriptures, liturgy and other religious works; and (iv) forming a residence for European missionaries on their arrival in India. The first Principal was the Rev. William Hodges Mill, DD (1792-1853).

The college was originally situated at the present premises of the Bengal Engineering College, Shibpore. In 1879, these buildings were sold to the Government and the college was removed temporarily to 33 Circular Road and finally to the buildings and grounds of 224 Lower Circular Road, which were purchased by the Society for the Propagation of the Gospel.

Here we cross the present Ballygunge Circular Road, which in the early nineteenth century was a narrow road called 'Ballygunge Road' leading to the Viceroy's Bodyguard Lines at Ballygunge Maidan. Next to the petrol pump at the corner there is a part of a very old house, 225 Lower Circular Road, which was also called Tivoli Park or Tivoli Gardens. The modern residence-cum-office complex, Tivoli Court, occupies the site of Tivoli Park. In 1933, 225 was J.D. Scott's Stables and the Japanese Club. Probably at this site stood St. James' Theatre, as described by Montague Massey. Giving an account of the devastation after the great cyclone of 1864 he says:

> Many of the buildings had also suffered very severely. Some had their verandahs and sides blown in, and others had corners literally cut off where the fury of the storm had struck at a particular angle. Amongst some others that had fared so badly was unhappily St. James's Theatre at Circular Road, the home of the "CATS". All the members at once felt that it had become a thing of the past, as the owner, Mr. Jimmy Brown, who had built it at a cost of Rs. 30,000 could never afford the expense of repairing it.

Next is a blind alley, Lower Rawdon Street, with very few houses, but with gardens and compounds, which in the last few decades have been replaced by residential high-rises, and a college.

Between Lower Rawdon Street and Lansdowne Road there were seven old houses, all now replaced by modern buildings. In the early twentieth century 227/1 was the residence of the Maharaja of Gidhour. In the Plan of Schalch and Prinsep (1825-32), Lansdowne Road is shown as a road leading to Chakraberia; in Heysham's Map of Calcutta, showing the latest improvements in 1856, it is called Kaseea Bagaun Road. The name Lansdowne Road was approved by the Corporation as late as 1889. Massey describes it as *Peepul Puttee Rasta*. Where the high-rises now vie with each other on the old plot No. 2, J.C. Galstaun had his famous stable of race horses.

In Schalch's Plan, Cussiah Bagan Bustee is shown opposite Bhamun Bustee, with some English houses shown west of the *bustee*. But in Heysham's Map of 1856 the entire stretch from the present Lansdowne Road to Chowringhee is shown as Kaseea Bagaun, with two Kaseea Bagaun Roads, one of them the present Lansdowne Road and the other the present Woodburn Park Road. The *bustee* had a Mahomedan Burial Ground in the centre. The Calcutta Corporation took an initiative to improve the Kaseea Bagan Roads and the *bustees* were removed to give way to building plots. The Kaseea Bagan Road opposite Loudon Street became Lansdowne Road, renamed Sarat Bose Road after Independence, when the road was widened and improved up to Hazra Road at a cost of Rs. 3,28,000. The second Kaseea Bagan Road was renamed Woodburn Park Road. The Mahomedan Burial Ground inside the *bustee* was removed and now there is no sign of it.

As we cross Lansdowne Road we come across some modern office complexes which have replaced old residential houses. Premises No. 230 served as the office and workshop of J.E. Tomlin & Co., furniture and billiard table manufacturers, decorators, upholsterers and gilders, their premises extending into a narrow lane leading to the eastern end of Woodburn Park and No. 231. On the rear part of the site now stands a Girls' School— Ashok Hall. No. 231 still stands as an old house surrounded by a compound, housing the Calcutta Nursing Home. Sarat Chandra Bose, the well-known lawyer and nationalist leader, once lived in this house for some time. No. 233 is Lord's Building, an old residential house which still exists; 233/4 and 233/5 were the premises of Victor & Co. and United Motor Co., both motor engineers.

In 1905 No. 234/3 was Calcutta Corporation's Kassia Bagan *dhobi khana* (washerman's facilities). In McCluskie's *Directory and Guide to Calcutta* of 1906 Woodburn Park Road is shown as Woolfut Bagan Road. The name Woodburn Park Road came much later, commemorating Sir John Woodburn, ICS, Lieutenant Governor of Bengal from April 1898 till his death on 21 November 1902.

The Woodburn Park covers the site of the old Kassia Bagan burial ground, which was given as a Wakf to the Mahomedan community by Nawab Saadat Ali Khan Bahadur, the last independent ruler of Oudh. The burial ground was about 37 *bighas* in area and different parts were used for burial of Mahomedans and Low Caste Hindus. It was closed in July 1858 on sanitary grounds, and the Commissioners provided another cemetery at Tiljala, at a cost of Rs. 4272. In 1888 the Mahomedan Burial Board moved the Chairman of the Corporation for preserving the old burial ground from encroachment and defilement and for its decent maintenance, but nothing was done until 1896, when it was proposed to acquire the land and reserve it as an open space. Government claimed that the property had vested in itself, and sued one Fazlar Rahman, who was in possession of a portion of the site. The suit however was compromised, Fazlar Rahman being left in possession of about 12 *bighas*, and the remainder being passed over to the Government (1901). In 1903 the land was passed over to the Corporation to be converted into a public square, and Woodburn Park Road was constructed in 1905-06. The square (19½ *bighas* in area) was fenced in, but it was only in 1913-14 that a comprehensive scheme of improvement was prepared; the park to be laid out as a garden on the lines suggested by Mr. Lane of the Royal Botanical Gardens (Sibpur).[5] The Calcutta South Club was established on this site. This is one of the finest Tennis clubs in the East and has held a number of important tournaments on its courts.

After crossing Woodburn Park Road we come to No. 234/3, where the French Motor Car & Electric Co. Ltd. has its showroom and a huge workshop extending well into the Woodburn Park Road. The old showroom was a fine building where the latest imported cars were kept on display, many a Rolls Royce car passing through their hands. The old showroom has been demolished and a new office complex-cum-showroom has taken its place.

GALSTAUN PARK–NIZAM'S PALACE

In the Armenian Church at Calcutta there is a black marble slab with white border fixed on the north wall of the nave, with the following inscription:

> Sacred to the memory of the late Rose Catherine Galstaun, the beloved wife of Johannes Carapiet Galstaun. Born in Batavia on 26th November 1866 Died in Calcutta on 14th August 1910 and buried at the Armenian Cemetery in Lower Circular Road. This tablet was erected by the Church Committee AD 1911, in recognition of Mr. Galstaun's many acts of kindness to his community.

J.C. Galstaun built the magnificent edifice with a large garden and stables at No. 234/4 for his beloved Rose Catherine in the early twentieth century. The house was an 'art deco palace' with a fine silvery dome, the inside all Italian marble. Galstaun lost interest in the house after the death of his wife, but continued to live there. During the First World War he put the Galstaun Park at the disposal of the military authorities for the use of sick and invalid soldiers. In this house he received the Prince of Wales (later King Edward VIII) in 1921. He used to keep his prized race horses in the stable. A legend goes:

One morning, the champion race-horse, Paddy's Darling, trespassed into the convent of the Little Sisters of the Poor on the opposite side of the road. The good nuns had just lost their old buggy horse and saw in the Darling an answer to their prayer. It was only after a suitable replacement was made that the champion was released.[6]

Later this property was acquired by the Nizam of Hyderabad and Galstaun Park is now known by the name of Nizam's Palace. After Independence the Government of India acquired the building, the palatial building now accommodating a number of offices; with new residential buildings erected in the compound as residential apartments for senior Government of India officers. The next two houses in the old days were mainly residential houses, which have since been swallowed up by a five-star hotel, Hotel Hindusthan International. The old buildings before Lee Road have all been demolished and new multistoreyed complexes have taken their place.

The next road leading south is Lee Road, which is a thoroughfare for the area. It does not appear in the Calcutta Directories of 1905, when it was still a part of Kassia Bagan Bustee. When the bustee was removed the Calcutta Corporation built a huge reservoir for the supply of filtered water, a road called Reservoir Road South was constructed up to Lower Circular Road. This was renamed by the Corporation as Lee Road to honour Harry Lee, ICS, who was chairman of the municipal body from 16.4.1890 to 31.3.1895.[7]

After Lee Road the site of the old No. 237 has an interesting history. Indira Devi Chowdhurani, Tagore's brilliant niece, recalled in her memoirs that her parents stayed in this area when she was a student in the Loreto House and her elder brother Suren was studying at the St. Xavier's School. One of the addresses she remembered was 237, which then (in the closing years of the nineteenth century) belonged to Mr. Bhuban Mohan Das. In 1905 this was the residence of Mr. Behari Lal Gupta, ICS, who later became a judge at the Calcutta High Court. After retirement from service he acted for some years as Secretary to the Maharaja of Baroda. The present house on the site is a modern one, 'Ranjani', built by Nalini Ranjan Sircar, his nameplate still adorning the eastern gate of the house. Sircar (1882-1953) was a leading figure in Bengal politics, who became a member of the Bengal Legislative Assembly in 1923 and Mayor of Calcutta in 1935. He served as a minister in undivided Bengal under Fazlul Haque, and after Independence he was Finance Minister of West Bengal, and in 1949 acting Chief Minister for some time. The house is now used by the Calcutta Police as Foreigners' Registration Office.

No. 239 is the residence of the Raja of Jharia and is still called the Jharia House, as the shining brass nameplate proclaims.

No. 240, the last house before Chowringhee Road, was the residence of Mr. T.B. Sookias and Mr. and Mrs. Firpo, owners of the Firpo's Restaurant. Here we cross Chowringhee Road and come to the western part of the Lower Circular Road. The whole area was called

Dehee Birjee and an old tank opposite the Calcutta Club was called Birjee Talao, the area later assuming the same name.

Dehee Birjee in the Eighteenth Century

The records of a few transactions of properties in the area conjure up an image of Dehee Birjee.

October 4-5, 1787: The Reverend John Zachariah Kiernander mortgages to Matthew Leslie of Chittra for Sicca Rs. 16,000 a new built upper-roomed dwelling house and ground (3 bighas 5½ cottas) 'in Bobanypore adjoining to the Great Garden of the said John Zachariah Kiernander and bounded as follows: on the east by the garden of the said John Zachariah Kiernander, on the south by the said garden, on the west by the garden of the said John Zachariah Kiernander, and the high road leading from Chowringhee to Russa Pugla, and on the north by a new road leading to the ground of Richard Johnson Esq.;' and also 'the dwelling house and ground (1 biga 16 cottas and 6 chitacks), the property of R.W. Kiernander bounded on the south by the great road leading from the Hospital to the English Burying Ground, to the east by an avenue commonly called or known by the name of Vansittart's Avenue, on the north by a new built house belonging to the said Robert William Kiernander and to the west by one other brick house belonging to the said Robert William Kiernander.'

July 1-2, 1787: John Zachariah Kiernander and Robert William Kiernander mortgage for Sicca Rs. 23,513 to Stephen Fivey an upper-roomed dwelling house and ground (2 bigas 13 cottas and 1 chitack) in Dehee Birjee 'bounded on the east by the avenue formerly belonging to Mr. Vansittart, on the west and north by some ground belonging to Robert William Kiernander, and on the south by the upper-roomed house belonging to Robert William Kiernander;' and an upper-roomed dwelling-house and ground (1 biga 16 cottas and 9 chitacks) in Dehee Birjee, 'bounded on the east by the avenue of trees formerly belonging to Mr. Vansittart, on the west by a new built house belonging to Robert William Kiernander, on the north by some ground belonging to Mr. Robert William Kiernander, and on the south by the public road leading from the Hospital to the Burial Ground.'

January 18, 1785: Patta granted by John Scott, Collector to R.W. Kiernander for 23 bigas and 12 cottas of land in Dehee Birjee, formerly the property of George Vansittart Esq.

August 22, 1788: Joseph Bernard mortgages to Wm. Smoult for Sicca Rs. 2,000 a lower-roomed dwelling-house in Dehee Birjee and ground (4 bigas), bounded on the north by the garden house of Burgh and Barber, on the south by the house of Mons. Ponchelet, on the east by ground belonging to Mr. Camac, and on the west by the high road fronting Mr. Boileau's house.

July 1-2, 1788: Wm. Smoult sells to Solomon Hamilton for Sicca Rs. 4,500 an upper-roomed house and ground (5 bigas 13 cottas and 9 chittacks) in Dehee Birjee, bounded on the east by the avenue formerly belonging to Mr. Vansittart, on the north and south by properties of R.W. Kiernander, and on the west by a highway.[8]

In A. Upjohn's *Map of Calcutta and its Environs 1892-93* the site opposite the Birjee Talao is shown as a vacant land with a tank in the centre. The *Map of the Suburbs of Calcutta* in 1817 by Steepleton shows a part of the vacant land occupied by a bazar called Setaram's Bazar. In Schalch and Prinsep's Plan of 1825-32 Setaram Ghosh's Bazar appears further south and the front portion opposite Birjee Talao is described as Nimoo Mullick Ka Bustee and between it and the General Hospital was Bediah Parrah. Setaram Ghosh's Bazar was probably burnt down in a fire, and the area assumed the name of Pora Bazar. The Pora Bazar Lane off 71 Chowringhee Road commemorates the fire. Houses were built on the site of Nimoo Mullick's Bustee.

Indira Devi Chowdhurani, daughter of Satyendranath Tagore and niece of Rabindranath Tagore, in her reminiscenses, described a house at Birjee Talao, where her family lived for a number of years, when she was a student at the Loreto House. It was a large house with tennis and badminton courts. Rabindranath's drama *Raja O Rani* was staged here by the family, the cast including Rabindranath and his wife and Satyendranath and his wife. The second staging of Rabindranath's *Mayar Khela* took place in this house where Indira took the leading role. The cast included Rabindranath and his elder brother Jyotirindranath Tagore. Once the Tagores moved elsewhere, the laughter, music and drama disappeared

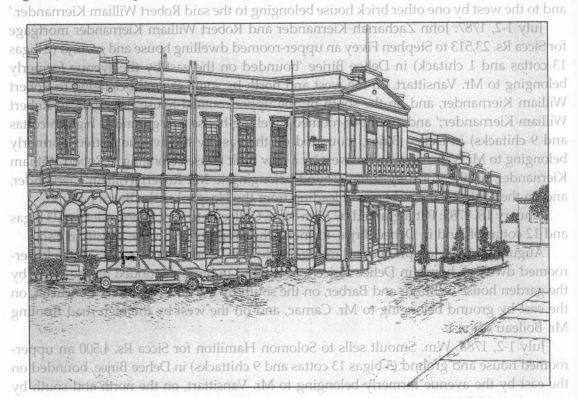

Figure 63: Calcutta Club, Sketch courtesy Rathin Mitra

for years to come; the old house was demolished; in the Calcutta Directories of 1906, No. 241 Lower Circular Road is shown as vacant land.

Since 1915, 241 Lower Circular Road is the address of the Calcutta Club.

CALCUTTA CLUB LTD.

The formation of the Calcutta Club was the result of an incident that took place at the Bengal Club when Rajendranath Mookherjee was the guest of the then Governor of Bengal, Sir John Woodburn. Sir John was asked to take his Indian guest along with others to an ante-room as the European members of the Bengal Club could not then think of having an Indian in the Main Dining Hall. There was immediate consultation among some of the guests and they all decided to form a club where respectable citizens, both Indians and Europeans, would have equal status, facility and treatment and would be the top Club of Calcutta.

In the chapter dealing with the Theatre Royal and Grand Hotel, I have already referred to the old Calcutta Club, which was only for Europeans, and mostly patronized by the mercantile community.

In 1905 a group of men, both Indians and Europeans, had formed a society called the Union Club which met monthly at the Bishop's College under the guiding spirit of Reverend Milburn for dinner and discussion over papers read by members on subjects of general interest. At a garden party given in December 1906 by the members of the Union Club and held at Bishop's College, Mr. Noel Paton on behalf of the guests broached the idea of an institution on the lines of the Orient Club which had been in existence for some years at Bombay. The idea met with general approval and a committee with Mr. Justice Geidt as President, the Rev. Milburn as Secretary, Sir Charles Allen, Mr. Justice Holmwood, Mr. R.N. Mookherjee, Mr. P.L. Roy as members was constituted to go into the prospects of setting up such a club. The committee called a meeting at the Town Hall on 19 March 1907 at which Mr. Justice Geidt presided. At this meeting the Calcutta Club was formed with a number of founder members. A provisional committee was also constituted to draft rules and by-laws, secure suitable premises and arrange other details. Sir Edward Fitzgerald Law, member of the Governor-General's Council and Minister of Finance, drafted the constitution of the club. Arrangements were made to rent 17 Elysium Row as temporary quarters. Meetings were held at the Town Hall on 5 and 12 April, the rules and by-laws as drafted were adopted, other arrangements confirmed and the first Committee of Management elected. The first committee was as follows:

His Highness the Maharaja of Cooch Behar, President
Sir Charles Allen

Mr. G. Lane Anderson
The Hon'ble Mr. A.A. Apcar
Mr. Bhupendranath Basu
The Maharajadhiraj of Burdwan
Mr. A. Chaudhuri
The Maharaja of Durbhanga
Mr. W.R. Gourlay
The Hon'ble Mr. Justice Holmwood
Mr. D. King
Mr. C.W. Walsh
The Hon'ble Mr. Justice Mitter
Mr. Manmatha Nath Mitter
The Nawab of Murshidabad
Mr. C.A. Oldham
Mr. F. Noel Paton
Mr. A. Rahim
Mr. P.L. Roy
Mr. Lockhart Smith
Maharaja Sir P.K. Tagore
Hony. Secretaries:
Mr. D. Lindsay
Mr. R.N. Mookherjee

The club was formally opened on 15 April 1907 with an inaugural dinner at which 45 members were present.

A plot of land measuring roughly 8 3/4 bighas or 4.66 acres known as Pora Bazar at the prime location of the junction of Chowringhee Road and Lower Circular Road (No. 241) was selected. Lease was taken with approval from the Government of India for a term of 90 years at a rent of approximately Rs. 650 per month.

An imposing two-storey club house designed by Mr. Thornton was constructed by Martin & Co. and others. The club building was formally opened by the Governor of Bengal, Sir Thomas David Gibson Carmichael, on 3 February 1915.

Additions which offered greater facilities were to come over the years. The Maharaja of Cooch Behar gave to the club a Lawn House for the use of the ladies. Till then ladies, not allowed into the main building of the club, were compelled to wait in the carriages for their husbands to come down. The ladies' annexe was formally opened on 3 January 1920. In 1918 Mr. Prafulla Nath Tagore funded the tennis court.

From the beginning it was the custom that an Indian and a European would become President of the club for alternate years, but now there are hardly any European residents left in Calcutta, who would be interested in the position of the President of the Club.

The club has a well-stocked library and the general ambience is excellent. The Prince of Wales (later King Edward VIII) was the first Royal Guest at the Club, when he was invited to a lunch on 28 December 1921.

The club has always had distinguished members from every community, who have enjoyed the club and served it well. After the Maharaja of Cooch Behar, the Hon'ble Mr. Justice Holmwood was the President followed by the Maharaja of Burdwan. Sir Rajen Mookherjee was President in 1913 and 1921. Nawab Sir K.G.M. Faroqui of Ratanpur was the first Muslim President in 1953.

It seems his name was on the list of ministers chosen to serve the newly created East Pakistan after the partition of India. He was politely asked when he was going to Dacca. The Nawab had only one condition, viz. that the Calcutta Club with all its members had to be shifted to Dacca! How could he leave his old friends, the Maharaja of Burdwan and Sir Biren Mookherjee?

The Tagore brothers, Gaganendranath and Abanindranath, were regular visitors to the club, so were other respectable members throughout the years. Satyajit Ray was a member too. The club is still there, a popular landmark in Calcutta.

After Calcutta Club we come to a small street linking Lower Circular Road with Sambhu Nath Pandit Street. The street is of recent origin. 'The Corporation, vide notification dated May 9, 1931, proposed that the new 40 feet road connecting Sambhunath Pandit Street and Lower Circular Road be called Gokhale Road in honour of the reputed Indian Political leader Gopal Krishna Gokhale.'[11]

In Schalch and Prinsep's Plan of 1825-32, the entire area from Nimoo Mullick ka Bustee to the Presidency General Hospital is shown as Bediah Parrah. Much later, Numbers 242 and 243 were acquired by the Bengal Government, the former used for the hospital staff quarters and the corner plot for a fine house with a large compound as the residence of the Surgeon Superintendent of the General Hospital.

Next we come to a main thoroughfare which separates the hospital quarters from the hospital itself, viz. Harish Mukherjee Road.

The original name of Harish Mukherjee Road (from Acharya Jagadish Bose Road to Sambhu Nath Pandit Street) was Bediapara Road. Bediapara Road formerly ran from Lower Circular Road to Peepulputty (modern Sambhu Nath Pandit Street). With the sale of the last plot of land measuring about 2 cottahs and 4 chittacks used as the Corporation stone-metal depot on the west of 8 Harish Mukherjee Road, the major portion of the road became incorporated in the Presidency General Hospital premises and consequently the road was closed in 1917.[12]

The Corporation, on 1 October 1913, named the whole length of the road from the end of Lower Circular Road near the Great Maidan, passing through Bhowanipore, the heart of

Figure 64: The Presidency General Hospital

the respectable Indian quarter in South Calcutta, up to the end of Hazra Road (which was formerly known as New Kalighat Road) as Harish Mukherjee Road in recognition of the invaluable services rendered to the country by Hurrish Chunder Mookerjee, the editor of the *Hindoo Patriot*. Hurrish Chunder, the father of Indian journalism, was born in 1824 and died in 1861.[13]

PRESIDENCY GENERAL HOSPITAL

Now located at 244 Lower Circular Road, the hospital, since rechristened Seth Sukhlal Karnani Memorial Hospital, is more than 230 years old.

The need for a hospital for Europeans, particularly for military personnel, was felt by the East India Company. A Board Meeting was held at the Fort William on 29 September 1766, in which the following were present: Lord Clive, President, Brigadier General John Carnac, Henry Verelst, Randolph Mariott, Hugh Watts, Claude Russell, Thomas Rumboldt, William Aldersey, Thomas Keplsall and Charles Floyer, as members. From the transactions we find that

The Board taking into consideration the great inconveniency attending the want of a proper Hospital for the Military, the present one being only a temporary building in the Old Fort destitute of proper accommodations, it is judged expedient that a commodious one be erected as soon as possible and the Civil Architect attending the Board on this occasion, he is ordered to point out a proper spot for an Hospital to be built upon, and at the same time to deliver in a Plan of one with an estimate of the expense.

The Civil Architect, Colonel Fortnom, who submitted his proposal in December 1766, wanted the hospital to be built on a high ground near the river, viz. Point Sumatra near Surman's Bridge.

At the consultations of the Board, the President (H. Verelst) acquainted the Board that the Reverend Mr. J.H. Kiernander (of the Old Mission Church) had built a very large commodious Garden House at a proper distance from the new Fort which he imagined with a few additions might be converted into a very convenient hospital and which he was willing to dispose of. 'He therefore recommends having it surveyed and the value estimated. He is further induced to recommend the purchasing this House as every Member of this Board must be fully sensible of the tediousness of erecting public buildings and the extravagant charges attendant thereon.'[14] The East India Company accepted the proposals and the price for the Garden House was determined at Rs. 98,000. Rev. Kiernander agreed to be builder of the hospital, the newly-built Garden House to be converted into the Central Block of the Hospital. He offered to supervise the addition of the east and west blocks. The first house or centre building was delivered up and taken possession of on 20 June 1769. The West Wing was begun to be inhabited by the sick people on 2 April 1770, and the East Wing on 2 June.

The hospital was open to all members of His Majesty's civil, military and naval services, and to seamen belonging to private and foreign ships, and also to European paupers. All Europeans of whatever class were admitted. The first picture of the Presidency General Hospital was the handiwork of James Moffat in 1800, in the form of an aquatint showing the hospital and the surgeon's quarters west of it from the Maidan. Sophia Goldborne in *Hartly House* describes:

Near the fort is the hospital I have already mentioned, erected for the reception of all indisposed persons, from whatever cause; throughout which, the wards of chambers are so neat and accommodating, that wretchedness reposes and malady is put to flight. It is lighted and cooled by verandas, and every possible means are adopted to procure the free circulation of air, etc., etc., and it is allowed, by all who have seen it, to be superior to everything under that appellation in the universe... . It was built by the united contributions of the Europeans of Calcutta, and the Company,—Yes Arabella, this blessed asylum owes its support solely to commerce... . To gain admittance into the hospital of Calcutta, there is no other interest or recommendation necessary, than being an European, and deprived of health.[15]

The present Main Building was built to the east of the original Hospital in 1901. The Woodburn Ward was built north-west of the Main Building, facing the Maidan. The Obstetrics and Gynaecology Building stands north of the Main Building.

The Presidency General Hospital has an outstanding claim to distinction throughout the world, for it was in a small laboratory in this hospital that Surgeon-Major (afterwards Sir) Ronald Ross of the Indian Medical Service discovered in 1898 how malaria is conveyed by mosquitoes of the anopheles breed. This epoch-making discovery is worthily commemorated by an iron gate set in a masonry wall to the right of the main entrance on Lower Circular Road. This gate now remains closed, without a gatekeeper to man it. Over the gate is a medallion portrait of Sir Ronald Ross, and let into the wall on either side of the portrait, are two marble tablets, one bearing the inscription:

In this small laboratory seventy yards to the south-east of this gate, Surgeon-Major Ronald Ross of the I.M.S., in 1898 discovered the manner in which malaria is conveyed by mosquitoes.

And the other:

This day relenting God
Hath placed within my hand
A wondrous thing; and God
Be praised at His Command.

Seeking His secret deeds
With tears and toiling health
I find thy cunning seeds
O million murdering death.

I know this little thing
A myriad men will save
O death where is thy sting
The Victory O Grave?

Ronald Ross's laboratory, just east of the Administrative Block, was once the Hospital's Clinical Laboratory. Now the laboratory has shifted to a new building, and the old building has been put to several uses other than research.

The old hospital had beautifully laid gardens, at least two tanks and tennis and badminton courts.

After Independence, the gates were opened to Indian patients too and the hospital acquired a new name—Seth Sukhlal Karnani Memorial Hospital. It was never quite clear what prompted the West Bengal Government to change such a historic name or what the late Karnani's contribution was to the welfare of the suffering humanity of the state.

Remarkable changes took place, as the tank bordering Harish Mukherjee Road was filled up and a four-storey building came up. The ground floor was occupied by the Emergency Department and various outdoor departments. The first floor has the Radiology Department, the second and third occupied by the Pathology Department. In the 1960s the Institute of Post-Graduate Medical Education and Research was established here.

The bicentenary was celebrated in 1970 and a high-rise new building was erected and named Sir Ronald Ross Building.

A large plot of land from the garden in front of the Woodburn Ward bordering Lower Circular Road was given away to the University of Calcutta, to set up the University College of Medicine.

No. 245 in the same compound with a separate gate is probably the oldest surviving building in the Hospital campus. This was the old Surgeon's Quarters, shown as such in Schalch and Prinsep's Plan of 1825-32.

After the Surgeon Superintendent's new residential house was built at No. 243 in 1902, this house at 245 was converted to accommodate several other medical officers. Next we come to a road going south, viz. Bhowanipore Road.

On this road, behind the General Hospital there is an Insane Hospital mentioned in Steepleton's *Map of the Suburbs of Calcutta* of 1817. Later it was called Lunatic Asylum, before it came to be known the Mental Observation Ward.

A little further ahead on the opposite side of the road is the Bhowanipore Military Cemetery, opened in 1782. Some of the notable persons buried here are General Sir Thomas Valiant (1784-1845), who died while commanding a garrison at Fort William, Calcutta; Sir William Lockhart (1841-1900), Commander-in-Chief, India; Lt. Dickens, a descendant of the novelist Charles Dickens, who died in a ship near Calcutta; Henry W.M. Thackeray, Surgeon of the Bengal Artillery (1813); and Esther Leach, the greatest actress of her day in Calcutta, who was burnt on the stage of the Sans Souci Theatre at Calcutta and succumbed to her wounds on 18 November 1843. She found her place in this cemetery as the wife of a sergeant in the army.

As we come back to Lower Circular Road and proceed west, the first buildings on our left are a number of residential buildings for the army erected more recently. Formerly, this was part of a large compound and a building, which appears for the first time in Schalch & Prinsep's Plan of the City of 1825-32 as the Sailors' Hospital.

SUDDER DEWANY ADALAT

This was first situated at a house near Chowringhee, in Speke Street, constructed for William Speke in 1790. It was rented by the Government for the use of the Sudder Dewany Adalat, one of the two courts for appeal, this one reserved for civil cases for Indians in the Presidency outside Calcutta, for whom justice was administered under Hindu or Muslim Legal Codes as appropriate. At this time the name of the street was changed to Sudder Street.

The court in the 1830s was transferred to a new building erected south of the Maidan, for a military hospital, which had been commandeered by Lord William Bentinck for this purpose. This was the building or the site of the Sailors' Hospital. The *adalat* functioned here for many years. In 1862, after many changes, the Supreme Court was united with the Sudder Dewany Adalat, and became the High Court. The building south of the Maidan was given back to the Army and it again became the Military Hospital and remained so until the late twentieth century, when the new extensive complex of the Command Hospital was built in Alipore. Now the fine old house is used by the Army as the Bengal Area Command Headquarters.

No. 247 was Dallanda Buildings, Office of the Controller of Stationery in charge of forms. Later, the Calcutta Police Training School was established here. This is followed by No. 248, occupied by the Telecommunication Factory of the Government of India.

Next is a road going left towards the Zoological Gardens and Belvedere, described in old directories as Zeerut Bridge Road. The Lower Circular Road actually ends at Kidderpore Road near the bridge, but now it has been extended to the approach road to the latest bridge over the Hooghly, the Vidyasagar Setu.

The Corporation, vide notification dated September 24, 1957, proposed that Lower Circular Road be renamed as Acharya Jagadish Chandra Bose Road (*Calcutta Municipal Gazette*, 12 October 1957, p. 570). The road was renamed as such at the Coporation's meeting held on August 26, 1960.[16]

Near the junction of Lower Circular Road with Kidderpore Road on the west, stretches Hastings, an area named after the Marquis of Hastings, Governor-General of India. This area came up as a labour settlement when the new Fort William was being built and was once known as Coolie Bazar.

References

1. Chatterjee, Subir K. 'From Victoria to Gorky—From Home to Hospital,' in *Souvenir of the Park Clinic*, Calcutta 1998.

2. Cotton, H.E.A. *Calcutta Old and New*, p. 775.

3. *Calcutta Review*, vols. XIII & XIV, 1850, p. 447.

4. Massey, Montague, *Recollections of Old Calcutta*, p. 32.

5. Goode. *Municipal Calcutta*, pp. 348-49.

6. Gupta, Bunny & Chaliha, Jaya. In *Calcutta Portraits*, Calcutta 1995, p. 46.

7. Nair, P.T. *A History of Calcutta Streets*, p. 369.

8. Firminger, W.K. 'History of Calcutta Streets and Houses 1786-1834,' in *Bengal Past & Present*, vol. XIV, 1917, pp. 159-222.

9. Roy, Biren. *From Marshes to Metropolis*, Calcutta. p. 118.

10. *Calcutta Club 75th Anniversary Booklet*.

11. Nair, P.T. op. cit. p. 640.

12. Ibid. p. 399.

13. Ibid. p. 399.

14. Moir, D.M. *Bengal Past & Present*.

15. Losty, J.P. *Calcutta, City of Palaces*, London, 1990, p. 78.

16. Nair, P.T. op. cit. p. 131.

Chapter Fourteen

The Vast Expanse of the Maidan

When the new Fort William was built in the village of Gobindapore, the adjoining jungle was cleared and a vast expanse was created for the fort's gunners to have a clear line of fire. But what the future Calcutta got was its lungs. It is an open space about two miles long, its narrowest part in the north ¾th of a mile in breadth and the widest part on the south, at the Lower Circular Road end, where it is 1½ mile wide. It lies in the heart of the city surrounding the Fort, and is bounded on the west by the river Hooghly, on the east by Chowringhee Road; with its northern end at Esplanade East and the southern end at Lower Circular Road. Fine wide roads crisscross the Maidan, all of them the creation of Colonel Henry Watson, the Engineer of Bengal, along with the Red Road and the Secretary's Walk beside it. He is best remembered as the Engineer who supervised the final stages of the construction of the new Fort William.

Of the several large tanks in the Maidan, the Serpentine Tank, within the Race Course, the Manohar Dass Tank opposite Lindsay Street, the Birjee Talao at the south-eastern fringe and the General's Tank opposite the old Hall and Anderson building have survived. The Dhoba Pookur, at the site of the Brigade Parade Ground, the Elliot's Tank, opposite Harrington Street, and the Dhurrumtollah Tank in the Curzon Park have been filled up.

A. Upjohn's Map of 1792-93 shows the Course (later the Race Course) and the Common Jail (now the site of the Victorial Memorial Hall) as the only names in the Maidan, besides the new Fort William.

The oldest road in the Maidan was the Course. It was described in 1768 as being out of town in a sort of angle, made to take the air in; although an old song tells us that those who frequented it swallowed ten mouthfuls of dust for one of fresh air.[1]

THE OLD PRESIDENCY JAIL

According to tradition this was once the site of the hunting box of Nawab Siraj-ud-Daula. Firminger writes:

The basis of this belief is two-fold: (1) the Jail is still called by natives *hurrinbari*, i.e. the deer house; (2) Siraj-ud-Daula is the only name of a Nawab of Dacca familiar to Calcutta ears. *Hurrinbari*, however, was the playful native name for the place, where His Majesty's pets were constrained to dwell, long before the present Jail came into use.'[2]

In 1767 Calcutta had two jails, one in Lal Bazar, the other in Burra Bazar. Of these two places of incarceration one was the House of Correction for petty offenders committed by the Police Magistrates; the other the jail proper for convicted felons and debtors. A letter of the Board to the Court of the Hon. East India Company, dated 30 November 1778, establishes that the present jail was erected in this year. The wall round the jail dated from the end of the year 1783. So far it was only the jail which had been removed to the Maidan, but in 1783 a Mr. Hare, late Sheriff of Calcutta, offered to erect a new House of Correction or 'New Hurrinbari' within the precincts of the jail, in return for the site of the 'Old Hurrinbari' and the sum which had been thought necessary for its repairs.

The Lal Bazar Jail was converted into the Company's Printing Works in 1787. The Debtors' Prison was included within the jail. In the presentment of the Grand Jury in June 1784, we find the complaint:

In every civilized Government the measure of punishment should be ever regulated by the weight of the offence, but in the present state of the jail the convicted felon who is led out to execution, is happier than the unfortunate debtor, who is left to a lingering destruction amidst the gloom of a confined and unwholesome prison, in a damp and stagnated air, without a hope of relief, but what depends upon the caprice of a merciless creditor.[3]

Here was imprisoned in 1782 John Augustus Hickey, the founder of the first Indian newspaper, the *Bengal Gazette*. For a time the unfortunate debtor was able to maintain his family outside the jail in a small brick house, but as Christmas came round, stern necessity led to the incarceration of his children also. A Report of the House of Commons in 1872 gives us a picture of the Calcutta Jail in Hickey's time.

It was the ruin of a house, formerly the residence of some black native. Natives and Europeans were huddled together promiscuously, and many died for want of the necessities of life.

In the middle of the Jail enclosure was a tank about thirty yards square, in which the prisoners promiscuously bathed and washed their clothes. Europeans were generally indulged by the gaoler with the permission to erect and live in small bamboo and matting huts near this tank; it would be impossible for any European to exist for any length of time within the prison. The stench was dreadful. There was no infirmery or provision for the sick that he ever heard of. Debtors and criminals were not separated, nor men from women (but of this he was not positive). An old woman prisoner who begged of him said, in answer to his question, that she wanted the money to buy water.[4]

A road opposite the Presidency General Hospital led to this jail; past the vegetable garden cultivated by the native inmates was the central gateway of the jail.

Frederick Fiebig's *Panoramic Views of Calcutta* in six plates was published by the Asiatic Lithographic Press, Calcutta in 1847. The views were taken through 360° from the top of the Ochterlony Monument. The first view, looking south, gives a rare view of the Jail. In the compound was a tank and a huge barrack.

Until 1865 there were two separate institutions within the walls of the jail—the Great Jail, under the jurisdiction of the Sheriff, where were confined prisoners sentenced by the High Court, military convicts awaiting deportation, and the debtors; and the House of Correction, under the Commissioner of Police for petty offenders.

In February 1865, a bill was passed which united the two prisons under a Superintendent, and from that time the jail was known as the Presidency jail.

In the beautiful surroundings of the Maidan the jail stood as an eyesore for a long time,

Figure 65: Victorial Memorial Hall

till a new jail was constructed at Alipore in 1906. The old jail then fell into disrepair and the scene was even more hideous and ugly until it was demolished to make way for the Victoria Memorial Hall.

THE VICTORIA MEMORIAL HALL

On the site of the old Presidency Jail stands one of the finest buildings of the modern world.

When Queen Victoria died in 1901, the British Government first wanted smaller memorial halls or monuments in the state capitals of India, but Lord Curzon, the then Viceroy of India, had other ideas.

> From the time of his arrival in India he had dreamed of the creation of a building which should contain "a standing record of our wonderful history, a visible monument of Indian glories, and an illustration, more eloquent than any spoken address or printed page, of the lessons of public patriotism and civil duty". He had worked out the details of the proposal, and even prepared tentative designs of the building, when the lamented death of Queen Victoria aroused throughout India a desire for an Imperial Memorial worthy of the late Queen-Empress.[5]
>
> Let us therefore, have a building, stately, spacious, monumental, and grand, to which every newcomer in Calcutta will turn, to which all the resident population, European and Native, will flock, where all classes will learn the lessons of history, and see revived before their eyes the marvels of the past.[6]

With these words Lord Curzon submitted his scheme first at a meeting at the Town Hall, Calcutta on 6 February 1901, and later at a meeting of the Asiatic Society of Bengal.

The Victoria Hall, he explained, was to be an Historical Museum, a National Gallery, and it was essential that "the art, the science, the literature, the history, the men, the events which are therein commemorated must be those of India, and of Great Britain in India, alone".[7]

The scheme encountered criticism. Questions arose whether only one all-India memorial will be built at the expense of many regional ones. However, opposition gradually died as no other alternatives were forthcoming. The British Government ultimately accepted his plan of a single Memorial Hall at Calcutta, a fitting yet memorable tribute to the departed Queen.

This enormous yet symmetrical pile of white marble, conceived by the genius of Lord Curzon, is regarded as one of the great buildings of the modern world and is unsurpassed as a priceless collection of pictures, statues, historical documents and other objects of art and interest, illustrative of Indian History in general and the Victorian era in particular.

Again, it was Lord Curzon, who started the collection for the future Hall, by asking the Indian Maharajas and important collectors to donate pictures, statues and other objects. Before the Hall was finished these objects were displayed in a separate section of the Indian Museum.

The design was completed by the architect, Sir William Emerson, in 1903. The foundation stone was laid in 1906, when King George V visited India as Prince of Wales. The King inspected the progress of the building operations during his visit to Calcutta in 1912. The building took fifteen years to complete. The building, of Renaissance architecture with traces of Saracenic influence, was constructed by Messrs. Martin & Co. under the supervision of Mr. V.J. Esch, C.V.O (architect) at a cost of Rs. 76,00,000, entirely from donations from the people and Princes of India. It was formally opened on 28 December 1921, by the Prince of Wales (later King Edward VIII).

The building is situated in a well laid out garden, interspersed with stone-lined ornamental waters. The main entrance is to the north, on a new road created and called the Queen's Way. Opposite the entrance once stood a striking bronze statue of Lord Curzon by Pomeroy. Surrounding his statue at the four corners were groups of statuary representing Commerce, Famine Relief, Agriculture and Peace. Today only the statuary at the base remains, but the statue of Lord Curzon has been removed from its pedestal and is replaced by a grotesque statue of Sri Aurobindo, totally out of proportion to the base or the pedestal.

Proceeding up the gravel drive, we come to the bronze statue of Queen Victoria by Sir George Frampton. The Queen is represented seated on a throne, wearing the Robes of the Order of the Star of India; on her head a crown, in her right hand the Sceptre and in her left hand the Orb of State adorned with the figure of St. George. Surmounting the throne are bronze figures representing Art, Literature and Justice, while at the back in relief, side by side, are the lion of Britain and the Tiger of India, and above them the Sun that never sets on the British Empire. The pedestal is of green marble, adorned in front with the Royal Coat of Arms encircled by palms of Victory. On the base of the pedestal are bronze bas-reliefs, depicting Indian State Processions.

The south gate approached from the Lower Circular Road has a lofty white marble arch surmounted by a fine equestrian statue of King Edward VII in a Field Marshall's uniform. It was unveiled by His Royal Highness The Duke of Connaught (the youngest son of Queen Victoria), in front of the steps of the south entrance on 29 January 1921.

The dimensions of the Hall at the corner towers are 339 feet by 228 feet. The dome of the building, 182 feet above ground level, is surmounted by a figure of Victory, 16 feet high, weighing 3 tons, revolving on a sphere 2 feet in diameter. The ornamental statuary groups over the entrance and the figures surrounding the dome were designed and executed in Italy.

As we ascend the marble steps of the Hall and enter through the Entrance Hall, we come upon galleries full of treasures so carefully collected for the public. The collection and arrangement of the material was entrusted to Sir William Foster, CIE, while the later work of revision and completion was supervised by Sir Evan Cotton, CIE.

The collections of the Victoria Memorial Hall include a remarkable group of oil paintings by European artists active in India between 1780 and 1830. It is larger and more important than those of the Tate Gallery, London, and the Mellon Collection of Art at Yale University, USA, with extensive holdings of works by Thomas and William Daniell, some of the finest examples of John Zoffany and William Hodges, Thomas Hickey, James Wales and Balthazar Solvyns. The complementary works of art on paper—drawings, watercolours, aquatints—include many hitherto unknown works, notably by Samuel Davis, and natural history studies by both Indian and European artists.[8]

The administration of the Hall is vested with a Board of Trustees, where both Government of India and Government of West Bengal are represented. The Hall today needs repair and more care in the preservation and restoration of priceless paintings and art objects. Though there is a Son et Lumiere show on the history of Calcutta within its precincts, the trustees often make the hall and the grounds available for various functions like filming of a pop and classical music show and even for marriage parties, which cause harm to the flowerbeds and the grass lawn, and disturb the sombre ambience of the place.

THE COURSE TO CALCUTTA
RACE COURSE

The first racing in Calcutta took place at Akra, near Garden Reach. Racing at Akra was

Figure 66: The Grandstand, Race Course

spasmodic. The first known year of the meeting there is 1794, but there must have been racing before that even as early as 1769. Racing probably moved to the Course on the Maidan from Akra in 1809. This was just west of the Victoria Memorial Hall. Certain alterations and improvements to the Course were made in 1812 and again in 1818. A substantial and elaborate stand was built in 1820 from subscriptions paid by race enthusiasts; the Bengal Jockey Club, formed some years earlier at Akra contributing Rs. 3000. The stand was a solid two-storeyed affair with the Lottery Room on the ground floor and the entertaining rooms above, with space for spectators on the roof. The stand stood approximately where the present 1000 metres marker stands and backed on to the jail. Racing was in the morning and was to continue so for many years to come. This explains why the stand was built in that position rather than on the western side of the Course where they are situated today for afternoon racing, which was introduced only in 1876, when it became necessary to turn the Course round and build stands on their present site. The first to be built was what came to be known as 'the old iron Stand'. It was built in 1880 and stood approximately between the present Members' and Grand Stands.

On 22 February 1847, a meeting of race enthusiasts was held at the Stand and a decision was taken to form the Calcutta Turf Club, which later became the Royal Calcutta Turf Club in 1912 during the visit of King George V.

The Course is almost triangular in shape and consists of the Winter, the Training, and the Monsoon tracks, the first named measuring about 1 mile, 5 furlongs and 58 yards. In the centre lies the age-old Serpentine Tank and the great tree.

Calcutta was the first centre in the subcontinent to stage a Derby race called the Calcutta Derby Stakes in 1842 and carried the fabulous prize of Rs. 5000. Royalty came to the races while in Calcutta: King Edward VII (when Prince of Wales) came in 1876; King George V in 1912; his son the Prince of Wales (later King Edward VIII) in 1921; and Queen Elizabeth II in 1961. As popularity of racing grew the Indian Maharajas flocked to the Race Course; every ruler including the Maharaja of Nepal would be in Calcutta during the winter racing season. The Maharajadhiraj of Burdwan, Sir Bejoy Chand Mahtab, was the first Indian to be elected full member of the Club. Lord Ulrich Brown, Lord William Beresford, Sir A.A. Apcar and the legendary J.C. Galstaun left their mark in the racing arena. In 1997 the Royal Calcutta Turf Club celebrated its 150th anniversary with great pomp.

The Race Course had other uses too. In December 1912 two French aviators, Mark Pourpe and George Verminck, came to Calcutta with their tiny Bleriot monoplanes. Aeroplanes at that time were quite small and had a very limited range, and were mainly used for joyriding and demonstration flights. By the kind permission of the Calcutta Turf Club, they had their first demonstration flights over Calcutta starting and coming back to the Race Course.

The rates of admission to the air display were as follows:

Grand Stand	Rs. 5
Second Stand	Rs. 2
Ground entry only	2 annas

Entry was free for the Calcutta Turf Club Members.

In 1918, a Handley-Page plane piloted by Capt. Ross Smith with Generals Salmond and Burton left Cairo on 30 November for Calcutta.

It flew via Damascus, Baghdad, Basra, Bushire, Bandar Abbas, Chahbar, Karachi, Nasirabad, Delhi and Allahabad. On 17 December the plane landed at the Calcutta Race Course; while landing its right wing hit the great Tree by the Serpentine Tank and the plane was slightly damaged. A special *shamiana* had been set up at the Course to receive the crew, and the Viceroy Lord Chelmsford, the Bengal Governor Lord Ronaldshay, Lady Ronaldshay and other dignitaries were present to give them a hearty welcome.

Next year Capt. Ross Smith and Lt. Kieth Smith landed at the Calcutta Race Course on 28 December. This was a part of their historic England–Australia First Flight in a Vickers Vimy biplane.

To the west of the Race Course across the Kidderpore Road lies the Ellenborough Course and the old polo grounds. The Ellenborough Course was also used as an airstrip. A Handley-Page H.P. 9 aeroplane left the Course on 2 March 1920 for Bombay, commanded by Captain F. Clarke, and carried Mr. R.K. Minney, Mr. Mitra, Mr. Abdul Ghafoor and seven other passengers.

Roads in the Southern Part of the Maidan

Kidderpore Road runs west of the Maidan, starting from the end of Red Road in the north and ending at the Kidderpore Bridge in the south. The Hospital Road starts from Kidderpore Road in the north and runs between the Race Course and the Victoria Memorial Hall and ends at the Lower Circular Road opposite the Presidency General Hospital.

Casuarina Avenue is a fine road starting at the end of Red Road in the north to end at the Hospital Road in the south after touching the Queen's Way. In the triangular plot of land between the Kidderpore Road, Casuarina Avenue and a part of the Hospital Road stand the Ladies' Golf Club Tent and the Course.

To the east of the Victoria Memorial Hall is the Cathedral Road which runs north and ends at the Chowringhee Road opposite Harrington Street.

Between Cathedral Road and Chowringhee Road, the easternmost part of the Maidan is fully built-up. The first structure to appear was the St. Paul's Cathedral consecrated in 1847. The other buildings came in the twentieth century. Immediately to the south of the cathedral is the Nehru Children's Museum on Chowringhee Road, followed by the Rotary Club of Calcutta's Rotary Sadan and an Electric Supply Corporation sub-station. Behind the latter building and the Calcutta Police Outpost opposite the Calcutta Club is the old tank Birjee Talao. Next is the Sainik Bhawan followed by the West Bengal Government's Calcutta Information Centre and an auditorium Sisir Mancha, named after the late Sisir Kumar Bhaduri, a noted Bengali actor of the first half of the twentieth century. This is followed by the Nandan Complex, containing a multiplex of three film theatres, a theatre-cum-gallery, a film archive, a library of film books. Nandan is a popular venue for International Film Festivals. Just behind the Nandan is the three-storey building of the Bangla Akademi, an institution devoted to the study of the Bengali language and culture. Next to it stands the Rabindra Sadan, a theatre hall of modern architecture named after Rabindranath Tagore; the idea conceived in 1961, the birth centenary of the poet.

Here we come to Cathedral Road, near its junction with Lower Circular Road. As we proceed north along the Cathedral Road and come to the end of the Nandan-Bangla Akademi-Rabindra Sadan complex we come to a fine building in traditional Indian design—the Academy of Fine Arts.

The Academy is a private art foundation and is the dreamchild of Lady Ranu Mukherjee, wife of the late industrialist Sir Biren Mukherjee and the daughter-in-law of Sir Rajen Mookerjee of Martin & Co. The Academy has permanent exhibits of art objects of eastern India, works of Rabindranath Tagore and eminent artists of Bengal. It has four galleries available for solo and group shows by artists from all over India and abroad throughout the year. It holds an annual art exhibition by young artists. It has also a theatre hall where regular shows are staged.

Next is the compound of the Cathedral and opposite the main entrance of the latter stands the planetarium of Calcutta, the Birla Planetarium. This is a modern structure and one of the most popular spots in the city. There are daily shows in English, Bengali and Hindi.

Just behind it on the Chowringhee side stands the structure of a once popular club of the city, The Calcutta Racket Club, which still has very fine squash courts. The club had a new lease of life recently and is once again active in sport.

ST. PAUL'S CATHEDRAL

St. Paul's, the Anglican Cathedral of Calcutta and the Metropolitan Church of India, occupies the south-eastern part of the Maidan. The Cathedral has an architectural dignity of its own.

The Bishopric of Calcutta was created in 1813, and the first four incumbents of the See—Middleton, Heber, James and Turner—were enthroned in the old Cathedral Church of St. John's, which for 32 years remained the Cathedral of the Diocese. By 1819, the idea of a new Cathedral Church was mooted, and a design and plan on a grand scale were prepared,

Figure 67: St. Paul's Cathedral with the Old Steeple

but the project fell through. After twenty years the idea was revived by Bishop Wilson, who succeeded Turner in 1833, and took up the challenge very earnestly.

He applied to the Government for a site, and the moment the present one, so well situated, was granted, he took possession. A committee was appointed and the foundation stone was laid by him on 8 October 1839. The design and plan were prepared by Major (afterwards General) W.N. Forbes of the Bengal Engineers, the architect of the Calcutta Mint, and carried out under his superintendence. The style of the building is Indo-Gothic, that is to say 'spurious Gothic adapted to the exigencies of Indian climate'.[9]

The Cathedral is 247 feet in length, 81 feet in width and 114 feet at the transept; the spire, since demolished, was 201 feet high and almost a replica of that of Norwich Cathedral, England. The new tower, modelled on the 'Bell Harry' Tower of Canterbury Cathedral, was designed by Mr. W.L. Kier and built by Mackintosh Burn Ltd., at a cost of about Rs. 70,000. The top of the flagstaff rises to a height of 175 feet above ground level. The walls to the top of the battlements are 59 feet. The western vestibule which contains the principal entrance is 36 feet by 22 feet 8 inches. The lantern beneath the tower is 27 feet square, and opens by lofty arches to the transepts. The dimensions of the main body of the Cathedral are 127 feet by 61 feet, and it is spanned by an iron-trussed roof, adorned with gothic tracery. The chimes of the clock which is the work of Vulliamy, are very melodious. The great bell bears the inscription—'Its sound is gone out into all lands'. During the great earthquake of 12 June 1897 the upper part of the steeple fell, to be later restored; but it was completely destroyed in the earthquake of 1934, after which the tower was constructed in place of the spire.

The Cathedral was consecrated by Bishop Wilson on 8 October 1847.

The expenditure on the building was about Rs. 5 lakh. About seven and a half lakh were raised, the Bishop himself donating two lakh, one lakh for the building and one for the endowment. The East India Company appointed two additional chaplains, and contributed a lakh and a half for the building. The subscription raised in India amounted to a lakh and quarter: in England to £13,000, besides a grant from the Society for the Propagation of the Gospel of £5000; one from the Society for the Promotion of Christian Knowledge of £5000; and a gift of £4000 from Thomas Nutt of London. The Communion Plate was the gift of Her Majesty Queen Victoria.[10]

The grounds of the Cathedral are tastefully laid out with colourful flowerbeds, rolling lawns and shady trees. . The main entrance is in the north made of fine ornamented wrought iron and called Sir William Prentice Memorial Gate.

Entering by this gate we come to the large western porch 61 feet high and 21 feet in length. Over the porch is the Cathedral Library, containing a good collection of books in divinity and general literature, the bulk of which was bequeathed by Bishop Wilson. The Library contains a fine marble bust of the Bishop and a clock presented to him by the parishioners of St. Mary's, Islington in 1832. As we enter the church we find a handsome Baptismal Font of white marble, resting on two circular pedestals of grey marble, erected to the memory of Sir W.H. Carnduff, a puisne judge of the Calcutta High Court. The Cathedral is full of memorials, medallion portraits, busts, etc. of those who have served India. Facing the entrance is a memorial depicting two Eastern scenes, crowned with a seated figure of Justice, to the memory of Chief Justice John Paxton Norman who was assassinated in 1871 as he was entering the Calcutta Town Hall. On the right of the entrance, stands a white marble memorial, supported by two figures and surmounted by a bust, erected in memory of Major General Forbes, architect of the Cathedral.

The great west window was designed by Sir Edward Burne Jones as a memorial to Lord Mayo, Viceroy of India from 1869 to 1872, who was assassinated at Port Blair in February of the latter year. In the vestry, which is on the ground floor, will be found a large folio manuscript volume, entitled 'History of the Erection of St. Paul's Cathedral, Calcutta drawn up by the Reverend J.H. Pratt, Bishop's chaplain' which contains a plan of the building at page 265.

The first painting of the new Cathedral was by the hand of Sir Charles D'Oyly, in a view of the south end of the Maidan. D'Oyly had left India in 1838, retiring eventually to Italy, where he died in 1845. Clearly he cannot have seen the building, but it is possible that he may have seen the architect William Forbes's designs before he left Calcutta, or indeed Forbes may have sent him copies.

We have a clear view of the Cathedral from the north-east in a tinted lithograph by William Clerihew in 1844, again from before the Cathedral was consecrated.

The eastern end of the Cathedral has several features of interest. The original east window was the gift of the Dean and Chapter of Windsor. The subject was 'The Crucifixion', after a design by Benjamin West, R.A. It was originally intended as a present from King George III to St. George's Chapel, Windsor, but due to some unknown cause was never erected in Windsor. This window was destroyed in the cyclone of 1864, and the present one was erected by subscription from designs by Messrs Clayton & Bell. The window to the right of the great eastern window was erected in 1880 by the Government of India to the memory of the Right Reverend Robert Milman who succeeded Cotton as Bishop of Calcutta in 1867.

On the other side of the great eastern window is a white marble tablet to the memory of the Right Reverend Daniel Wilson, fifth Bishop of Calcutta (1832-58) and first Metropolitan of India, who died in Calcutta on 2 January 1858. Bishop Wilson's remains are buried beneath the altar of the Cathedral.

An interesting article published in the *Bengal Past & Present* in 1939—'Some Recent Discoveries etc. Including a Large Vault in the Calcutta Cathedral by Mr. William S. Birney'—came up with the following information:

> The discovery of this spacious vault, the only one of its kind in an Indian Cathedral, is narrated in the following article which appeared in the Calcutta Diocesan Record in July, 1934 and which was reproduced by *The Statesman* on 4th July and *The Times*, London on 20th July.
>
> We are informed by Mr. W.S. Birney, who has been investigating the matter, that a large vault thirty feet by eighteen feet by six feet exists under the high altar of St. Paul's Cathedral, Calcutta, and that this was intended as a sepulchre for the Metropolitan Bishops of Calcutta. The descent into it was by means of steps leading from a moveable slab of marble in front of the altar. All traces of the vault have been lost, but Mr. Birney is of the opinion, that it exists in the position indicated and if he had been buried in accordance with his expressed wish, the vault will contain the mortal remains of Bishop Wilson, the founder of the Cathedral. This wish is contained in the following extract from the Bishop's will: "I desire that if I die in India, my body be interred in the vault which has been erected under the Communion Table of St. Paul's Cathedral, Calcutta.
>
> '...With regard to his remains being laid to rest in this vault, there can be no doubt, for

sufficient proof of this is given in the account of the burial service, which took place on the evening of Monday, 4 January 1858. Among other details it is stated:

1. The mortal remains of the Venerable Prelate were consigned to their last resting place at the St. Paul's Cathedral etc.

2. The coffin is laid immediately under the Communion Table in a vault constructed for this purpose.
3. Everyone vied with each other to have a last parting look at the place where the Venerable Divine's remains were laid... .

The writer (Mr. Birney) has also often viewed the coffin, which appears to be in a perfect state of preservation.

It may be of interest perhaps to mention here that no provision was made in the original plans of the Cathedral to build a vault. This was done at a later date when the foundations were extended to build a larger edifice, and probably also with a view to avoid any contravention of the conditions under which the Government gave the Bishop the land to build his Cathedral. One of these conditions was:

> The ground to be thus attached to the Cathedral, it is expressly conditioned shall in no case be made use of for the purpose of Sepulchre and that no Monument or other structure of any description whatsoever shall be raised hereafter within the space enclosed. Any breach of these injunctions will involve the forefeiture of the permission now granted.'

It is regretable that all traces of this vault appear to have been lost at the time of Bishop Lefroy's death, or else he would surely have been laid to rest within the vault.

In the Bishop's library there still remains a quaint-looking old-fashioned chair of great historical interest. The origin of this chair may be known to a few persons, but most people seem to have the impression that it was brought to this city by some 'Indiaman' in the dim and distant past.

Its history however dates back to January 1835, and recalls the first visit of Bishop Wilson to South India. With his keen interest in the work of the pioneer missionaries to South India, the Bishop visited the various centres at which they laboured and arrived in due course at Tanjore, where the great missionary Schwartz had spent the concluding twenty years of his life. Before leaving the house, the Bishop was glad to be able to secure a few relics of the missionary, which he treasured. They were Schwartz's Pocket Testament, a lock of his silvery hair and an 'Old Danish Chair' with round back and rattan sides, in which Schwartz used to sit and study. This chair the Bishop ordered to be repaired, after which it was sent to his study in Calcutta, where it still remains.'

To the right of the Lantern below the Belfry is a blue screen marking the entrance to Jesus Chapel, where high above on the wall, preserved in a glass case, are two flags, the old colours of the 18th Bengal Infantry, and the Alipore Regiment deposited in 1886. Pictures illustrative of the Life of Christ adorn the walls. On the left is a passage leading to the Chapel of Remembrance.

The Episcopal Throne, which stands to the south of the altar, is a memorial to the Right Reverend Ralph Johnson, who succeeded Milman in 1876.

The lighting system in the Cathedral consists of reflectors which throw the light on to the ceiling and thus diffuse it evenly throughout the building. This system also throws into relief the carved ceiling.

The organ loft contains a gigantic organ of 41 stops, built by Joseph Willis and Sons, London, which was opened on St. Paul's Day, 23 January 1881.

The wall behind the altar is adorned with a reredos depicting incidents from the life of St. Paul, portrayed in alabaster set with coloured mosaic, and above are three stained glass windows separated from one another by two Florentine frescoes. The altar is a gift from the Bengal Chamber of Commerce in memory of their late President, Sir William Ironside.

In addition to the seating accommodation in the centre, there are raised lines of pews on either side; some of them once reserved for the Viceroy, the Governor of Bengal and the Chief Justice of Bengal.

Inside the Cathedral compound close to the southern end stands the Parish Hall, a large hall with a stage meant for social functions, and a popular venue for marriage and other receptions for people of all religions.

The Reverend Aurobindo Mukherjee was the first Indian Bishop and Metropolitan of India. St. Paul's still remains the principal Anglican Church of the city.

BRIGADE PARADE GROUND

North of the Victoria Memorial Hall is the main body of the Maidan, a mostly unspoilt lush green with shady trees and the pride of the city. This stretch lies between the Queen's Way in the south, Outram Road in the north, Chowringhee Road in the east and Casuarina Avenue and a part of Red Road on the west. Outram Road is the short street which starts from Chowringhee Road nearly opposite Park Street and ends at the circle in front of the Chowringhee Gate of the Fort William. There were three tanks in this area, of which only the General's Tank near the Outram Road-Chowringhee Road juction has survived. The Elliot's Tank opposite Harrington Street has been filled up. If any one desires to see how the jungle looked like before the Esplanade, one should visit the site of the Elliot's Tank, where a dense jungle on the Chowringhee end can be seen, no doubt due to the carelessness of the people who are paid to look after this area.

In the middle was the Dhoba Pooker, which was filled up to create the lush green of the Brigade Parade Ground once exclusively the ceremonial parade ground of the military, paramilitary, militia and the police forces; in more democratic times it is now more often the venue of political meetings. The Pat Williamson ground on the south is a venue for the dwindling number of polo enthusiasts. The Royal Calcutta Golf Club's Maidan Pavilion and golf course and the ITF Pavilion border the Outram Road.

Figure 68: The Equestrian State of General Outram in the Maidan and the Ochterloney Monument

The Rest of the Maidan

Cutting the Maidan from north to south is the finest road in Calcutta, the Red Road, constructed in 1781 by Colonel Henry Watson. During the Second World War the road was barricaded for traffic at the Ochterlony Road end and the Chowringhee Gate end and the wide stretch was used as a runway for fighter and bomber planes. The balustrade railings on both sides were removed partly to provide for parking of the planes. The other road in the area to be used as an airfield is the Kidderpore Road.

There were some fine statues of the British era on both sides of the road, all removed now, and the original pedestals are now being used for statues of Indian leaders, some of whom deserve a place on this fine avenue, but others definitely do not. Lords Roberts and Kitchener were Commander in Chief of India, Ripon and Lansdowne made their mark as Viceroys, and deserve better than to be dumped in an obscure park or a filthy godown. On the Outram Road-Chowringhee junction there was an equestrian statue of Sir James Outram by J.H. Foley, R.A., unveiled in 1874 with great ceremony by Lord Napier of Magdala, then Commander in Chief of India. This has often been acclaimed as one of the finest equestrian statues in the world. Naturally, after Independence it disappeared from the public eye and was replaced by a fine artistic statue of Mahatma Gandhi by the renowned artist and sculptor Devi Prasad Roychowdhury. But due to reasons unknown this fine statue, perhaps the best erected in Calcutta in the post-Independence period, was removed to a less important position in the Maidan and a very ordinary one of Pandit Jawaharlal Nehru, the first Prime Minister of India, was put up in its original place.

At the point where the Red Road meets the King's Way in front of the south gate of the Government House stands The Cenotaph, a memorial to the Allied soldiers who lost their lives in the First World War of 1914-18. Diagonally right to this memorial is a statue of Netaji Subhas Chandra Bose. The Indian National Army memorial stands at the corner of Mayo Road (now Guru Nanak Sarani) and Red Road. This is a replica of the original one erected under orders of Netaji at the Singapore seafront. As Singapore fell to the British in 1945, this memorial was dynamited under orders of Lord Mountbatten, then Chief of the South-East Asia Command. This is a flagrant example of a victorious army showing disrespect to the enemy dead by destroying a memorial erected in their memory.

The Red Road lost its name in 1985, again pointlessly, as it was renamed Indira Gandhi Sarani.

To the west of Red Road are the enclosed football and cricket grounds of Mohammedan Sporting Club, East Bengal Club and Mohun Bagan Club. Earlier Mohun Bagan and East Bengal Clubs shared the same ground on the Plassey Gate Road, and Calcutta Football Club (European) had its separate ground almost opposite the Eden Gardens. But after Independence, Calcutta Football Club merged with the Calcutta Cricket Club and became Calcutta Cricket and Football Club and moved to the Ballygunge Maidan home ground of the Calcutta Cricket Club. The Calcutta Football Club's ground was taken over by Mohun Bagan Club.

The north-eastern part of the Maidan is crisscrossed by two roads forming the letter X. The Dufferin Road starts from the Chowringhee Gate circle just east of the Red Road and ends at Ochterlony Road near Chowringhee Road. The Kidderpore-Esplanade Tram tracks pass through this road, and cross Mayo Road. There was a beautiful statue once of Lord Mayo at the traffic circle at the jucntion of the two roads. The Mayo Road starts from Chowringhee Road opposite Park Street, crosses the Dufferin Road and ends at Red Road. On the Maidan, near Mayo Road there used to be a quaint little wooden structure painted milk white, which used to be the Police Traffic Post. In the days of computerized automatic signalling, this little building has vanished into thin air. This stretch of the Maidan has the tents of a large number of sporting clubs.

OCHTERLONY MONUMENT

One of the most prominent landmarks of the city, it was erected by public subscription in 1828 in honour of a distinguished soldier, Major-General Sir Lord David Ochterlony, Bart., GCB, Resident in Malwa and Rajputana and conqueror of Nepal.

Sir David Ochterlony was born in February 1758 at Boston, USA, joined the East India Company's army as a cadet in 1777, and rose to the rank of Major General. He married a

Mughal princess of Delhi, who was later locally known as Akhtar-loony Begum. She was a pious Muslim and built a mosque near her house in Delhi for public use, but no one visited the mosque for prayers, as she was married to a Christian. Ochterlony died at Meerut in 1825.

The monument, a fluted column of brickwork, was built in 1828 by J.P. Parker, from the designs of Charles Knowles Robinson, at a cost of about Rs. 35,000, met by public subscription. It is made of a rare combination of three distinct styles of Muslim architecture. The abse is purely Egyptian, the fluted column Syrian, while the dome with its metal cupola is Turkish.

The monument is 158 feet high; the spiral staircase within has 198 steps from the ground level to the first balcony, and another 25 from the first to the second balcony.

From the top one can have a splendid panoramic view of the city and its surroundings. There is an inscription reading:

Sir David Ochterlony, Baronet, Grand Cross of the Military Order of the Bath, Major General in the Army of Bengal, died at Meerut on the 15th July 1825. The people of Bengal, natives and European, to commemorate his services as a statesman and a soldier, have in grateful admiration raised this column.

There is a story that just before the monument was completed, a dinner party was held on the top of the shaft, which was then 3 feet above the floor of the second gallery, at an elevation of 145 feet above the plain. The seats were disposed around the gallery, and secure temporary railing provided for the occasion. Old chronicles describe the party as a 'unique and hilarious function' which did not terminate until the 'unusual hour' of nine o'clock at night.[13]

The Ochterlony Monument still stands today, but it has lost its original name. The Government of West Bengal has renamed it Shaheed Minar (Martyrs' Column). The cupola has been painted bright red, otherwise it is all the same. The area is still a popular venue for political meetings. But it is being gradually taken over by the inter-state bus terminus, which gives the whole area a very shabby look, made uglier still with the conglomeration of dark, gloomy shops of wretched construction.

This part of the Calcutta Maidan needs urgent cleaning and beautification to restore it to its former glory.

References

1. Cotton, H.E.A. *Calcutta Old and New*, p. 775, p. 220.
2. Firminger, W.K. quoting *Seton-Kerr Selections*, vol. 1, p. 21.

3. Ibid. p. 104-5.

4. Ibid. p. 105.

5. Fraser, Lovat. *India under Curzon and After,* London 1911, p. 236.

6. Tillotson, G.H.R. in Philippa Vaugham (ed.) *Victoria Memorial Hall, Calcutta,* Bombay 1997, p. 8.

7. Fraser, Lovat. op. cit. p. 236.

8. *Victoria Memorial Hall*, p. 2.

9. Cotton. op. cit. p. 479.

10. Ibid. p. 480.

11. Losty, J.P. Calcutta, City of Palaces, p. 118.

12. Birney, W.S. 'Some Recent Discoveries etc. including a Large Vault in the Calcutta Cathedral,' in *Bengal Past & Present,* vol. LVII, 1939, pp. 77-80.

13. Cotton. op. cit. p. 330.

Chapter Fifteen

The Fort William of Today

The formidable Fort William stands west of the Maidan, bounded by the Red Road on the east, the Strand Road on the west, King's Way on the north and Hastings lines on the south.

After the battle of Plassey, plans were afoot for a new fort for the town, as the old Fort William was partly destroyed by the Nawab's army during the siege of 1756, and was proved only too vulnerable. A plan had been brought forward by Captain Robert Barker, afterwards Commander-in-Chief, for the placing of the New Fort in the centre of the settlement. He examined the ground eastward of the old factory, and reported that with a little expense a proper spot might be cleared to the distance of about six hundred yards sufficient for a fort and an esplanade. Two months later Captain John Brohier, who was in the same year to level the houses and fortifications of Chandernagore with the ground, came forward with another proposal to build a hexagonal citadel to the south of the Old Dock, which stood somewhere about Bankshall Street. Three of the sides were to flank the river, and extensive works were to be carried round the town to a point above the Portuguese and Armenian churches. On this line the houses were to be demolished for the space of at least five hundred yards, and the owners were to be provided for in the Park, which was to be laid out in streets. The suggestions were considered by the Committee of Fortifications, and Clive arrived just in time from Murshidabad to prevent the carrying into effect of the orders, which had been actually given, to pull down all the buildings south of the Dock and of the Park. Clive's conception of a suitable site was of a different kind. On the riverside to the south of the settlement was the village of Gobindapore, founded two centuries earlier by the Setts and Bysacks, the Hindu Founding Fathers of Calcutta; and surrounding it was a thick jungle infested with tigers, which could easily be cut down. The whole colony, with their tutelary deity Gobindajee and its historic shrine, migrated to the northern part of the town and liberal compensation in money and grants of lands was made to them for their dispossession.[1]

Figure 69: Chowringhee Gate Fort William

Figure 70: Plassey Gate Fort William

Captain Brohier modified his earlier plan and was given the task of building at a brisk pace the finest fort on earth, a showpiece of the East India Company's Army. A Standing Committee of Works to survey all stores and material was constituted. Brohier laid out the lines of the New Fort William in August 1757, and work began in October. An Esplanade was formed out of the jungle surrounding the New Fort, extending northwards to a new road (now leading to Kalighat), and southwards to a new road in continuation of the Marhatta Ditch. This whole area was cleared and levelled to form a great Esplanade, with an absolute prohibition on building thereon, so that the New Fort should not be dominated by the surrounding buildings as the old one had been.[2] But from the beginning Brohier faced problems, including an inadequate supply of labourers. Orders forbidding the employment of labour by private persons were repeated more than once but produced no effect. In 1762 the engineer renewed his complaint of being in constant want of workers, and was empowered by Government to seize all the brick-layers in Calcutta.

Brohier was a competent engineer, but a financial controversy destroyed his career. On 10 January 1761 the Calcutta authorities informed the Court

of a great fraud committed in carrying on the new works by combination of those who were employed upon them... . By the confession of Gobindram Taccor was found that the sum of Rs. 344,565 had been shared by different persons employed on the works, besides the sum of Rs. 99,484 which Captain Brohier acknowledged in his letter of the 25th June to have come to the share of those immediately under him.

The Calcutta authorities believed that the latter amount was Brohier's own share of the gain. A sum of Rs. 61,609.9.10 was charged to two Indian agents but which upon examination was found to have been embezzled by John Louis, for some time assistant engineer. In the same way Rs. 31,639.11.6 was proved to have been taken by Louis da Costa, a Portuguese writer employed in the works. Both John Louis and Louis da Costa absconded before enquiry and neither could be traced.

Brohier was arrested immediately after discovery of the fraud. A few days later he was released on parole. Thereafter he too seemed to have vanished into thin air. 'But the use he made of this indulgence will stand as proof of his guilt. For in the night between 29 and 30 of July he also absconded and has evaded all our searches notwithstanding.'[3]

Despite all these hindrances the main work of the fort was completed in ten years.

The new Fort conformed to the very latest thinking in siege tactics. It was in outline an irregular octagon with seven gates, surrounded by most extensive defences, and was large enough to afford refuge to the entire population at the time or any then imaginable increase in it... . The whole cost £2 million. A Government House was built in the new Fort, but rarely occupied... . The oldest barracks, the Royal Barracks facing the river, were completed in 1764, and the North and South barracks on either side shortly thereafter. Near the Water Gate is the Armoury built under the auspices of Warren Hastings in 1777. The powder magazine capable of holding 2,200 barrels of gunpowder and impervious at the time to any shot, was completed in 1778. From this same year the Treasure was also kept in the Fort. The great granary was begun in 1779, sufficient to contain 120,000 maunds of grain and rice; it was planned by Hastings as one of a chain of such places to alleviate the dreadful consequences of famines such as that which devastated Bengal in 1770. In 1780 it was completed and by 1782 over 70,000 maunds of rice and paddy were deposited in it. A Bazar was erected about 1787 with a complete range of shops. Although a church was planned, none was built until the 1820s.

The earliest view of the new Fort is probably that found as part of a panoramic view of Calcutta from the opposite bank of the river as it appeared in 1768, although this errs in omitting the half-mile of Esplanade, the work of Major Antoine Polier, who became Chief Engineer of the Bengal Army in 1762...although Mark Wood's three maps of Calcutta and its environs of 1780-85 show the buildings which had then been completed, as well of course as the plan of the glacis and fortifications. The earliest printed view of it is a view from the Esplanade engraved by William Baillie in Calcutta in 1791: a further three views appear in Baillie's set of 12 views of Calcutta published in 1794.[4]

One of these views shows the magnificent Water Gate and the Royal Barracks.

As has been said already, the Fort is in shape an irregular octagon, five of its sides facing the land and three the river. It is surrounded by a dry ditch, which can be filled with water by a sluice from the river. There are seven gates to the Fort: the Calcutta Gate leading to the Eden Gardens; the Plassey Gate to the south of the Government House, called *Lal Darwaza* in the local vernacular, possibly as it leads to the Lal Dighi or the Lal Bazar; the Chowringhee or the Royal Gate, which faces Chowringhee; the Treasury Gate or the *Pias Darwaza* or Thirsty Gate, from the proximity of the old drinking tanks or reservoirs; the Hospital Gate which faces the Race Course; St. George's Gate or *Coolie Darwaza* as it gives access to the Hastings or Coolie Bazar; and the Water Gate or *Paani Darwaza* facing the river bank near the Gwalior Monument. The various bastions have also names allotted to them in 1766, e.g. the King's, Queen's, Prince of Wales' and Duke of Cumberland's Bastions; and the demibastions were named as the Duke of York's and the King of Prussia's.[5]

The Commander-in-Chief used to reside over the Treasury Gate; and each of the other gates has likewise a house over it; the houses used as residences for senior military officers. At one time the Fort mounted 600 guns of various calibres and could accommodate 10,000 men. But by the time the Fort was finished, the East India Company ruled over a large part of India and the city of Calcutta was in no danger of being invaded by an attacking army and the Fort remained as showpiece of the English East India Company.

In most contemporary accounts the new Fort drew admiration. 'We are invited to dine in the New Fort,' says Miss Sophia Goldborne in 1780, 'at the Commanding Officer's, the Fort Major whose house is situated within its circumference: and it is deemed one of the finest forts in the world, has a chain across the river, to secure the harbour from invasion, covers nearly five miles of ground, and has all the bustling charms of a garrison.

A later description from Mrs. Fay:

The town of Calcutta reaches along the eastern bank of the Hooghly: as you come up past Fort William and the Esplanade, it has a beautiful appearance.... . Our Fort is also so well kept and everything in such excellent order that it is quite a curiosity to see it, all the slopes, banks and ramparts are covered with the richest verdure, which competes the enchantment of the scene.

At an earlier date it would seem that it was proposed to allow private individuals to build residences in the Fort: for we find the Dutch Admiral Stavorinus, who visited Calcutta about 1770, writing that 'permission has likewise been given to every inhabitant of Calcutta to build, if he chooses it, a house in the Fort, provided it be equally bombproof: but in the year 1770 no one had yet felt any inclination to avail himself of this privilege.'[6]

William Hodges, a British artist, described his arrival in Calcutta in 1781:

This capital of British dominions in the East is marked by a considerable fortress . . . superior to any in India. On the foreground is the Water Gate of the Fort, which reflects great honour on the talents of the engineer—the ingenious Colonel Polier. The glacis and esplanade are seen in perspective, bounded by a range of beautiful and regular buildings and a considerable reach of the river.[7]

A line engraving with etching by W. Byrne from William Hodges' painting, *A View of Calcutta taken from Fort William in 1781*, was published in Hodges' *Travels in India* in 1794. The picture shows the Water Gate and its surroundings.

INSIDE THE FORT

The Government House

This was built as a residence for the Governor-General. But Lord Wellesley seems to have been the only one to have resided in it, when the new Government House was being built. It was also used as a residence for distinguished guests. A tablet on the wall bears the following inscription: 'This house was built for the Governor General and was sometimes occupied by him. Bishop Heber was accommodated in it by Lord Amherst when he first arrived in India in October 1823.' The Bishop has described the house in the following manner:

The house consisted of a lofty and well-proportioned hall, 40 feet by 25 feet, a drawing room of the same length, and six or seven rooms all on the same floor, one of which served as a Chapel, the lower storey being chiefly occupied as offices or lobbies. All these rooms were lofty, with many doors and windows on every side, the floors of plasters covered with mats, the ceilings of bricks, plastered also, flat, and supported by massive beams, which were visible from the rooms below, but being painted neatly had not at all a bad effect. Punkas, large frames of wood covered with white cotton and looking not unlike enormous fireboards, hung from the ceiling of principal apartments: to which cords were fastened, which were drawn backwards and forwards by one or more servants, so as to agitate and cool the air very agreeably. The walls were white or unadorned except with a number of glass lamps filled with cocoanut oil, and the furniture, though sufficient for the climate, was scanty in comparison with that of an English house. The beds instead of curtains had mosquito nets: they were raised high from the ground and very hard, admirably adapted for a hot climate.[8]

Upon the deposition in February 1856, of Wazed Ali Shah, the last King of Oudh, he was brought down to Calcutta and lodged in this building in the Fort. He occupied it for three years before he went to the palace in Metia Buruz. Since that time until recently it was used as a soldiers' institute and a garrison school and was called Outram Institute. Now it houses the Fort William Canteen.

Barracks

The early barracks in the Fort were all of a single storey; the oldest were the Royal, North and South barracks. In the nineteenth century these barracks were considered unhealthy, as their height was lower than that of the walls of the Fort. Some of the older barracks were reconstructed by raising their heights. Among the new barracks to be constructed, the first was the three-storeyed Queen's Barrack in 1859 followed by the Dalhousie Barrack two years later. The old Granary Barrack has a black stone slab on its wall with the following inscription: 'This building contains 51,258 maunds of rice and 20,023½ maunds of paddy which were deposited by order of the Governor-General and Council, under the inspection and charge of John Belli, Agent for Providing Victualling Stores to this Garrison, in the months of March, April and May 1782'. For some time in 1871 this was used as a prison. But the original Military Prison in the Fort was located in a low building in the Ravelin of the St. George's Gate. The *Calcutta Gazette* of 7 January 1808 records that 'in the course of Monday night, eighteen of the French prisoners of war, confined in Fort William, continued to make their escape by cutting a hole through the building in which they were confined. They are supposed to have gone down the river towards Kedgeree in the hope of seizing a pilot schooner or some other small vessel in which they may endeavour to get to sea.'[9]

'Possibly, this was also the place of confinement of Vizir Ali (Wazir Ali), the successor of Asaf-ud-Daula in the nawabship of Awadh, Vizir Ali who was deposed by the Government of Fort William for his refusal to pay an additional subsidy for the Company's troops stationed in Awadh, staged his rebellion against the British at Benares in 1799. The rebellion was put down very easily and Vizir Ali was brought to Calcutta and confined in the Fort's prison where he breathed his last.[10]

Churches in the Fort

In about the centre of the Fort is the Anglican St. Peter's Church, built during 1822-28, and considered to be the finest garrison church in India. The church was adorned with a baptismal font, two stained glass windows, a handsome marble pulpit and arcades adorned on either side by figures of angels, and a stone reredos* behind the altar representing the Lord's Last Super. The walls and pillars were lined with tablets erected to the memory of the brave. These have since been removed and the church is now used as the Fort's Library. About a hundred yards to this church stands St. Patrick's Roman Catholic Chapel, opened on 18 January 1859.

The Grand Arsenal

This is situated near the Water Gate and probably stands on the site of the old Artillery Barracks and gun-sheds. The building contains many interesting relics of war. The Armoury is a magnificent room, built under the orders of Warren Hastings, in 1777. Over the entrance is the following inscription: 'Anno Domini 1777. These arms were arranged by order and under the auspices of the Honourable Warren Hastings, Esquire, Governor-General.'

With time, the Fort has changed, new buildings have come up; with the advent of modern artillery the old faithful guns are now only showpieces. Some illustrious generals left their mark in the Fort William. The Duke of Wellington, who in future was to defeat Napoleon at Waterloo, spent quite some time in the Fort. He was not popular as he had a social contempt of his intellectual equals, and an intellectual contempt for his social equals.' When the British Cabinet sought the Duke's advice as to who should lead the expedition to Burma, he is said to have replied: 'Send Lord Combermere!'

'But we have always understood that your Grace thought Lord Combermere a fool?'

'So he is a fool and a damned fool, but he can take Rangoon.' Lord Curzon as Viceory recommended the name of Lord Kitchener as the new Commander-in-Chief of India. Kitchener occupied the residence over the Treasury Gate, giving it its new name Kitchener's House. Curzon and Kitchener had divergent views on the issue of the Military Member's post in the Viceroy's Council. Kitchener wanted absolute control of the Army. Ultimately, Lord Curzon had to resign from his post.

---

* Ornamental screens covering the wall behind an altar.

The Fort William became busy during the Second World War, when Singapore fell to the Japanese. Fort William became the nucleus around which the Allied army gathered for the assault. It was the headquarters of the Eastern Command.

Before we come to the end of the British era, here are a few anecdotes from the time published in older issues of the *Bengal Past & Present*:

An Army Doctor has come to India very recently, and not conversant with the language, he depends entirely on the Medical Orderly.

He enters the hospital ward and comes to the first patient and asks the orderly:

'This man?'
'Diarrhoea Sir.'
'One pill.'
'This man?'
'Fever Sir.'
'Two pills.'
'This man?'
'Dead Sir.'
'Three pills.'

'The European soldiers were a shabby-looking stunted set of men, because the Company would only enlist Protestants, diminutive, dwarfish, crooked recruits. The ban on Roman Catholics lasted well into the 19th Century. When the soldiers broke down in health they were posted to various Corps of Invalids, stationed in places like Chunar etc. where they eked out life with an Indian woman on Rs. 8 a month. One of these pensioners was cut off in his prime at the age of 119 years. His tombstone in Chunar is:

In Downing Street red tapeworms thrive,
In Somerset House they are all alive.
And slimy tracks mark where they fall,
Within the precincts of White Hall.'[11]

A Fine Poem on Khaki

Khaki from the Persian *kak* (dust) came into general use in the 1880s. The following poem appeared in an Indian paper:

Oh the Daughty-Dash were a Khaki Corps
And nothing but Khaki dress they wore;

And every evening they sat down to dinner,
With the whole of their mess kit provided by Spinner [E. Spinner & Co.],
They wore Khaki jackets and Khaki 'bags',
And in lieu of pocket handkerchief, Khaki rags;
They had Khaki boots (which you need not clean)
And a Khaki tie which was scarcely seen;
They had Khaki cloth and Khaki braid,
And the board with a Khaki cloth was laid;
And the pride of their kit was a Khaki shirt,
Which you need not wash,
for it would never show dirt

B.B.

THE FORT AFTER INDEPENDENCE

On 15 August 1947, the Union Jack was lowered from the flagposts in the Fort and the Indian Tricolour was hoisted. The Eastern Command Headquarters was moved to Ranchi.

During the Chinese aggression in 1962, the Eastern Command Headquarters was located at Lucknow. But due to the conflict it was moved back to Calcutta on 1 May 1963.

During the Indo-Pakistan War of 1971, the Eastern Command Headquarters in the Fort William played a glorious role.

It was here that the planning of the offensive in East Pakistan was made and executed in a fine manner. On 16 December 1971 the Pakistan Eastern Command with all other troops under the leadership of Lt. General A.A.K. Niazi tendered unconditional surrender to the General Officer Commanding, Eastern Command, Lt. General J.S. Arora.

Fort William today has modern functional structures side by side with the older ones of the Raj. The Royal Barracks are now used as family quarters for other ranks.

The Dalhousie Barrack, now a four-storey building can house an entire battalion with its stores, arms, ammunition and offices. The North Barrack previously used as living accommodation for soldiers have now been converted into offices.

The Queen's Barracks have been partly converted into offices. A new Eastern Command Headquarters complex has come up; still some of the offices are in the old building.

The Bell Tower is an interesting sight on the waterfront. This was erected in 1824 and used for signalling by semaphore to ships passing along the river. In 1881 Calcutta Port Commissioners installed the bell to act as a timepiece for shipping. The Fort William Army Officers' Institute has a lush green 18 hole golf course, a swimming pool of international standard, a tennis court, squash courts and posh holiday homes.

Figure 71: Dalhousie Barrack Fort William

Many new quarters have come up to accommodate the increasing number of officers. Fort William, erected more that two hundred and forty years ago, is still there, full of activity, a part of Calcutta.

References

1. Cotton. op. cit. pp. 687-88.
2. Losty. op. cit. pp. 35-36.
3. *Fort William, Calcutta*, Calcutta 1997, p. 39.
4. Losty. op. cit. p. 36.
5. Cotton. op. cit. p. 690.
6. Ibid. pp. 689-90.
7. Losty. op. cit. p. 44.
8. Cotton. op. cit. p. 693.
9. Ibid. p. 696.
10. *Fort William, Calcutta*, p. 50.
11. *Bengal Past & Present*, vol III, p. 7.
12. Ibid. vol. LIV, p. 83.

Chapter Sixteen

Here and There

The Europeans, generally confined to the area between Dalhousie Square and Lower Circular Road in the south, did nonetheless choose some parts of the city and outskirts for their residence and leisure. These include Hastings, Kidderpore, Garden Reach, Alipore, Tollygunge, Barrackpore and Dum Dum. Without a brief visit to these places the history of the White Town in Calcutta will not be complete.

Hastings

This is just south of the Fort William. Before the Fort was built the site was a Muslim burial ground. When construction of the new Fort started in 1757, the workmen or 'coolies' camped here and the area acquired a new name 'Coolie Bazar'. It was here near the Hastings Bridge that scaffoldings were erected to hang Maharaja Nandakumar. Later, it became a Government colony, accommodating chiefly warrant officers, officers connected with the Ordnance and Commissariat Departments and personnel of the Harbour Master's Department of the Calcutta Port Commissioners. The Commissariat Department's godowns were also located here. Coolie Bazar was re-named Hastings after the Marquess of Hastings, Governor-General of India. The area still has quaint houses, the serene Hastings Chapel and the popular Ordnance Club.

Tolly's Nullah

As we venture out of Hastings we have to cross the bridge to go further south. The bridge is on what has come to be known as Tolly's Nullah, starting from the river Hooghly, to course down east towards Alipore, run south from there through Kalighat (the famous Kali temple is nearby) and run through Tollygunge to end in the Vidyadhari river further south. Many believe that this was the original course of the Ganga. The Rev. James Long writes:

Our readers may deem it incredible, but we have a firm conviction that the Ganges itself which now flows by Bishop's College, once took its course on the site of Tolly's Nala. With the natives, to the south of Calcutta, Tollygunge is a sacred place of cremation, and so is Baripur, where there is now not a drop of water, because they believe the stream of the Ganges rolled here once: the traveller never sees any funeral pyres smoking near the Hughli, south of Calcutta, as the native has a notion that this is 'Khata Ganga', or a modern channel—the ancient channel, and not merely the water, is accounted sacred by them. Geological observations confirm this. In borings made at Kidderpur in 1822, it was found, there were no vegetable remains or trees, hence there must have been a river or large body of water here.[1]

In 1775 Captain Tolly was permitted by the Government to excavate this ancient silted up river-bed and open a way into the Sundarbans. He reimbursed himself for this toll by setting up a bazar or *ganj* at the place which still bears his name—Tollyganj—and by collecting tolls on crafts making use of his canal. Tolly, at one time, owned and lived in the house, which was later named Belvedere.

Garden Reach

This area started developing in 1768. The approach from Calcutta in the eighteenth century was over the Surman's Bridge.

William Hickey who arrived in Calcutta in November 1777 was impressed by Garden Reach 'by a rich and magnificent view of a number of spendid houses, the residences of gentlemen of the highest rank in the Company's service.' His host Colonel Watson's house was situated 'upon an elevation...commanding a noble view of Garden Reach with all its palaces downwards.'[2] From the Calcutta Collectorate's deeds and leases we know the names of several persons owning garden houses in Garden Reach. They included Colonel Watson, Mr. Petrie, Mr. Reid, Mr. Dacre, Mr. Wheler, with Mr. Stewart's inland, Mr. Stark, Mr. Vansittart, Colonel Pearse, Mr. Hannay, Mr. Charters, Mr. Goodwin, Col. Parker, Mr. Murray, and Col. Macpherson.[3] Colonel Watson, the Chief Engineer in Fort William, constructed in his private capacity in 1776 his dockyard, with his house beside it.

It was here that the enterprising Colonel Henry Watson domesticated the act of shipbuilding in Bengal. It is true that Grose, in speaking of the year 1756, says on the other side of the water there were docks for repairing and careening the ships, near which the Armenians had a good garden, but his statements are generally too loose to command confidence... . To Colonel Watson unquestionably belongs the honour of having established the first dock-yard in Bengal. His penetration led him to perceive the advantageous situation of the Bay of Bengal in reference to the countries lying to the east and west of it. He felt that if the English Marine was placed on an efficient footing, we must remain masters of the Eastern Seas. He, therefore, obtained a grant of land at Kidderpore, from the Government for the establishment of wet and dry docks, and of a marine yard in which every facility should be created for building, repairing and equipping vessels of war and merchantmen. His works were commenced in 1780; and the next year he launched the Nonsuch, a frigate of 36 guns, which was constructed under his own directions by native workmen, and proved remarkable for her speed. The Nonsuch was lost in 1801 when hauling into port. She was quite rotten at the time. Watson devoted his time and fortune to this national undertaking for eight years, and in 1788 launched another frigate, the Surprise, of 36 guns; but his resources were by this time exhausted: and after having sunk ten lakhs of rupees in his dockyard, he was obliged to relinquish it.[4]

In 1780 Mrs. Fay writes about Garden Reach:

The banks of the river are, as one may say, studded with elegant mansions, called here, as in Madras, garden houses. These houses are surrounded with groves and lawns, which descend to the water's edge, and present a constant succession of whatever can delight the eye or bespeak the wealth and elegance in the owners.[5]

Many of the garden houses seem to have been of the nature of rural taverns and a snare and a delusion to the young writers in the Company's service. In granting a licence for a garden house to a certain William Parkes in 1762, we find the Board expressly stipulating that the house was not to be open in the morning.

When the Governor General, Lord Wellesley, established the College of Fort William in 1800, his original plans were to shift it to Garden Reach, for which a suitable land was selected. He had also proposed to attach a Natural History Institution to the college. For this purpose a number of animals had been collected, and between the years 1800 and 1804 £350 was spent for their upkeep. The college having been vetoed, the undefeated Governor General turned to Barrackpore; where a miniature zoo was set up.[6]

Immediately after passing the dock bridges, we find on our right a strip of ground on which but a year ago stood No. 6 Garden Reach (1904). It was a fine old house and belonged to the Prinsep family. It passed through Messrs. Carr, Tagore & Co., of which William Prinsep was one of the partners, to the Indian General Navigation Co., and for fifty years it was the headquarters of the Company's fleet. In 1879 the Company acquired a plot of ground known as Rajah Bagan some three miles lower down the river, in 1898 most of their works were removed thither from Nos. 6 & 7, Garden Reach. The old Indian General Steam Navigation Co. went into liquidation in 1899, and a new Company—the India General Navigation and Railway Co.—was formed to take its place.

No. 8 was probably the residence of Sir William Jones, who used to walk to the Supreme Court in the morning and walk back home in the evening. The house has completely disappeared.

No. 12, the residence of the Chief of the Bengal Nagpore Railway Company (now South Eastern Railway), was described by J.C. Marshman as 'distinguished above all others for its classical elegance. It was erected after a design by Mr. C.K. Robinson, to whose architectural taste the city is indebted for some of its noblest buildings.' In 1845 it was the residence of the Agent of the P. & O. Company, and off its banks was the anchorage 'of those magnificent steamers which ply monthly between Suez and Calcutta in six weeks from England'. The building is a fine example of Greek architecture with Ionic pillars just by the river. At present this house is called Serall House and is the residence of the General Manager of South Eastern Railway (as the Bengal Nagpore Railway is called after nationalization.)

The Numbers 51 to 55 were the palace, garden and estate of Wajid Ali Shah, the deposed King of Oudh. The King resided in a magnificent palace with his *harem* and a large entourage. He built a beautiful *imambarah* for his followers. During the Sepoy Mutiny, the King was incarcerated in the Fort William from 1857 to 1859, from the fear that the rebellious sepoys might gather around him and fight against the British. The breakup of the Garden Reach establishment after the King's death has been described by Lady Dufferin (January 1888):

The King of Oudh died in the autumn, and we all went to see his place and his house. I had visited the animals there before, but the Viceroy had never been able to go to this King's habitation, so it was all new to him. Most of the animals have been sold, and the grounds look tidy and well kept. They are very large, and we drove about for half an hour, winding round bungalows, and bear houses, and tanks for waterfowl, and cages for monkeys, deer, and birds, and sheds for camels and palaces for pigeons. The bungalows all had marble floors, and in every room there was a bed with silver feet, and no other furniture whatever. The walls, however, were covered with pictures— questionable French prints and Scripture subjects mixed indiscriminately. The park is situated on the river, and would be lovely were it a little less zoological. The King died in a room on the ground floor, opening into a small court which was full of monkeys and pigeons—extremely suggestive of fleas. Upstairs there were some nicer rooms, and we saw some books of prints which he had coloured himself, they were really very well done. His ladies were nearly as numerous as his animals, and they are now being despatched to their own homes as quickly as possible. They go at the rate of seven or eight a day, but there are still a great number left; and when the Viceroy approached their habitation they collected behind some venetian shutters, and set to work to howl and weep with all their might. The effect was most extraordinary, but did not excite the pity it was intended to evoke.[8]

Figure 72: Bengal Nagpore Railways Head Office at Garden Reach
Photo courtesy South Eastern Railway

The greater part of the King's grounds was bought up by the Bengal Nagpore Railway for their headquarters. The building is in Indo-Saracenic style, in red brick, occasionally relieved by stone/terracotta, the architectural features are based on the building's own proportions and not unnecessary decoration. The plan is square with large central quadrangles. The architect was Mr. V.J. Esch, who designed the Victoria Memorial Hall, Calcutta; and the structure was built by Martin & Co. in 1908. The cost came to Rs. 7,01,995.

The entrance porch, *verandah* around the Agent's room and the inside of the Central Hall were for officers and visitors only. Clerks and peons were supposed to use the smaller stairways, so arranged as to keep staff of each department separate to avoid overcrowding on stairways. Records were to be stored either in lofts under the roof or in the ground floor. The ground floor level kept 5 feet above the actual ground level. The open quadrangles had patent stone flooring to keep the building free from dampness. Foundations were taken only three feet to four feet deep with a wide spread. All rooms open on both sides allowing a through current of air; and most rooms get northern light. The smaller rooms are 16 feet 6 inches wide, while the large ones are 30 feet wide in order to keep the structure as light as possible. The roof over the main building is mansard or curb roof covered with corrugated iron or uralite patent asbestos roof. With emphasis on avoiding long wide roof areas and flat roofs of any kind, there was a dome placed over the Central Hall.

The ground floor had the offices of the Superintendent of Transportation, the District Engineer, Calcutta, the Superintendent of Goods, the Marine Superintendent, a Telegraph and Telephone Exchange, a waiting room and an enquiry office. The first foor accommodated the Agent and his office, the Engineering Department, the Engineer-in-Chief of Construction, the Government Consulting Engineer, the Traffic Manager, the Chief Store Keeper, the Auditor and Government Examiner of Accounts.

The second floor was taken up by drawing offices, record rooms, Construction Survey Office, the Chief Medical Officer, the Signal Engineer, the Architect, the Government Consulting Engineer and their offices. The entire ground area is 53,613 square feet.[9]

Today the building is as magnificent as it was when constructed in 1908. After nationalization BNR has become South Eastern Railway and instead of the Agent there is a General Manager. The huge compound no longer contains the animals of the King of Oudh, but has spacious staff quarters, the Officers' Club and the Railways Hospital.

There are two roads to Garden Reach; one, the old Garden Reach Road; and the other, the later Circular Garden Reach Road which, starting from Kidderpore, Bridge meets Garden Reach Road, the latter recently renamed Karl Marx Sarani. Notable addresses on Garden Reach Road included the Upper Hooghly Jute Mills, near the BNR office, the Army Remount Department, the Clive Mills, various Port Commissioners' offices and the Pilots' Chummery at No. 71. Further south is the present Garden Reach Ship Builders' and Engineers' establishment where naval frigates and other vessels are constructed as in Henry Watson's in the bygone days.

Next to Garden Reach is Metia Buruz, literally 'a mud fortress'. In the days of the Nawabs of Bengal, the river was protected by a fort here and another on the wesern bank of the river at Tannah, where the Botanical Gardens now flourish. In 1760 the Government ordered a boom to be thrown across the river, between these two forts, to prevent the Mugs, coming up the river to ravage Calcutta.

Now we proceed back towards the city along the Garden Reach Road and at one point we turn right to get into Kidderpore, by Watgunge Road, originally named Watsongunge after Col. Henry Watson, but later Watgunge, a filthy market, a dingy area.

Kidderpore

According to P.T. Nair:

> Kidderpore is the anglice of Kedarpore, i.e. the pore (Pura in Sanskrit) of Kedar, Lord Siva. When the altar of the goddess Kali was situated in Govindapore, in the Maidan, it is but natural that her consort should have a place nearby; hence Kedarpore. An antiquarian has derived it from Khettarpore, meaning the town near *khetar* (Sanskrit *kshetra*, a field). The name Kidderpore does not come from Col. Robert Kyd who laid

out the Botanical Gardens. Kidderpore is shown in the map of the Hooghly drawn by Thomas Bowery in 1670. All other maps of the Hooghly of the seventeenth century show Kidderpore very clearly, long before the arrival of Col. Kyd in India.[10]

Col. Henry Watson's dockyard was acquired in 1807 by James and Alexander Kyd, the shipbuilding sons of Col. Robert Kyd. This dockyard formed the nucleus of the famous Kidderpore Docks, which have grown over the years into a major exit point for export of goods. King George's Docks were a later welcome addition.

The approach to Kidderpore was across the Kidderpore Bridge over Tolly's Nullah. The Kidderpore Road starts from the Red Road in the Maidan and leads straight to the bridge keeping the Coolie Bazar or Hastings on the west. The bridge was erected in 1826, as the earliest suspension bridge of stone and iron constructed in India. It can be seen well depicted by William Wood in 1830.

Next to Orphangunge Bazar (derived from the Military Orphanage to which we shall come shortly) stands St. Stephen's Church with its lofty spire, one of the finest churches in Bengal. This is the Parish Church of Kidderpore, Hastings (Civil), Garden Reach, Alipore and Belvedere. The Church was built in 1846, but, for one reason or the other, not consecrated until December 1870. The handsome marble pulpit is worthy of mention. Designed by some master in the Gothic revival of the nineteenth century, and courageously true to mediaeval ideas, this magnificent pulpit remained for nearly half a century hidden away in an undertaker's shop in Bentinck Street. In 1901 Archdeacon Walter K. Firminger, then Parish of St. Stephen's, was able to purchase it for the Church.

KIDDERPORE HOUSE

A gateway to the south of the principal entrance to the Church leads into a house called Kidderpore House standing amidst extensive grounds. This house was the country residence of Richard Barwell, friend and supporter of Warren Hastings, who with the Governor General formed the minority, while Philip Francis, with Col. Monson and General Clavering formed the majority in the Governor General's Council. Mr. Barwell belonged to the Bengal Civil Service and was the owner of Writers' Buildings and of several other extensive estates from which he got a handsome income. His house was famous for its grand entertainments and was frequented by every social belle and literary light of the period, and was noted for gambling at high stakes.

Sir Philip Francis' regard for Barwell was by no means increased by the winnings he drew from that youth by high stakes. Sir Philip is supposed to have once said: 'If money be his blood, I feel and can very well afford it.'

In 1775 Sir Philip wrote:

Mr. Barwell in Council supports the Government, but abroad is endeavouring to make a bank apart in order to screen his own iniquities. He is to marry Miss Clavering, a damnable match, which can produce nothing but misery and dishonour to the lady and her family and disappointment to himself. He is cunning, cruel, rapacious, tyrannical and profligate beyond all European ideas of these qualities.

Barwell, as a matter of fact, married Miss Elizabeth Jane Sanderson in November 1776. She died two years later, leaving her husband, two infant sons, and was buried beneath a nameless but lofty pyramid in the South Park Street Burial Ground.[11]

The Orphan Institution of the Bengal Military Orphan Society had a two-fold aim—to educate and settle in life children of both sexes of officers and soldiers on the Bengal Establishment. The Lower Orphan School was situated at Alipore, and was intended for all children, whether orphans or not, of non-commissioned officers and private soldiers of the Bengal Establishment. This institution disappeared long ago, but as late as 1902 there were a few wards living in what was originally the hospital of the Upper School.

The Upper School itself was a charitable institution founded in August 1782 by Major William Kirkpatrick, and its first home until persistent outbreaks of ophthalmia called for a change, was in a building in Howrah. The building was originally constructed by Mr. Levett as a distillery; after the School moved from here this became in Bishop Heber's days the Episcopal Chapel and in later years the Magistrate's Cutchery. In 1789-90 the Military Orphan School moved to Kidderpore House, calling for structural changes to adapt the fine house to the needs of the School. But the old ball room, with its glittering chandeliers, was left untouched.

Perhaps the only room now remaining in Calcutta, in which all this grace and comeliness were often gathered together, is the ball room of Richard Barwell's garden house at Alipore. What generations of exiled feet—the gayest and lightest—have not disported on this floor! The very lamps and wall-shades which were lighted in the consulship of Warren Hastings are sometimes lighted still. What stately minutes and cotilions and romping country dances long obsolete have those old lustres not looked down on. Who does not wish that they could speak of the past and its faded scenes and tell us stories of the merry "ladies and gentlemen of the Settlement"—of their frolics and their wooings—their laughter and their love.[12]

This house was a harbour of refuge for unmarried Europeans in search for a wife; for a gala dancing night, they would gather here often travelling 500 miles.

William Baillie made a coloured etching of this house in 1794, which was published as a part of his *Views of Calcutta.*

The Boys' Orphanage which opened on to Belvedere Road was amalgamated with the St. Paul's School in Chowringhee Road in 1846, but the girls' department remained in Kidderpore House. But a lot from the estate was carved away to accommodate the Mazuchelli Bazar, a good deal of the Zoological Gardens and the Meteorological Observatory.

> The southern part of the Kidderpore Park is about to be handed over to the public by Lord Curzon to be added to the grounds of the Zoological Gardens. As soon as the number of orphans (now 15) is reduced to 13, the house and the remainder of the grounds will be similarly utilised for the benefit of the community, the surviving inmates being moved to a suitable residence elswhere.[13]

But the Kidderpore House survived, St. Thomas's School's Girls' department taking the place of the Military Orphan School. The age-old Kidderpore House was demolished to construct the modern school building. During the Second World War, the Free School premises at Free School Street was requisitioned by the Army and the school was transferred to Kidderpore. It is still at the same site. St. Thomas's Girls' and Boys' Schools are situated in large premises at Kidderpore. Beyond the playground of the Boys' school is the parsonage of the church. Next to it on Diamond Harbour Road was the Hospital for Indian Troops; its site later taken over by a commodious Old People's Home. Next was the Cavalry Barracks, for the Governor of Bengal's bodyguards. It is still called the bodyguard Lines, but now the extensive compound houses the headquarters of the Calcutta Armed Police in new buildings; with one of the gates leading to the Meteorological Observatory. After crossing the road leading to Belvedere we come to the site of Woodlands, palace and grounds of the Maharaja of Coochbehar. It had a full size cricket ground, where the legendary cricketer prince Ranji once played in a friendly match. Woodlands was demolished later and a lot of new constructions have appeared in its place.

ALIPORE METEOROLOGICAL OFFICE AND OBSERVATORY

In Calcutta systematic observation of weather conditions commenced in 1840 in an Observatory at the Survey of India Office in Wood Street.

Impetus for the study of meteorology grew after the great cyclone of 1864 which swept over Calcutta. Over 80,000 people perished and a considerable number of shipping damaged. Later, as the outcome of a Government scheme for an all-India service, which was launched in 1875, the Alipore Observatory was founded, where the work included the recording of observations of various meteorological phenomena. A very important project in this scheme was the transmission of daily weather reports: the first to begin in Calcutta was in 1877. Observational data at that time were collected by post and charts prepared at the Central Office. The droughts and famines of 1876 and 1877 made

Government anxious for quicker weather information, and in 1878 observations began to be telegraphed in code to weather report centres.

Gradually the Office grew in importance and today advance weather information is available through the satellites.

THE ZOOLOGICAL GARDENS

This is situated between Kidderpore and Alipore in the area which is shown as Jerrut in old plans of Calcutta.

The idea of establishing a zoo in Calcutta appears to have originated with Dr. Fayrer, CSI, in 1867; the subject was again raised in 1873 by Mr. C.L. Schwendler, who strongly stressed the necessity of a Zoological Garden. Sir Richard Temple, Lieutenant Governor of Bengal (1874-77), supported the scheme and on the representation of the Asiatic and the Agri-horticultural Societies, the Government granted the present site. The grounds were laid out with fine trees, plants, ornamental lakes and animal cages and houses. It was inaugurated on 1 January 1876 by H.R.H. the Prince of Wales, later King Edward VII, and opened to the public in May of the same year, with Mr. Schwendler as its first Superintendent. The entire area is about 45 acres.

This is one of the most popular places in Calcutta, with little children and grownups, city sophisticates and people from remote villages standing patiently in long queues to enter the zoo to see the rare specimens of animals, birds, reptiles, etc.

Figure 73: A View of the Zoological Gardens

Alipore

East of Kidderpore, this was the most fashonable suburb of Calcutta favoured by the English. The origin of the name is not very certain. Siraj-ud-Daula renamed Calcutta as Alinagar after capturing the city in 1756. There is a notion that the suburb got its name from Alinagar. There is another notion that the name originated from Mir Zafar Ali Khan's residence in the locality when he was deposed from the *musnud* of Murshidabad by Governor Vansittart in 1760. And it is a fact that names such as Begum Bari and Sahib Bagan survived in the neighbourhood. The site of the Nawab's house has been placed by some where Belvedere stands today. Others prefer a spot close to the Modern Court of the Judge of 24-Parganas and the presence of Mohammedan tombs in the garden of the house at the southern corner of Alipore Lane and Alipore Road lends colour to the conjecture. It is further claimed that when Mir Zafar was restored to the throne of Murshidabad in 1763, he made over his entire property at Alipore to Warren Hastings as a gift.[14]

BELVEDERE HOUSE

Perhaps the most historic house in Alipore is the Belvedere House, originally called Belvidere House, which now houses the National Library (previously the Imperial Library). Mr. A.K. Ray is convinced that Emperor Aurangzeb's son Prince Azim-us-Shan constructed

Figure 74: Belvedere House, Alipore

it in 1700. But it is certain that Belvedere was the garden house of Mr. Frankland, the official who in 1758 conducted a survey of the South Parganas of Calcutta.[15]

In the proceedings of the Council on 20 June 1763, permission is given to Warren Hastings to 'build a bridge over the Callighaut [Kalighat] Nullah on the road to his Garden House.' Walter K. Firminger tends to believe that Hastings' Garden House at Alipore in 1763 could not have been Belvedere (he was not then Governor), but another old residence still standing on Judge's Court Road. Verelst, Governor of Bengal from January 1767 to December 1769, and Cartier, Governor, December 1769 to April 1772, resided at Belvedere, but can it be the present Belvedere? Stavorinus, the Dutch Admiral, writes:

(February 26th 1779). 'At 6 o'clock in the evening Mr. Cartier came to fetch the Director V, and his company to ride to his country seat Belvedere, about two Dutch miles from Calcutta, where we were entertained with an excellent concert by amateurs and an elegant supper.'

Mrs. Fay who visited Mrs. Hastings at Belvedere House in May 1780, estimates the journey from Calcutta at five miles—'a great distance at this season'.

The house is a perfect gem; most superbly fitted up with all that unbounded affluence can display; but still deficient in that simple elegance which the wealthy so seldom attain, from the circumstance of not being obliged to search for effect without much cost, which those moderately rich find to be so indispensable. The grounds are said to be very tastefully laid out.

But was the house where Mrs. Fay paid court to the 'elegant Marian' the former home of Verelst and Cartier? Apparently not, or only so in part, for Macrabie, Francis' brother-in-law and secretary, writes in February 1778: 'Colonel Monson dined with us in the country: after dinner we walked over to the Governor's new-built house. This a pretty thing but very small, tho' airy and lofty. These milk-white buildings with smooth shiny surface utterly blind one.'[16]

But whatever the controversy be, that Hastings owned a house in the vicinity of Belvedere House is probably beyond doubt.

This house too was probably called Belvedere House, as there are records that this property was bequeathed by Hastings to his stepsons, the Imhoff children, from Marian's first marriage. After the death of the last Imhoff, who was in the Bengal Civil Service, this property was demolished and disappeared in the extensions of the garden of Belvedere House.

Hastings, who came to own the original Belvedere House, sold it to Major Tolly in February 1780. Tolly, after residing at the house for some time, leased it to W.A. Brooke, and after Tolly's death, subject to a yearly rent of £350 on that lease, in 1802 it was put up for auction 'By order of Richard Johnson Esq., Attorney to the Administrator of the late

Colonel William Tolly.' The property passed through the hands of John Brereton Birch (1810), Sambhu Chunder Mukerji (1824) and James Mackillop (1841).

Sir Edward Paget, Commander-in-Chief, lived in this house from 1823 to 1825. On arrival at Belvedere he writes to Lady Harriet Paget on 8 February 1823: 'We reached Belvedere about two o'clock and I pronounce it to be a delightful residence... . It is most cheerful, clean and gentleman-like, and I would not change it.'[17]

Before we pass on from the days of Warren Hastings, let us have a look at the famous duel fought between Warren Hastings and his arch rival Sir Philip Francis near the north-west boundary of the Belvedere House which came to be known as Duel Avenue. This took place in the early morning of 17 August 1780. At his wit's end for money, dogged by a relentless opposition, Hastings decided to bring matters into a crisis by penning the celebrated minute of July 3rd in which he wrote of Francis: 'I judge of his public conduct by my experience of his private, which I have found void of truth and honour. This is a severe charge, but temperately and deliberately made.' A duel was the result. Lieut. Col. Pearse, Hastings' second, tells us what took place:

The next morning, Thursday August 17, I waited on Mr. Hastings in my chariot to carry him to the place of appointment. When we arrived there we found Mr. Francis and Colonel Watson walking together, and therefore soon after we alighted, I looked at my watch and mentioned aloud that it was half past five and Francis looked at his and said it was near six. This induced me to tell him that my watch was set by my astronomical clock to solar time. The place they were at was very improper for the business; it was the road leading to Alipore, at the crossing of it through a double row of trees that formerly had been a walk of Belvedere Garden, on the western side of the house. Whilst Col. Watson went, by the desire of Mr. Francis, to fetch his pistols, that gentleman proposed to go aside from the road into the walk; but Mr. Hastings disapproved of the place, because it was full of weeds and dark. The road itself was next mentioned, but was thought by everybody too public, as it was near riding time, and people want to pass that way; it was therefore agreed to walk towards Mr. Barwell's House on an old road that separated his ground from Belvedere, and before he had gone far a retired dry spot was chosen as a proper place.

As soon as the suitable place was selected, I proceeded to load Mr. Hastings' pistols; those of Mr. Francis were already loaded. When I had delivered one to Mr. Hastings, and Colonel Watson had done the same to Mr. Francis, finding the gentlemen were both unacquainted with the modes usually observed on those occasions, I took the liberty to tell them that if they would fix their distance, it was the business of the seconds to measure it. Colonel Watson immediately mentioned that Fox and Adam had taken fourteen paces, and he recommended the distance. Mr. Hastings observed it was a great distance for pistols; but as no actual objection was made to it, Watson measured and I counted. When the gentlemen had got to their ground, Mr. Hastings asked Mr. Francis if he stood before the line or behind it, and being told behind the mark, he said he would do the same and immediately took his stand. I then told them it was a rule that neither of them were to quit the ground till they had discharged their pistols, and Colonel Watson proposed that both should fire together without taking any advantage. Mr. Hastings asked if he meant they ought to fire by word of command, and was told he only meant they should fire together as nearly as could be. The preliminaries were all agreed to, and both parties presented; but Mr. Francis raised his hand and again came down to the present; he did so a second time, when he came down to his present—which was the third time of doing so—he drew his trigger, but his powder being damp, the pistol did not fire. Mr. Hastings came down from his present to give Mr. Francis time to rectify his priming, and this was done out of a cartridge with which I supplied him upon finding that they had no spare powder. Again, the gentlemen took their stands, both presented together, and Mr. Francis fired. Mr. Hastings did the same at the distance of time equal to counting of one, two, three distinctly, but not greater. His shot took place. Mr. Francis staggered, and, in attempting to sit down, he fell and said he was a dead man. Mr. Hastings hearing this, cried out, 'Good God! I hope not,' and immediately went up to him, as did Col. Watson, but I ran to call the servants.

Col. Pearse goes on to say:

I ran to call the servants and to order a sheet to be brought to bind up the wound. I was absent about two minutes. On my return I found Mr. Hastings standing by Mr. Francis, but Col. Watson was gone to fetch a cot or palanquin from Belvedere to carry him to town. When the sheet was brought, Mr. Hastings and myself bound it around his body, and we had the satisfaction to find it was not to a vital part, and Mr. Francis agreed with me in opinion as soon as it was mentioned. I offered to attend him to town in my carriage, and Mr. Hastings urged him to go, as my carriage was remarkably easy. Mr. Francis agreed to go, and therefore, when the cot came, we proceeded towards the chariot, but were stopped by a deep, broad ditch, over which we could not carry the cot; for this reason Mr. Francis was conveyed to Belvedere.[18]

It seems strange that Francis was carried to Belvedere House, as his own country house was very near, at the site of the present day Presidency Jail. Coming back to Belvedere House, we find in a minute dated 24 September 1854, Lord Dalhousie asked the Court of Directors 'that a furnished house should be found for the Lieutenant-Governor of Bengal, as is done for the Governor General and for the Governors of the Presidencies,' adding, 'I wish it to be clearly understood that I do so without the knowledge of the Lieutenant Governor.' Belvedere, which had in 1841 come into the hands of Charles Robert Prinsep, the Advocate General, was therefore purchased.[19] The house was completely renovated with additions and alterations.

The house has been enlarged and improved from time to time by successive Lieutenant Governors. Its architecture is of a free Italian renaissance style, developed on an ordinary Anglo-Indian building. The construction of a *verandah* on the east side, and the reconstruction of a more commodious west wing, were carried out in 1868-70 by Sir W. Grey. Alterations and additions to other parts of the building were effected, and the boundary fences to the new grounds and a guard-room was constructed. Sir Ashley Eden added the whole of the centre main facade, with the steps, on the north side, Mr. E.J. Martin being the Government architect; he also had the wooden floor put to the centre ball room. In Sir S. Bayley's time the wooden-glazed dining room was made on the north-east side of the house. Sir C. Elliot had the rooms on the upper storey of the west wing constructed, and the archway leading into the drawing room from the main staircase substituted for a door. Sir A. Mackenzie introduced the electric lighting. Sir W. Grey had the honour of receiving H.R.H. the Duke of Edinburgh (Queen Victoria's second son) at a Ball and Reception at Belvedere in December 1869-January 1870. Sir R. Temple had the honour of entertaining H.R.H. the Prince of Wales (later King Edward VII), at a dinner and a garden party in December 1875. Sir C. Elliot entertained the Czarevich of Russia (later Czar Nicholas II, the last Czar), at a dinner and an evening party in January 1891. It was on this occasion that the sudden explosion of a soda water bottle created some momentary alarm, which was promptly met by the ready wit of the hostess. The Russian staff were much more alarmed by the incident than the Czarevich himself.[20]

Belvedere House still stands today with its long history of changing fortunes. The main entrance is to the north, a lofty gateway surmounted by a carved figure of a vigilant tiger. A road called Belvedere Road leads straight to the imposing gateway from Lower Circular Road over the bridge on Tolly's Nullah with the Zoological Gardens on the right and the spanking new Taj Bengal Hotel on the left. The first bridge on this site was an iron suspension bridge, beautifully depicted by Sir Charles D'Oyly in his coloured lithograph of 1835, *Suspension Bridge at Alipore over Tolly's Nullah*. The lofty scaffolding in the distance is for fire watching.

Back to Belvedere House, the drive from the main gateway sweeps round smooth lawns to a flight of steps guarded by two brass cannons, which were cast at Cossipore and bear the arms of the East India Company. The facade was adorned with the Royal Coat of Arms and supported by a double row of Ionic pillars crowned by Doric capitals.

Up to 1912, the house continued to be the residence of the Lieutenant Governors of Bengal, but upon the transfer of Capital to New Delhi in 1912, the Governor of Bengal moved to the more gorgeous Government House; Belvedere being reserved for the use of the Viceroys on their visits to the city.

The Viceroy used to descend upon the city during the winter season, for races, gala parties, balls etc. On ceremonial occasions, the superbly attired Viceroy's Bodyguard lined the drive and the steps, and when Indian ladies in their colourful saris, and Indian gentlemen in elegant dresses, mingled with the European guests, Belvedere and its surrounding lawns came alive in a beautiful pageant.

After Independence the Viceroys and Vicerines were gone and Belvedere House was again vacant, till it was decided that the National Library (before Independence the Imperial Library) would be shifted here. In making over Belvedere to the Ministry of Education, the Prime Minister, Pandit Jawaharlal Nehru, expressed himself as follows:

> I do not want Belvedere for the mere purpose of stacking books. We want to convert it into a fine Central Library where large numbers of research students can work and where there would be all other amenities which a modern library gives. The place must not be judged as something just like the present Imperial Library. It is not merely a question of accommodation, but of something much more.[21]

*Figure 75: Woodlands, The Maharaja of Cooch Behar's Palace in Alipore 'during my father's time",
writes Rajmata Gayatri Devi of Jaipur. Photo courtesy the Rajmata*

The work of shifting the Library to Belvedere began in 1948, when it was enriched by the donation of 80,000 volumes of books covering a phenomenal range of subjects and languages, the whole collection of Sir Asutosh Mukherjee, by his heirs. Similar collections of books were donated by other sources, particularly the Library of the Residency at Hyderabad.

Many additions of new buildings have been made in the compound to house various sections of the Library, but the old Belvedere House still stands resplendent in its glory.

West of Belvedere there stood a house within a spacious compound, which was probably Hastings' 'Old House' which was purchased by Jackson in 1785. This was the site of Woodlands, the Maharaja of Coochbehar's palace in Calcutta. To the north of this house and within the compound were two smaller buildings, tenanted in 1780 by Lieutenant Foley of the commissariat and Dr. Clement Francis, the Governor-General's Body-surgeon. Immediately behind Belvedere on the south are the seventy *bighas* of land not included in the sale of Hastings' property. Here was the site of the house built by Julius Imhoff, the younger of the stepsons of Hastings, who had made him a gift of the land. He was married to a Mohammedan lady, and the grave of his mother-in-law, the Begum, was alongside the house and was to be seen as late as 1896-98 with a large Bougainville creeper growing over it. This was the only house owned by Julius Imhoff (who died in 1799) and is the one mentioned by him in his will as 'my grounds situated behind that House or Mansion commonly known by the name of Belvedere House and at present occupied by William Augustus Brooke'.[22] The house in 1891 belonged to Sir Charles Imhoff, a descendant of Julius, and was once occupied by Sir C.T. Metcalfe. One of the houses was sold by Sir Charles Imhoff to the Nawab Nazim of Murshidabad and was known as 'Nawab Sahib ka Kothi'.

In 1864 the latter was purhased by Sir Cecil Beadon on behalf of the Government of Bengal and the house was demolished. A portion of the land was added to Belvedere and the remainder, at one time set apart for an extension of the Alipore Cantonment, became the property of the Agri-horticultural Society of India.

THE AGRI-HORTICULTURAL SOCIETY OF INDIA

This is situated south of Belvedere, as described above, the frontage being on Alipore Road. The garden covers about thirty acres, well planted and laid out. Just inside the gate on Alipore Road, is an ornamented miniature lake, lined with tall shady trees, and encircled by a cinder pathway. The main road, laid in tarmac, goes past both sides of the lake in symmetrical curves, and criss-crossing the grounds, leads to various nurseries, hot-houses and ferneries.

In the centre of the garden is the society's office, which was transferred here from the Metcalfe Hall in 1903. It had some marvellous portraits of Sir Edward Ryan, Sir Lawrence

Peel, and a small but unique portrait in chalk of Colonel Robert Kyd. There is a fine bust (that first stood in the Metcalfe Hall) by J.C. Lough of Dr. William Carey, the famous Serampore missionary, founder of The Agri-horticultural Society in 1820.

The society's gardens, during the early years, had to be frequently moved from place to place; notwithstanding this handicap, its progress remained unimpeded. It was only in 1870 that the present site at Alipore was acquired. The society is still there and its annual flower show is an important event in the city's calendar.

Opposite the garden was the old Number 4 Alipore Road, called Woodlands, the Coochbehar palace in the city, long disappeared. No. 5 was 'Dil Khush', the Calcutta Suburbs Survey Office. The Military Command Hospital now stands on the spacious site of the Native Infantry Lines.

Alipore, always considered as a very healthy suburb, had its influx of European residents after the Judge's Court Road was constructed, in place of the conglomeration of stables, paddocks and occasional huts.

This area had once been of considerable interest, as is evident from the old issues of *Calcutta Gazette* announcing sales of property. In 1785 the *Gazette* announces the sale of Hastings' property after his departure, by Messrs. William and Lee at the Old Court House on 10 May.

Lot 1 was 'the house opposite the paddock gate consisting of a hall, a large *verandah* to the southward, and six rooms;' and included therewith are 'two small bungalows, a large tank of excellent water, and above 63 bighas of land, partly lawn, but chiefly garden ground in high cultivation, and well stocked with a great variety of fruit trees.' The second lot is described as 'an upper-roomed house consisting of a hall and two rooms on each floor, a handsome stone staircase and a back staircase all finished with Madras Chunam;' and 'a lower-roomed house containing a large hall and four good bedchambers: a complete bathing house with two rooms finished with Madras Chunam: a convenient bungalow containing two rooms and a *verandah* all round, a large range of *pucka* buildings containing stabling for 14 horses and four coach houses: other stables also thatched for 12 horses and 6 carriages and 46 *bighas* of ground.' Lot 3 is the 'paddock containing 52 *bighas* of ground surrounded with railed fence.'

In the map of 1780 only three houses are distinctly shown; the first at the south-eastern corner of the paddock, and if the modern Judge's Court Road follows the alignment of the old continuation of Alipore Lane, its site was on the north-eastern portion of the compound of Hastings House as it is now demarcated. Its foundations are stated by Dr. Chambers to have been visible in 1897. There is another house behind it, slightly to the south-west, which from its situation may very reasonably be identified with the Hastings House, and the subject of Lot 2: while its companion, the 'lower-roomed house', as indicated on the map, standing to the west of both the others, has been swallowed up by the Judge's Court compound. The large tank of excellent water has survived, however, and may still be seen within the *cutchery* precincts.[23]

Before coming to the Hastings House, we should have a look at the western and south-western areas of Alipore. In the old Alipore Lane, which was later widened and named Judge's Court Road, the Maharajadhiraj of Burdwan built his palace Vijay Manjil; in the southward extension of Alipore Road the Maharaja of Santosh built his palace. Montague Massey writes that where Alipore Park is now situated there was once a big open field with a factory, which was called the Arrowroot Farm.[24] As we travel east along Judge's Court Road, the first block of buildings are the Alipore Judge's Court, which is situated mostly on property belonging to Warren Hastings. The next building now enclosed within high walls is the Hastings House.

HASTINGS HOUSE

This was Warren Hastings' favourite house in Alipore, corresponding to the Lot 2 of the sale of his properties in 1785 as described above.

It was constructed around 1776, as corroborated by Macrabie. The original house, the central building with its portico, is the little house which Mrs. Fay describes as 'a perfect Bijou'. In this house, then called the Alipore Gardens, Warren Hastings lived with his second wife, the 'beloved Marian', the celebrated Baroness Imhoff, to whom he was passionately devoted. John Zoffany painted a picture of Warren Hastings, the second Mrs. Hastings and a lady attendant standing in a park, with the old Hastings House in the background. Hastings had planted cinnamon and other valuable trees on the grounds which he had laid out wonderfully.

> The stone staircase still stands, but can hardly be called handsome, being narrow, winding and steep. The back staircase is also in good preservation; it is built into an odd corner cupboard like a wooden shaft within a bathroom and is lighted by a small barred window which opens into the room. The Madras *chunam* of the advertisement is lost under successive coats of whitewash. The hall and two rooms on each floor form the original house, the central block, while the wings are distinctly of a later date, as is evidenced by the style of the beams and *burgahs*, and by the stucco work. The entire building is raised four feet from the ground, but only the wings are flued—another mark of the later period, and finally the walls of the wings do not bond into those of the central block. This is very apparent on the southern front of the building.[25]

After the departure of Hastings the building and its spacious grounds were neglected for many years leading to decay and desolation. In 1901 the Hastings House along with the grounds were bought for the Government by Lord Curzon; after a thorough renovation it was converted into a State Guest House, where Lord Curzon entertained the Indian Princes and Nobles during the winter season. The eldest son of the Amir of Afghanistan was

Figure 76: Hastings House, Alipore

accommodated here as a State Guest in 1904. Lord Curzon also laid out the grounds and built a second bungalow for the convenience of the guests. Hastings House contains a big pillared *durbar* room which was used for the exchange of state visits. Lord Curzon put up a marble tablet above the entrance with the following inscription:

> This House known as Hastings House, originally the country seat of Warren Hastings, Governor General of Fort William in Bengal, 1774 to 1785, was bought as State Guest House by Lord Curzon, Viceroy and Governor General of India in 1901.

After the transfer of Capital to Delhi, Hastings House remained unoccupied until 1915, when it was converted into a residential Boys' School for the sons of well-to-do Indian gentlemen in imitation of an English Public School. The arrangements were unsuitable; the experiment did not prove a success and the school was closed in 1920 and for a number of years the buildings remained vacant. Hastings House has been since used as offices of the Government for a long time. In 1954 the Institute for Education for Women, a B.Ed. College, was established here; and the college continues at the same building. But changes have occurred; a wooden staircase has replaced the stone steps and there is no sign of the staircase at the back. A Multipurpose Girls' High School has come up in the compound; and in a separate compound to the east the Vihari Lal College for Home Sciences occupies a new building. The latter too has a large compound, but neither of the compounds carries traces of the beautifully laid out gardens, whose place has been taken by grassless meadows or unkempt jungle. Even the marble tablet installed by Lord Curzon, and later replaced by a brass plaque, was allegedly removed under orders of the Education Minister of the West Bengal Government.

For a long time a ghost story has been associated with Hastings House. The apparition of Hastings is said to appear from time to time driving in a coach and four up the avenue and on alighting at the portico of the house, to go up the stairs in search of something. A curious corroboration of the story is furnished by a letter from Hastings to his great friend and late Private Secretary, Nesbitt Thompson, in Calcutta, dated 21 July 1785, and is referred to in the volume of Gleig's biography. 'It pains me,' he writes, 'to recur to the subject of my bureau. I have not as yet received any intelligence from you or Larkins about it. You cannot conceive my anxiety about it.' The contents of the bureau were evidently highly prized by Hastings, for on 6 September 1787, the following advertisement regarding it appears in the *Calcutta Gazette*:

Whereas an old Black Wood Bureau, the property of Warren Hastings, Esq., containing, amongst other things, two small miniature pictures and some private papers, was about the time of his departure from Bengal either stolen from his house on the Esplanade, or by mistake sold at the auction of his effects: This is to give notice that Mr. Larkins and Mr. Thompson will pay the sum of two thousand sicca rupees to any person who shall give them such information as shall enable them to recover the contents of the bureau.'

The loss seems never to have been made good: and it is impossible not to trace some connection between it and the ghostly visits so constantly paid by Hastings to his old haunts at Alipore.'[26]

Francis Grand and Madame Grand had a country house near Hastings House, probably in the vicinity of the old Alipore Lane. Many believe that the Philip Francis incident took place at Alipore.

Opposite Hastings House is a small lane ending in Belvedere Road in the north, a lane of palaces. On the corner was the house of Mr. Hugh Knight, Bar-at-Law, the 'Sans Souci,' a fine colonial house in a large compound. Number 1 was Hong Kong Bank House which now is the German Consulate in Calcutta. Number 2 was the house of Mr. E.J. Oakley and others of Kilburn and Co. It was the residence of the British Deputy High Commissioner in Calcutta and a very fine house laid out in marble and a large dance hall. Recently a Bengali gentleman has bought the house. Coming back to the corner of the lane with Judge's Court Road one comes to the site of the old Number 6, the palatial residence of Sir Acquin Martin, one of the partners of Martin & Company. After his death, this became the

Gillanders House. The old building was later demolished and a twin block of apartments, Rajshri and Rajhans, built on the site.

Proceeding east along the Judge's Court Road we pass the National Test House, previously known as Alipore Test House to our left; as we cross Gopalnagar Road, we pass to our right the lofty building of the West Bengal Survey Department and an extensive Map Printing Press. Next and south to it is the West Bengal Government Press. As we proceed towards the Tolly's Nullah we reach the entrance and high walls of the Alipore Jail built in 1906.

Now we retrace our steps and come to the crossing of Judge's Court Road and Gopalnagar Road and turn right northwards. This was once Baker Road, probably named after Alfred Baker of the Calcutta Municipal Corporation.

To our right is the Alipore Post Office followed by the extensive compound of the South 24-Parganas District Magistrate's Office and Court and the Alipore Criminal Court and Bhavani Bhawan (old Anderson House), a large administrative building of the state government, housing different departments of the government and some of the important police offices. This is followed by the Bengal Police Lines. To our left a road goes west towards Alipore Road—called Belvedere Road or Park. This road accommodates the Calcutta Municipal Corporation Birth Registration Office, some old buildings, a modern giant complex containing the Eastern Railway Officers' Quarters and Club, and also forms the southern boundary of the Agri-Horticultural Society's gardens. After Hastings Park Road there is a small lane called Penn Road which ends in Alipore Road. P.T. Nair writes that 'the Penn Road finds entry in the Calcutta street directories from the beginning of this [i.e. the twentieth] century. It is not clear whether the road derived its name from the cattle pen of Warren Hastings situated in this locality.'[27] According to other sources the road owes its name to Mr. William Penn, an English civilian.

Now we come back to Baker Road and proceed north towards Belvedere House. A lane to our left leads to an old and spacious bungalow, the residence of the Superintendent of Police, South 24-Parganas. At one time this house had a large kitchen-garden and stables to the south; later demolished to make way for residences for senior police officers fronting Belvedere Road. There are a few old houses followed by the Army's Clothing Department. Baker Road meets Belvedere Road and to the right a road called Thackeray Road goes on to a historic house in Alipore—The Lodge, the country house of Sir Philip Francis, the compound of which extended up to the present Presidency Jail and the building with its grounds was considerably larger than the Belvedere House.

THE LODGE

In 1775 Sir Philip Francis purchased this property, according to his brother-in-law and Secretary, Macrabie. The Lodge consisted of 'a spacious hall and four chambers, and

Figure 77: Thackeray House, Alipore. Photo couresty Mr. Arun Bhattacharya I.A.S.

standing in the midst of twenty acres of ground, pleasant to the last degree.'[28] The property included the site of the present Presidency Jail and Reformatory and its boundary on the north and east was Tolly's Nullah. Early in 1776, the indefatigable Macrabie writes in his diary: 'At the Gardens, being Sunday, we rode special hard all the morning. Colonel Monsoon, Mr. Farren and Mr. Thompson dined with us, so did Major Tolly, he is cutting a navigable canal close by.' The Lodge has also been described as Francis' 'villa inter palludes'. There is a tradition that Francis, being a Roman Catholic, built the ecclesiastical-looking erection now used as a stable in the neighbouring compound. Francis was the son of an English clergyman, and it is doubted 'if he ever was sufficiently interested in religious matters to go to the pains of a secession, which would have cost him a seat in Parliament'.[29] Six months before he left India, Francis sold the house and grounds in April 1780 to his friend Livius. The Lodge still survives at the end of Thackeray Road. For nearly 190 years it has served for the official residence of the Collector and Magistrate of the 24-Parganas, now the District Magistrate of South 24-Parganas. A wing and an upper storey have been added, otherwise it is the same house where Francis held his weekly symposia. Towards the end of 1811, Richmond Thackeray, father of the novelist, William Makepeace Thackeray, was appointed Collector of 24-Parganas and came to reside in this house. His little son was then only five months old, having been born on 18 July 1811 at their Free School Street residence. Richmond lived in the house with his wife and little son, until 13 September 1815 when he died, aged about thirty-three years.

The Lodge still stands there, as a witness to the bygone days. There was a ghost story associated with the house. Many occupants claimed to have heard someone playing on a piano at night, but there was no piano in the house.

Now we turn away from the Lodge, and proceed towards Lower Circular Road over yet another bridge on the Tolly's Nullah, the Zeerut Bridge, constructed in 1932. We pass the Bhowanipore Military Cemetery, the Minto Park and the new Army quarters. Legend goes that the entire area of the army's buildings was at one time the stables of the Maharaja of Sholapur.

Tollygunge

Tollygunge takes its name from Major Tolly, and begins about four miles south of the Government House. Major Tolly established a market and a settlement here, which drew the Europeans to turn it into a country seat, like Alipore.

One of the earliest settlers in the area was Alexander Dow, Lieutenant Colonel in the service of the Honourable the United Company of Merchants of Calcutta trading to the East Indies, who bought his three-storeyed house in Russapaglah from Major Andrew Williams in 1776.[30] Tilman Henckell bought a plot of land close to Dow's house in 1796. But at his death in 1800, Tilman Henckell's estate not being sufficient to pay off and discharge the debts that were due and owing by him at the time of his death, it became proper and necessary to sell and dispose of the messuage, tenement or garden house; it was sold by the auctioners Tulloh and Company, to Richard Johnson for 3,600 sicca rupees.[31]

Johnson had started acquiring property in Tollygunge from 1781. Between 1785 and 1790 he was Accountant, Revenue Department; Member, Board of Revenue; Chairman, General Bank of India; and Accountant General. This great landowner was interested in the culture of the Orient. On 29 January 1789, Sir William Jones sent back to Johnson his copy of the *Shahnama,* and promised in a letter to 'pass Saturday or Sunday at your Garden', and enquired about his neighbour in Russapughlah, Jeremiah Church, then Sheriff of Calcutta and an advocate at the Supreme Court since 1782. A couple of months earlier, Jones had made the same Promise in a letter dated 1 November 1788: 'will visit you soon at Russapuglah: but a Hindu Goddess must visit you first, and you may expect her next week'. The Hindu Goddess Jones promised to send Johnson was only a Hymn to the Hindu Goddess of wealth and prosperity, Lakshmi. John Owen, Chaplain to the Garrison of Fort William, in a letter dated 10 March 1788, described Johnson as 'a gentleman of the first quality, both intellectual and moral,' with whom he had 'lived a little out of town'.[32]

The Calcutta grapevine recorded that Richard Johnson played a major role in the divorce settlement of Baroness Imhoff, the second Mrs. Warren Hastings. After a satisfactory financial deal, the Baron was packed off to Europe. At the turn of the century, when Johnson resettled at Russapuglah, his neighbours included Richard Waite Cox, Accountant General; Gabriel Vrignon, Ship Chandler; Jeremiah Church, Sheriff; Charles Wyatt, son of James Wyatt (President of the Royal Academy in 1806) an indigo merchant; a considerable community of Europeans. The landscape was made of garden houses in the picturesque settings of woods and cool jheels, with the road belonging to Richard Johnson and Tolly's Nullah forming the border. In spite of scattered Indian homesteads, Tollygunge remained mainly European until 1806.

After the fall of Seringapattam during the storming of which Tipu Sultan was killed, the Mysore princes and their families were confined in the fort of Vellore, near Madras. The family were suspected of complicity in the mutiny at Vellore in 1806. This led the British Government to transfer them from Madras presidency to Bengal, but on their arrival in Calcutta they were given full liberty and allowed to build houses for themselves in Tollygunge.

One of Tipu Sultan's surviving sons, Prince Gholam Mohammad, bought Richard Johnson's Russapuglah garden house, made extensive development of the property and named it 'Bara Bagh'. The original owner Richard Johnson, such a wealthy man in 1800, died seven years later penniless in Brighton.

Moizuddin Sultan was the younger of the two princes taken hostage by Lord Cornwallis, and was the third son of Tipu Sultan. He lived with his brother Sultan Shobhan Shah in Khas Mahal on what is now Anwar Shah Road. Muniruddin Shah was another son of Tipu Sultan and the grandfather of Bakhtiar Shah. He lived in the Nach Kothi or Dancing House. The Pul-par palace, so called as it was beyond the bridge away from the other palaces, was a place well known to Calcutta people. Fateh Hyder Shah was the eldest son of Tipu Sultan and was so named, as he was born immediately after a successful campaign against the Marhattas. His residence was called Bara Mahal to signify his seniority and is opposite the Tollygunge Club on the road to the Royal Calcutta Golf Links.

Another son of Tipu Sultan lived in the house later called Aldeen, which was taken over by ITC Ltd., who have established a classical music research centre there.

Coming back to Prince Gholam Mohammad, we find him living happily in Bara Bagh, sending petitions and memorials to the Gvoernment, claiming all the benefits promised to him in terms of the treaty of 1799. He was a protege of Queen Victoria. He built two fine mosques, one at the junction of Anwar Shah Road, and the other at the junction of Bentinck Street and Dhurrumtolla Street. The latter, popularly known as Tipu Sultan's Mosque, bears the following inscription:

> This Musjeed was erected during the Government of Lord Auckland, G.C.B.,—by the Prince Ghoolam Mahomud, son of the late Tipoo Sultan, in gratitude to God and in commemoration of the Hon'ble the Court of Directors granting him the arrears of his stipend in 1840.

He died in 1872 aged seventy-seven. At the time of his death, his properties included two three-storey houses on Bankshall Street, a two-storeyed house with extensive godown and stable accommodation on Hastings Street, a string of shops on Bentinck Street, the large estate at Tollygunge then known as Bara Bagh (305 *bighas* of land with a large upper-roomed house and several smaller houses), a smaller Tollygunge estate of 83 *bighas* then known as Cutchery Bagh and now part of the Royal Calcutta Golf Club, a few more plots of land with several tanks and small houses and gardens on the banks of Tolly's Nullah and a string of shops and godowns next to the Tollygunge mosque.

The nineteenth century saw the Mysore Princes well established in Tollygunge and the early British settlers moving elsewhere, till Tollygunge became almost a Muslim town. But by the end of the century the Mysore Princes were on the decline and the white men returned to Tollygunge, now for sports and pleasure. In 1871 the Ballygunge Steeplechase Association developed the Tollygunge steeplechase course in Regents Park. In 1895 the Tollygunge Club acquired the original Johnson estate from the descendants of Prince Gholam Mohammad, and laid the Golf Course, the Race Course, and set up the Gymkhana. In 1910 opened the Calcutta Golf Links.

In the early 1930s, several film studios sprouted in Tollygunge. All the major ones were located here later giving Tollygunge a new name, Tollywood, in imitation of Hollywood. With the partition of India in 1947 there was an exodus of settlers in Tollygunge and adjoining areas—Hindu refugees fleeing from East Pakistan. The Government did very little for their proper rehabilitation, driving them to live in thatched cottages built by themselves in insanitary conditions. But they survived. The settlers' colonies have by now taken the shape of ill-planned townships spread all over Tollygunge and the neighbouring areas.

THE TOLLYGUNGE CLUB

The club was established in 1895 in the old Richard Johnson estate acquired from the descendants of Prince Gholam Mohammad. Sir William Dickson Cruickshank, CIE, Secretary and Treasurer of the Bank of Bengal, was the first President and Mr. C.P. Symes Scutt was the first Honorary Secretary. The administrative office of the club was in the Bank of Bengal office. As in other clubs of this nature, membership was restricted to Europeans only. Racing in Tollygunge has stopped in the 1980s. The main sport now is golf. The Club House, once the garden house of Johnson and the Mysore Prince, is very well maintained. It is still one of the best clubs in Calcutta with its lush green and eco-friendly atmosphere. The club has also a unique record in India; the first ever aeroplane flight in India took place on 28 December 1910 in the Tollygunge Club. Two French aviators, Baron de Caters and Jules Tyck brought their small mono and biplanes to the city for demonstration flights. The entry fees for better seats were Rs. 10 and stand tickets were priced at Rs. 3. According to *The Statesman* of 29 December, traffic near the club was in a state of utter confusion from 12 noon onwards; there were 1000 people in the Rs. 10 enclosure and double that number in the cheaper one.

The Baron first went up in his Farman biplane and showed aerobatics at a small height. He also took a few passengers for a joy ride. Mrs. Mrinalini Sen was one of the lucky ones, and she probably is the first Indian woman to fly in an aeroplane. Later Mr. Tyck went up in his Bleriot monoplane and showed aerobatics at a height of 2000 feet. The exciting Air Display was witnessed by the Lieutenant-Governor of Bengal and other distinguished guests.

Like all other 'whites only' clubs in Calcutta, Tollygunge Club also had to open its doors to Indian members, at a point of time. Today Tollygunge Club enjoys extremely popular patronage; on one side is the old Club House evoking nostalgia about the Raj era, on the other is the newly erected Tolly Towers, a residential complex for members and guests. The club had to give up a lot of ground for the Tollygunge Metro Station and a sports stadium but its lush green and its ambience attract Calcuttans and visitors away from the pollution in the city.

THE ROYAL CALCUTTA GOLF CLUB

The club was originally founded in the Maidan in 1829 and a Ladies section with a separate tent in the Maidan came up in 1891. The club is the oldest golf club in India and also the second oldest outside Great Britain. The club acquired the Tollygunge property in 1910 and the very English Club House took shape in 1919.

The club is still popular as more and more Indians have become interested in the sport. The club has extensive grounds and is now facing problems from unruly poachers.

Ballygunge

The European Ballygunge grew up around the Ballygunge Maidan, which in 1775 became the Governor General's bodyguard camp. The area was bounded by the Ballygunge Circular Road on the west and south, Gariahat Road and Syed Amir Ali Avenue on the east and Store Road (today's Gurusaday Road) on the north.

In A. Upjohn's Map of 1792 the name Ballygunge is mentioned. In Steepleton's Map of 1817 we find the first mention of the Bodyguard Lines. In later maps and plans we see further development of the area and the establishment of a Bodyguards Hospital in the south-western corner. The Ballygunge Maidan was used for sports also, in the Bodyguard Lines, where the Ballygunge Steeplechase Association was formed and the Ballygunge Cricket Club was established in the north-eastern corner. Around the lines many fine garden houses were built for Europeans. Montague Massey, coming to the city in the 1860s, gives an account of 'Rainey Park, Ballygunge, where there was a big building called Rainey

Castle, standing in its own extensive grounds, owned by a Mr. Griffiths, and occupied as a chummery. On the other side was a large building with an enormous compound called the Park Chummery*, now converted into the Park, Ballygunge, while Queen's Park and Sunny Park were waste jungly land.'[33]

In the late nineteenth and early twentieth centuries, the Bengali gentry ventured out to live in European Ballygunge in their own palaces. From the corner of Rowland Road and Ballygunge Circular Road there are some interesting houses. Number 11 was once the Calcutta residence of Maulana Abul Kalam Azad, a noted Indian National Congress leader. Number 14 at the corner of Mullen Street was once a fine European house, where Pramatha Chowdhury and his newly-wed bride Indira, niece of Rabindranath Tagore, came to live after their marriage towards the close of the nineteenth century. The premises were taken on rent, while Indira's own house at 1, Rainey Park was being renovated. In 1905 this was taken on rent by the Bengal Government for the residence of Mr. Alex P. Kinney, Deputy Administrator, Bengal. In 1934 it was the residence of the Raja of Gouripore (Assam), none other than the noted film actor-director Pramathes Barua, after whom the part of Ballygunge Circular Road from Lower Circular Road to Mullen Street has been recently re-named. Number 18 in the 1930s was the residence of the Swedish Consul in Calcutta. Number 22/1 was Kilgraston House, a fine building with a stately portico, owned by Jas B. Crichton, a noted jute-broker. The property was purchased by a noted Bengali gentleman, Mr. J.N. Bose, whose son Sir S.M. Bose was at one time Advocate General, Bengal, and a noted personality of Bengal. This fine building, one of the last of the grand old mansions, is being demolished to give way to yet another residential complex. Where the Ballygunge Circular Road takes a turn to the left, on the right hand corner stands Number 26. A historic house with a large garden and a sizeable tank within its gates, this was the residence of Mr. Janaki Nath Ghosal and Swarnakumari Devi, one of the elder sisters of Rabindranath Tagore. This was the house where eminent people of the time would converge in the evening, where Janakinath, Swarnakumari Devi and their daughter Sarala would be the main attraction. Janakinath was active in Indian National Congress politics and attended all the Congress sessions in his time. One particular year, the Congress session was to be held at Calcutta and Janaki Nath was the Organizing Secretary. One day a young man newly arrived from South Africa approached him to volunteer his services for the forthcoming session. Janaki Nath appointed him his secretary, and asked him to go through all the mail and take necessary action. He was none other than Mohandas Karamchand Gandhi. Sarala was very active in helping the young Bengali revolutionaries, provoking the British Government to auction off the property. In 1934 Number 26 appears as R. Scott Thompson's Aerated Water Depot. In our younger days, the Maddox Square Park, a stone's throw from Number 26, was dug up with trenches, during the war years (1939-45). We

---

* A common accomodation shared by a number of men/women/friends.

went to play football in the compound of Number 26, which we found deserted. Later, the site was bought by others and a housing complex has since come up, called Udayan Park.

Turning left we find to our right the St. Lawrence Boys' High School set in its extensive grounds, once the site of the garden house of Raja Rajendralal Mullick, of Marble Palace fame. Number 34 has for a long time been the residence of the Chaudhuris, a family of lawyers, who have served Bengal in various capacities. In 1905 the house belonged to the Hon. Mr. J. Chaudhuri, Bar-at-Law, Member of the Bengal Legislative Council. Jogesh Chandra Chaudhuri started legal practice at Calcutta in 1895. He was associated with the Indian National Congress, and was founder-editor of the famous law journal, *Calcutta Weekly Notes*. He had extensive properties in the area.

Number 35 was the extensive garden house of Sir Tarak Nath Palit and his son Lokendra Nath Palit. Sir Tarak Nath became a Bar-at-Law in 1871. After coming back to Calcutta he started legal practice and became a very successful lawyer. He was one of the founders of the National Council of Education. He donated Rs. fifteen lakh for the establishment of the Calcutta University Science College in Upper Circular Road. In 1886 he joined the Indian Civil Service and served in various parts of Bengal and Bihar. He donated the property at Number 35 to Calcutta University for a college and research centre on Botany and Zoology. His house with its gardens and ponds were still there in 1964-65. These were later demolished to make way for the new modern building.

On the opposite side, now mostly taken over by high-rises, there were shacks and shanties jostling with European residences. In 1905, Number 59 was 'Green Park', the residence of Mr. E.T. Sandys, Manager of the Maharaja of Tripura state. Later on this site came up the fine palace of the Maharaja of Tripura in an extensive park. The palace is still there.

Now we turn back to the east and come to the junction of Ballygunge Circular Road and Old Ballygunge Road and proceed north. The Old Ballygunge Road was once occupied mostly by *bustees* and huts, before it came to be developed and many European and Indian gentlemen built their garden houses in the neighbourhood. Queen's Park and Sunny Park were turned from woody lands to streets with fine houses. The road was renamed Ashutosh Chaudhury Avenue in 1965. Justice Ashutosh Chaudhury lived at 47 Old Ballygunge Road for a number of years. He belonged to the famous Chaudhury family of Bengal and had extensive properties in the area, particulary in and around Ballygunge Store Road (Gurusaday Road). As we come to the junction of Old Ballygunge Road and Ballygunge Store Road, to our left at the corner is a full-size cricket ground, once the home ground of Ballygunge Cricket Club formed in 1864. One of those early 'whites only' clubs, Calcutta Cricket Club developed the Eden Gardens cricket arena and was the oldest existing cricket club outside Great Britain. The Calcutta Cricket Club ultimately moved out of Eden Gardens and to Ballygunge, to merge with the Ballygunge Cricket Club. It brought the Lagden Memorial Gate, which was the gateway to the Eden Gardens pavilion, to Ballygunge,

Figure 77A: The Club House, Calcutta Cricket & Football Club, Ballygunge
Photo courtesy C.C.F & C.

where it still rests. The Calcutta Football Club, which had its enclosed football ground in the Maidan opposite Eden Gardens, handed it to Mohun Bagan Club and merged with the Calcutta Cricket Club to form the Calcutta Cricket and Football Club in 1965. The C.C. & F.C. still enjoys great popularity, and is now open to Indians as well. The Club House is full of old trophies and memories.

Ballygunge Store Road (Gurusaday Road)

The name probably came from the Body Guard Stores situated on this street, or from a number of wine and provision stores on the stretch. Just opposite the Cricket Club ground was 19 Store Road, at the corner. In the closing years of the nineteenth century, Satyendranath Tagore bought the property and came to live here. It consisted of twenty-two *bighas* of land, three ponds and a large house, at least 100 years old (according to Indira Devi Chowdhurani's memoirs), the back gate opened on 93 Karaya Road. There were beautiful flowering trees, ideal for the intellectual Tagores. Rabindranath visited regularly, as Ashutosh Chaudhuri, the well-known lawyer, at 16 Store Road.

After Satyendranath, his only son Surendranath inherited the property and lived there until 1923.

Surendranath Tagore (1872-1940) was highly educated and considered a pioneer in the fields of Indian banking and life insurance. He was the founder of the Hindustan Co-operative Insurance Company. He was a writer of some eminence but, like the later Tagores, none too good in business acumen. To pay off his debts he had to sell his house at Number 19.

Mr. Ghanashyam Das Birla, the doyen of the upcoming business house of the Birlas, bought a house at 6, Rainey Park around 1915 and came to live in Ballygunge. Every morning he would take a walk around the cricket ground, where he met Suren Tagore and a friendship grew up between them. They would talk sitting on a bench by the side of the ground. G.D. Birla told Suren that if the latter ever contemplated selling Number 19, he would be interested in buying it for Rs. four lakh. When the time came for Suren to sell off the house, he was offered higher prices, but he sold the plot to his friend G.D. Birla at the promised price of Rs. four lakh in 1923.

The plot then had nineteen *bighas* of land; the old house was demolished, and G.D. himself made the plans for a large house for his family. The Bengali firm of N. Guin was entrusted with the 'engineering'. The plan was to have a separate wing for each brother—each section having three rooms, two bathrooms and a long *verandah*. It was a beautiful, elegant Victorian-style edifice completed in 1923. The house was named Birla Park, and the Birla family stayed in it till 2 February 1955, when it was gifted to the Government of India and transformed to the Birla Industrial and Technological Museum. The museum is now a favourite haunt of scientifically inclined young people and an important landmark of Calcutta.[34]

Number 18 was for several years the residence of Manook Zorab, Bar-at-Law and others, and the next two garden houses, Crimson Villa and Primrose Villa, of European gentlemen. At Number 16 lived Ashutosh Chaudhuri, Bar-at-Law (1860-1924). Sir Ashutosh was a friend of Rabindranath Tagore and married Tagore's niece, Prativa Devi. His younger brother, Pramatha, also a Bar-at-Law, married another niece of Rabindranath, Indira, in February 1899. Sir Ashutosh had a lucrative practice at the Calcutta High Court and was associated with many social and political activities of Bengal. From 1912 to 1920 he was a judge of the High Court. The Chaudhuris no longer reside in Number 16.

The fine garden houses and villas have mostly disappeared or taken over by corporate houses, but memories linger. Number 10 was the 'Red House', the residence of Mordie Arakie in 1934. Arakie was a well-known Jewish businessman of the city. An earlier resident of the Red House was Mr. J.H. Lewes of Messrs. Lovelock & Lewes. Number 9 was Cook & Company's Ballygunge Stables. Number 6 was 'Tara Lodge', in 1905 the residence of the Hon. K.G. Gupta, ICS.

After Ahiripukur Road there was a large house with a big compound, 'Baragunda House' at Number 2, where quite a number of European families lived. In 1934 this was the residence of Baron H. Rudt von Collenberg, the Consul-General of Germany. In 1950, Mr. B.K. Birla, son of Mr. G.D. Birla, decided to build his own house. Ten *bighas* of land on this site were acquired, and a fine house with a sprawling garden, 'Basant Vihar', was finally ready in January 1955.[35]

At the corner of Store Road and Ballygunge Circular Road on the south side was a prominent landmark, the Ballygunge Pharmacy of Bathgate & Co. Two large vases filled with coloured water, representing syrups, attracted everybody. The pharmacy has been closed for a long time, and the landmark has fallen into disrepair. The south side of the road also has a few old houses, some with lovely old gateways, reminders of a bygone era and its architecture.

Ballygunge Store Road was renamed Gurusaday Road in 1942, after an eminent son of Bengal. Gurusaday Dutt, ICS, was a great social reformer and founder of the Bratachari Movement. He joined the Indian Civil Service in 1905 and after working in various places, came to the Bengal Secretariat in 1923. He retired in 1940 after 35 years of service. He lived in a house in Store Road, where he died on 25 June 1941.[36]

Rainey Park

This is a part of old Ballygunge, parallel to Store Road on the south, starting from Ballygunge Circular Road on the west and ending at Store Road near the military camps. Almost all the houses on this road were inhabited by Europeans, but the castle at Number 1 was a gift to Indira Devi Chaudhurani from her father Satyendranath Tagore, before her marriage in 1899. Like many houses in the vicinity, as in Mayfair Road and Bright Street, she lived here for some time and the property passed on to others.

Dum Dum

A part of Greater Calcutta now, Dum Dum is about four miles north-east from the centre of the city. In early times the site of Dum Dum seems to have been covered by an ancient forest—a home of wild buffaloes and tigers. In the eighteenth century Calcutta sportsmen established their Jockey Club and Refreshment Room (the 'bread and cheese bungalow') at the south corner of Sealdah, opposite the Baithakkhana, and thence went in search of tigers and wild boars at Dum Dum. The neighbourhood of Sealdah was the site of skirmishes between the armies of Clive and Nawab Siraj-ud-Daula on the foggy morning of 5 February 1757. The consequent treaty was signed at Dum Dum, where Clive later erected his country house.

Dum Dum as an artillery station dates back from 1783; but for many years it was only used in the cold weather. It subsequently remained the headquarters of the Bengal

Artillery until the year 1853. The presence of the artillery probably was the origin of the name, Dum Dum, or where there is the sound of gunfire.

The chief places of European interest in Dum Dum are the following:

ST. STEPHEN'S CHURCH

This was built in 1822 and consecrated by the Bishop Heber next year. The walls are covered with memorial monuments to officers of the Bengal Artillery.

In the Churchyard a tall column in progressive disrepair commemorates Colonel Thomas Deane Pearse, the trusted friend of Warren Hastings. The Colonel lies buried in the South Park Street Cemetery in Calcutta.

THE SMALL ARMS FACTORY

This is an old establishment, now taken over by the Government of India and still in production. The Old Bengal Artillery Officers' Mess was a fine bungalow close to the church, later used as a soldiers' club.

LORD CLIVE'S HOUSE

A description has been recorded by Bishop Heber in his Journals:

> November 1824—The Commandant, General Hardwicke, with whom we spent the day, resides in a large house, built on an artificial mound of considerable height above the neighbouring country, and surrounded by very pretty walks and shrubberies. The house has a venerable appearance, and its lower storey, as well as the mound on which it stands, is said to be of some antiquity, at least for Bengal, where so many powerful agents of destruction are always at work that no architecture can be durable,—and though ruins and buildings of apparently remote date are extremely common, it would perhaps be difficult to find a single edifice 150 years old. This building is of brick, with small windows and enormous buttresses. The upper storey, which is of the style usual in Calcutta, was added by Lord Clive, who also laid out the gardens and made this his country house.[37]

There are diverse opinions about the origin of the house, with sources suggesting that the house was built by either the Portuguese or the Dutch as a fortress-cum-godown. But other sources describe it as an observation post-cum-fortress built by the Nawab of Bengal. But it was Lord Clive, who renovated the house and laid out the gardens as Bishop Heber confirms. A stone tablet at the gate tells us that it was Lord Clive's Country House, 1757-60 and 1765-67.

The house stood on 126 *bighas* of land, with a large hall, five bedrooms, a wide *verandah* and two staircases. The house still stands near the junction of Jessore Road and

Nager Bazar. The house has fallen in disrepair and has become a squatters' colony after the partition of Bengal.

Close to the Church was Fairley Hall, the residence of Henry Lawrence in his early days in India.

Walter K. Firminger informs us that 'Not so many years ago Dum Dum enjoyed an evil reputation on account of cholera—one house in particular being known as "Cholera Hall".'[38]

In the early twentieth century Dum Dum started developing into an industrial district, with companies like Jessop and Company and the Gramophone Company Ltd. opening their workshops in the area.

Much greater glory was waiting for Dum Dum. On 13 April 1920, *The Statesman*, Calcutta, reported that the Government of India had selected Dum Dum as the airport of Calcutta. After the end of the First Wold War passenger aeroplanes had started regular air services in Europe and the USA. A large tract of land was selected for the new airport, an airstrip was cleared and hangars constructed in due course. The first plane to land at Dum Dum was a Havilland DH 9 with Major Blake and Captain McMillan as pilots, touching down on 12 August 1922. But regular passenger service through Dum Dum was started by the Dutch airline KLM in 1927 on their route from Amsterdam to Batavia.

On 2 February 1929, the Bengal Flying Club was formed in Dum Dum. This was the second flying club in India (undivided), the first being at Karachi. The club house was the Old Bengal Artillery Mess.

Dum Dum Airport has come a long way from the days of small planes landing on grass airstrips. There are separate International and Domestic terminals now, and it is now known as Netaji Subhas Chandra Bose International Airport.

Barrackpore

Fourteen miles north of Calcutta, Barrackpore on the river bank occupies an important niche in the history of India's Independence. The Great Mutiny against the English, later described as the First War of India's Independence, started here in 1857. The name probably came from army barracks situated in the area. According to tradition Job Charnock built a bungalow and a bazar grew up under his protection, before he moved downstream and settled in Calcutta. The Charnock legend owed its origin solely to the native name of Chanak. To quote from Rainey, 'Even the natives, whom Governor Charnock is reputed to have treated with great severity, have perpetuated his name by calling Barrackpore, where he had a *bangalah* and a small bazar, after him, Charnock or Chanak.'[39] This has been corroborated by other contemporary British historians.

Refuting the above theory Lord Curzon wrote:

But as a matter of fact Chanak is not only a common village name in Bengal (which it is thought may perhaps have been derived from Chanakya, the famous Minister of the great King Chandra Gupta), but it appears to have been the actual name of a native village on this very site, at a period when Job Charnock was still living far away at Patna, and before he had moved to Lower Bengal. A letter from the Court of Directors in England to Fort St. George, dated 14 December, 1677, is conclusive of this point: "It is ordered that if any ships shall go up to the said river as high as Hughley, or at least as Channock, etc."

Other and earlier evidence supports the same conclusion. The learned Pandit Hara Prasad Shastri read a paper before the Asiatic Society at Calcutta in December 1892, about an old Bengali MS. of the year AD 1495 describing a journey made by one Chand Saudagar on the Ganges at that date.

With a fleet of seven vessels he descended the river, and at this spot he is described as passing "Chanak". The same name appears as Tsjannok in much the same locality in a Dutch atlas of Bengal which I have seen, of the year 1678; and in an English map of Barrackpore, in the early part of the nineteenth century, the name Achanak is printed immediately south of the present railway station of Barrackpore. We may be confident, therefore, that this is the original name of the place, and that Job Charnock, even if he ever called and traded here, is at any rate not its eponymous hero.[40]

English troops were first quartered here in 1775, and till the Mutiny it was the principal garrison station of Calcutta, though it was stated to be the most unhealthy military station in Bengal. Civilians however did not think so; and with the establishment of the garrison station, bungalows built by Englishmen followed. The first of these was erected in February 1775. Ten years later, the Government appeared on the scene as owner; for Captain John Macintyre having offered, in April 1785, to sell a property of 220 *bighas* and two bungalows to the Government, either for the extension of the Cantonment or the convenience of the Commander-in-Chief, they were purchased with the approval of the Acting Governor-General, Sir John Macpherson, for the substantial sum of Rs. 25,000, in August of the same year, and the bungalows were handed over for occupation to the Commander-in-Chief. This house and grounds were the nucleus of the famous Barrackpore Park.

Lord Cornwallis, who succeeded Macpherson, was both Governor General and Commander-in-Chief, and it seems to have been in the latter capacity that he took possession of the bungalow. Lord Wellesley appropriated the house as the property of the Governor General in Council, on the retirement of Sir A. Clarke, the Commander-in-Chief, in 1801. Two days later the Governor General wrote a letter dated 27 June 1801, to Lady Anne Barnard:

I have been very well..., residing almost entirely at Barrackpore, a charming spot which, in my usual spirit of tyranny, I have plucked from the Commander-in-Chief.[41]

But Lord Wellesley was not satisfied with the old bungalow; again, without permission of the Court of Directors in England, he planned a magnificent palace at Barrackpore. We turn to the inimitable William Hickey's account:

> Not content with having works of such magnitude and unbounded expence on foot, he at the same time commenced a second palace at Barrackpore, almost rivalling in magnificence the Calcutta one, which he intended as a country residence for future Governor Generals as he could not expect it would be completed within his own reign. The grounds which of themselves were very pretty he laid out with extraordinary taste and elegance, upon different parts of which he erected a theatre, a riding-house, with probably the finest aviary and menagerie in the world, the two latter buildings being stocked with the rarest and most beautiful birds, and beasts equally uncommon, collected from every quarter of the globe.[42]

These were most certainly transferred to Barrackpore from Garden Reach, where Lord Wellesley wanted to shift the College of Fort William.

But at this point the Court of Directors intervened and placed a veto on the expenditure, and the building was stopped. In Lord Hastings' days all traces of Wellesley's intended palace were finally removed. As the original house had been dismantled, Wellesley had set up a temporary building to serve his needs as long as it took his dream palace to be erected. This new building was considerably enlarged by Lord Minto (1807-13). In Lord Hastings' time it took a final shape as the Governor-General's country seat.

But everything in Barrackpore had not been destroyed to make way for the great palace. Lord Valentia describes Barrackpore in 1803:

> The situation of the house is much more pleasing than anything I have yet seen. It is considerably elevated above the Hooghly river, on a very extended reach of which it stands: directly opposite is the Danish settlement of Serampore: on the sides are pagodas, villages, and groves of lofty trees. The water itself is much clearer than at Calcutta, and covered with the state barges and cutters of the Governor General.... . The park is laid out in the English style; and the house, at present unfinished, is well adapted to the climate, having a beautiful *verandah* on every side, and the rooms being on a very ample scale.... . Several of the bungalows belonging to the lines have been taken into the park, and are fitted for the reception of Secretaries, Aides-de Camp, and visitors...at his Excellency's request, I left Mr. Salt behind me to take views of the place.[43]

The house described by Valentia which appears in the drawing by Henry Salt published as a vignette at the head of Valentia's *Voyages and Travels,* was the new, temporary bungalow erected by Wellesley, while his new palace was being built.

Tom Raw (Sir C. D'Oyly) is very caustic at the expense of Lord Wellesley's unfinished structure:

> Here from the cares of Government released
> Our Indian Governors their ease enjoy,
> In pleasures by the contrast much increased
> Their intermediate moments they employ.
> Wellesley first stampt it his. He was the boy
> For making ducks and drakes with public cash,
> Planted a great house that time might not destroy;
> Built the first floor, prepared brick, beam, and sash,
> And then returned, and left it in this dismal hash.[44]

But the unfinished palace was not immediately dismantled. The next Governor General, Lord Cornwallis, issued instructions for the unroofed building to be covered in, but shortly afterwards he fell sick and died. The Acting Governor General, Sir George Barlow, did not carry out the instructions left by his predecessor. Lord Minto, the next Governor General, who liked Barrackpore, was anxious to get rid of the unfinished building. His successor, Lord Hastings (1813-1823) once contemplated to finish the structure at a reduced scale. Instead he devoted himself to the enlargement and completion of the present house. In his day the empty shell was finally pulled down, and Lady Hastings built a greenhouse or conservatory in its place.

The exact location of Wellesley's proposed palace continued to puzzle Calcutta topographers for a long time. Mrs. Graham, who came up the river to visit Barrackpore in 1810, said:

> When we came to the port of Barrackpore, the tamarind, acacia, and peepil tree, through whose branches the moon threw her flickering beams on the river, seemed to hang over our heads, and formed a strong contrast to the white buildings of Serampore which shone on the opposite shore. We landed at the palace begun by the Marquis Wellesley, but discontinued by the frugality of the Indian Company; its unfinished arches showed by the moonlight like an ancient ruin and completed the beauty of the scenery.[45]

According to old maps and accounts, the palace, and later the greenhouse, was situated on the banks of the river Hooghly; the greenhouse built by Lady Hastings also disappeared from the scene.

Now let us go back to the temporary house built by Lord Wellesley for his stay, while the palace was coming up. It consisted of three large rooms opening into a *verandah*. Sir

George Barlow, the Acting Governing-General, converted each corner of the *verandah* into a small room, greatly improving the comfort of the house. And this became the nucleus of the Barrackpore House. The house in this state can be seen in a watercolour drawn in 1808 by Edward Hawke Locker. The first Lord Minto, Governor-General (1807-12), loved the simple beauty of Barrackpore, and was glad that Wellesley's grand scheme had come to nothing:

> It would have been magnificent, I have no doubt, but in perfect contradiction with every purpose of the place. It would have been to come from Calcutta to Calcutta again; and you must have had the same multitude of troublesome attendants, and have lived the same full-dress intolerable life at your country house as in town. I am extremely glad it has been stopped.[46]

On yet another occasion, Minto wrote:

> Barrackpore surpasses all my expectations in the beauty of the ground, the beauty of the situation, and the comfort of its ways, compared to Calcutta. The grounds are a mixture of park and pleasure-grounds. They are laid out with the greatest judgement and taste, and their extent is very considerable. There is a great variety of fine timber and curious ornamental shrubs and flowering trees. Pools of water of very pretty forms and certain inequalities of surface have been artificially produced, but the real beauties consist in the rich verdure which covers the whole, the magnificent timber, and the fine river which forms one side of the place from end to end. Although it is a tide river, there is no mud on the sides; the grass extends to low watermark.... . The present house is what is called a bungalow or cottage, and was intended only as a makeshift while the great house was erecting. It is a cottage indeed, but a very considerable building compared with the European scale... . The *verandah* next the room is a charming apartment. It affords a long shaded, airy walk with a most beautiful prospect, and we find it an excellent eating-room. It is within forty or fifty paces off the water's edge. Besides this principal bungalow there are a number of smaller ones like neat Swiss cottages scattered about the lawn. These afford accommodation for aides-de-camp, guests, etc., etc. A better or more regular house will certainly be proper.[47]

But Lord Hastings (1813-23) carried out improvements, more than doubling its size and giving it its present form. The summer exodus to Simla was not there at the time, the Governor General had to spend the summer in Bengal, and Barrackpore became the summer residence of the Governor General. Bishop Heber, who came to Barrackpore on 28 October 1828, as a guest of Lord and Lady Amherst, writes with admiration:

The house itself of Barrackpore is handsome, containing three fine sitting rooms, though but few bedchambers. Indeed, as in this climate no sleeping rooms are even tolerable unless they admit the Southern breeze, there can be but few in any house. Accordingly that of Barrackpore barely accommodates Lord Amherst's family, and his Aides-de-Camp and visitors sleep in bungalows, built at some distance from it in the park. "Bungalow", a corruption of Bengalee, is the general name in this country for any structure in the cottage style, and only of one floor. Some of these are spacious and comfortable dwellings, generally with high thatched roofs, surrounded with a *verandah*, and containing three or four good apartments, with bathrooms and dressing-rooms enclosed from the eastern, western, or northern *verandahs*. The south is always left open.[48]

These bungalows in the Barrackpore Park had thatched roofs until 1863, when pucca structures were built.

Governors General and their families in succession have loved Barrackpore and spent their summers here; during Lord Auckland's stint in office, his sisters, the famous Misses Eden loved Barrackpore as is evident from their letters. Lord Dalhousie writes:

I spent Sunday, Monday, Tuesday and Wednesday at Barrackpore with Lady Dalhousie, went into Calcutta very early on Thursday morning, remained there Thursday, Friday

Figure 78: A view of Barrackpore Government House. Photo courtesy Calcutta Historical Society

and Saturday, and returned to the country on Saturday night "at e'en". We used to have a dinner party of twenty-five at Barrackpore on Tuesdays, one of fifty at Calcutta on Fridays. My Lady during the summer months had an evening dancing party once a month, and we had three very large balls at Calcutta, and one at Barrackpore.[49]

When Lady Dalhousie died at sea on her way to England in 1853, her husband was so grief-stricken that for two years he did not visit Barrackpore.

As the popularity of Barrackpore grew, a Royal Mail Coach was instituted by order of the Government between Calcutta and Barrackpore, carrying six passengers inside, and six out. Lady Charlotte Canning, wife of the Governor-General, Lord Canning, describing her first visit to Barrackpore, wrote (19 March 1856):

> The last ten or twelve miles of the road are as straight as an arrow, and bordered all the way with beautiful trees, planted in Lord Wellesley's time, mango, banyan, india-rubber, peepul—like white poplars—teak, with enormous leaves, laurel of several sorts, mimosas, tamarinds, etc. But it all looks poisonously green, and gives a notion of unwholesome damp, yet this is not all an unwholesome part of the country. The roads are pounded red brick, and the country brighter and richer in colour than anything European. We have a half-way house to which our horses are sent, and where we change the escorts, and the red and gold servants and soldiers looked bright and gay at this place.[50]

There was another means of transport to Barrackpore for the Governor General, viz. his fleet of colourful boats, pinnace or yachts (or in Bengali *budgerows*). The principal boat would be called *Sonamukhi* (golden face). Sir Charles D'Oyly, in his *European in India* (published in 1813), gave a coloured illustration of the Sonamukhi. According to contemporary records the state yacht was built by Warren Hastings of teakwood, sheathed with copper. It was a mixture of European and Oriental naval architecture, at a cost of Rs. 45,000. It was manned by thirty oars, but was too heavy to be rowed, and was commonly pulled by a number of towboats or sailed (having two masts) and tracked. More than half the boat was constructed so as to represent cabins, saloons, etc., with green venetians. It had a flat roof and awning. Its attendant *pheel cherra*, or elephant head, was a long narrow boat. It was pulled or paddled by boatmen in scarlet and gold livery, and had a small cabin in the afterpart of the boat. Another favourite boat was the *Mayurpankhee*. In Wellesley's time a new *Sonamukhi* was built, costing Rs. 47,000.

Official records from the early nineteenth century show that the State Boat Establishment, as it was called, was kept at Barrackpore, where additional ground was purchased in 1814 for its accommodation. With the advent of steam launches, the old boats were scrapped.[51]

Coming back to Lady Canning, we find that she had fallen in love with the Barrackpore House and Park, and came to make several improvements. She constructed the raised walk leading straight down from the south front of the house to the main landing-stage, and planted *poinsettias* along it, and placed a stone bench at the end; and she also made the terrace and pillared balustrade round the small Italian Garden on the same side, and planted the bamboos and the blue *convolvulus* behind it. Lady Canning also opened out the big banyan tree (previously closed by shrubs).

Lady Canning was a painter, and her watercolours and drawings of Barrackpore portray a vivid picture of her time there. These are now preserved at Harewood House, the seat of the Earl of Harewood in England. One of the watercolours depicts her sitting-room at Government House, Barrackpore, with its thirteen doors and three windows. 'I am getting so fond of this place,' she wrote in her journal on 22 October 1856. 'I believe it would look rather nice even as an English country-house, so marvellously it is improved by 450 yards of rose-chintz, a great many armchairs, small round tables, framed drawings, etc., & flowerpots in number.'[52] Other watercolous include 'The Garden Reach at Barrackpore, Near the main gate of the Park,' 'The Banyan tree,' 'The Verandah at Government House looking out on the river' (1856), 'The Burning Ghat at Barrackpore' (1857), her 'newly-laid out terrace' (1859).

Lady Canning went for a trip to Darjeeling with her drawing book and camera; on her return journey, she had a fever and reached Calcutta in a state of collapse. She died at the Government House, Calcutta, on the night of 18 November 1861. Her body was placed on a gun-carriage, drawn by six black horses, and taken to Barrackpore during the night.

Early next morning, as the rays of the sun shone over the river, Lady Canning was laid to rest in a grassy knoll in the private park, which was a favourite place for her days in Barrackpore. Only eleven people were present at the graveside. D'Oyly has recorded the scene at the graveside on 19 November 1861. The grief-stricken Governor-General thanked everyone present and walked back alone and locked himself in for an entire day.

Three days later he wrote the following tribute, which was subsequently placed upon the headstone of the grave:

Honours and praises written on a tomb are at best a vain glory; but that her charity, humility, meekness, and watchful faith in her Saviour will, for that Saviour's sake, be accepted of God, and be to her a glory everlasting, is the firm trust of those who knew her best, and most dearly loved her in life, and who cherish the memory of her, departed. Sacred to the Memory of Charlotte Elizabeth, eldest daughter of Lord Stuart De Rothsay, wife of Charles John, Viscount and Earl Canning, first Viceroy of India. Born at Paris 31 March 1817, Died at Calcutta 18 November 1861.

Earl Canning lived only for seven months after his wife's death. He died in England on 17 June 1862.

The enclosure of the tomb was protected by an iron railing, formed of the intertwined initials of Lady Canning (C.C) at the cost of the Government of India, and early in March 1862, previous to Lord Canning's departure, Bishop Cotton consecrated this spot, henceforth to be set apart, as the petition for consecration declared, 'for the families of the Governor Generals of India'.

'When all was concluded, he kindly greeted the few present; he turned to the Bishop and said, "I think the ground is large enough to justify consecration," and then walked slowly and alone to the desolate house hard by.'[53]

Lady Canning's sister, Louisa Lady Waterford, designed a marvellous monument which consisted of an immense marble platform ornamented with inlaid mosaic in the Agra fashion, and with a headstone rising at one end. When it was found to be damaged by the heavy monsoon downpours, there was a proposal to shelter it under a canopy of timber or stone.

The idea was however abandoned. In 1873 the original monument was transferred by Lord Northbrook, with the assent of the family, to St. John's Church in Calcutta, in the southern transept of which it stood till 1913. A simpler reproduction without the inlaid work, but with the same inscription, was erected above the grave.

The original monument made another migration in 1913, as the Church authorities thought that its great size blocked the south transept, which they desired to use as a chapel, and obtained the permission of the successors of Lord Canning to move it to the north portico of St. John's Church, where it stands today.

Lady Canning still lies in her grave in Barrackpore, in her favourite corner of the park, in the company of her husband's equestrian statue. The statue originally stood in front of the Government House, until removed from its pedestal after Independence, and some kindred spirit in the Government of West Bengal had the statue re-erected within the enclosure that surrounds Lady Canning's tomb.

Lady Canning's name lived on in Bengal in the shape of an Indian sweetmeat known as 'Ladykeny', a ball of milk-solids, flour and sugar, deep fried in syrup, to which she is reputed to have had a particular liking. The Government House had alterations in 1870 and 1903. After the shifting of the Capital to Delhi, it became the residence of the Governor of Bengal. After Independence Barrackpore House with the park was given to the Police Department, and the house has now become the Police Hospital.

BARRACKPORE PARK

The park, stretching over 250 acres, has been mentioned already in connection with the house. It had a vast menagerie with exotic animals. The Governor Generals' wives and guests had elephant rides in the park. There were fine trees and flower gardens, with bungalows for the park-keeper, staff, band masters and others. The park was gradually opened to the public. Lord Lytton lent the Viceregal Band Barracks as a Library and Reading Room to the Barrackpore Club in 1878. At a later date the members of the club were permitted to make, and to keep up lawn-tennis courts in the Viceregal grounds. In 1891 Lord Lansdowne gave leave to the Barrackpore Golf Club to establish links and play in the Park.

The Hall of Fame, a fine memorial hall, was erected by Lord Minto in 1813 'to the memory of the brave'. It contains tablets commemorating the officers who fell at the conquest of the Isle of France (Mauritius) in 1810 and of Java in 1811. In 1843 inscriptions were added by Lord Ellenborough to the officers who fell at Maharajpore and Punniar. The hall is said to have an extraordinary echo.[54]

Vast areas of the park have been converted into today's West Bengal Police Training Centre with large barracks and officers' quarters. The Parade Ground has been named after Mangal Pande, the hero of the Sepoy Mutiny in 1857.

THE ARMY AT BARRACKPORE

From its inception, Barrackpore was one of the major garrison towns in India. The Military Parade Ground was a witness to three abortive mutinies. The first was in 1824, when three Indian regiments, ordered from the Barrackpore Cantonment to the war in Burma, mutinied from dread of the Burmese climate, and caste prejudice against crossing the sea. The Governor General and Lady Amherst and the Commander-in-Chief, Sir E. Paget, hurried from Calcutta to quell the revolt. Lady Amherst has left a vivid description of the event in her journal:

November 1824. On the evening of October 31, General Dalzell informed Lord Amherst that a mutinous spirit has manifested itself among the troops in the cantonment, that the 47th Native Infantry had refused to march and had demanded increase of pay, and in short resolved to resist their officers. Early on the morning of the 1st, General Dalzell went up to the Commander-in-Chief, and before 3 O'clock that day himself and all his staff arrived at Barrackpore. Soon after, the bodyguard consisting of 300 men, went up in a boat to overtake General Cotton's regiment... . Some artillery also arrived from Dum Dum... . The cannon from Dum Dum was stationed in the park to fire over the pales on the insurgents, if necessary. Captain Macan and two other officers were sent to them. He addressed the mutineers in their own language in very conciliatory manner, endeavouring to persuade them of the folly and danger of persisting in their mutiny, and refusal to deliver up their arms. No argument availed. He then told them the dire consequence that must ensue, and that at his return without their laying down their arms, the signal would be given to fire upon them. Their ringleaders laughed at him, and on his report to the Commander-in-Chief, the signal was given. The mutineers instantly fled. The cannons fired several volleys afterwards, as did the musketry, four or five were killed & wounded, and many hundreds were taken prisoners. They fled in all directions, and were instantly dispersed. About 800 muskets and uniforms were found in the adjacent fields and roads. The Court-Martial sat immediately. The ringleaders (six) were hanged next morning. Many hundreds since have been found guilty and sentenced to death, but this was commuted to hard labour for fourteen years on the public roads. Five other ringleaders were executed afterwards, and one man whom the mutineers regarded as their Commander-in-Chief was hung in chains in front of the lines. Everyone of these unfortunate deluded wretched declared that their native officers had instigated them to mutiny by all sorts of means. To the Hindus they told them they would be compelled to eat beef, and to the Mussalmans, pork. All the officers (native) were dismissed the service and their guilt proclaimed at the head of every regiment in their native language.[55]

Another such mutinous situation was averted at Barrackpore when preparations were being made by Lord Dalhousie for the Burmese Expedition. The 38th Native Infantry declined to proceed by sea. The situation was tackled in a clever and lenient manner.

Five years later, the outbreak of the Great Mutiny, called Sepoy Mutiny, began here on the same Parade Ground. Everybody knows the background of the story of the new cartridge containing beef grease, which must be opened by mouth before loading into a musket. This was a great sacrilege to the Hindus. The problem could have been solved earlier, as Major General Hearsey, the officer in charge of this Bengal Division, states in a letter as early as 23 January 1857. He represented to Government the extreme difficulty of eradicating the notion which had taken hold in the mind of the Indian soldiers, and urged, as the only remedy, that despite the trouble and expense it would occasion, the sepoys should be allowed to obtain from the bazar the ingredients necessary to grease the cartridges.[56]

On Sunday 29 March 1857, Mangal Pande, a sepoy of the 34th Native Infantry, Bengal Army, appeared in front of the quarter-guard of the regiment at Barrackpore, calling for his comrades to join him in defending and dying for their religion and their caste. He was a man of character, but has been described to have acted under the influence of *bhang* or opium, but it is significant that General Hearsey speaks of his motivation as 'religious frenzy', not intoxication. He fired at a British sergeant, Hewson, but missed, and fired at the Adjutant, Lieutenant Baugh, and brought down his horse. Baugh's life was saved by a sepoy called Sheikh Phul, who restrained Mangal Pande and deterred others: around 400 men were passive onlookers. The regimental commander, Colonel Wheeler, ordered the Jemadar of the guard to arrest Mangal Pande, but he refused to do so. General Hearsey rode up and Mangal Pande turned his musket upon himself and pulled the trigger with his foot, but was not killed by the shot. He was arrested and the native regiments were ordered to lay down their arms. This was obeyed, meanwhile Mangal Pande was tried by a court-martial, condemned and hanged on 7 or 8 April 1857.[57] The Great Revolt started in Meerut in May.

After the Mutiny, Barrackpore lost its position as a garrison town, but in Independent India, the Indian Air Force has an important centre there. Near the Military Parade Ground is the Garrison Church.

There is a tradition that the present Church, dedicated to St. Bartholomew, and consecrated on the festival of that Saint by Bishop Wilson in 1847, was originally the Assembly Room of the station. The Chancel, Tower and the Western Porch are later additions, probably dating back to 1868. The Church organ was partly funded by Lord Dalhousie, the Font in the Transept was the gift of Lord Ellenborough.

Barrackpore today has changed. There is a memorial, of modern non-descript architecture, to Mohandas Karamchand Gandhi, who fell to an assassin's bullet on 30 January 1948 at New Delhi. A part of his ashes were strewn in the river Hooghly and the memorial called Gandhi Ghat came up in the precincts of the park. The park has been considerably built up to accommodate policemen; the town has become overcrowded, dirty and dingy.

The Upper Strand

THE OLD HOWRAH BRIDGE

In 1855-56 a committee was appointed to consider proposals for a bridge across the Hooghly to connect with the newly-opened terminus of the East Indian Railway at Howrah. Nothing came of the proposals until 1868 when the idea was revived. Sir W. Grey, the then Lt. Governor of Bengal, was in favour of a road-bridge at Armenian Ghat, but suggested a floating-bridge as a temporary measure.

The question of a more permanent structure was apparently connected to the question of a central railway station at Calcutta. The Government of India concluded that it would be wiser to construct a bridge higher up the river and bring passengers by rail into Sealdah. In the meanwhile they were prepared to give their support to the proposed floating road-bridge. In 1871 an Act was passed to enable the Lieutenant Governor, Sir G. Campbell, to construct, at the expense of Government, a bridge across the Hooghly, to fix tolls, and to appoint the Port Commissioners to carry out the purposes of the Act. In moving for leave to bring in this Bill, the Hon'ble Sir Ashley Eden stated that a contract had been entered into with Sir Bradford Leslie and that it was hoped that the bridge would be completed by the beginning of 1873, at a cost not exceeding £150,000. Several portions of the bridge were manufactured in England and put together in Bengal.

Figure 79: The Strand Calcutta

Figure 80: The Old Pontoon Howrah Bridge

The construction of this floating or pontoon bridge connecting Calcutta and Howrah was completed in 1874. An unfortunate accident by which two sections of the bridge were destroyed, occurred on 20 March 1874. The steamer *Egeria* broke from her moorings in the river, and came into collision with the bridge, damaging and sinking three pontoons, and completely destroying two hundred feet of the superstructure of the bridge, especially the main truss-girders which were twisted and torn to pieces. It was opened to the public on 17 October 1874, and proved to be of great utility, with men, animals, carriages and cars crossing over it daily. At specific notified periods the bridge was closed to traffic and the central portions were opened wide to let the river traffic move. It was described at the time as a structure of considerable novelty and originality in its design. It was dismantled after the new Howrah Bridge was opened to traffic in 1943.

THE NEW HOWRAH BRIDGE (RABINDRA SETU)

Built north of the old pontoon bridge, the majestic bridge with two towers at the ends is a marvel of engineering. It is one of the few cantilever bridges in the world. It was constructed by a British firm, Cleveland Bridge and Engineering Company. Two massive creeper cranes started out from either bank moving along the superstructure as they constructed it until they met in the middle and the halves were joined.

About 25,000 tons of steel went into the construction of the superstructure and most of the fabrication of the structural steelwork was carried out at Calcutta, mainly by the Martin Burn Ltd.

THE ROYAL MINT

The Strand Road north from the Chandpaul Ghat was laid out in the 1820s, reclaiming land from the river, which was receding westwards. The Old Mint, which was situated by the river between Hastings Street and Hare Street, moved to a new palatial building north of the New Howrah Bridge on the Strand in 1831. The New Royal Mint was built in a large space of ground and is really two separate mints, Silver and Copper; the former a much larger and finer building and built first. The foundations were laid in October 1823. It was designed and constructed by Major W.N. Forbes, R.E. of the Engineers, and took six years to build. The foundations were built up to the depth of a little more that 26 feet; so there is more brickwork below the ground than above it. The central portico facing Strand Road is said to be a copy of the Temple of Minerva at Athens, calculated down to half its dimensions. The building was completed in six years and opened in 1831. A watercolour painted by Thomas Prinsep in 1829 shows the external features of the New Mint, which were completed. Up to 30 April 1833, Rs. 24 lakh had been expended on the New Mint—eleven for the machinery and thirteen for the buildings. Another three lakh (mainly on building) were expended during the years 1833-40.

The year 1835 saw the passing of the Act establishing a uniform coinage with a British device for the whole of British India. The East India Company started to strike here coins in its own name without reference to the Mughal Emperor in Delhi.

The Copper Mint, opened in 1865, consists of a very large block of buildings, to the north-east of the Silver Mint. The Mint Master's Office, the Accountant's Office, the Record Room, Library, and Mint Master's residence occupy a block in front of the Copper Mint opposite to the Assay Office and Laboratory. In the centre of the Silver Mint is a quadrangle where the Bullion Vaults were located; and between the Silver and Copper mints was an extensive workshop including a brass and iron foundry, carpenters' shops and the blacksmith's shop. At its zenith the Royal Mint was the largest in the world. When employed to its full capacity, it could turn out 800,000 pieces of coins in a working day of seven hours. Besides Indian coins it used to supply copper coins to the Governments of Ceylon (Sri Lanka) and the Straits Settlements, and made medals for the Indian Army or to the order of private individuals.

In the Bullion Room there is a fine marble bust of Major General Forbes, who constructed the mint and presided over it for many years.

After a modern mint was constructed on Diamond Harbour Road, the hub of activity shifted there and the Royal Mint today stands abandoned, still a fine building. The Government has been considering a proposal to have a permanent Coin Museum in it.

References

1. Long, the Reverend James, in *Calcutta Review,* p. 287.

2. Losty. op. cit. p. 45.

3. Ibid. p. 48.

4. Long, in *Calcutta Review,* vol. XVIII, p. 430.

5. Quoted in *Thacker's Guide to Calcutta* 1906, p.110.

6. Curzon, Lord. *British Government in India,* vol. II, p. 22.

7. Firminger, W.K. op. cit. p. 110.

8. Dufferin, Lady, *Our Viceregal Life in India,* vol. II, pp. 240-41.

9. Bhandari, R.R. *The Blue Chip Railway B.N.R. 1887 to South Eastern Railway 1987,* Calcutta 1987, pp. 49-50.

10. Nair, P.T. *A History of Calcutta Streets,* p. 490.

11. Firminger, W.K. op. cit. p. 115.

12. Busteed, *Echoes from Old Calcutta.*

13. Firminger, W.K. op. cit. p. 117.

14. Cotton. op. cit. p. 703.

15. Firminger. op. cit. p. 119.

16. Ibid. p. 120.

17. 'Letters of Sir Edward Paget,' in *Bengal Past & Present*, vol. xxiv, 1922, p. 97.

18. Quoted in Firminger. op. cit. pp. 123-24.

19. Firminger. op. cit. p. 121.

20. Buckland, C.E. *Bengal Under Lieutenant Governors*, vol. ii.

21. Barry, John. *Calcutta Illustrated*, p. 159.

22. Cotton. op. cit. pp. 708-09.

23. Ibid. pp. 709-10.

24. Massey. op. cit. p. 23.

25. Cotton. op. cit. p. 728.

26. Ibid. pp. 729-30.

27. Nair, P.T. *A History of Calcutta Streets*, p. 670.

28. Cotton. op. cit. p. 714.

29. Firminger. op. cit. p. 126.

30. *Calcutta 200 Years*, p. 12.

31. Ibid. p. 15.

32. Ibid. p. 111.

33. Massey. op. cit. p. 23.

34. Birla, B.K. *A Rare Legacy*, Calcutta 1994, pp. 212-13.

35. Ibid. p. 118.

36. Nair, P.T. *A History of Calcutta Streets*, p. 384.

37. Heber, Bishop. *Journals*, quoted in Firminger. op. cit. p. 160.

38. Firminger. op. cit. p. 160.

39. Rainey, *Historical & Topographical Sketch of Calcutta*, p. 16.

40. Curzon, Lord. *British Government in India*, vol. ii, pp. 2-3.

41. Quoted in above, p. 6.

42. Quoted in Losty. op. cit. p. 80.

43. Ibid. p. 80.

44. *Tom Raw & Griffin*, p. 109, quoted in Curzon. op. cit. vol. ii, p. 9.

45. Quoted in Curzon, op. cit. vol. ii, p. 10.

46. Quoted in Losty. op. cit. p. 8.

47. Countess of Minto. *Lord Minto in India*, quoted in Curzon. op. cit. Vol. ii, p. 17.

48. Heber. op. cit. vol. I, p. 36.

49. Curzon. op. cit. vol. II, p. 21.

50. Quoted in Curzon. op. cit. vol. II, pp. 13-14.

51. Curzon. op. cit. vol. I, pp. 250-54.

52. Allen, Charles. *Glimpses of the Burning Plain*, London 1986, p. 34.

53. Firminger. op. cit. p. 233.

54. Cotton. op. cit. p. 810.

55. Amherst, Lord, quoted in Firminger. op. cit. pp. 226-27.

56. Taylor, P.J.O. *ed. A Companion to the Indian Mutiny 1857*, Delhi 1996, p. 39.

57. Ibid. p. 209.

Epilogue

Thus ends a journey that began more than five hundred year ago. Meandering along the muddy banks of the Hooghly, past the three little hamlets, we come to the time of Job Charnock's arrival and the British East India Company. That was the turning point in the history of this city. The little hamlets metamorphosed into a great metropolis. It was the kind of change that legends are made of. The legend still lives; it is the city of Calcutta. At first the Europeans settled around the Lal Dighi and traded at Sutanuti. Then the centre of gravity shifted.

After the Fort William was built and the Maidan came into being, the Esplanade Row area became the most fashionable place to live in. It housed all the important people, including the judges and attorneys of the Supreme Court.

Later on, with the building of the High Court, Town Hall and the Government House, the residential hub of European Calcutta moved to the east, to Chowringhee. The Bamun Basti and other slums surrendered to the onslaught of colonisation. Trade flourished, making Calcutta the place to be for the Europeans. They flocked to the rising capital, the land of plenty.

The new settlers moved south: Park Street and the adjoining areas, beyond Lower Circular Road, ultimately stopping at Elgin Road. Here ends Calcutta's 'White Town'. As for the Native Town, that too has an equally fascinating history of its own... Some year, some day, maybe it will be another book.

Index

Act of 1920, 126
Act XI of 1835, 55
Acton, Lord, 21
Adam, John, 116
Adam, Robert, 150
Adam, William, 50
Adaulat, Sudder Dewani, 178
Adi Saptagram, 4
administration, 31
Advocates Act of 1961, 142
Agarpara, 7
Agg, Lieutenant, 114
Agra, 84, 333
Agricultural and Horticultural Society, 51-52,
    301, 308-310
Ahmed, Aziz, 180
Akhtar-loony Begum, 280
Akra, 269-270
Alam, Shah, 32
Albert, Prince, 203
Alefounder, John, 35
Ali, Vizir (Wazir Ali), 288
Alinagar, 24, 302
Allahabad, 88, 271
    Allahabad Bank building
    historic association, 80-81
Allen Gardens, 207
Allen, C.G.H., 207
Allen, Sir Charles, 255
Altham, James, 83
Amherst, Lord, 329, 334
Amir, Shaikh Muhammad, 75, 146
Andaman islands, 154
Anderson, Bishop, 23
Anderson, G. Lane, 256
Anderson, John Alexander, 80
Anderson, William, 221
Andrew, Major, 315
Andrew, Yule, 90
Anstruther, Sir John, 43
Antoinette, Queen Marie, 116
ANZ Grindlays Bank, 38, 123, 238
Apcar, A.G., 236
Apcar, A.T., 208
Apcar, J.G., 236
Armenian Church graveyard, 7
Armenian Church of St. Nagareth (1724), 91-92
Armenian Club, 195
Armenian College, 194-195
Armenian Ghat, 103
Armenian Philanthropic Academy (1821)
    establishment, 195
Armenians, 24

Army and Navy Sports, 230-240
Arnot, William, 105
Arora, Lt. General J.S., 291
Arundel, Sir A.T., 208
Asansol, 106
Ashutosh Centenary Hall, 187
Asiatic Society (1784) of Bengal, 4, 10, 29, 35, 53,
    129, 183, 188, 190-193
    Buddhist manuscript, 192
    formation, 191
    funds problem, 193
    library, 191
    Museum, 192
    oil paintings, 192
    rare Asoka edict in Prakrit and Sanskrit
        written in Brahmi script, 192
    rare books, 192
Assam, 89
Auckland, Lord, 50, 129-131, 133, 214, 316, 330
Aurangzeb, 17
Aylmer Rose, 36-37
Azad, Maulana Abul Kalam, 319
Azim-us-Shan, Prince, 302

B.C. Roy Club House, 132
Bada Sikh Sangat Gurdwara, 3
Bagan, Hydra, 172
Baghdad, 271
Bahadur, Rai Buddree Das Mukkim, 104
Baillie, William, 14, 115, 137, 285, 299
Baker, Alfred, 313
Baker, Sir William Erskine, 122
Balasore
    factories, 4
Ball, Mother Mary Teresa, 213
Ballygunge, 165
Ballygunge Cricket Club, 317, 320
Ballygunge Maidan, Governor General's
    bodyguards' camp, 31
Balrampur, Maharaja, 76
Balthazar Solvyns, 269
Banerjee, Surendra Nath, 146, 160
Banerji, Dr. Lalit Mohan, 247
Banerji, Sir Gooroodas, 141
Bangalore, 230
Bangla Academy, 272
Bank of Bengal, 125-127
Bankshall Street or Marine House, 38, 42, 44-48,
    56, 101-102, 163, 316-317
    destruction and rebuilding, 46
    governor's residence, 46
    siege, 46
    Siraj-ud-Daula's army attack, 46

baptism, 8
Bar Library Club, 142
Bara Bagh, 207, 316-317
Baranagore, 7
Barker, Captain Robert, 282
Barlow, Sir George, 328-329
Barnard, Lady Anne, 326
Barrackpore, 31, 325-333
Barrackpore, Army, 334-336
Barrackpore Club (1878), 334
Barreto, Joseph, 102
Barretto, Louis, 93, 196
Barretto's Lane, 102-103
Barwell, Richárd, 64, 78, 298-299
Barwell's children's trust fund, 78-79
Basra, 271
Basu, Bhupendranath, 256
Basu, Binoy, 15-16
Batson, Stanlake, 45
Battle of Plassey, 44, 282
Bandar Abbas, 271
Baugh, Lieutenant, 335
Bayley, Sir S., 306
Bayne, Roskell, 25, 42
Beadon, Sir Cecil, 15, 308
Becher, Richard, 201
Beck Bagan Row, 245
Benares, 219, 288
Bengal British India Society, 102
Bengal Chamber of Commerce and Industry
    aim, 86
    building, 84
    donation, 84
    founder members, 84
    golden jubilee year, 84
    jubilee dinner, 84
    new building inauguration (1918), 84
Bengal Club, 50, 55, 72, 161, 223, 227
    Indian members, 226
Bengal Club Chambers, 220-221
Bengal Flying Club, 325
Bengal Gazette or Calcutta General Advertiser, 33-34,
    50, 265
Bengal Harkaru, 50, 56
Bengal Jockey Club, 218, 270
Bengal Landholders' Association, 197
Bengal Legislative Council, 78, 80, 84
Bengal Military Club or Bengal United Service
    Club, 185
Bengal National Chamber of Commerce and
    Industry, 104
Bengal Pilot Service (1669), 44
Bengal Presidency, 43, 59

Bengali revolutionaries, 15-16, 319
Benthal, Sir Paul, 86, 89
Benthall, Sir Edward, 89
Bentinck, Lady William, 196
Bentinck, Lord William Cavendish, 50, 100, 128, 262
Bepin Behari Ganguly Street, 99
Beresford, Lord William, 70, 270
Bernard, Joseph, 253
Bhadrachalam, 230
Bahadur, Nawab Saadat Ali Khan, 250
Bhaduri, Sisir Kumar, 272
Bhagat Singh Udyan, 247
Bhamun Bustee, 246, 250
Bhattacharya, Bikash, 147
Bhoop Bahadur of Cooch Behar, Maharaja Sir Nripendra Narayan, 193
Bhowanipore, 105
Bhowanipore Military Cemetery, 261
Bible Society Building, 177
Bibliotheca Indica, 192
Bihar, 233
Bikaner, 88
Binoy-Badal-Dinesh Bagh East (BBD Bagh), 15, 63
Birch, John Brereton, 304
Bird, Sir Wilberforce, 242
Biren, Sir, 235
Birkmyre Hostel Club, 215
Birla Park, 322
Birla Planetarium, 272
Birla, B.K., 323
Birla, Ghanashyam Das, 322
Bishop's College, 251
Bishop's Palace, 242-243
Bishopric of Calcutta, 1813, 272
'black acts' agitation, 102
Black Hole tragedy, 19-21, 25, 27, 41
Blackwood, 87
Blair, Lieutenant, 131
Blanford, Henry F., 1
Blechynden, Kathleen, 13, 184
boat races (1813), 134
Bogden Garden, 95
Bombay, 271
Bonaparte, Napoleon, 101, 288
Bonnerjee, W.C., 210
Boscolo, F.A., 169
Bose, J.N., 319
Bose, Netaji Subash Chandra, 22, 63
Bose, Sir Jagadish Chandra, 146
Bose, Sir S.M., 319
Botanical Gardens, 297, 298
Botanical Survey of India, 181
Bourchier, Robert, 73
Bow Bazar, 3, 49, 96, 99
Bower, Polly, 90
Bowman, A.H., 177
Box, Mrs., 235
Brabourne, Lord, 94
Brabourne Road or Biplabi Trailokya Maharaj Sarani, 75, 79, 92
Brahmachari, Sir U.N., 192, 202
Brahman Nandakumar bribery case, 32-33, 74
Bridge, Cleveland, 338
Brigade Parade Ground, 277-278
Bristol Hotel, 166
Bristow, John Charles, 213
British Club, 185
British Constitution, 58
British Indian Association, 102
British Indian Street, 101-102

British Library, 65
British Museum, 52
Brohier, Captain, 24, 284
Brooke, William Augustus, 303, 308
Brown, David, 58, 201
Brown, Jimmy, 249
Brown, Lord Ulrich, 270
Browne, William Adolphus, 79
Bryce, Dr. James, 55
Buckingham House, 32, 65, 109, 119, 123, 136, 138-139, 147, 150
Buckingham, James Silk, 55
Buddha, Gautama, 130
Burial Ground Road (later Park Street), 95
Burke, W.S., 34, 53
Burma, 158, 209, 288
Burman, Subir, 124
Burmese Pagoda, 130
Burra Bazar jail, 265
Burra Bazar Setts, 81
Burrows, Sir Frederick, 158
Burton, 271
bustees, 245, 250
Bysacks,
    founding fathers of Calcutta, 282

Cable, Ernest, 88
Cairo, 271
Calcutta Amateur Theatrical Society or CATS, 206
Calcutta Chamber of Commerce, 84
Calcutta Club, 170, 256-258, 272
Calcutta Collectorate, 29, 40-41
Calcutta Corporation, 54, 72, 84, 90, 94, 101, 107, 113, 145-147, 163, 175, 206, 232
Calcutta Cricket Club (1825-26), 131-132, 279, 320-321
Calcutta Derby Stakes, 1842, 270
Calcutta Directory, 63, 110, 190, 252
Calcutta Exchange, 61
    number of lines and subscribers, 54-55
Calcutta Football Club, 279, 321
Calcutta Free School, 195-196
Calcutta Gate Road, 130
Calcutta Gazette, The, 35, 43, 56-57, 95-97, 88, 100, 105, 109, 136, 174, 207, 287, 309, 312
Calcutta Golf Links, 317
Calcutta Historical Society (1907), 21, 98
Calcutta Improvement Trust, 80, 92-94, 103
Calcutta Light Horse Club, 210
Calcutta Magazine, 70
Calcutta Maidan, 217
Calcutta Plan of 1742, 14
Calcutta Port Commissioners, 44
Calcutta Port Improvement Act of 1870, 44
Calcutta Port Trust, 44
Calcutta Race Course, 269-272
Calcutta Review, 73, 248
Calcutta Rowing Club (1858), 134-135
Calcutta School of Planning, 209
Calcutta Society for Prevention of Cruelty to Animals (CSPCA), 15, 65
Calcutta South Club, 251
Calcutta Stamp Act, 51
Calcutta Stock Exchange, 79
Calcutta Stock Exchange Association (1908), 81
Calcutta Swimming Bath (1887)
    opening, 134
Calcutta Swimming Club, 134
Calcutta Traders Club, 15
Calcutta Turf Club or Royal Calcutta Turf Club, 42, 270

Camac, Burges, 207
Camac, Jacob, 207
Camac, William, 207
Camac Street, 207-211, 215, 245-246
Cameron, Major General, 151
Campbell, George, 183
Canabletti, 192
Canada, 186
Canning, Lord, 112, 331-333
Canning Street or Murgihatta Street, now Biplabi Rashhephari Basu Sarani, 87-91
Canning Town, 1
Cape of Good Hope, 97
Carew, 213
Carey, Dr. William, 61, 134, 309
Carmichael, Sir Thomas David Gibson, 256
Carnac, John, 258
Carnduff, Sir W.H., 274
Cartier, 303
Casanova, Jacques, 95
Chakravarti, P.B., 141
Chambers, Sir Robert, 135-136, 141
Chandernagore, 64, 74
Chandi goddess, 3
Chandra, Gopal, 232
Chandra, Sarat, 246
Chapel, St. George, 274
Chaplain, 190
Chapuzet, Anna-Maria Apollonia, 116
Charity School, 73-74, 104, 195
Charlotte, Lady, 331
Charnock grave digging, 10
Charnock Place, 38, 41, 84
Charnock, Job, 4-5, 17, 91, 114, 325-326
Charnock's Mausoleum at St John's Church, 8-9, 117
Chartered Bank Building, 88
Chatterjee International Centre, 227
Chatterjee, Bankim Chandra, 146
Chatterjee, Benoy K., 227
Chatterjee, Dr. S.C., 246
Chatterjee, Dr. Subir, 246
Chatterjee, N.C., 237
Chaudhuri, Jogesh Chandra, 320
Chaudhuri, Sir Ashutosh, 141, 256, 320-321
Cheese, Michael, 116
Chelmsford, Viceroy Lord, 271
Chhiattarer Manvantar, 32
China, 89, 97, 180
China Bazar, 91, 94
Chinnery, George, 141, 192
Chitpore Road, 3, 95-99
Chittagong English trading centre, 7
Chittagong port, 3
cholera,
    European community death toll, 31
Choudhurani, Indira Devi, 214, 252, 254, 321, 323
Chowdhury, Maharaja Suryyakanta Acharyya, 197
Chowdhury, Prematha, 319, 322
Chowringhee, 4, 32, 37, 41, 89, 100, 122, 160, 165, 221, 236-237
Chowringhee Gate, 278
Chowringhee Lane, 181
Chowringhee Mansion, 187-188
Chowringhee Road or Jawaharlal Nehru Road, 72, 169, 177, 211, 218, 220, 243, 264, 271
Chowringhee Square, 56, 163
Chowringhee Street, 43
Chowringhee Theatre (1813), 68, 204, 237, 240-242
Christ, Jesus, 10, 216

Christianity, 8
Church Committee AD 1911, 251
Church Lane, 39, 41, 48-49, 53, 117, 122-123
Church of England, 58
Churchill, Winston, 156, 168
Circular Road or *Bahar Sarak*, 245
Civil Rights Act of 1964, 206
Clarke, Captain F., 271
Clarke, Longueville, 51, 55
Clarke, Sir A., 326
Clavering, General Sir John, 67, 105-106, 195, 198
Clavering, Miss, 299
Clerihew, William, 275
climate or weather, 5, 31
Clive Ghat Street, 81, 88
Clive Lord, 24, 32, 81, 104, 137, 210, 258, 282, 323
Clive Row, 81, 87, 89-91
Clive Street, 14, 38, 42
College of Fort William (1800), 56-57, 153, 192
    curriculum, 59
    foundation, 58
    objectives, 58
    opening, 59
    Governor General Council meeting minutes, 58
College Street, 49
Collins, Capt., 165
Colombo, 112
Colvin, Alexander, 116
Colvin's Bazar, 245
Combermere, Lord, 288
Committee of Fortifications, 282
Comptroller General and Deputy Comptroller office, 45
Consort, Prince, 203
Coomer, Nun, hanging, 34
Coote, Sir Eyre, 104
Corkscrew Lane, 109
Cornwallis, Lord, 31, 114, 140, 207, 232, 328
Corporation Street (Surendra Nath Banerjee Road), 145
Corrie, Archdeacon, 219
Cossim Bazar, 4, 20, 83
Cotton, Bishop, 333
Cotton, Evan, 110, 268
Cotton, H.E.A., 33, 165, 202, 206, 236, 242
Cotton, Sir Henry, 236
Council Chamber, 78
Council House, 32, 109, 136-138, 150
Council House Street, 56, 57, 60, 66, 80, 109-11, 113, 119, 123, 125
Cox, Richard Waite, 316
Creek Lane, 5
Creek Row, 5
Cricket Association of Bengal, 132
Criterion Hotel, 46
Crouching Tiger Fort, 117
Crown Court, 128
Cruttenden, George, 116
Cuddalore, 104
Curzon Park, 163, 264
Customs House, 25, 27, 29, 41
Customs House Wharf, 25
Curzon, Lord, 13, 15, 22, 25-26, 29, 45, 52-53, 84, 109-110, 117, 119, 122, 152, 160, 211, 267-268, 288, 300, 311, 325
cyclone, 1864, 48

D'Oyly, Sir Charles, 14, 25, 75, 84, 274, 306, 321
Darbhanga, Maharaja, 15, 246, 256
Dacca or Dhaka, 42, 173-174, 257
    factories, 4

da Costa, Louis, 284
Dacre, 293
Dacres Lane, 101
Dalhousie Institute (1865), 14-15, 57, 62, 177
Dalhousie, Lord, 42, 61, 130-131, 205, 305, 330, 335
Dalhousie Square (B.B.D. Bagh East), 14-15, 26, 38, 40, 56, 62, 67, 71-73, 76, 84, 94, 96, 103-104, 142, 157, 292
Dalhousie Street, 203, 246
Dalhousie Testimonial Fund, 15
Damascus, 271
Daniell, Thomas paintings, 14, 21, 25, 36, 63, 74, 77, 81, 105, 115, 137-138, 165
Daniell, William, 36, 192, 269
Darjeeling, 72, 171, 215, 221, 332
Das, Bhuban Mohan, 252
Das, Deshbandhu Chittaranjan, 123
David, Maghan, 94
Davies, Thomas Henry, 36, 66
Davis, Samuel, 269
Day, Sir John, 66
de Grandpre, M., 138
de Mevell, Martin Boutant, 104
De Souza, Sir Walter, 72
de St. Valentine, Anna Maria Apollonia Chapuzet, 35, 123
Deb, A.K., 236
Deb, Maharaja Nabakrishna, 114
Deb, Raja Radha Kant, 192
defamation case (1780), 34
Dehee Birjee, 253-255
Dehra Dun, 88
Delhi, transfer of capital (1912), 78, 121, 134, 158, 271, 280, 306, 311, 330
den Broucke, Van, 3
DeRothsay, Lord Stuart, 332
Derozio, Henry Louis Vivian, 201
Desouza, Sir Walter, 63
Devi, Prativa, 322
Devi, Swarnakumari, 319
Dey, Mukul, 184, 187
Dey, Ramdayal, 143
Dhaka High Court, 141
Dhakuria Lakes (Rabindra Sarovar), 133
Dhar, Sanat, 86
Dharamtolla Street (now Lenin Sarani), 119, 160, 163, 225
Dharamtollah Tank, 160, 264
Dickens, Charles, 261
Dickens, Lt., 261
Diemer, Christian, 201
Doljatra festival, 12
Doss, Baboo Rajchunder, 128
Doughty, William, 56
Douglas, Melvyn, 180
Doveton Protestant College, Madras, 194
Doveton, Capt. John, 194
Down, Alexander, 315
Drake, Roger, 20
Dublin, 213
Dufferin, Lady, 295
Dufferin Road, 229
Duke of Connaught, 268
Duke of Cumberland, 285
Duke of Edinburgh (Queen Victoria's second son), 306
Duke of Wellington, 288
Dum Dum, 31, 87, 323-325, 334
Duncan House, 88
Dundas, Henry, 173
Dunkin, Sir William, 135, 217

Dunlop India Ltd., 196-198
Dunlop, John Boyd, 196
Dutt, Gurusaday, 323
Dutt, Prosunno Coomar, 193
Dutt, Russick Lall, 218-219
Dutt, Woody Chand, 219
Dutta, Michael Madhusudan, 143
Dutta, Ram Das, 71
Dutta, Sagar, 55

Earl of Minto, 100
East Bengal, 2
East Bengal Club, 279
East India Company, 4-5, 12, 22, 31, 40, 44, 51, 54-55, 61, 72, 81, 90, 97, 104, 111-112, 115, 125, 128-129, 142, 219, 258-259, 265, 274, 284-285, 306, 339
East India Company's criminal court, 102
East India Railway, now Eastern Railways, 25, 27-29, 42
East Wick, Edward B., 70
East, Sir Edward Hyde, 49, 140
Eden Gardens Cricket Ground, 131
Eden, Fanny, 130
Eden Gardens, 54, 128-134, 320-321
Eden, Miss Emily, 155
Eden, Sir Ashley, 15, 78, 133, 337
Edward VIII, King (Prince of Wales), 107, 154, 251, 257, 270
Elgin, Lord, 157
Elizabeth, 9, 111
Elizabeth, Charlotte, 332
Elizabeth, Lady Sarah, 152
Elizabeth II, Queen, 216, 270
Ellenborough course, 271
Ellenborough, Lord, 152, 334, 336
Elliot, Sir C., 306
Elliot, Sir Charles A., 146
Elliot's Tank, 264
Ellis, 65
Enemy Property Act, 88
English arrival in 1651, 7
    called *nabobs*, 30
    interest in Bengal, 17
    Mughal Fauzdar of Hooghly attack, 7
English Club House, 318
English laws, 34
Englishman, The, newspaper, 55-56, 90
Emmerson, Sir William, 107, 268
Esch, Vincent, 226, 268-269
Esplanade, 14, 35, 43, 66, 100, 146, 160-165
Esplanade Mansions, 66, 160
Esplanade Row, 24, 32, 74, 124, 130, 139, 150, 217
Europeans
    Chowringhee area, 32
    Mughal culture adoption, 30
    rainy season weather killer, 31
    watching dancing girls perform a native song, 30
European artists arrival, 35
European Ballygunge, 318-319
European Burial Ground digging, 8, 10
European sailors, 8
European traders, 30
Exchange Gazette, The, 61
export warehouse, 45
Eyles, Maria, 10
Eyre, Charles, 9-10
Ezra, Elias David Joseph, 93-94
Ezra, Sir David, 160, 180, 185-186

Fairlie Place, 28-29, 38, 42-43

Fairlie, William, 43
famine (1770), 32
Fancy Lane, 110-113
Faroqui, Sri K.G.M., 257
Fay, Mrs. Eliza, 123, 286, 294, 303
Fayrer, Dr., 301
Fayrer, Sir Joseph, 234
Fazal, Abul, 3
Fenwick's Bazar, 175
Fergusson, W.F., 218
Fiebig, Frederick, 14, 65
Figgis, A.W., 54
Finlay, Kirman, 80
Firpo, Mrs., 252
Firmeirger, Walter K., 21, 98, 161, 264, 298, 303, 325
first postage stamp (1854), 39
First World War, 89, 210, 248, 251, 279, 325
first horse-drawn carriage (1740), 31
first war of India's independence, 325
Fitzgerald, Capt., 129
Foley, J.H., 278
Forbes, Lieut N., 219
Forbes, Major General W.N., 273-274, 338, 339
forgery case, 33-34
Forresti, Theodore, 14
Foster, Sir William, 268
Frampton, Sir George, 268
Francis, Sir Phillip, 32, 64, 77, 78, 81, 127-128, 298, 304-305, 313
Frankland, William, 211-212, 303
Fraser, James Baillie, 14, 65, 75, 97, 119, 146, 157
Fraser, Sir Andrew, 15
Free School Society (1789), 73, 195
Free School Street, 76, 193-196
freedom of press, 49, 50, 55
Freemasons' Hall, 193-194
French interests, 17
Fiebig, Frederick, 266
Friend, Capt. Curling, 111
Friend, Mary Ann, 111
Friends of India, The, 100

GPO, Philatelic Bureau, 40
Galstaun Park or Nizam's Palace, 207-208, 251-255
Galstaun, J.C., 195, 208, 216, 218, 250-251
Galstaun, Rose Catherine, 251
Gandhi, Mohandas Karamchand, 319
Gandhi, Mrs. Indira, 227
Ganesh Chandra Avenue, 104
Ganesh Chandra Chunder, 104
Ganga, 129, 245, 292
garden houses construction, 32
Garden Reach, 7, 31, 293-297, 327
Garrick, David, 96, 184
Garstein House, 53-54
Garstin, Colonel J., 145
Garstin, Edward, 145, 219
Garth, Sir Richard, 235
Geidt, Justice, 255
General Post Office, 1868, 17, 22, 25-27, 29, 38, 40-41, 46-47
Geological Survey of India, 181-182, 186
George V, King, 76, 107, 128, 154, 157, 185, 268, 270
German Club, 240
German Musical Club (1872), 195
Ghafoor, Abdul, 271
Ghat Armenian, 336
Ghosal, Janaki Nath, 319
Ghose, Sir C.C., 237

Ghosh, Babu Ram Gopal, 146
Ghosh, Girish Chandra, 102
Ghosh, Monohar, 3
Ghosh, Ramgopal, 102
Ghosh, Sir Chunder Madhah, 141
Ghosh, Sri Hari, 3
Gibbon, 105
Gidhour, Maharaja of, 250
Gigantic Granary, Bankipore, Patna, 54
Gillanders House, 313
Global Trust Bank, 223, 264, 282
Goa, 7
Gobindapore, 3-4, 17, 97
Goenkas, 88
Goethal, Archbishop Paul, 93, 245
Gokhale, Gopal Krishna, 257
Goldborne, Miss Sophia, 200, 259, 286
Goldborough, Sir John, 17
Gooptu, Dr. Samaresh, 232
Goswami, Baboo Hem Chander, 177, 203
Goswami, Raghu Ram, 203
Gough, Lt. Gen. Sir Hugh, 152
Gouripore (Assam), Raja, 319
Gourlay, W.R., 256
Government House (Raj Bhavan), 62, 74, 147-160, 287-288
Government Place East, 63, 66-67, 100-101
Graham Street, 234
Graham, C.A., 199
Graham, Maria, 78
Graham, Robert, 234
Graham, Thomas, 234
Grand, Francis, 312
Grand, George Francis, 116
Grand Hotel, 169-175, 208
Grand, Madame, 312
Grand, Mrs. Catherine, 64-65
Grant, Charles, 105
Grant, Colesworthy, 15, 63, 65, 141
Grant, Sir John Peter, 209
Granville, Walter B., 39, 140, 182
Great Eastern Hotel, 68-72, 163
Greenlaw, Charles Beckett, 145
Grey, Sir William, 44, 49, 306, 336
Griffiths, 319
Grove, D.W., 171-172
Gupta era, 3
Gupta, Badal (Sudhir), 15-16
Gupta, Behari Lal, 252
Gupta, Dinesh, 15-16, 232
Gupta, K.G., 322
Gupta, King Chandra, 326
Gymkhana, 1910, 317

Haksar, A.N., 230
Haldia Port, 44
Hall, P.N., 221
Halliday, F.L., 185
Halsey, Henry, 213
Hamilton, Alexander, 5, 8, 19, 23
Hamilton, Solomon, 253
Hamilton, William, 10
hanging cases, 33-34
Haque, Fazlul, 252
Hardinge, Lord, 65, 157
Hare Street, 38, 46, 53-56, 113, 122, 163
Hare, Dr., 65
Hare, John, 49
Hare, L., 235
Hare, David,
    watch-maker, 49-50, 53, 122
Harrington, John Herbert, 234, 236

Harrington Street, 190, 208, 233-236, 264
Harrison Road (Mahatma Gandhi Road), 3, 84, 87
Hart, Mother Mary Delphine, 214
Hartford Lane, 180
Hardwicke, General, 324
Hastie, William, 145
Hastings Bridge, 292
Hastings House, 309-313
Hastings Street (now Kiran Shankar Roy Road), 39, 109, 112-114, 119, 122-124, 138
Hastings, Mrs. Warren, 303, 315, 328
Hastings, Warren, 13, 31-36, 41, 45, 64, 66, 77, 81, 95, 97, 114, 123, 128, 137-138, 150, 154, 192, 285, 288, 298, 303-305, 310, 327-328, 331
Havell, E.B., 187, 209
Hearsey, Maj. General, 335
Heber, Bishop, 212-213, 272, 286, 299, 324, 329
Hebrew, 198
Heilgers, F.W., 88-89
Henckell, Tilman, 315
Heritage Building, 41
Hickey, James Augustus, 50
Hickey, John Augustus, 265
Hickey, Thomas, 269
Highfield, H.G, 179
Hindu College (1817) or Presidency College, 140, 153
Hodges, William, 269, 286
Hogg, Sir Stuart, 175
Holden Cruttenden, Eduard, 43
Holdwell, 46
Holland, Thomas H., 10
Holland, William, 173
Holmwood, Justice H., 239, 255-256
Holwell, John Zephania, 13, 20-21, 41, 46, 63
Holwell Monument, 14, 78, 81
Homage Trust, 147
Hong Kong, 180
Honon, Moung, 130
Hooghly, 4, 105, 262
Hooghly bridge, 129
Hooghly river, 3-4, 7, 17, 44, 112, 197, 210, 264, 292, 326-327
hookah
    Europeans enjoying, 30
Hotel Continental, 169
House of Commons Report, 265
Howrah bridge, 44, 94, 107
Howrah station, 42, 44, 75, 94, 229
Humayun Place, 172-173
Hume, James, 204
Humphry, Ozias, 35
Hungerford Street, 202-203
Hyde, Archdeadon, 112
Hyde, Chaplain H.B., 10, 117
Hyde, John, 142
Hyde, Judge, 64, 135
Hyderabad, 308

Ibbetson, Sir Denzil, 208
ICI (Imperial Chemical Industries) House, 228
Ikramullah, Begum Shaista, 214
Ilbert Bill, 153
Imhoff, Baroness, 35-36, 123, 138, 315
Imhoff, Charles, 308
impeachment,
    Elija Impey, 34
Imperial Legislative Council, 78
Imperial Library,
    (now National Library), 52-53, 158, 163
Imperial Secretariat (1880), 110, 113, 117-119, 122-123

Imperial Tobacco Company, 43, 89
Impey, Sir Elija, 32-34, 64, 128, 134-135, 140-142, 196, 212, 215
Import and Export House Establishment, 81
India Exchange Place, house of Birlas, Kotharis and others, 80
India Patent Office, 46
Indian Daily News (1924), 56
Indian Gazette, The, 45, 56
Indian Museum, 182-183
    birth, 192
indigenous education
    in Bengal, 50
Indira
    (Tagore's niece), 322
Indo-American trade, 48
Infants School, 198
Inland, Stewart, 293
insane Hospital or Lunatic Asylum, 261
institution of divorce, beginning, 123
Iran society, 184, 187
Ishaque, Dr. M., 184
Ispahan, Iran, 72
Israel, 186
ITC (India Tobacco Company), 220, 230

Jackson Ghat Road, 90, 91
Jackson, Louis, 206
Jafar, Mir, 24, 32, 198, 302
James, Bishop, 219, 272
Jan Bazar, 195
Jang, Nawab Dilawar, 139, 150
Japan, 106
Japanese Club, 249
Jardine, David, 89
Java, 97
Jellicoe, 229
Jessore, 1
Jewish Girls School, 198-199
Jewish synagogue, 93-94
Jharia, Raja, 252
Jockey Club, 323
John Bull in the East, 55
John Palmer's House in Lal Bazar, 97-98
John Zacharia Kiernander, 104
John, Elton, 36
John's, St., 115
Johnson, Begum, 81, 117
Johnson, Chaplain, 116
Johnson, Reverend Ralph, 119, 277
Johnson, Reverend William, 83, 114
Johnson, Richard, 66, 315-316
Jones, Sir Edward Burne, 274
Jones, Sir William, 35, 134, 192, 200, 295, 315
Journal of the Asiatic Society of Bengal, 192
Jyotirindranath, 180

Kadambari, 180
Kala Mandir, 238
Kali, 3
Kali temple, 292, 297
Kalighat, 3, 24
Kalighat temple, 100
Kalikata, 3-4, 17
Kaloos, Aratoon, 194
Kanga, D.P.M., 226
Kar, Chintamani, 184
Karachi, 271, 325
Karnani Mansions, 193
Kassia Bagan Bustee, 252
Kaye, Sir John William, 204
Keddleston Hall, Derbyshire, 150

Keddleston, Lord, 150-151
Keighley, 114
Keir, Archibald, 134
Khan, Ali Verdi, 83
Khan, Fouzdar Nawab Shaista, 4
Khan, Ibrahim, 4
Khan, Mirza Asadullah, 194
Khan, Mohammed Reza, 32, 113, 138, 139
Khan, Nawab Golam Hosain, 20
Khudiram Anushilan Kendra, 132
Khulna, 1-2
Kidderpore, 31, 63-64, 262, 293, 297-298, 301
Kidderpore House, 298-300
Kidderpore Road, 262, 271
Kier, W.L., 273
Kiernander, John K., 104-105, 259
Kiernander, John Zachariah, 200, 253
Kiernander, R.W., 253
Kiev, Chicken, 238
Kilburn and Company Building, 43
Kindersley's letters from the East Indies, 30-31,
Kipling, Rudyard, 161, 201
Kitchener, Lord, 208-209, 278, 288
Kitson, Sidney, 181
Knight, Hugh, 312
Knight, Robert, founder of *The Statesman*, 167
Knowles, Sheridan, 62, 68
Kumar, Maharaja Nanda, 142
Kyd, Alexander, 184, 298
Kyd, Lt. Col. Robert, 184, 187, 297-298
Kyd, James, 184
Kyd Street (Dr. M. Ishaque Road), 180-185, 187

L'Etang, Chevalier Antoine, 116
La Martiniere Schools, 247-249
Lafont, Father E., 54
Lahiri, Dipak, 203
Laidlaw, Whiteaway, 99
Lake Club, 134
Lal Bazar, 5, 32-33, 41, 63, 95-99, 104, 193
Lal Bazar jail, 265
Lal Bazar Street, 75, 96, 107
Lal Dighi or Lal Bag, 5, 12-13, 17, 19, 21, 32, 44, 46, 56-57, 63, 65, 71, 74, 77, 96, 104, 113, 124, 195
Lambert, George, 19, 23
Land Acquisition Act, 126
Lansdowne, Lord, 133, 278
Larkin, John Pascal, 55
Larkin's Lane, 63, 66, 112
Larkins, William, 66
Law, Doorga Churn, 146
Law, Sir Edward Fitgerald, 255
Lawrence, Henry, 325
Lawrie, Balmer, 89
Le Maistre, 33, 201
Leach, Mrs Esther, 68, 204, 241
Lee Road, 252
Lee, Harry, 252
Le Gallais, Francis, 64
Leslie, Matthew, 253
Leslie, Sir Bradford, 336
Leuba, Favre, 70
Leveson-Gower, Frederick, 116
Lewes, John Herbert, 79
Lindsay Street, 48, 173-175, 177, 195, 264
Lindsay, D., 256
Lindsay, Robert, 173
Little Russell Street, 233-234
Little Sisters, 245-246
Little, J.H., 21
Locker, Edward Hawke, 329

Lockhart, Allan, 238
Lockhart, Sir William, 261
Lodge, 313-315
London Missionary School, 105
Long, Rev. James, 46, 96, 100, 212, 292
Loring, Henry Lloyd, 116
Loudon Building, 110-111, 119, 177
Loudon Hotel, 96
Loudon Street or Lansdowne Road, 239, 247, 250
Lough, J.C., 309
Louis, John, 284
Louis, XV, 116
Lovelock, Arthur Samuel, 79
Lower Circular Road Cemetery,
    opening (1840), 190, 201
Lower Circular Road or Acharya Jagdish
    Chandra Bose Road, 31, 97, 200, 237, 240, 243, 245-246, 258, 262, 264, 268, 292
Lucknow, 290, 247
Luddy, Miss Ramah, 198
Luddy, Sam, 198
Lumley, Colonel, 55
Lyall, James Napier, 61
Lyon, Thomas, 75, 77-78, 81, 136
Lyon's Range, 60-61, 78-80
Lyons (France), 247
Lytton, Bulwer, 62
Lytton, Lady, 334
Lytton, Lord, 54, 157

Macan, Captain, 334
Macaulay, Thomas Babington, 223-226
Macintyre, Captain John, 326
Mackay, James L., 84
Mackenzie, Murdoch, 61
Mackenzie, Sir A., 306
Mackillop, M. James, 304
Mackrabie, Alexander, 127
Macleod, Duncan, 213
Macpherson, Sir John, 35, 293, 326
Macpherson, Sir William, 239
Macropolo, D., 70
Madge, E.W., 175
Madge, James, 175
Madge, W.C., 175
Madras, 35, 112, 123, 150, 153, 316
Maharaja Rama Nath Tagore statue, 145
Mahomedan Burial Board, 251
Mahtab, Sir Bejoy Chand, 270
Maidan horse-racing, 32
Maitraya, Akshaya Kumar, 21
Majumdar, Zamindar Lakshmi Kanta (Sabarna Roy Chowdhury), 5, 17
Ma Kin, 130
malaria,
    death of one-third European community, 31
Mangoe Lane, 71, 76, 102-103
Manik Chand, Raja, 24
Manohar Dass Tank, 264
Marconi, Signor, 146
Marine House, 46-47
Markley, Sir William, 242
Martin, Dr. J.R., 51
Marquess of Hastings, 14, 22, 74
Marris, W.S., 208
Marryat, Capt., 62
Marshman, John Clark, 46, 295
Marten, Charles, 106
Martin, Col. Claude, 153, 155, 247-248
Martin, E.J., 306
Martin, Sir Acquin, 106, 312
Martin, Thomas Acquin, 86

Martyn, 60
Mary, Queen, 10, 157
Mary, Virgin, 213
Massey, Montague, 48, 91, 162, 172, 177, 178, 232, 310
Mathewson, R.N., 160
Mauritius, 97, 334
Mayo, Lord, 153-154, 157, 274
Mayo Road, now Guru Nanak Sarani, 188, 279
Mayor's court
    elevation, 32
Mayurbhanj, Maharani, 215
McCluskie, E.T., 177, 211, 250
Mckilligan, J.P., 218
Mcleod House, 38
Mcleod Street, 199
McIntosh, John, 56
McMillan, Captain, 325
Medical College, Bengal (1835), 49
Meerut, 280
Meerut revolt, 336
Melville, Lord, 173
Metcalfe Hall, 50-52, 192, 202, 308
Metcalfe, Sir C.T., 50-51, 55, 58, 72, 308
metro railway, 227-228
Metropolitan Building, 167-168
Meyer, 223
Middleton Row, 61, 211, 213-215
Middleton, Samuel, 213, 215, 272
Middleton Street, 190, 215, 230-233
Middleton, Dr. Thomas Fanshawe, 116, 187, 232
Milburn, Rev., 255
Military Parade Ground, 334
Mill, Rev. William Hodges, 249
Miller, Hoare, 79
Mills, Captain, 21
Milman, Rev. Robert, 274, 277
Minchin, Captain-Commandant, 20
Minney, R.K., 271
Minto Park, 315
Minto, Lord, 117, 125, 175, 324, 327-329
Mission Church, 14, 63, 105
Mission Row Extension, 75, 107
Mission School (1773)
    construction, 104-105
Mitra, Govindram, 40, 271
Mitra, Raja Digambar, 102
Mitra, Reary Chand, 102
Mitter, Justice Dwaraka Nath, 141, 239
Mitter, Manmatha Nath, 256
Mitter, Ramesh Chandra, 141
Mody, Russi, 89
Moffat, James, 151, 157
Mohammad, Prince Gholam, 242, 316-317
Mohun Bagan Club, 279, 321
Moira, Earl of, 74, 203
Moira Street, 203
Monik, Mrs. Annie, 169, 171-172, 208, 235
Monson, Colonel, 105, 298, 303, 314
Mookerjee, Hurrish Chunder, 258
Mookherjee, Rajan, 257
Mookherjee, Rajendra Nath, 256
Mookherjee, Sir Biren, 257, 272
Mookherjee, Sir Rajen, 107
Moonghyr, 229-230
Morrison, Goldie, 112
Morrison, Turner, 79
Mount, Captain, Sir James, 179
Mount, Sir George, 180
Mountbatten, Lord, 279
Mowbray, John, 234
Mughal Empire, 3

Mukerji, Sambhu Chunder, 304
Mukherjee, Dr. Harendra Coomer, 153
Mukherjee, Harish Chandra, 102
Mukherjee, Lady Ranu, 235
Mukherjee, O.N., 238
Mukherjee, Raja Baidyanath, 49
Mukherjee, Reverend Aurobindo, 277
Mukherjee, Sir Asutosh, 141, 192, 308
Mukherjee, Sir Rajendranath, 235, 255
Mukhopadhyay, Harisadhan, 96
Mullick, Jadulal, 102
Mullick, Raja Rajendra Lal, 124, 320
Mulling, Edward, 45
Municipal Council Chamber (1905)
    opening, 145
municipal water supply
    introduction, 13
Munni Begum, 32
Murghihatta, Chapel, 93
Murray, Col., 165, 293
Murshidabad, Nawab of, 256
Murshidabad, 20, 24, 32, 83, 140, 282, 302
Mussoorie, 221
Mysore Princes, 76, 317

Nahoum, David, 198
Naidu, Sarojini, 202
Nair, P.T., 10, 46, 122, 203, 206, 216, 313
Nanak, Guru, 3
Nandakumar, Maharaja, 34, 201, 292
    bribery case and arrest, 32-33, 74
    trial and judgement, 33, 196
Nandan Complex, venue for International Film
    Festival, 272
Napier, Lord, 278
Nasirabad, 271
Nath, Janaki, 319
National & Grindlays Bank, 226-227
National Library, 234, 307-308
National Test House or Alipore Test House, 313
Naval and Military League (1895), 181
Nawab Bahadur of Dacca, 238
Nazar, Aga, 92
Nazargunje, Raja, 239
Nazim of Murshidabad, Nawab, 198, 308
Nehru, Jawaharlal, 243, 279, 307
Neill, 15
Nepal, Maharaja, 240
Netaji Indoor Stadium, 132, 134
Netaji Subhas Road, 38, 88-89
Niazi, Lt. General A.A.K., 290
Nicco House, 49, 53
Nicholas II, Czar, 306
Nicholls, C.G., 234
Nicholson Fund, 15
Nicholson, Dr. Simon, 188
Nizam of Hyderabad, 172, 252
Norman, John Paxton, 146, 274
North Park Street Cemetery, 98
Northbrook, Lord, 154, 157, 333
Nuremberg, 35
Nutt, Thomas, 274

Oakley, E.J., 312
Oaten, E.F., 21
Oberoi, Mohan Singh, 171-172
Ochterlony, Major-General Sir Lord David, 279
Octherlony Monument or Shaheed Minar, 160, 279-280
Ogilvie, Miss Margaret, 43
old Bengal Club, 216
old burial ground (later St. John's Church)
    closure, 8, 31, 190

old Calcutta
    legend, 2-3
Oldham, C.A., 256
Oldham, Samuel 200
Oliffres, John, 14
old Archiepiscopal Palace, 93
Omichund, 33, 73
Ordnance Club, 292
Orient Club, 255
Orme, Robert, 19
Orphan Institution of the Bengal Military Orphan
    Society, 299
Outram Street, 202
Outram, Lt General Sir James, 202, 225, 278
Owen, John, 315

Paget, Lady Harriet, 304
Paget, Sir Edward, 304, 334
paintings of European artists, 13
Pal, Dr. Radha Benode, 143
Palace Hotel, 160
Palit, Sir Tarak Nath, 320
Palmer, John, 97, 145, 203, 213, 233
Panckridge, H.R., 55
Pande, Mangal, 336
Pandit Sambhu Nath, 141
Pandit, Mrs. Vijayalakshmi, 153
panch pir or five saints in Bihar, 8
Pannala, Banerjee Lane, 113
Parental Academic Institution, 194
Parer, Raymond, 56
Park Children's Centre (1977), 247
Park Nursing Home (now Park Clinic), 246-247
Park Plaza, 198
Park, R.J.C., 196
Park Street, 4, 41, 76, 166, 177, 187, 190, 193-194,
    197-198, 206-207, 215-216
Parkeh, V.V., 226
Parker, J.P., 219, 247, 280, 293
Parker, Sir William, 152
Partition of Bengal, 78
    protest, 146
Patna, 8
Paton, F. Noel, 255-256
Patterson, Sir C, 146
Paul, Butta Kristo, 175
Payne, Thomas, 162
Peacock, Sir Barnes, 143, 225
Pearse, Colonel, 201, 293, 304-305
Pearson, John, 124
Peel, Sir Lawrence, 141, 308-309
Petheram, Sir Comer, 234
Penn, William, 313
Philatelic Museum, 26, 46
Philip Francis House, 84
Phul, Sheikh, 335
Picasso, Pablo, 203
plague (1770), 32
Planter's Journal, 61
Plaza Hotel, 180
Polier, Major Antoine, 35, 285-286
Pomfret, George, 193
Port Blair, 154, 274
Port of Calcutta, 44
Portuguese, 3, 92-93
Portuguese churches, 97, 102, 104
Portuguese sailors, 7
Potato Bazar, 91
Pourpe, Mark, 270
Prasad, Dr. Rajendra (first President of India),
    joins Calcutta High Court as a *vakeel* in
    1911, 143

Pratt, Reverend J.H., 274
Presidency General Hospital, 258-262, 266
press censorship, 50, 51
Preston, Arthur, 199
Pringle, John Alexander, 31
Pringle, Mrs. Christina, 66
Prinsep Capt., 245-246
Prinsep, Charles Robert, 305
Prinsep, James, 29, 63, 192
Prinsep, Thomas, 338
Prinsep, William, 240-241
Prinsep's Plan, 257, 261
Public Department Notification of 1798, 58
public toilet complex, 65
Pugla, Russa, 253

Queen's Park, 320

Rabindra Sadan, 272
Radha Bazar, 12, 76
Radha Bazar Lane, 43, 230
Radha Bazar Street, 75, 99
radio transmission, 54
Ragamuffin Hall, 97
Rahim, A., 256
Rahman, Fazar, 251
Rainey Park, 318, 319, 322-323
Raj Bhavan,
    total cost of the land, 150
Rajagopalachari, C., 158
Rashmoni, Rani, 128
Rajmahal hills, 2
Ramjan, Sheikh, 179
Rampore, 117
Rangoon, 84, 131
Ranji, Prince, 300
Rattray, J.H., 247
Rawdon Street, 201-202, 239, 247
Rawdon, Earl of, 201
Ray, A.K., 2, 65, 302
Ray, Dr. Kumud Sankar, 246
Ray, Raja Janaki Nath, 246
Ray, Raja Pramada Nath, 197
Ray, Satyajit, 257
Ray, Sir P.C., 192
Rayen, Sir Edward, 141, 308
Red Cross Place or Wellesley Palace, 62, 109
Red Road or Indira Gandhi Sarani, 279, 282
    reform of 1921, 134
Reni, Guido, 192
Reserve Bank of India
    building, 17, 27-29, 142
revolutionary organisations, 112
Reynolds, Sir Joshua, 192
Richard Westmacott
    statue of Warren Hastings, 145
Ricketts, John William, 194
Ripon, Lord, 54, 153, 278
River Trust (1863), 44
Robertson, L., 208
Robertson, Mrs, 101
Robinson, Charles Knowles, 51, 280, 295
Robinson, Reverend John, 202
Robinson Street, 202
Roerich, Nicolas, 192
Roman Catholic Church (1950), 92-93, 97
Rome, 213
Ronaldshay, Lady, 271
Ross, R.L., 208, 260
Rotary Club, 271
Row, Tom, 328
rowing matches, 133

Rowlatt Committee Report, 112
Roy, Dr. Bidhan Chandra, 78, 227, 246
Roy, Kiran Shankar, 123
Roy, Maharaja, H.L., 181
Roy, P.L., 255-256
Roy, P.N., 89
Roy, Raja Ram Mohun, 49
Royal Asiatic Society of Great Britain and
    Ireland, 192
Royal Botanical Gardens, 251
Royal Calcutta Golf Links, 316, 317, 318-324
Royal Calcutta Turf Club (1847), 15, 217-221, 237
Royal Charter of 1853, 80
Royal Exchange, 81, 84
Roychowdhurys, Mrs. Subhadra, 110
Roychowdhurys, Sabarna, 46
Royd, Sir John, 197
Rubens, Peter Paul, 192
Rudra, Chandra Sekhar, 227
Rudt, Baron, H., 323
Rumboldt, Thomas, 258
Rundell, Franics, 80
Russell, Claude, 258
Russell, Lady, 105
Russell, Sir Henry, 37, 141, 217-218
Russell Street, 213, 216-218, 220, 227, 232-233, 237,
    242
Ryan, Sir Edward, 51

Saharanpore, 230
Sanderson, Robert, 64
Salim, Golam Hosain, 20-21
Salimullah, H.H. Nawab, 239
Salt Lakes, 5, 96, 99, 109
salt water marshes, 96
Salt, Henry, 327
Sanderson, Miss Elizabeth Jane, 299
Sandys, E.T., 320
Sarani, Abdul Hamid, 102
Sarani, Anandi Lal Poddar, 232
Sarani, Hemanta Basu, 63, 66-67
Sarani, Martin Luther King, 206
Sarani, Sir William Jones, 215
Saraswati, Pundit P., 175
Satgaon, 3-4, 7
Saturday Club, 206, 238
Scarsdale, Lord, 150
Scott Thomson's Corner, 66
Scott, Charles, 213
Scott, Henry, 101
Scott, John, 253
Scott, Miss Ivy, 169
Scutt, C.P. Symes, 317
Selby's Club, 105
Second World War, 107, 163, 179, 196-197, 210,
    278, 289, 299
Sen, Aparna, 181
Sen, Mrs. Mrinalini, 318
Sengupta, Dr. Naresh Chandra, 143
Sengupta, Jatindra Mohan, 174
Sengupta, Nellie, 174
Sepoy Mutiny, 14, 160, 295, 325-326, 334-335
Sett, Harinarayan, 51
Sett, Lalmohan, 5, 12, 96
Sett, Mukunda Ram, 5
Setts, Hindu founding fathers of Calcutta, 4, 282
Shah, Bakhtiar, 316
Shah, Fateh Hyder, 316
Shah, Muhammad Farooque, 146
Shah, Muniruddin, 316
Shah, Sultan Shobhan, 316
Shah, Viren, J., 159

Shah, Wajid Ali, 287, 295
Shakespeare, William, 237-240, 242
Shan, Azim Us, 17
Shaw, David Thomas, 47
Shaw, R. Gordon, 47
Shaw Wallace and Company (1886), 47
Shiva temple, 4
Shore, Sir John, 64
Short Street, 202
Short, Charles, 165, 201
Simla, 171, 181, 329
Singapore, 279, 289
Singh, Duleep, 111-112
Singh, Harihar Prasad, 247
Singh, Jagonnaut, 60
Singh, Raja Sobha, 17
Singh, Saum, 60
Singh, Kumar Arun Chandra, 236
Sinha, Balu Kaliprasanna, 223
Sinha, Lord, 240
Sinha, Satyendra Prasanna, 240
Sir Stuart Hogg Market or New Market, 175, 177
Siraj-ud-Daula, 20, 23-24, 28, 42, 46, 81, 96, 102,
    264-265, 301, 323
Sircar, Nalini Ranjan, 252
Skinner, Charles, 89
Sloper, General, 119
Smith, Capt. Ross, 271
Smith, E.F., 180
Smith, Lt. Kieth, 271
Smyth, Capt. R, 130
Society for the Promotion of Christian
    Knowledge (SPCK) (1740), 104
Solvyns, Francois Balthazar, 35, 76, 97
Sookias, T.B., 252
Sorabjee, Miss Cornelia, 208
South Africa, 319
South Park Street Cemetery, 95
Spence, John, 111
Spence, Mrs, 111
Spence's Hotel, 109, 111-112, 119
Spink, William, 161
Srpentine Tank, 264
St. Andrew's Church, 14, 65, 73-75, 78, 94
St. Andrew's Churchyard, 76
St. Andrew's Library, 75, 110
St. Anne's Church (1716), 22-24, 77-78, 122
St. John's Church Cemetery, 83
St. John's Church (1784), 8, 10, 32, 43, 55, 61, 66,
    75, 109, 113-117, 333
St. John's Churchyard, 8, 49, 54, 56, 117
St. Paul's Catherdal, 113, 272-276
St. Stephen's Church, 324
St. Thomas's Church, 196, 215-217
St. Xavier's College, 54, 204-205
Statesman, The (1933), 56, 84, 90, 167, 169, 179,
    318, 325
statue of Lord Cornwallis, 145
statue of Mahatma Gandhi, 278
statue of Marquess Cornwallis, 144
statue of Queen Victoria, 268
statue of Sri Aurobindo, 268
statue of Wellesley, 144
statue of Netaji Subash Chandra Bose, 279
Stavorinus, Dutch Admiral, 13, 74, 138
Steepleton's map of 1817, 318
Stephen, Aratoon, 170-172, 195, 208-209
Sternadale, R.C., 41
Stewart, Lewis, 72
Stocqueler, Joachim Hayward, 55, 68, 204
Strand Road, 5, 42, 44, 47, 50, 79, 81, 84, 94, 124

Stuart, Major General Charles, 201, 206
Sudder Street, 175, 178-181, 183, 195
Suez Canal (1866) opening, 112
Suhrawardy, Sir Hassan, 214
Sukhchar, 124
Sultan, Moizuddin, 316
Sultan, Tipu, 47, 150, 316
Sunderbans, 2-3, 96
Sunny Park, 320
Supreme Court (old Court House), 31-34, 57, 74,
    100, 102, 105, 115, 117, 124, 134, 139-140,
    197, 315
Surajpur, 157
Surman's bridge, 63, 293
Survey of India, 205
Swiss Club (1924) or International Club, 239
Sydney, 97
Sylhet, 174

Tagore, Abanindranath, 184, 209, 257
Tagore, Debendra Nath, 102
Tagore, Dwarkanath, 145-146, 209
Tagore, Gaganendranath, 257
Tagore, Jyotirindranath, 79, 254
Tagore, Maharaja Jatindra Mohan, 146
Tagore, Maharaja Rama Nath, 146
Tagore, Prafulla Nath, 256
Tagore, Rabindranath, 70, 79, 146, 161, 180, 187,
    209, 234, 272, 319, 321-322
Tagore, Satyendranath, 321-322
Tagore, Sir P.K., 256
Tagore, Surendranath, 322
Tanjore, 276
Tarag, Manohar Das, 165
Tata Centre, 89
Tatas, 80, 122
Tavern, J. Trenholm, 100
Temple of Kalighat, 3, 165
Temple of Minerva, Athens, 338
Temple of Winds, Athens, 52
Temple, Sir Richard, 301
Templer, Parry Purple, 81
Thacker's Directory of 1868, 90, 111
Thackeray, Charles, 55
Thackeray, Henry W.M., 261
Thackeray, Richmond, 194, 200, 314
Thackeray, William Makepiece, 55, 161, 194
Theatre Road (Shakespeare Sarani), 42, 68, 208,
    218, 245
Theophilus, Sir Charles, 50
Thomas, Robert, 106
Thompson, R. Scott, 67
Thomson, T.E., 163
Thornton, Ted, 235
Three Hundred Club, 238
Tipu Sultan's library, 192
Tiretta's Bazar, 95
Tiretta's or French cemetery, 199
Tirretta, Edward, 95, 151
Tollygunge, 315-317

Tolly, Colonel William, 303-304, 314-315
Tollygunge Club, 316-317
Tolly's Nullah, 32, 292-293, 306, 314-317
Town Hall (1807), 32, 43, 51, 53-54, 84, 111, 134-
    135, 140, 143-147, 255, 267
Town Hall Committee, 145
Town Hall lottery tickets, 144
Treasury buildings, 117-119, 147
Tremando, Antonio Angelo, 14, 63
Tretta, Count Edward, 95
Trevor, Binny, 141
Trevor, Captain S.T., 131
Tripura, Maharaja, 202, 320
Turner, Bishop, 219
Turner, John Mathias, 116, 272-273
Twain, Mark, 168
Tyck, Jules, 317-318

Udayan Park, 320
Union Club, 155
United Bengal Club, 197
United Missionary Girls High School, 105
United Service Club, 182, 184-188, 226
USA, 186

Valentia, Lord, 151, 327
Vallant, Sir Thomas, 261
Vansittart, George, 212
Vansittart, Henry, 45, 61, 190, 212, 253, 293
Venice, 95, 192
Verelst, Henry, 258, 303
Verminck, George, 270
Victoria House, 43
Victoria Memorial Hall, 71, 97, 145-147, 183, 192,
    266-267, 271, 277
Victoria Memorial Placement, 107
Victoria Terrace, 208
Victoria, Queen, 39, 246, 267, 316
Vidyalankar, Mrityunjy, 60
Vidyadhari river, 292
Vidyagagar, Ishwar Chandra, 60, 104, 146
Vidyasagar Setu, 129, 262
Virginia House, 228-230
Vrignon, Gabriel, 316

Wales, James, 269
Wallace, Charles William, 47
Ward, Mary, 213
Waterford, Louisa Lady, 333
Waterloo Street, 67, 100-101
Watson, Admiral, 33, 114
Watson, Col Henry, 63, 113, 184, 213, 264, 278,
    293, 297-298, 304-305
Watts, Hugh, 258
Watts, Mrs Frances, 81, 83
Watts, William, 81
Wellesley, Lord, 32, 43, 119, 137, 149, 150-151, 153,
    155, 207, 232, 257, 286, 294, 326-328
Wellesley,
    Marquis of, 58
Wellington Street, 103, 104

Wells map of 1753, 42, 122
Wells, William, 20
West Bengal Legislative Assembly House or
    Bidhan Sabha, 132-133
West, Benjamin, 274
Westmacott, Richard, 116
Westminister Abbey, Princes Diana's funeral, 36
Weston, Charles, 63, 95, 196Wheler, 77, 114, 293
Wheeler, Colonel, 335
Wheler Place, 65, 109, 150
Wheler, Sir Edward, 109, 201
White Town, 32
White, Campbell, 177
White, Jonathan, 10
White, Katharine, 10
White, W.H., 47
Wilkinson, Stephen, 208
William III, King, 17
William Wells' Plan, 46
William, Sir, Ironside, 277
Willis, Joseph, 277
Wilson, Dr. C.R., 2, 22
Wilson, David, 68
Wilson, Rev Daniel, 274
Wolley, Mrs. Anne, 104
Wood, Henry, 206
Wood, Lt. Col. Mark, 137, 165, 206, 218-219
Wood Street, 197-198, 203, 205-206
Woodburn Park Road, 250
Woodburn, Sir John, 15, 250, 255
Woodroffe, Justice, 220
Woods, W.T., 177
Writers' Building, 14-16, 60, 76-78, 134, 175
    Bengal Secretariat, 77-78
    dwelling place for East India Company's
        writers, 76
    extensions, 79
    first building with three stories, 77
    Fort William College, 76-77
    Graham's description, 78
    location, 77-78
    original *pattah*, 77
Wyatt, Captain, 150
Wyatt, Charles, 316
Wyatt, James, 150

Yate, Thomas, 201
YMCA Building, 177
Young Women's Christian Association, 216
Youngman's Christian Association Building, 177
Yule, Andrew, 86, 90
Yule, George, 86, 90
Yule, Sir David, 90

Zain-al-Din, Shaykh, 212
zamindar or collector, 40, 41
zamindari rights, 17
Zeerut Bridge, 315
Zoffany, John, 36, 115, 269, 310
Zoological Gardens, 301-302, 306
Zorab, Manook, 322